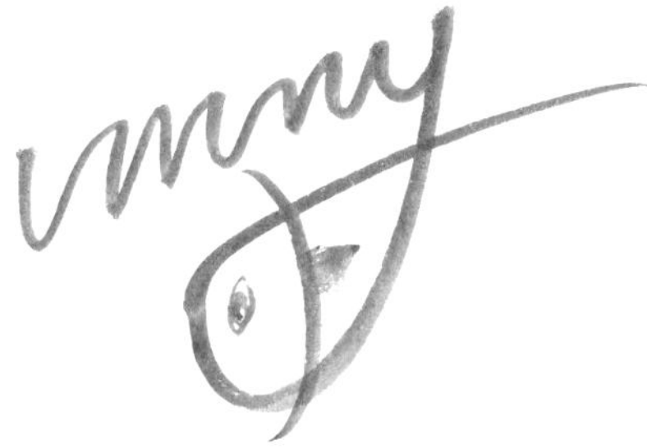

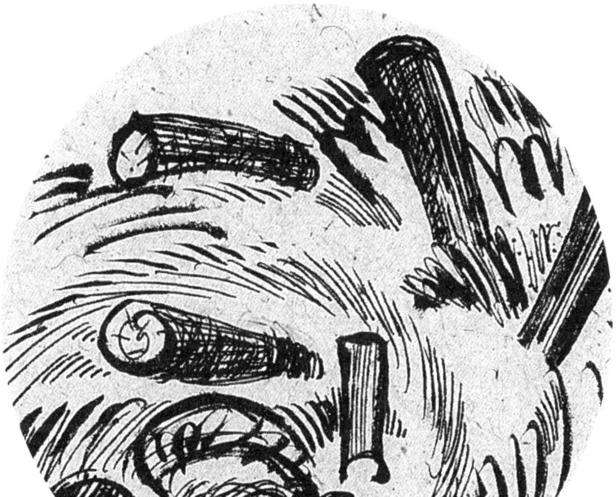

Big 7aawaa to all the tough-minded
big-hearted people who give a damn
and may this be us all.
- MNY

Old Growth

Michael Nicoll Yahgulanaas

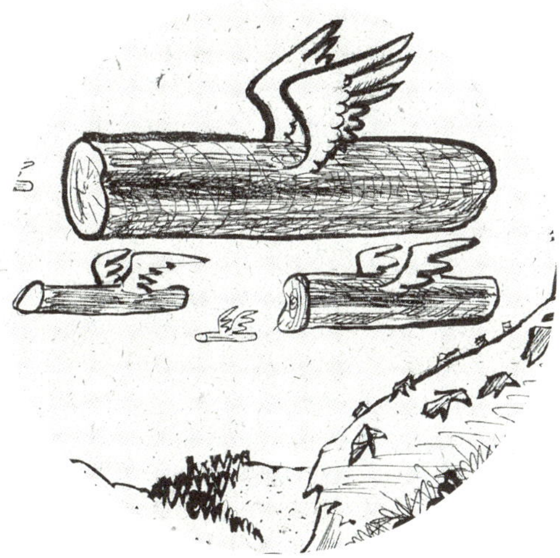

Edited by Liz Park

READ LEAF

grunt

Contents

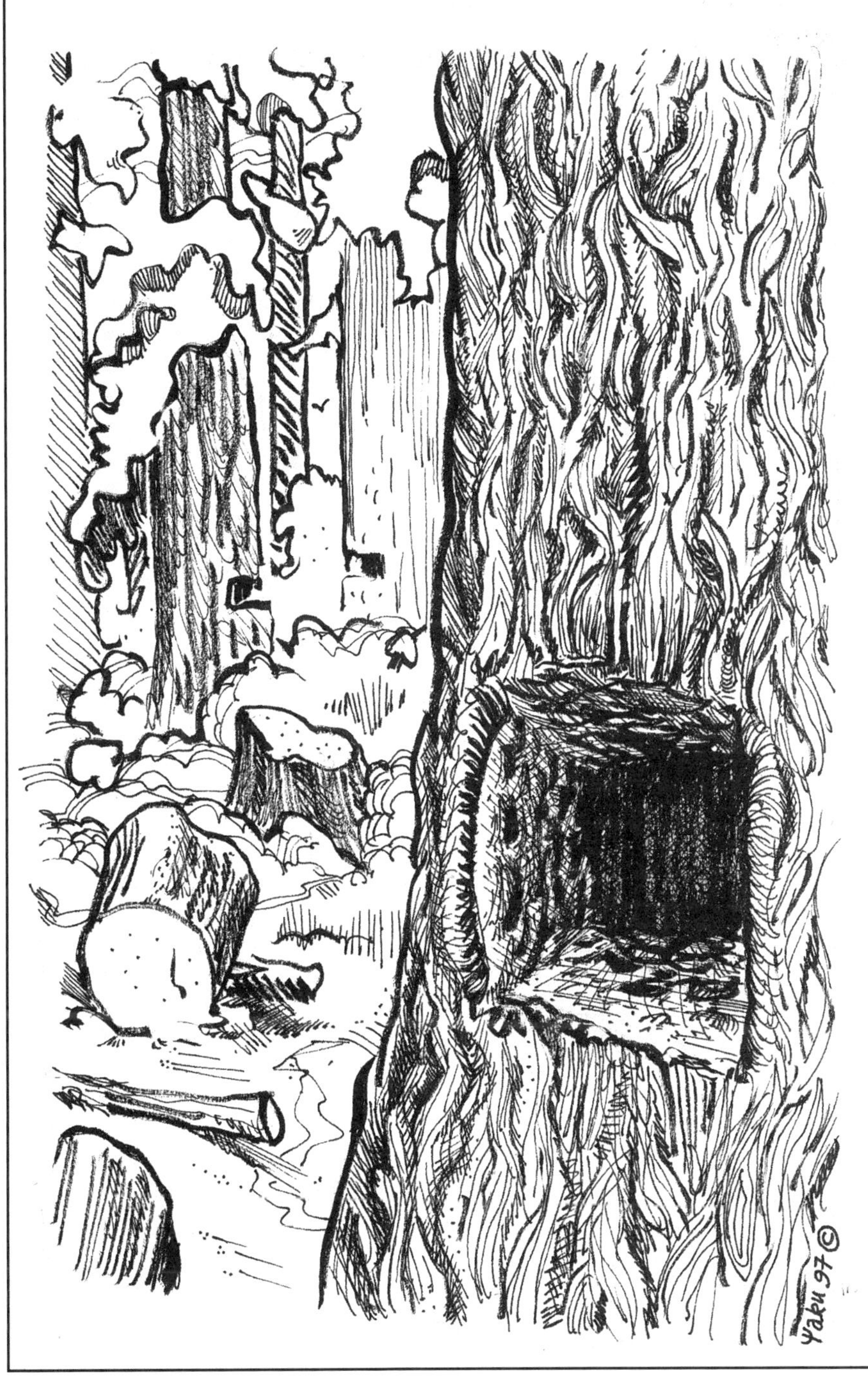

Untitled, 1997. Originally published in *SpruceRoots Magazine* (Haida Gwaii).

Preface

Liz Park

Mining the personal archive of Haida artist Michael Nicoll Yahgulanaas is akin to taking an alternative history lesson that reveals the struggles against unjust and short-sighted resource extraction on the Indigenous lands off the West Coast of Canada. His chests and trunks are time capsules, containing sketchbooks, pads of paper and scrap pieces of mat boards all filled with artwork and bound in three-ring binders. They chronicle over thirty years of the history of political negotiations and cultural conflict, from the 1970s to the early 2000s. As I delved into his archive, I intuitively sensed the importance of his works as historic documents and political statements.

I examined more than a thousand pages to gather those that were most representative of the artist's attitudes and opinions toward the current affairs of the time. In particular I chose studies and experiments, finished work previously unpublished, and works that few have seen – having only been published in community newsletters and in fundraising efforts. Ordered mostly chronologically, the material featured in this book charts some of the events that have influenced not only the artist's work, but also society at large. Rather than focusing on his more well known work such as large-scale watercolour murals, *RED* and *War of the Blink*, and sculptural installations involving car parts, *The Hood Series* and *Pedal to the Meddle*, this volume speaks to the experiences that have shaped the artist as an Indigenous person, a creative practitioner and a global citizen to demonstrate the decades of work that have informed his current practice. The works presented in the following pages interweave his personal narratives with issues that for the most part remain current – such as depletion of natural resources, global climate change and the fundamental question of 'how to live together.'

Michael's visual narratives refer to the generations past and to the cultural positions of the Haida. But he weaves into them slices from our shared contemporary reality. In the process, he retells some of the oldest Haida stories with currency and dynamism pertinent to today. By so doing, Michael invites readers to partake in his world. I am incredibly humbled to have had the opportunity to work with Michael in bringing much of his previously unseen work to a larger audience through this book.

This publication is the collective effort of many. Simply Read Books/Read Leaf and grunt gallery have been instrumental in bringing this book to publication. Thank you to Glenn Alteen, Demian Petryshyn and Meagan Kus from grunt gallery; Dimiter Savoff and Kallie George from Simply Read Books/Read Leaf; Tania Willard, book designer; Venge Dixon, copy-editor; Simon Davies, former editor of *SprueRoots*, and contributor to this publication; Charlotte Townsend-Gault and Beth Carter,

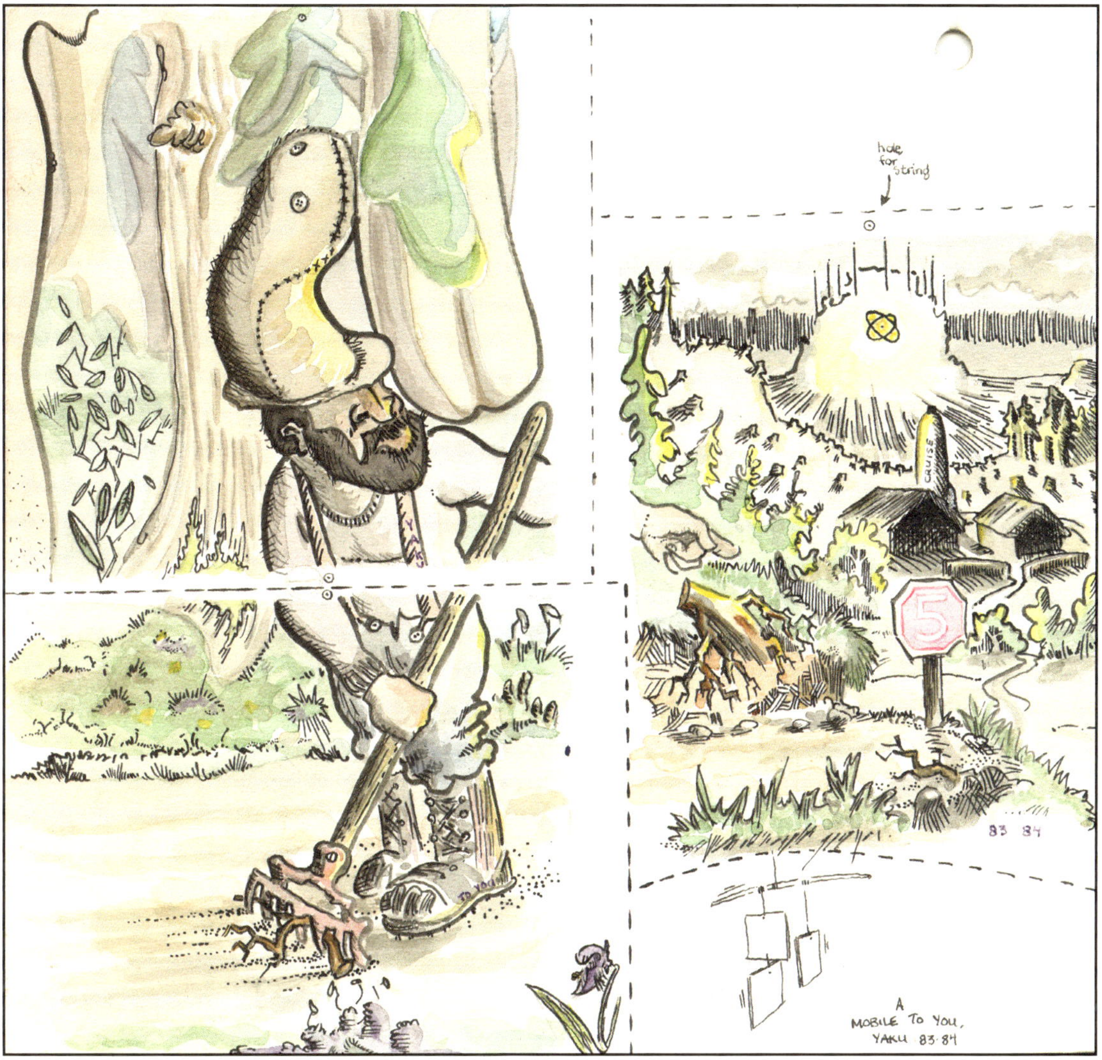

Untitled, 1983/84.

for their support along the way; Quyen Hoang and the staff at the Glenbow Museum, who provided an opportunity for Michael and I to try out the earliest iteration of the project as *Haida Manhwa Bang*; Maiko Tanaka, Yan Wu and Tad Hozumi, from Gendai Gallery for their support of my curatorial endeavour there; Joni Low and Mandy Ginson for their comments on the early drafts; and lastly and most importantly to Michael Nicoll Yahgulanaas for opening up his archive.

Introduction

Liz Park

This collection of graphic works by Haida artist Michael Nicoll Yahgulanaas spans nearly three decades of production, from 1976, when he was twenty-two years old, to 2001, when he was forty-seven, and had become a seasoned politician and respected artist. During this time span there were many changes in the way people along the Northwest Coast of North America imagined nature, understood sovereignty and constructed the place they call home. The political winds and popular perception of Indigenous rights and social issues shifted significantly during this time; the artist, too, underwent a transformation: from a young creator, scribing angry lines – driven by a sense of urgency and certainty in reason – to an experienced cultural ambassador with inflected thoughts, a robust sense of humour and a deep understanding of how the flowing lines carry his graphic narratives.

As you flip through the pages of this book, you will note his lines gradually become more fluid, connecting one part of the image to another in a harmonic yet non-linear way. Time and space flow in multiple directions in the narratives presented here, as Yahgulanaas draws on numerous references from both contemporary politics and generations-old Haida stories in a graphic form that is equally fluid, hybridized and ready to change. The artist has coined a brilliant name for this form and practice: *Haida Manga.*

Bestowing names holds importance on numerous levels. A name taken and given powerfully evokes the relationships that bind the name-givers and the named, as aptly illustrated by the terms America, Canada, British Columbia and the Queen Charlotte Islands. These names point to specific colonial encounters that are now institutionalized and have, through centuries, become naturalized. In Yahgulanaas' 1988 editorial cartoon *What's a Name?* a Haida man confronts a tourist wearing a camera slung around his neck and holding a *Guide to the Queen Charlotte Islands* in his hand [fig. 1]. The caption reads: "Haidas have called these islands 'Haida Gwaii' for thousands of years, but I suppose if we wanted to steal something we would change its name too."

Being bereft of the Indigenous names for places also means being bereft of the thousands of years of deep connection to the land that is made manifest in the languages of those peoples. Because language is the backbone of one's culture, the project of reclaiming Indigenous names – in this case, reclaiming the name Haida Gwaii for their archipelago – is an effort to re-establish this inherent relationship to the land and the culture. The reinstatement of the Indigenous name is also a major step in re-establishing sovereignty over traditional lands, in protest of how Indigenous nations in this country and many others have been placed under a stewardship of colonial states. On June 17, 2010, the Haida Nation held a Giving Back the Name with Respect ceremony, in which the colonial name, the Queen Charlotte Islands, for their archipelago, in use for more than two centuries, was returned, in a bentwood box, to then-Premier Gordon Campbell, the representative of the British Columbia provincial government.[1] This historic event illustrates the significance of a name, as a conscious marker of one's identity and as a reflection of one's relations and histories.*

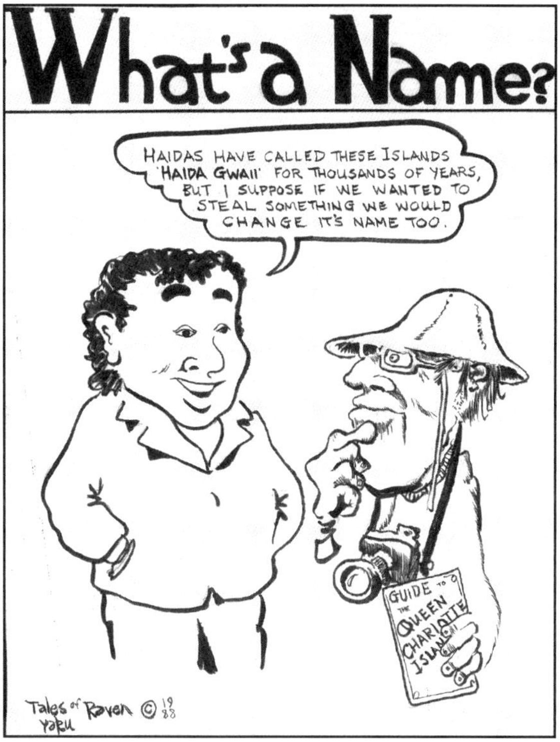

Fig. 1

On an individual level, the artist's name, Michael Nicoll Yahgulanaas, is a personal reclamation project. In the 1980s, Michael Nicoll added his clan name Yahgulanaas in an intentional, hybrid construction heralding his Scottish and Haida lineages. His penchant for cultural hybridity is also evident in *Haida Manga*, the term he coined for much of his work. Remarkably the name Haida Manga does not borrow from the colonial vocabulary that has framed much of Indigenous cultural production in North America: the artist appropriates the term from a genre of Japanese graphic narratives called 'manga' to consciously reject aligning his tales with mainstream North American and European comic cultures which largely centre on heroic protagonists in stories

* Yahgulanaas is acutely aware of the way nomenclature is used politically and legally as a tool of colonial control. In email communication dated March 16, 2011, he states, "I prefer the term Indigenous Peoples as it has a clear legal definition in international law. First Nations is a politically convenient and legally soft term used in Canada. The words don't even appear in the famous and much loved Section 35 of Canada's repatriated Constitution Act 1982. Because "First Nations" is such a squishy description and one unique to Canada, it suggests a distance between the application of Constitutional and International laws, treaties and covenant to the contemporary legislative experience. That is a dangerous proposition for all citizens regardless of ethnicity."

about good and evil. The Raven, a frequent star of Yahgulanaas' chronicles, modeled after the trickster figure of Haida oral tradition, is a complex character that does not fit into the established models of comic book superheroes in tights. The Raven cheats, lies, steals, while, at the same time, providing incredible insight, experience and opportunities to others.

Millennia-old stories and traditions are flexibly used in Yahgulanaas' work, and 'manga' itself is a term that the artist uses with a degree of elasticity. *Haida Manhwa* and *Manhua* are variant terms he has used, in Korean and Chinese contexts respectively. This changing term suggests that Haida cultural productions can adapt and evolve in an ever-shifting world without compromising their basic cultural integrity, thereby defiantly opposing pedestrian views of what is Indigenous or traditional. Yahgulanaas' work comes from a deep understanding of his cultural roots in the context of contemporary social and political environments, and the use of these hybrid names allows him and his work to navigate the global currents of image, cultures and commodities.

In Canada and across the globe, the Haida have become well-known for environmental activism, the work of world-famous artists like Bill Reid and their vigorous political muscles in the affairs of Indigenous sovereignty. Meanwhile, manga has increasingly become accepted as an important field of creative visual and literary production. Today, the word 'manga' and the concept it represents is accepted in common English usage and the word is found in a number of English dictionaries. Manga can quickly and easily present complex content through simple images. Haida Manga effectively translates some of the epic Haida tales and contemporary events into an accessible composition.

In the 1970s in Haida Gwaii, then called the Queen Charlotte Islands by the state, Yahgulanaas worked on creating the first issue of *Tales of Raven, No Tankers, T'anks*, an independently produced comic vividly illustrating the threats oil spills pose to marine life. At this time 'Haida' and 'manga' would have been a meaningless pairing of words, since there was little awareness, sympathy or interest in a Haida artist's comics about environmental devastation to his homeland and sea. Looking chronologically through the three decades of work following, presented in this volume, the roots of Haida Manga become clear. As Yahgulanaas and Simon Davies, an editor and publisher on Haida Gwaii, elucidate in an interview conducted for this publication, the mainstream media had and still has little interest in providing any depth of coverage to the affairs of Indigenous Peoples. In response, much of Yahgulanaas' earlier work was printed in local, alternative publications and dealt with issues especially pertinent to those on Haida Gwaii.

Yahgulanaas regularly injects a dose of humour into his drawings, even when their content deals with fraught and difficult moments – such as when logging on Haida Gwaii reached a peak in 1985, when forty-one million squared metres of the island was cleared.[2] Having worked as a forest surveyor for a logging company, as well as being involved on the Council of Haida Nation as an

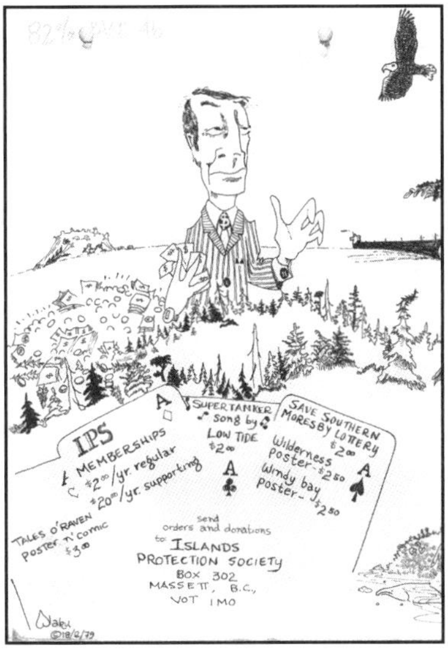

Fig. 2

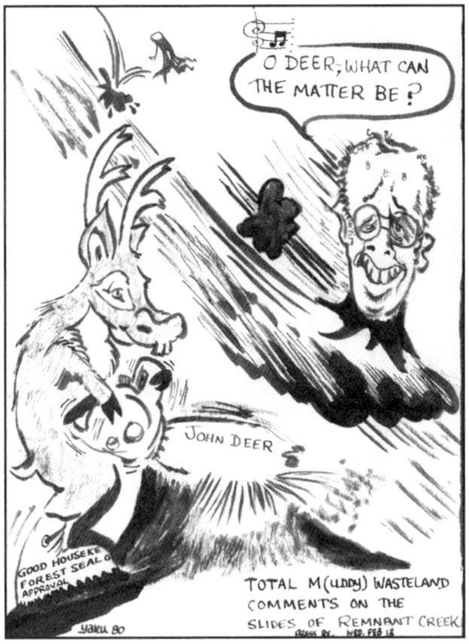

Fig. 3

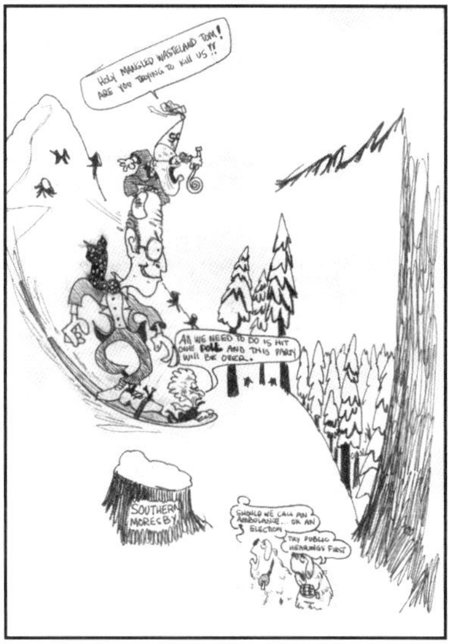

Fig. 4

elected Chief Councilor, Yahgulanaas' work stems from a place of knowledge and shared responsibility. Much of his earlier work was made to serve his community — to inform and entertain, to catalyze people into action and occasionally to fundraise. For instance, *Tales of Raven, No Tankers, T'anks* was produced for the Coalition Against Supertankers (COAST), an ad hoc group struck to raise money to send delegates to represent the Queen Charlotte Islands at the Federal Government's West Coast Oil Ports Inquiry in Vancouver.

Similarly, a number of Yahgulanaas' works were published as part of the collective effort of the Islands Protection Society (IPS), an organization formed on Haida Gwaii in 1974 by like-minded Haida and non-Haida, who tenaciously opposed the logging plans and environmentally destructive activities on Haida Gwaii [fig. 2].[3] Their mandate was to protect the wilderness areas on the islands from falling victim to indiscriminate logging practices. One of the first exploits of the IPS was to promote a proposal to preserve the South Moresby wilderness area, the southern fifteen percent of Haida Gwaii. Areas just north had already been clear-cut logged with devastating results, including massive landslides. South Moresby was a hotly contested area: for the Haida, protecting it was a matter of upholding cultural heritage and reclaiming sovereignty, while, for the forestry companies, proceeding to log there had become synonymous with maintaining their right to log not only on Haida Gwaii but elsewhere in British Columbia.

The gravity of the conflict on the Islands over this issue cannot be understated, but in Yahgulanaas' work, it is often peppered with humour. In particular, his 1980 map of Graham Island – located just north of Moresby – is layered with the artist's doubts, fears and characteristic wit, and delivers a wry commentary on the state of forestry on his homeland [fig. 5].

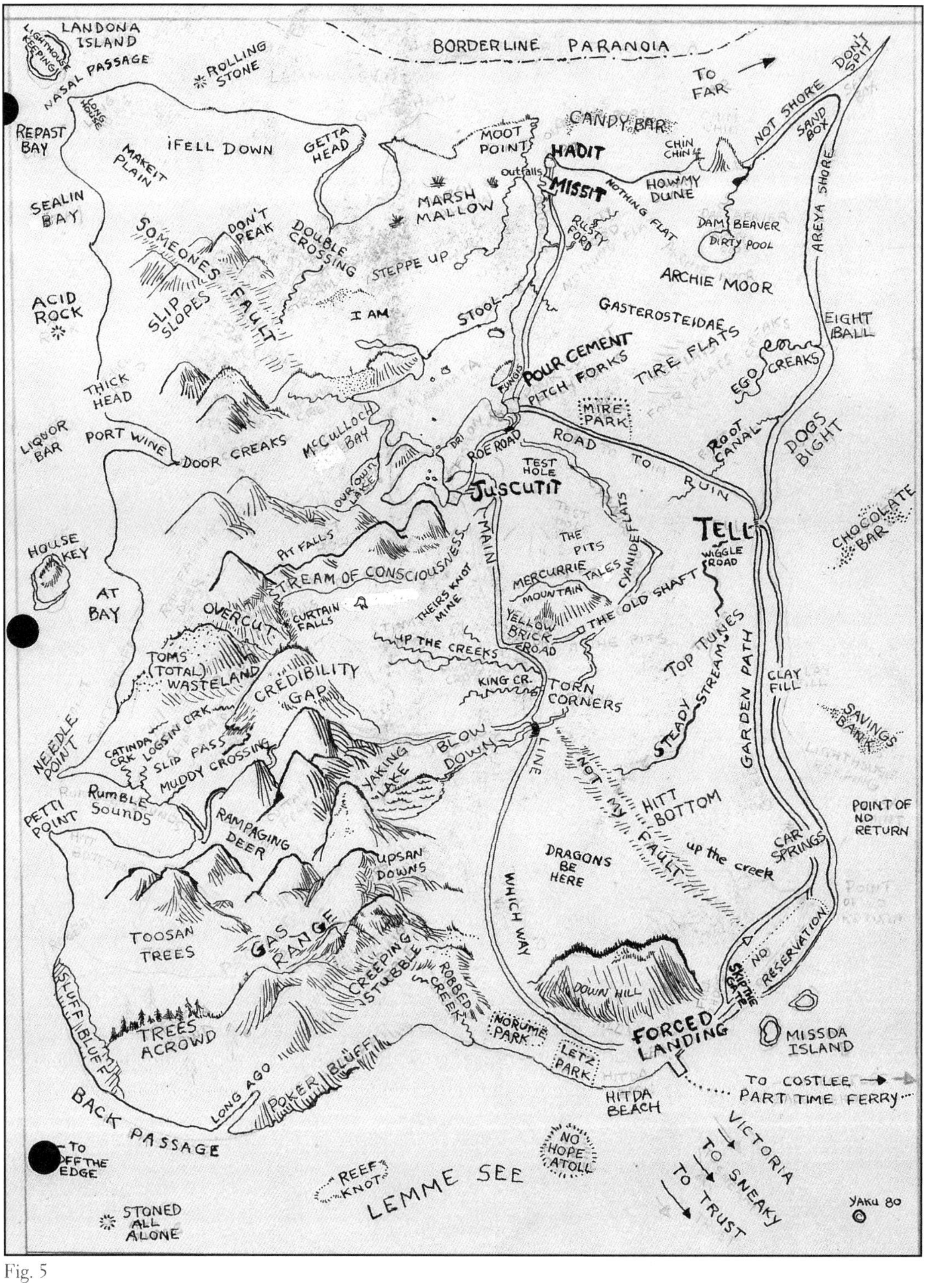
LANDONA ISLAND
LIGHTHOUSE KEEPING
NASAL PASSAGE
ROLLING STONE
BORDERLINE PARANOIA
TO FAR
DON'T SPIT
REPAST BAY
LONG HOUSE
iFELL DOWN
MAKEIT PLAIN
GETTA HEAD
MOOT POINT
CANDY BAR
HADIT
MISSIT
outfalls
CHIN CHIN
NOT SHORE
SAND BOX
AREYA SHORE
SEALIN BAY
SOMEONES FAULT
DON'T PEAK
DOUBLE CROSSING
MARSH MALLOW
STEPPE UP
RUSTY FORD
NOTHING FLAT
HOWMY DUNE
DAM BEAVER
DIRTY POOL
ARCHIE MOOR
ACID ROCK
SLIP SLOPES
I AM
STOOL
GASTEROSTEIDAE
EIGHT BALL
POUR CEMENT
FUNGUS
PITCH FORKS
TIRE FLATS
EGO CREAKS
THICK HEAD
MIRE PARK
LIQUOR BAR
PORT WINE
DOOR CREAKS
McCULLOCH BAY
DRI OUT
ROE ROAD
ROAD TO RUIN
ROOT CANAL
DOGS BIGHT
TEST HOLE
OUR OWN LAKE
JUSCUTIT
TELL
CHOCOLATE BAR
HOUSE KEY
PIT FALLS
MAIN
THE PITS
CYANIDE FLATS
WIGGLE ROAD
TREAM OF CONSCIOUSNESS
MERCURRIE TALES
MOUNTAIN
THE OLD SHAFT
AT BAY
OVERCUT
CURTAIN FALLS
THEIRS KNOT MINE
YELLOW BRICK ROAD
TOP TUNES
up THE CREEKS
TOMS (TOTAL) WASTELAND
CREDIBILITY GAP
CLAY FILL
GARDEN PATH
KING CR.
TORN CORNERS
STEADY STREAM
SAVINGS BANK
NEEDLE POINT
CATINDA CRK
LOGSIN CRK
SLIP PASS
MUDDY CROSSING
YAKING LAKE
BLOW DOWN
LINE
NOT MY FAULT
RUMBLE SOUNDS
PETTI POINT
RAMPAGING DEER
HITT BOTTOM
POINT OF NO RETURN
CAR SPRINGS
up the creek
DRAGONS BE HERE
UPSAN DOWNS
WHICH WAY
TOOSAN TREES
GAS RANGE
CREEPING STUBBLE
ROBBED CREEK
DOWN HILL
SKIP THE GATE
NO RESERVATION
SLUFF BLUFF
TREES ACROWD
NORUME PARK
LETZ PARK
FORCED LANDING
MISSDA ISLAND
TO COSTLEE
PART TIME FERRY
LONG AGO
POKER BLUFF
HITDA BEACH
BACK PASSAGE
VICTORIA
TO SNEAKY
TO TRUST
NO HOPE ATOLL
TO OFF THE EDGE
REEF KNOT
LEMME SEE
YAKU 80
©
STONED ALL ALONE

Fig. 5

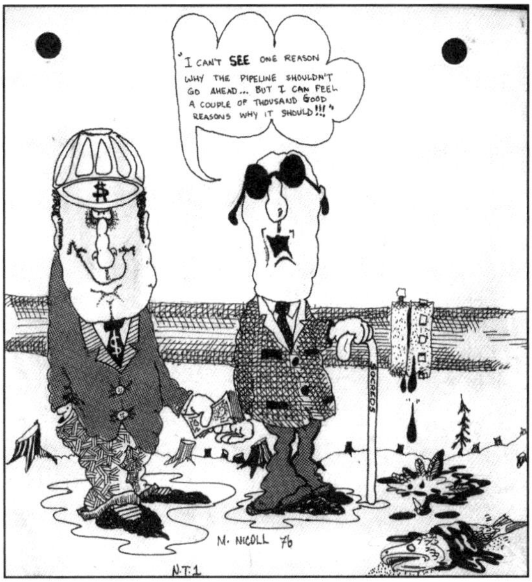

Fig. 6

In his map, Yahgulanaas alters and adjusts place names to reveal what was going on in the fraught landscape. Juskatla is "Juscutit." Massett is "Hadit Missit." There is more revealing play on names: "Someone's Fault," "Robbed Creek," "Ego Creaks." One of the most telling is "Toms (Total) Wasteland," nestled in by "Credibility Gap," "Muddy Crossing," "Slid Pass" and "Overcut." "Toms (Total) Wasteland" makes another appearance in the artist's 1980 cartoon featuring a caricature of Tom Waterland, then BC's Minister of Forests [fig. 3 & 4]. Serving from 1975 to 1986,[4] Waterland was one of the politicians to hold this post the longest. He was mired in the logging conflict in more than one way. During his term, Waterland invested as a shareholder in a logging company active on Haida Gwaii. He resigned in 1986 over this conflict-of-interest, only to return to the legislature in another capacity shortly thereafter.[5]

The public revelation of such an incestuous relationship between government and the logging industry came as no surprise to those who protested against the government's avid support of forestry companies. Yahgulanaas often depicted industry officials with their compadres, the provincial and federal politicians, in cozy collusion. In his earlier works, government and industry officials are represented as either blind, blundering fools or calculating fiends. Blindness as a motif appropriately characterizes the provincial government's blatant support for extractive industries in the 1970s and the 1980s. Visually literalized by men in dark glasses standing beside a leaking pipeline muttering such phrases as, "I can't see any reason why the pipelines shouldn't go ahead," and standing in a massive clearcut saying, "I know that second growth is around here some place!" Yahgulanaas' biting commentary exposes the enormous task that lay before the IPS and other concerned citizens [fig. 6, 7 & 8].

The fiercest frontline struggle for the Haida over their land took place during the nearly four-decade-long reign of the Social Credit Party. This party's legacy of fiscal and social conservatism, controversy and corruption, culminated in its precipitous decline and demise, following former Premier Bill Vander Zalm's 1991 resignation over a conflict of interest scandal. Yahgulanaas' opinion of the Socreds is clear: in a 1976 drawing, former Socred Premier Bill Bennett is called "Bill Bland BC, Bumbler" as he hands over a robbery kit to the Big Bad Wolf in a star-spangled suit (the

US), standing behind Red Riding Hood, who innocently carries a basket of "Resources of BC" [fig. 9]. In a 1984 drawing, Bill Bennett is depicted again, this time wearing a suit, logging boots and a hard hat, wielding a chain saw in a field of stumps labeled "fair play," "health," "responsible government," "education" and "labour" [fig. 10]. Scraggly new-growth of "mistrust," "fear," "hunger" and "crime" have sprouted to replace the old-growth trees. This image argues that this is the landscape the Social Credit party was leaving on Haida Gwaii and other places in BC.

The history of environmental activism in the province has always been colourful, both before and after the Socreds' poor track record of managing natural resources. Yet the province and its economy's utter dependency on logging, hydroelectricity, mining and other resource extractive industries can be likened to an addiction. To illustrate this, Yahgulanaas uses electric plugs as a motif in his work. In the 1970s, during the oil crisis and conflicts in the Middle East, Yahgulanaas developed a character: a man with an electric plug dangling out from his rear [fig. 11]. Surrounding him are stumps and dead birds, all bearing two unmistakable lines suggesting an outlet. He appears enraged as the last remaining bird feebly flies from his grip. In another image from 1980, a gargantuan figure with the same dangling electric plug is shown rampaging through a forest, eating up trees [fig. 12]. Behind it, a cityscape has an outlet for the monster to plug into, and a pipeline excretes the urban waste back into the environment. These images are extremely

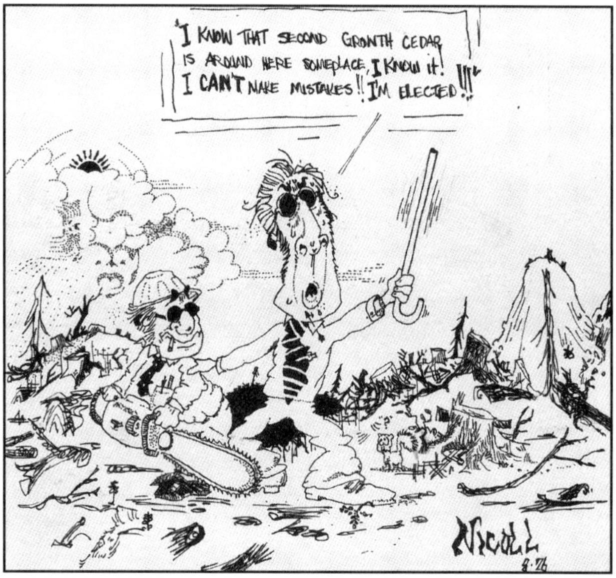

Fig. 7

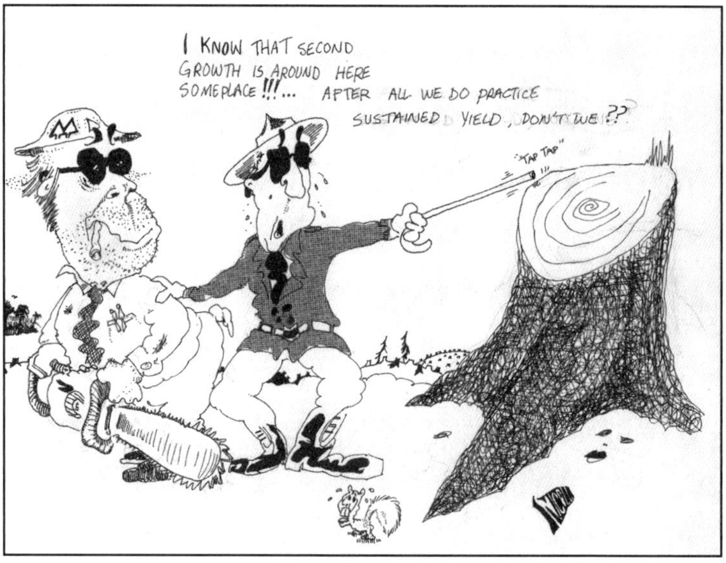

Fig. 8

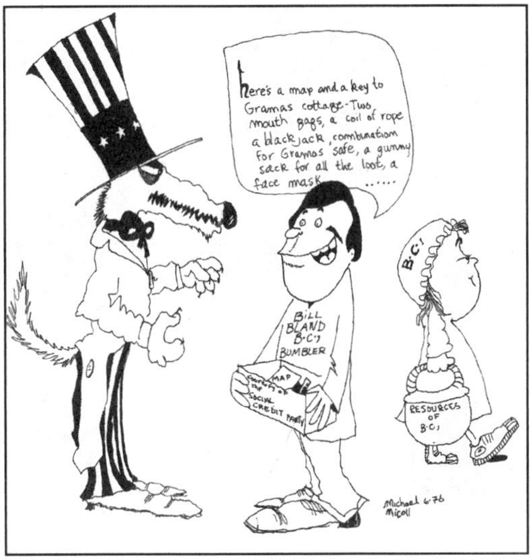

Fig. 9

pertinent today, with the United Nations predicting an eighty-four percent increase of world urban populations by 2050, which would concomitantly increase the human demand on our diminished natural resources.[6]

The question of how to sustain this system looms large. Yahgulanaas' 2002 Haida Manga *The Last Voyage of the Black Ship* addresses this question.[7] In this fantastical story, a young Haida woman, a talking bear and a supernatural being tackle an alien creature and the general population's addiction to lumber. The trio manages to redirect the alien to his home planet and break the spell of lumber dependency with the magical powers of a flying canoe carved out of an old-growth tree. Not only an amusing and endearing tale onto itself, *The Last Voyage* has grounding in the real life struggles of the Haida. The *Black Ship* in the book is based on an actual log hauling barge, ironically called the *Haida Brave*. The self-loading barge was capable

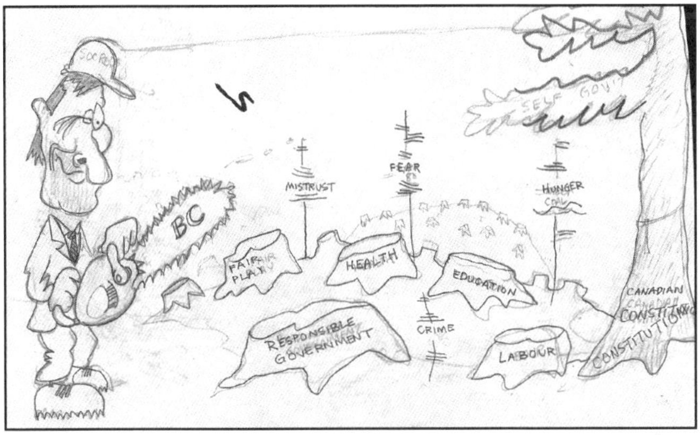

Fig. 10

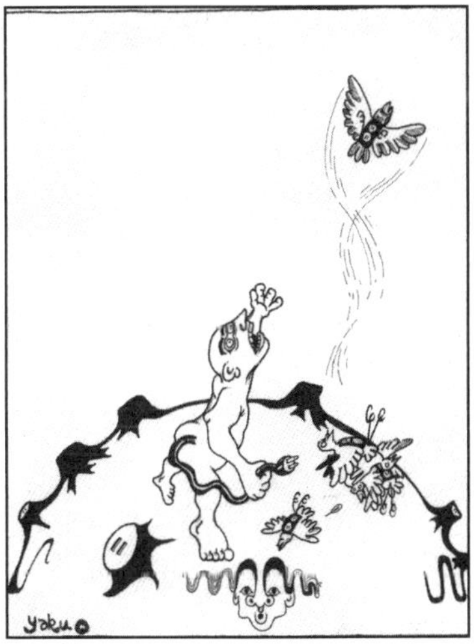

Fig. 11

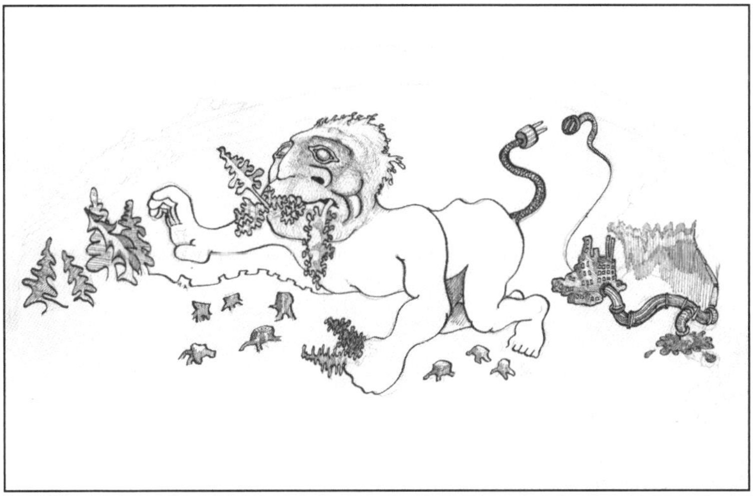

Fig. 12

of transporting twelve thousand logs per load. On August 1, 1996, a group of young environmentalists staged a marine blockade of the *Haida Brave*, or the *Black Ship*, as suggestively renamed by Yahgulanaas. Following this three-hour ordeal, a single canoe, with eight paddlers and flying the Haida flag, met the *Black Ship* in the mid-channel of Massett Inlet. Eventually the *Black Ship* changed its course and fled from the canoe. In addition to writing a story and photographing the event for Haida Gwaii-based *SpruceRoots Magazine*, Yahgulanaas documented this incident in a drawing titled *The Haida Brave Meets the Brave Haida* [fig. 13].[8]

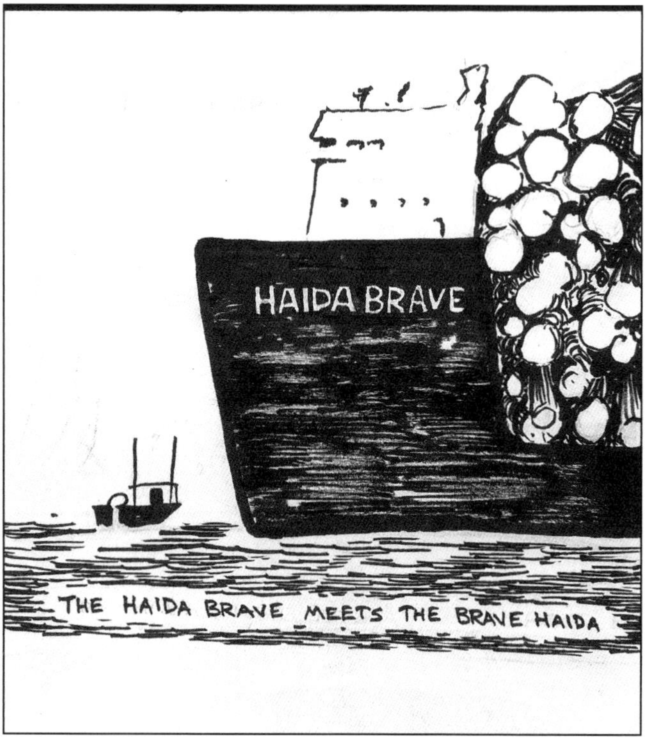

Fig. 13

This publication and many of his works focus on logging because timber has played a crucial part in Haida economy. The Haida are not against the harvesting of trees – in fact, they have been dependent on trees for millennia. In old-growth forests on the West Coast, the frequency of Culturally Modified Trees (called CMTs) which bear the mark of human use are proof of this long established relationship of the Haida and other Indigenous nations to their land. They have been used to establish their rights and title in the eyes of Western law. In the ongoing, uphill battle over resources, there is much onus put on the Indigenous Peoples to not only protect what remain in their hands, but also to prove their traditional use of their sovereign land in a judicial system that was forced upon them. Yahgulanaas' 1985 drawing of a man in a ceremonial blanket, standing in front of a judge, exudes this sense of burden [fig. 14]. The caption below reads, "Mr. Richardson, you are blocking the court. You are breaking the law. Will you please sit down and let me go to work." *

This drawing bears witness to a real event: the court proceedings that followed the arrests at the Ly-

*In Fig. 14, Yahgulanaas appropriates the words used by Frank Beban, a logging contractor, who addressed the logging protesters as law-breakers when they stood blockading his trucks and crews on the road into Lyell Island in the Fall of 1985.

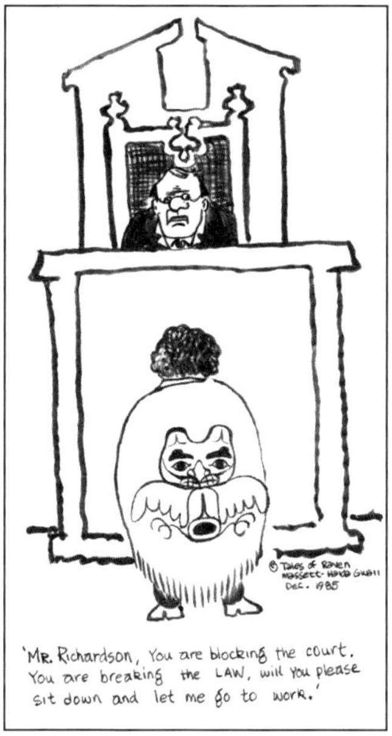

Fig. 14

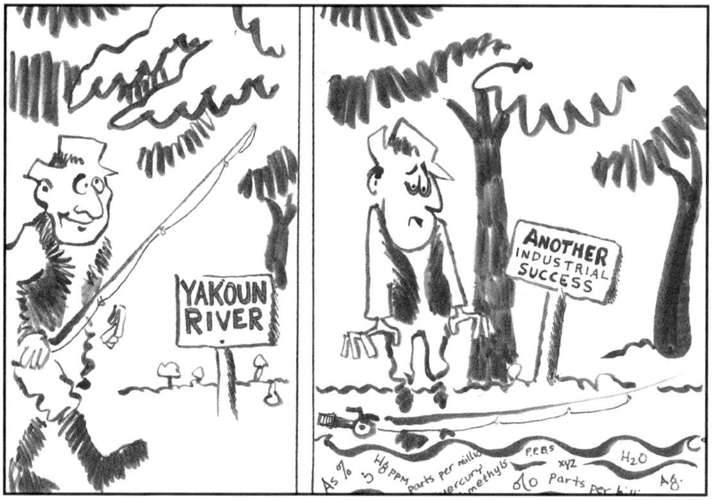

Fig. 15

ell Island – or Athili Gwaii, in Haida – logging-protest in the South Moresby region. On November 15, 1985, Miles Richardson, the then-elected President of the Haida Nation –who would later serve as BC Chief Treaty Commissioner – was in court defending the Haida citizens arrested. He stood before Justice Allan McEachern, who later became infamous for his draconian ruling in the landmark 1991 Delgamuukw case against the validity of Indigenous oral testimony.

The Lyell Island protest marked the point of eruption, after a frustrating string of legal actions and negotiations with the provincial government to protect South Moresby that led nowhere, ending with logging proceeding as usual. During the protest, seventy-two Haida, starting with a group of elders in their finest button blankets, were arrested for defying a court order to stop blockading a logging road. Their images were broadcast into people's living rooms fueling growing support for their Indigenous, sovereign control over their land and protection of the wilderness areas.[9] Of those arrested, a handful, including Yahgulanaas, were convicted and given jail sentences from four to six months, only to have their sentences dropped in response to the overwhelming outcry from different communities, including – significantly – labour unions with members in the logging industry.[10]

In many ways, this is a success story. The political, legal and cultural fight that Yahgulanaas' images depict, and are a part of, did not go unrewarded. Today the South Moresby wilderness area is protected as Gwaii Haanas National Park Reserve and Haida Heritage Site. Under a 1993 agreement between Ottawa and Haida Gwaii, it is co-managed by the Haida and federal governments.[11] The

Council of Haida Nation, formed in 1974, has recently concluded a land-use planning process with the provincial government, with a one thousand-year plan in mind.[12] However, the work is never finished, as there are constant encroachments by outside interests on Haida Gwaii, like the proposed oil tankers carrying tar sands crude oil through their waters.

Much of Yahgulanaas' work has been to inform and educate Island citizens through visually accessible materials that cut through the technical and legal jargon used by the government and the industry. For instance, *Mutants of the Pit* – the second issue of *Tales of the Raven*, published by IPS in 1987 – illustrates the effects of heightened mercury levels that would have spelled disaster for the fish stock, and those consuming it, if the proposed Cinola gold mine on Graham Island had been approved [for a related drawing, see fig. 15]. In the illustration *Gwaii Scientist*, Yahgulanaas explains how 3-Nitrobenzanthrone, a carcinogen found in diesel exhaust, poses great health risks to those who use diesel engine boats and vehicles [fig. 16]. And climate change, of course, is a subject to which the artist often returns in his work [fig. 17].

Beyond illustrating these issues, Yahgulanaas' new works encourage and inspire by providing a larger parable for contemporary reality. In his 2008 publication *Flight of the Hummingbird*, based on an Indigenous South American tale from the Quechua people, a lone hummingbird transports drops of water to a raging forest fire.[13] Not unlike the small group who set out in the 1970s to save an island from unsound logging practices that were enthusiastically backed by corrupt government officials, this seemingly small gesture resonates with people the world over who tackle mountainous tasks today. This story, however, ends with the hummingbird telling the other forest animals who have been merely watching her, "I'm doing what I can." Far from being happily-ever-after, this ending leaves open for speculation whether the other animals join in to put out the fire. Considering the subtitle – *A Parable for the Environment* – the story puts the onus on individual readers to do what they can.

It is a sad commentary on the current state of affairs that some of Yahgulanaas' oldest images of oil spills and their effects on marine life have even more urgency today. For example, a drawing made thirty-five years ago, of an oil tanker named OILLY II wears a large bandage on its side, not quite able to hold in the oil that gushes blood-like out of its leviathan-like body [fig. 18]. A screw with wings hovers overhead, as though it was supposed to have plugged OILLY II's open wound, or more likely as a symbol that if this traffic was allowed to happen everyone would be "screwed." Then there are studies of birds, fish and other marine life, as well as pages of character sketches that lead up to the creation of the very first issue of *Tales of Raven, No Tankers, T'anks* [fig. 19 & 20].

At the time of writing, Calgary-based company, Enbridge, proposed to build the Northern Gate-

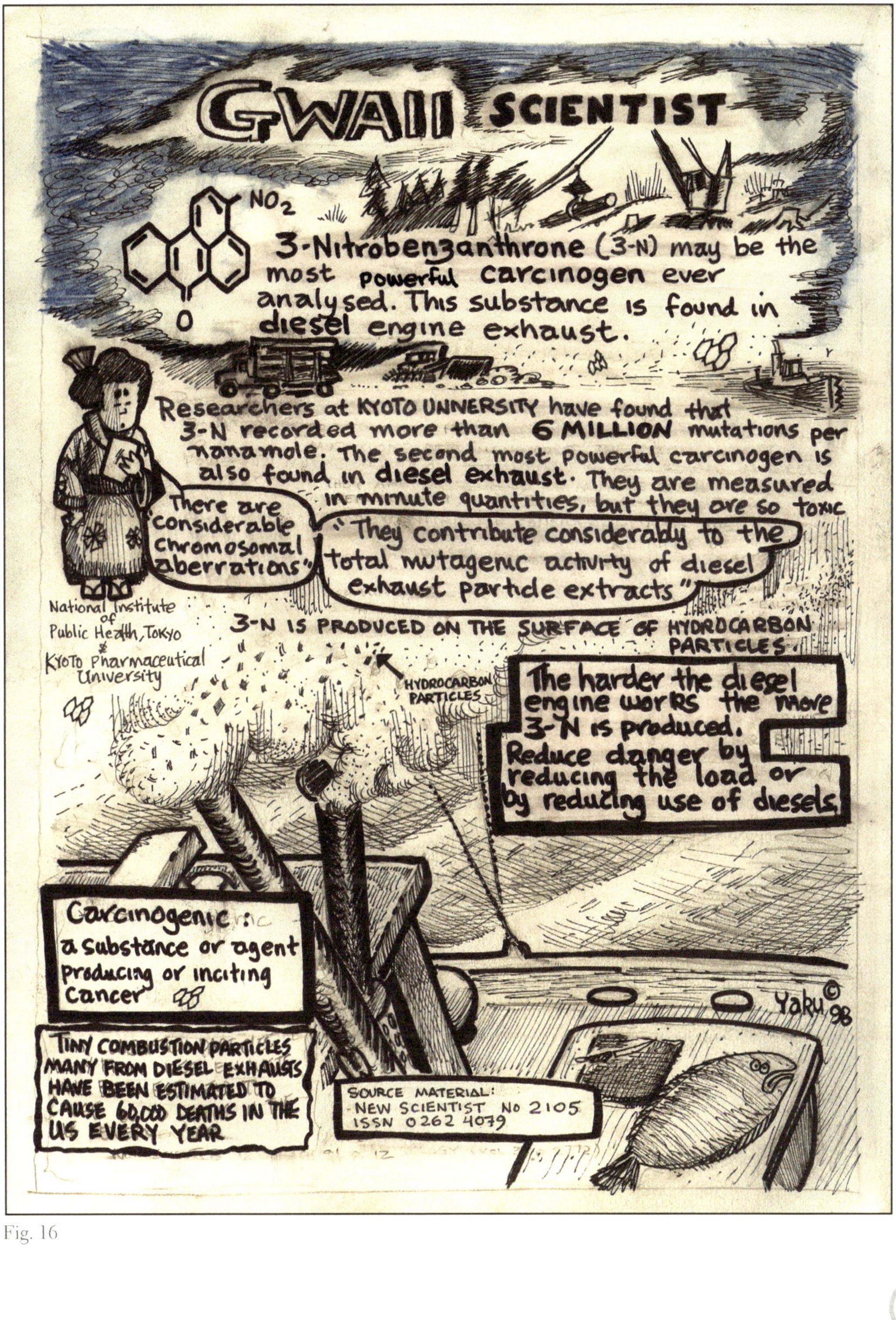

GWAII SCIENTIST
NO2
O
3-Nitrobenzanthrone (3-N) may be the most powerful carcinogen ever analysed. This substance is found in diesel engine exhaust.
Researchers at KYOTO UNIVERSITY have found that 3-N recorded more than 6 MILLION mutations per nanamole. The second most powerful carcinogen is also found in diesel exhaust. They are measured in minute quantities, but they are so toxic
"There are considerable chromosomal aberrations"
"They contribute considerably to the total mutagenic activity of diesel exhaust particle extracts"
National Institute of Public Health, Tokyo & Kyoto Pharmaceutical University
3-N IS PRODUCED ON THE SURFACE OF HYDROCARBON PARTICLES.
HYDROCARBON PARTICLES
The harder the diesel engine works the more 3-N is produced. Reduce danger by reducing the load or by reducing use of diesels.
Carcinogenic: a substance or agent producing or inciting cancer
Yaku © 98
TINY COMBUSTION PARTICLES MANY FROM DIESEL EXHAUSTS HAVE BEEN ESTIMATED TO CAUSE 60,000 DEATHS IN THE US EVERY YEAR
SOURCE MATERIAL: NEW SCIENTIST No 2105 ISSN 0262 4079

Fig. 16

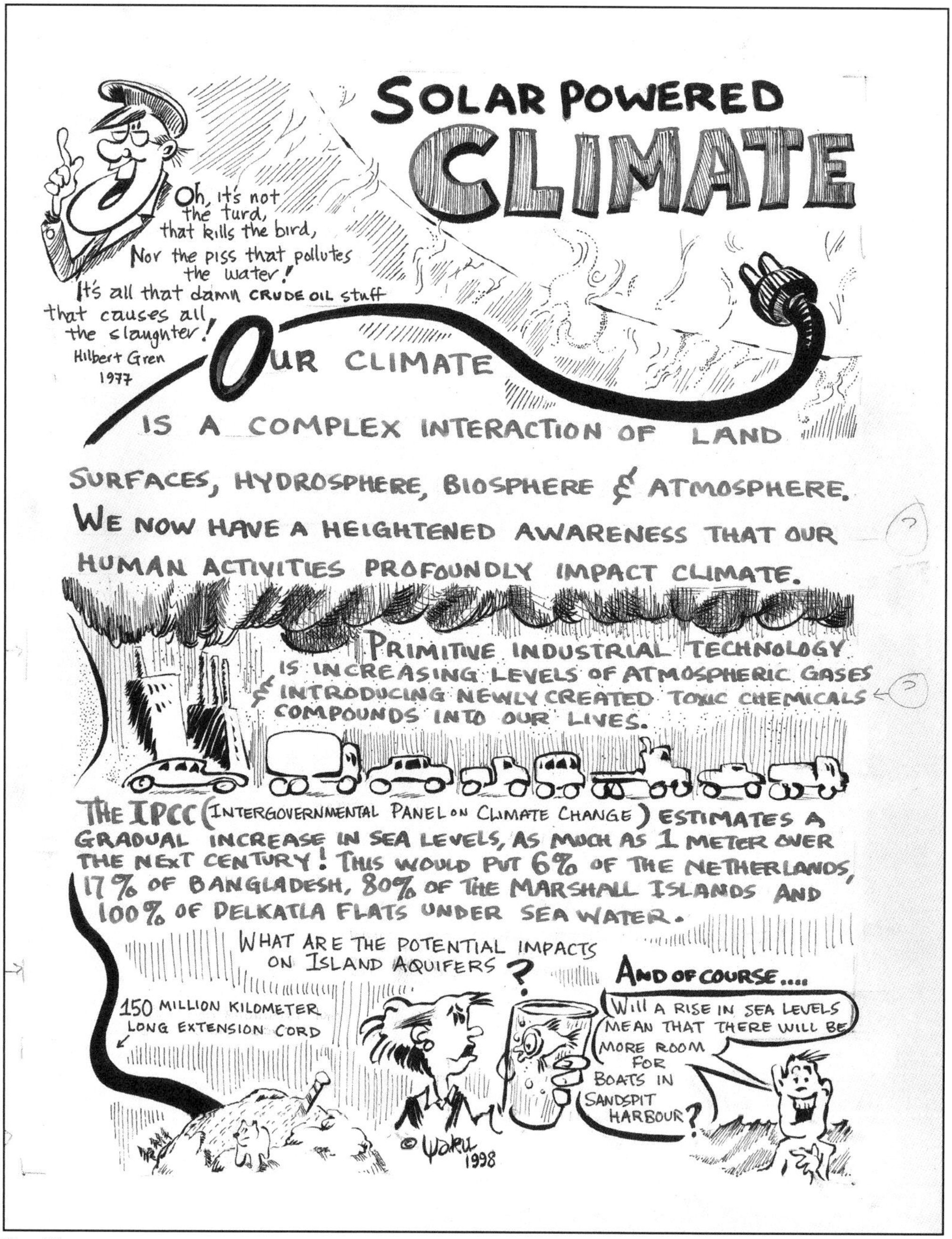

SOLAR POWERED
CLIMATE
Oh, it's not the turd, that kills the bird, Nor the piss that pollutes the water! It's all that damn CRUDE OIL stuff that causes all the slaughter!
Hilbert Gren 1977
OUR CLIMATE IS A COMPLEX INTERACTION OF LAND SURFACES, HYDROSPHERE, BIOSPHERE & ATMOSPHERE. WE NOW HAVE A HEIGHTENED AWARENESS THAT OUR HUMAN ACTIVITIES PROFOUNDLY IMPACT CLIMATE.
PRIMITIVE INDUSTRIAL TECHNOLOGY IS INCREASING LEVELS OF ATMOSPHERIC GASES & INTRODUCING NEWLY CREATED TOXIC CHEMICALS COMPOUNDS INTO OUR LIVES.
THE IPCC (INTERGOVERNMENTAL PANEL ON CLIMATE CHANGE) ESTIMATES A GRADUAL INCREASE IN SEA LEVELS, AS MUCH AS 1 METER OVER THE NEXT CENTURY! THIS WOULD PUT 6% OF THE NETHERLANDS, 17% OF BANGLADESH, 80% OF THE MARSHALL ISLANDS AND 100% OF DELKATLA FLATS UNDER SEA WATER.
WHAT ARE THE POTENTIAL IMPACTS ON ISLAND AQUIFERS?
150 MILLION KILOMETER LONG EXTENSION CORD
AND OF COURSE....
WILL A RISE IN SEA LEVELS MEAN THAT THERE WILL BE MORE ROOM FOR BOATS IN SANDSPIT HARBOUR?
© Waku 1998

Fig. 17

way Project — a pipeline that would stretch from the oil sands of Alberta to Kitimat port in BC, where tankers would transport an average of five hundred and twenty-five thousand barrels of oil per day along ecologically sensitive waterways, including that of Haida Gwaii, to the thirsty, developing markets across the Pacific Ocean.[14] This is happening in spite of Enbridge's record of three different pipeline leaks between July and September 2010.[15] Also, on April 20, 2010, BP's Deepwater Horizon rig in the Gulf of Mexico exploded, causing the largest marine oil spill in history, at a total estimated five million barrels.[16]

Since the industrial revolution, the search for and extraction of petroleum has continued, despite a growing consensus that the use of this energy source will soon ruin the global climate for humans. The world is powered by an engine that runs on fossil fuel and Yahgulanaas' pictures reveal the mechanics of this engine and how it is greased: a blind Socred taking a bribe in front of a leaking pipeline; the mayor of Kitimat in conversation with a broken oil tanker [fig. 21]; a willfully ignorant official from the National Energy Board confronting a group of angry marine creatures [fig. 22].

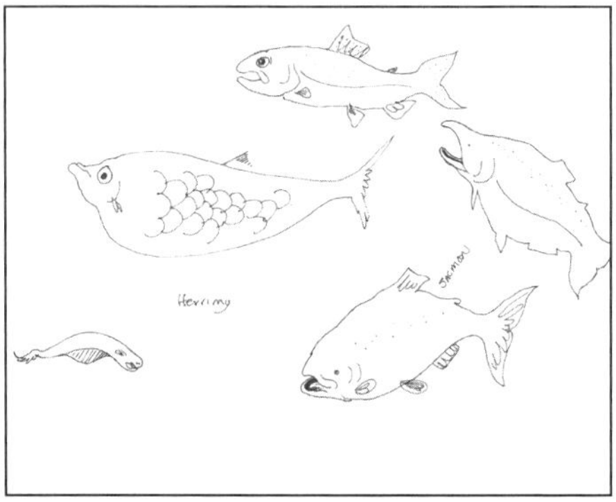

Fig. 19

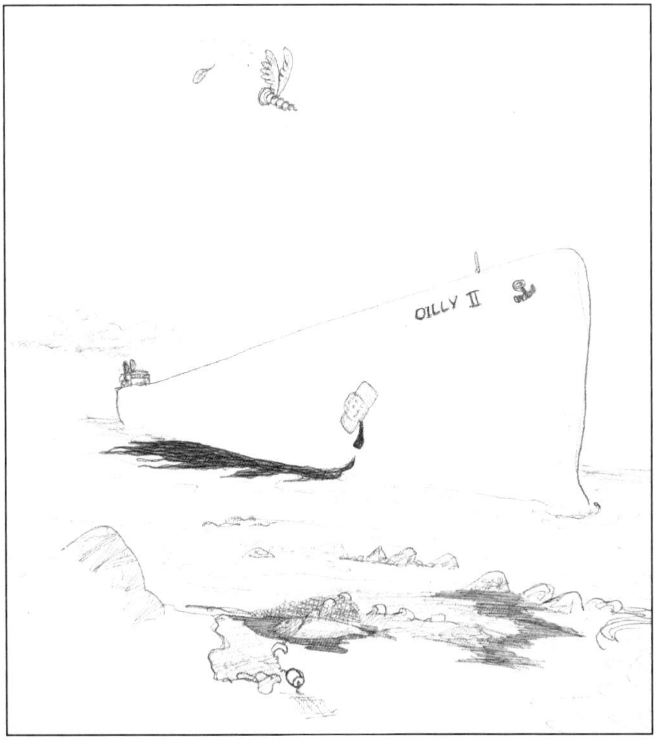

Fig. 18

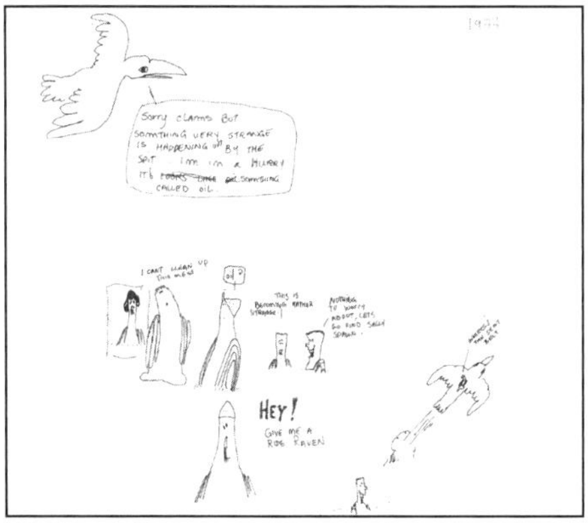

Fig. 20

These images stir people, whatever the reaction may be — laughter, discomfort or serious contemplation. The visual materials collected in the following pages provide a glimpse into the thousands of pages from Michael Nicoll Yahgulanaas' archive that document the decades of political and cultural work that have fostered the old-growth forests of Haida Gwaii. The four complete works of graphic narratives that punctuate this publication — *No Tankers, T'anks; Mutants of the Pit; Tree Spirit* and *Raven Kept Walking* — also underscore the importance of the natural world in the cultural imaginary and the identity of the Haida Nation. Yet, as it is demonstrated in the following interview, "Oblique Strategies," the artist's drawings speak to the larger world beyond Haida Gwaii, and beyond Canada. Any willing reader can establish a personal connection to the richness of these images, and the land and the stories that they depict. These connections nurture and sustain culture so that it may continue to shape-shift in the worlds to come.

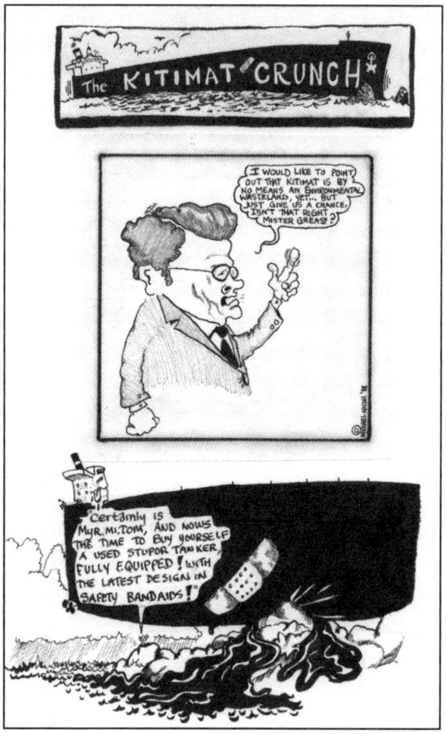

Fig. 21

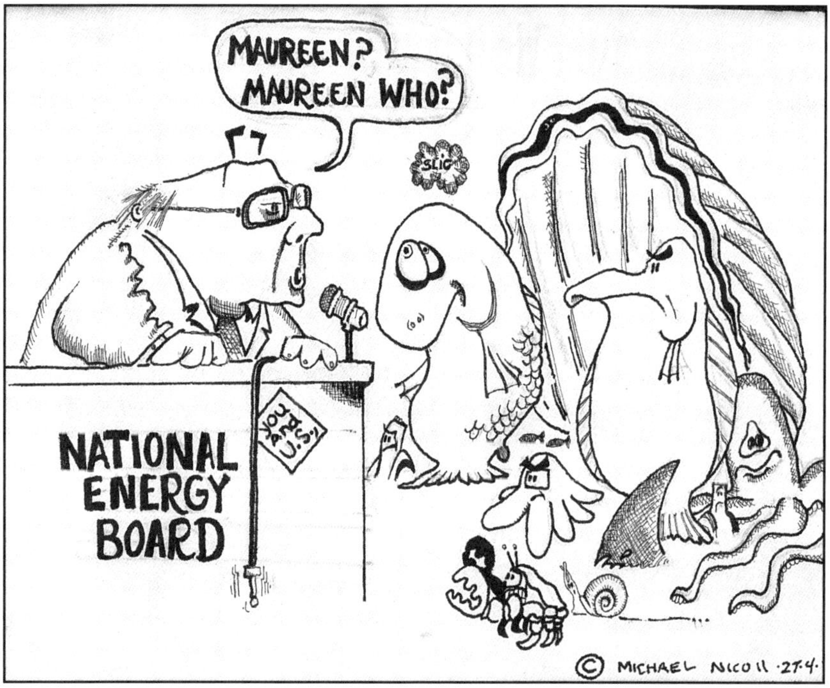

Fig. 22

Endnotes

1 Office of the Premier and Council of Haida Nation, "B.C., Haida Nation Restore Name 'Haida Gwaii' to Islands," news release, June 17, 2010, http://www2.news.gov.bc.ca/newsreleases_2009-2013/2010PREM0125-000719.htm.

2 Gowgaia Institute, "Logging Haida Gwaii 1900- 2005," *SpruceRoots Magazine*, July 2005, centrefold insert. Also available online. Accessed December 20, 2010, http://www.spruceroots.org/Maps/Logging05-BG.html.

3 "Athlii Gwaii: 25 Years Down the Road," *Haida Laas*, November 2010, 4. Accessed December 20, 2010, www.haidanation.ca/Pages/Haida_Laas/PDF/Journals/Athlii_Gwaii.72.pdf.

4 "British Columbia Forest Service History," *Province of British Columbia*, last modified October 2010, accessed December 27, 2010, http://www.for.gov.bc.ca/hfd/library/history.htm#Ministers.

5 Kenneth Freed, "British Columbia Officials Survive, Thrive in Scandals," *Los Angeles Times*, March 9, 1986, accessed December 27, 2010, http://articles.latimes.com/1986-03-09/news/mn17933_1_british-columbia.

6 *World Urbanization Prospects: The 2009 Revision, Highlights* (New York: United Nations Department of Economic and Social Affairs Population Division, 2010). 4. Accessed December 20, 2010, http://esa.un.org/unpd/wup/Documents/WUP2009_Highlights_Final.pdf.

7 Michael Nicoll Yahgulanaas, *The Last Voyage of the Black Ship* (Vancouver: Western Canada Wilderness Committee, 2002).

8 Michael Nicoll Yahgulanaas, "How Many Canoes are on that Black Ship?" *SpruceRoots Magazine*, August 1996, accessed December 27, 2010, http://www.spruceroots.org/BlackShip.html.

9 "A Chronology of Conflict" *Haida Laas*, Special Edition, February 1986. 3-5; Ian Gill, *All that we say is ours* (Vancouver: Douglas & McIntyre, 2009). 127-134; Caitlyn Vernon, "We Gathered to Say Haw'aa," *The Tyee*, November 25, 2010, accessed November 30, 2010, http:/thetyee.ca/Life/2010/11/25/SayHawaa/.

10 The numbers of people convicted vary from ten to thirteen depending on the reference. Ten are noted to have been convicted in Ian Gill, *All that we say is ours* (Vancouver: Douglas & McIntyre, 2009) pp. 127-134; twelve are noted to be convicted in "Athlii Gwaii: 25 Years Down the Road," *Haida Laas*, November 2010, 4; thirteen are noted to be convicted in personal email communication with the artist. Accessed January 23, 2011. Also in email communication dated March 16, 2011, the artist further elucidates the court proceeding and reflects on its implication. "The Judge had threatened us with a year in jail and gave us a week to think things over and if we apologized to the court all would be forgiven. However after that long week was over and we were back in his courtroom, he realized with some alarm that none of us were going to apologize to him. He recanted, saying, 'I don't know where you got that (idea of prison).' We were found guilty but immediately pardoned. This as to say that the courts apologized to us."

11 "Gwaii Haanas National Park Reserve and Haida Heritage Site," last modified October 12, 2010, accessed December 1, 2010. http://www.pc.gc.ca/pn-np/bc/gwaiihaanas/index.aspx.

12 "Haida Land Use Vision (HLUV)," *Council of the Haida Nation*, accessed December 27, 2010. http://www.haidanation.ca/Pages/Programs/Forests/Forest%20Guardians/Land%20Planning/HLUV.html.

13 Michael Nicoll Yahgulanaas, *Flight of the Hummingbird: a Parable for the Environment* (Vancouver: Greystone Books, 2008).
14 "Project Info: Northern Gateway at a Glance," *Enbridge Northern Gateway Pipelines*, accessed December 20, 2010, http://www.northerngateway.ca/project-info/northern-gateway-at-a-glance.
15 Nathan Vanderklippe, "Third Enbridge Line Springs Leak," *Globe and Mail*, September 13, 2010, accessed December 20, 2010, http://www.theglobeandmail.com/globe-investor/thirdenbridge-line-springs-leakarticle1705906/.
16 "BP oil spill by the numbers," *CBC News*, October 21, 2010, accessed December 27, 2010, http://www.cbc.ca/world/story/2010/10/19/f-bp-oil-spill-numbers.html.

Figures

Fig. 1 *What's a Name?*, 1988. Originally published in the *Queen Charlotte Islands Observer* (Haida Gwaii).
Fig. 2 Untitled, 1979. Originally published in *All Alone Stone* / Islands Protection Society (Haida Gwaii).
Fig. 3 Untitled, 1980.
Fig. 4 Untitled, 1980.
Fig. 5 Untitled, 1980.
Fig. 6 Untitled, 1976.
Fig. 7 Untitled, 1976.
Fig. 8 Untitled, 1976.
Fig. 9 Untitled, 1976.
Fig. 10 Untitled, 1981.
Fig. 11 Untitled, 1977.
Fig. 12 Untitled, 1977.
Fig. 13 *The Haida Brave Meets the Brave Haida*, 1996. Originally published in *SpruceRoots Magazine* (Haida Gwaii)
Fig. 14 Untitled, 1985.
Fig. 15 Untitled, 1988.
Fig. 16 *Gwaii Scientist*, 1998. Originally published in *SpruceRoots Magazine* (Haida Gwaii).
Fig. 17 *Solar Powered Climate*, 1998. Originally published in *SpruceRoots Magazine* (Haida Gwaii).
Fig. 18 Untitled, 1976.
Fig. 19 Untitled, 1976.
Fig. 20 Untitled, 1976. Character sketches from *Tales of Raven, No Tankers, T'anks.*
Fig. 21 *The Kitimat Crunch*, 1978.
Fig. 22 Untitled, 1978. Originally published in *The Northern Times* (Terrace, BC).

Comics

No Tankers, T'anks

Produced in 1977 for the Islands Protection Society, Tales of Raven, No. 1, No Tankers, T'anks *was a part of a successful organized effort to stop the proposal to transport Valdez oil through the northern coast of British Columbia. Most of the three-thousand copies of the first print were distributed on Haida Gwaii while a handful of copies made their way off the islands. This is its second printing.*

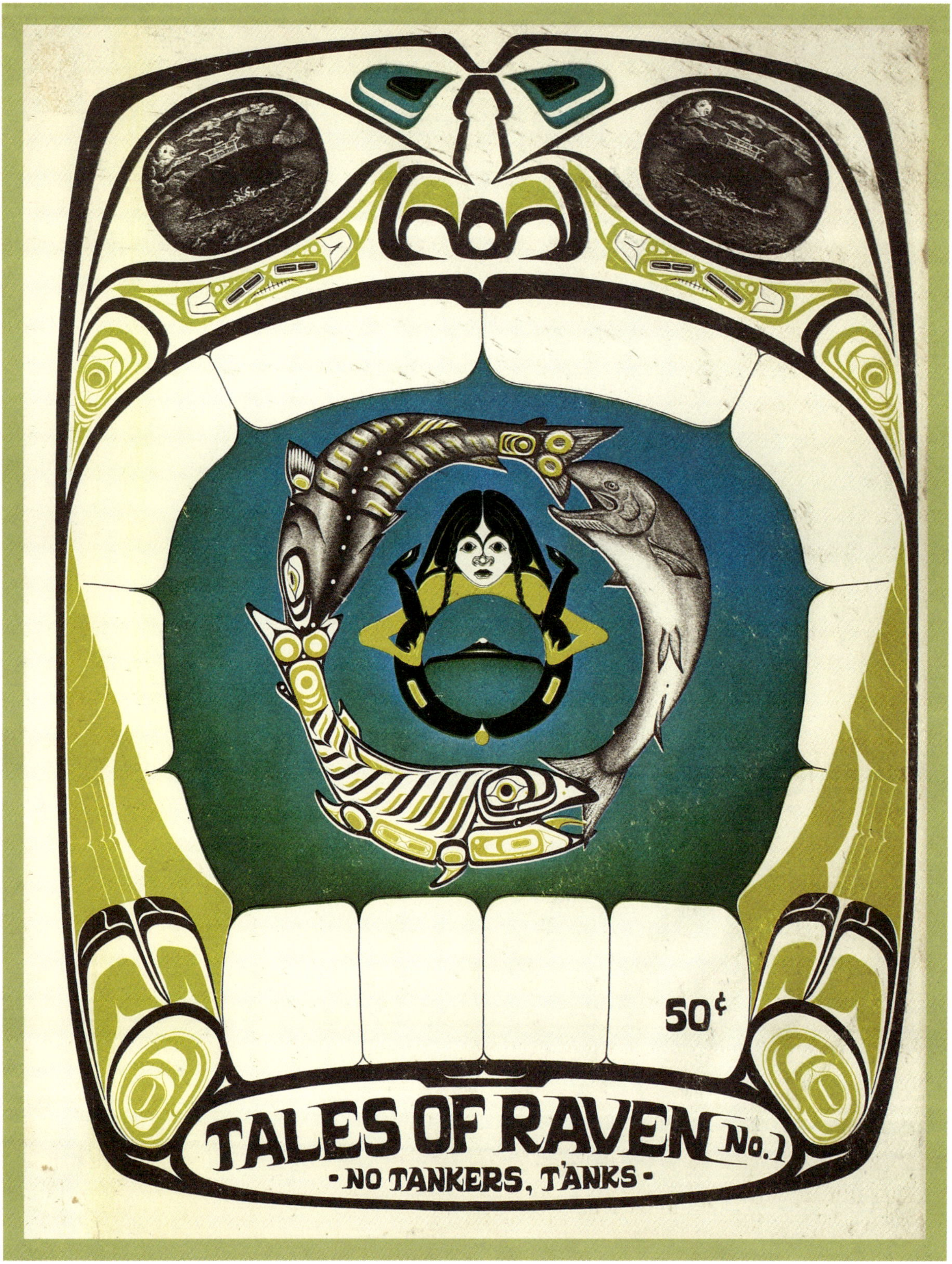

No Tankers, T'anks jointly produced by Michael Nicoll Yahgulanaas and John Broadhead.
Cover illustration and design by John Broadhead.

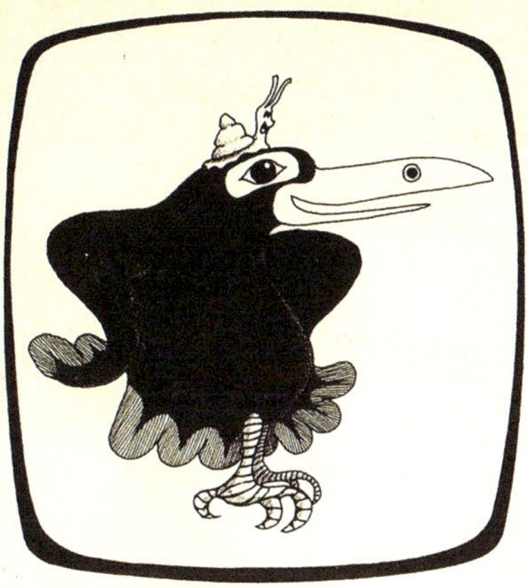

RAVEN, **HERO** OF THIS COMIC BOOK (AND **OTHERS** TO COME). **HAIDA** LEGENDS SOMETIMES PORTRAY **RAVEN** (A.K.A. ***YELTH***) AS A BIT OF A **TRICKSTER** WHO RARELY WAITS AROUND LONG ENOUGH TO TAKE RESPONSIBILITY FOR HIS DEEDS — ONE OF WHICH WAS COAXING THE **FIRST HUMAN BEINGS** TO COME OUT OF **HIDING** IN A **CLAM SHELL**...... THE LITTLE **MOLLUSC** ON **RAVEN'S** HEAD IS:

LIMPET, A TINY SNAIL-LIKE CREATURE, WHO **SIMULTANEOUSLY RUMINATES** ON VEGETABLES AND THE MEANING OF LIFE. THEIR LITTLE WHITE **CONICAL** SHELLS, OFTEN FOUND TOSSED UP ON BEACHES, ARE USUALLY TAKEN AS EVIDENCE OF ONE LESS LIMPET IN THE WORLD.... **THIS IS NOT THE CASE.** THEY ARE MERELY DISCARDED THINKING CAPS, WHICH THE **LIMPET** REMOVES AS NEW THOUGHTS GROW OLD AND **WEIGHTY.**

SUPPORTING CAST

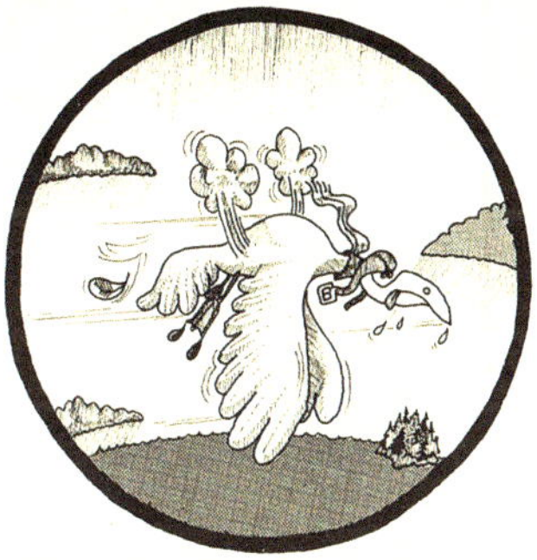

THE ALBATROSS:

DIOMEDEA NIGRIPES – A LARGE VAGRANT OF A BIRD WHICH ROAMS THE OCEANS OF THE WORLD, ONLY COMING WITHIN SIGHT OF LAND WHEN BURDENED WITH THE SOLEMN TASK OF DELIVERING **OMENS.** HE IS FOND OF FOLLOWING SHIPS AROUND, ALWAYS HAS BEEN — ONLY THE SHIPS HAVE CHANGED, AND SO HAVE THEIR CARGOES. **GONE ARE THE DAYS** OF SILKS AND SPICES – **COME ARE THE DAYS** OF BARRELS OF OIL, FROM WHICH WE MANUFACTURE SYNTHETIC FABRICS AND CONVINCING SALAD DRESSINGS AND JUST ABOUT ANYTHING ELSE YOU CARE TO READ THE LABEL ON, CLOSELY. THE **ALBATROSS** AMUSES HIMSELF BETWEEN JOBS BY RECITING TASTELESS VARIATIONS ON **THE RHYME OF THE ANCIENT MARINER.**

THE RAZOR CLAMS:

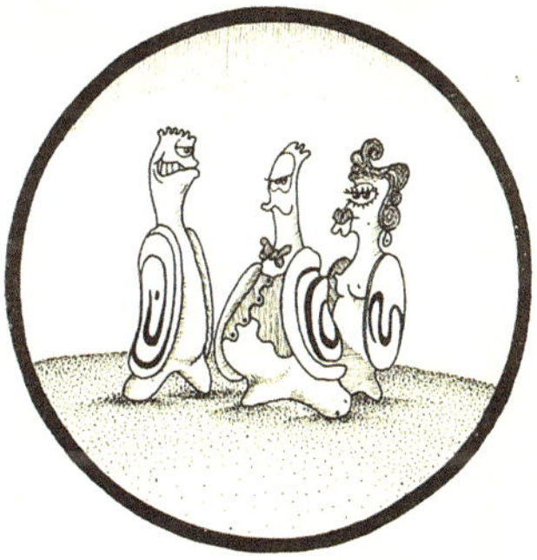

SILIQUE PATULA – A THIN, RAZOR-SHARP SHELLED BIVALVE, LIVING IN POPULOUS COMMUNITIES ON THE SURF-SWEPT BEACHES OF THE NORTHEASTERN PACIFIC OCEAN. AS ALREADY MENTIONED, **RAVEN** DISCOVERED TINY **HUMAN BEINGS** HIDING INSIDE A **RAZOR CLAM** SHELL AND BROUGHT THEM OUT INTO THE WORLD WITH A FRIENDLY WELCOME. AS YOU CAN SEE, HE DIDN'T QUITE GET THE HUMANS **COMPLETELY** OUT OF THE SHELL (THEY MUST HAVE LEFT SOME OF THEIR LUGGAGE BEHIND). WE ARE THEREBY ABSOLVED OF THE USUAL CHARGES AGAINST CARTOONISTS AS BEING UNTHINKING ANTHROPOMORPHISTS...

ABOUT THE COVER:

THE COVER DEPICTS THE HEAD OF AN **EARTH MOTHER** FIGURE. THE **OVOIDS** OF HER EYES ARE TWO PIECES OF **ARGYLLITE** WHICH HAVE BEEN POLISHED TO SUCH A FINE DEGREE THAT WE CAN SEE WHAT SHE IS SEEING. THE TWO PAIRS OF **RED OVOIDS** ARE TRADITIONAL **SALMON-TROUT HEAD** DESIGNS, AND REPRESENT THE **JOINTS** OF HER JAW AND WRISTS. HER **HANDS** ARE CUPPED BESIDE HER **MOUTH**, WHICH IS WIDE OPEN IN THE PROCESS OF YELLING SOMETHING AT US. THE FOUR FIGURES AGAINST THE BLUE-GREEN ARE HER MESSAGE. IN THE MIDDLE IS A **CHILD** WITH ITS LEGS TUCKED UP THROUGH ITS ARMS, WHICH ARE HOLDING ONTO ITS **ABDOMEN** — WHICH CONTAINS A SCHEMATIC VERSION OF AN ISLAND. IT IS A GESTURE OF **VULNERABILITY.** SURROUNDING THE CHILD ARE **THREE FISH:** ON THE **RIGHT** IS THE REAL THING, WHICH WE EAT. THE **BOTTOM** FISH REPRESENTS THE IDEA OF THE FISH, SHARED BY MANY CULTURES AS A RELIGIOUS **SYMBOL OF CONTINUITY** — IN ITS BELLY ARE TWO RED EGGS – THE EYES OF THE FUTURE. THE **THIRD** FISH IS THE TRANSITIONAL STEP, REPRESENTING THE HUMAN PENCHANT AND NEED TO THINK, TRANSFORM, TO **CONSTRUCT SYMBOLS** AS WE SEE FIT. THE **CHEEKS** BELOW THE EARTH MOTHER'S EYES ARE CANOES. HER **TEARS** OF ANGUISH CONTAIN MINIATURE OIL SLICKS.

THE GRAPHIC STYLE OF THE **NORTHWEST COAST INDIANS** USED HERE CANNOT BE CONSIDERED AS ACCURATE OR AUTHENTIC. IT WAS PRODUCED BY A MEMBER OF THE **CANUCK** TRIBE. THE "FORMLINE" STYLE WAS BORROWED FOR ITS ALLEGORICAL CAPABILITIES, AND ITS USE WAS INSPIRED BY THE FACT THAT, FOR WHATEVER REASONS, THE NATIVE PEOPLES AT ONE TIME DID A MUCH **CLEANER** JOB OF **CARETAKING** THE PLANET THAN WE SEEM TO BE DOING TODAY.

THE COVER ARTWORK IS AVAILABLE AS AN **18"X 24" POSTER.** SEE **INSIDE BACK COVER** FOR DETAILS ON HOW TO GET ONE.

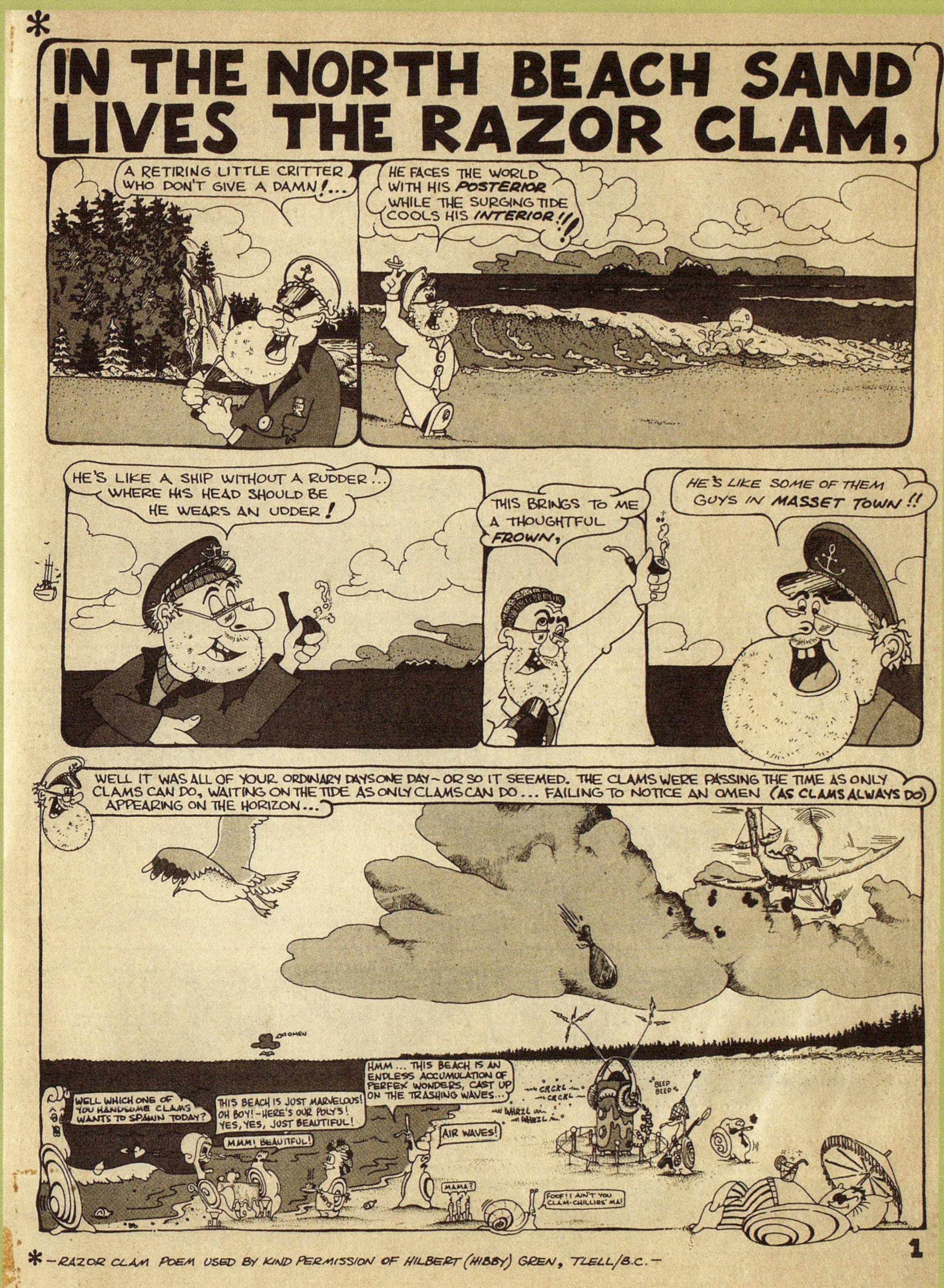
*
IN THE NORTH BEACH SAND LIVES THE RAZOR CLAM,
A RETIRING LITTLE CRITTER WHO DON'T GIVE A DAMN!...
HE FACES THE WORLD WITH HIS POSTERIOR WHILE THE SURGING TIDE COOLS HIS INTERIOR!!
HE'S LIKE A SHIP WITHOUT A RUDDER... WHERE HIS HEAD SHOULD BE HE WEARS AN UDDER!
THIS BRINGS TO ME A THOUGHTFUL FROWN,
HE'S LIKE SOME OF THEM GUYS IN MASSET TOWN!!
WELL IT WAS ALL OF YOUR ORDINARY DAYS ONE DAY ~ OR SO IT SEEMED. THE CLAMS WERE PASSING THE TIME AS ONLY CLAMS CAN DO, WAITING ON THE TIDE AS ONLY CLAMS CAN DO... FAILING TO NOTICE AN OMEN (AS CLAMS ALWAYS DO) APPEARING ON THE HORIZON...
OMEN
WELL WHICH ONE OF YOU HANDSOME CLAMS WANTS TO SPAWN TODAY?
THIS BEACH IS JUST MARVELOUS! OH BOY! - HERE'S OUR POLY'S! YES, YES, JUST BEAUTIFUL!
MMM! BEAUTIFUL!
HMM... THIS BEACH IS AN ENDLESS ACCUMULATION OF PERFEX WONDERS, CAST UP ON THE TRASHING WAVES...
AIR WAVES!
CRCKL CRCKL
WHRZL WHRZL
BEEP BEEP
MAMA?
FOOF!! AIN'T YOU CLAM-CHILLIES' MA!
* - RAZOR CLAM POEM USED BY KIND PERMISSION OF HILBERT (HIBBY) GREN, TLELL/B.C. -
1

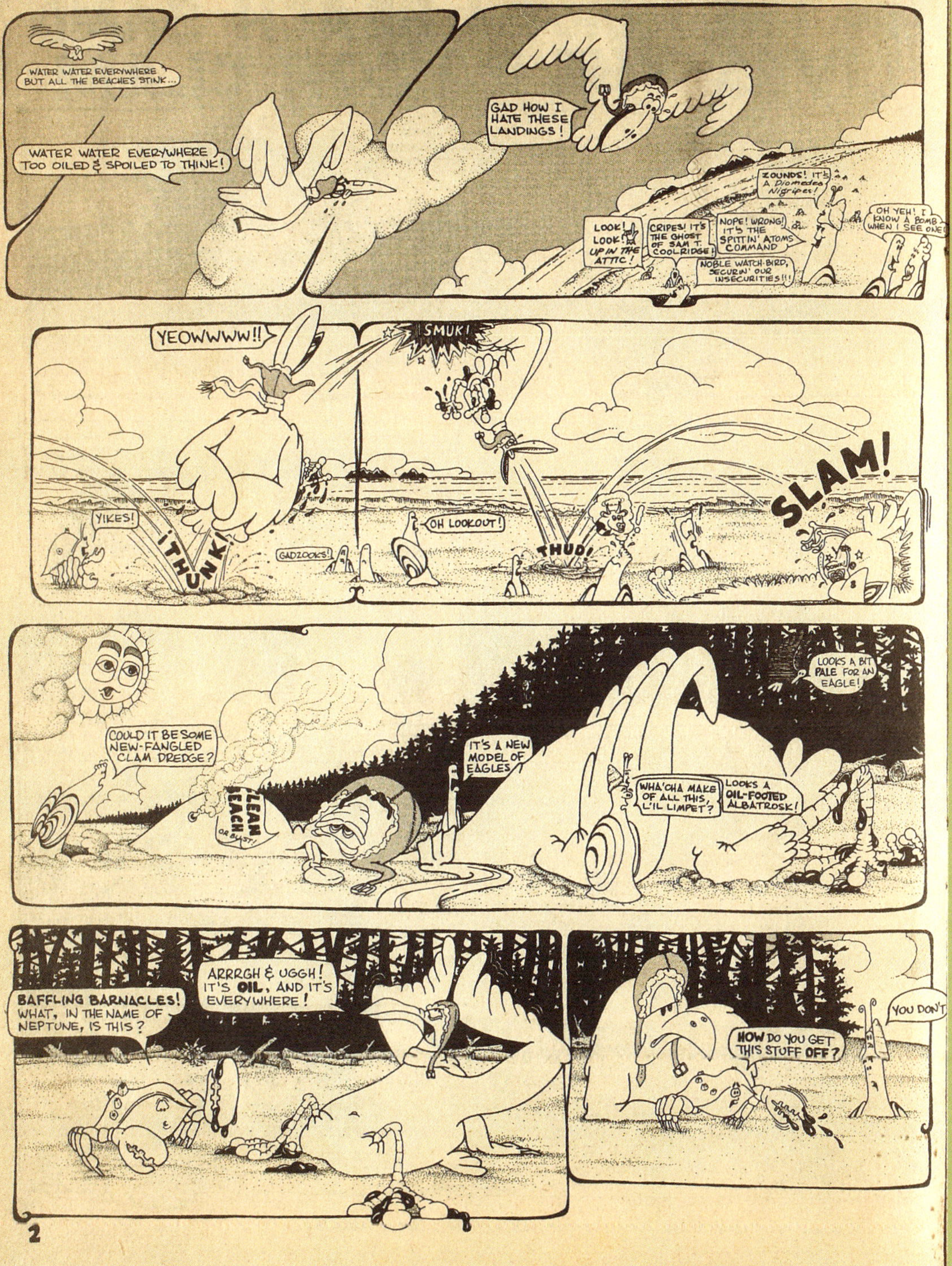
WATER WATER EVERYWHERE BUT ALL THE BEACHES STINK...
WATER WATER EVERYWHERE TOO OILED & SPOILED TO THINK!
GAD HOW I HATE THESE LANDINGS!
ZOUNDS! IT'S A Diomedea Nigripes!
LOOK! LOOK! UP IN THE ATTIC!
CRIPES! IT'S THE GHOST OF SAM T. COOLRIDGE!
NOPE! WRONG! IT'S THE SPITTIN' ATOMS COMMAND
NOBLE WATCH-BIRD, SECURIN' OUR INSECURITIES!!!
OH YEH! I KNOW A BOMB WHEN I SEE ONE!
YEOWWWW!!
SMUK!
YIKES!
¡THUNK!
GADZOOKS!
OH LOOKOUT!
THUD!
SLAM!
LOOKS A BIT PALE FOR AN EAGLE!
COULD IT BE SOME NEW-FANGLED CLAM DREDGE?
IT'S A NEW MODEL OF EAGLES
LEAN BEACH OR BUST!
WHA'CHA MAKE OF ALL THIS, L'IL LIMPET?
LOOKS A OIL-FOOTED ALBATROSK!
BAFFLING BARNACLES! WHAT, IN THE NAME OF NEPTUNE, IS THIS?
ARRRGH & UGGH! IT'S OIL, AND IT'S EVERYWHERE!
HOW DO YOU GET THIS STUFF OFF?
YOU DON'T
2

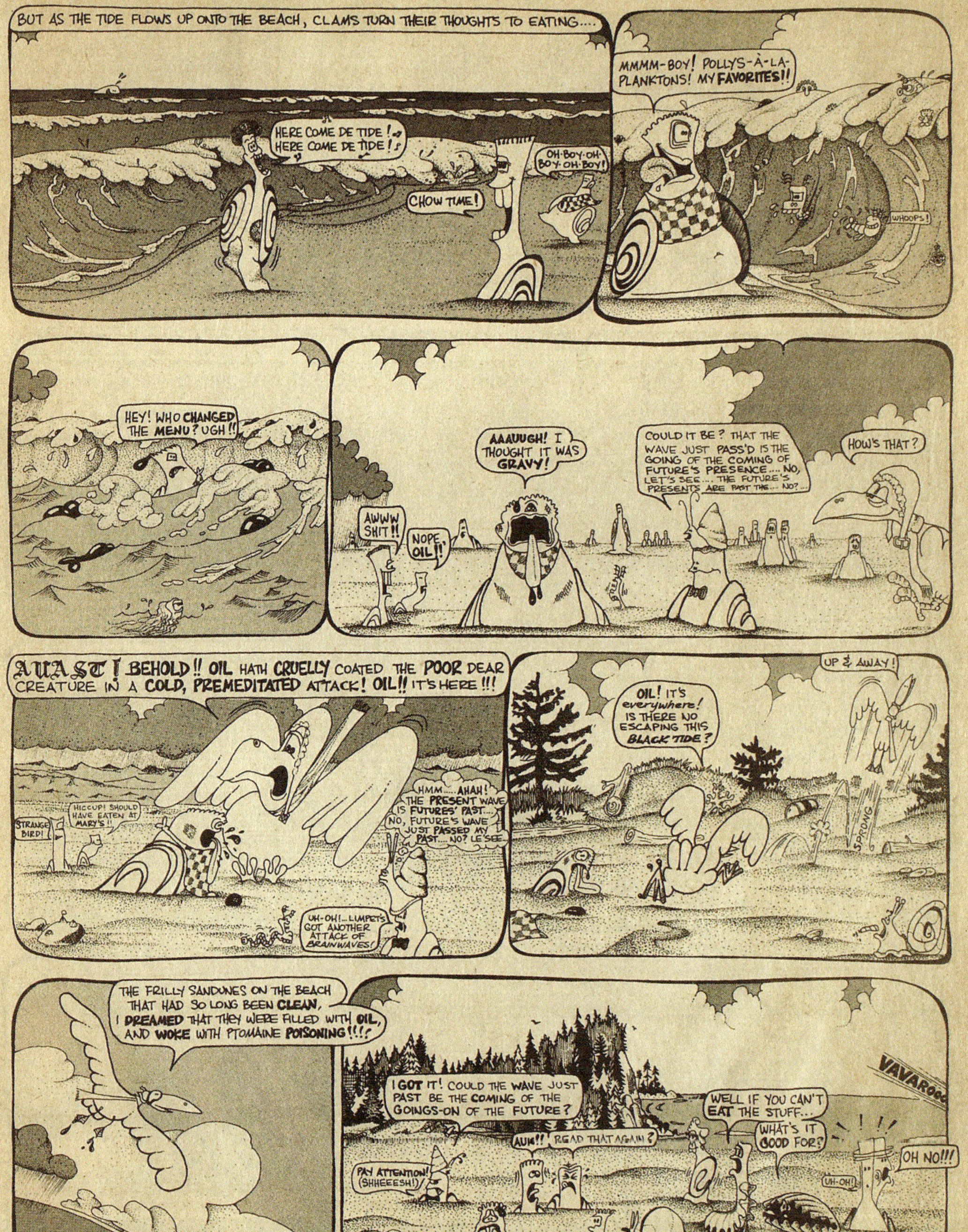

BUT AS THE TIDE FLOWS UP ONTO THE BEACH, CLAMS TURN THEIR THOUGHTS TO EATING....
HERE COME DE TIDE! HERE COME DE TIDE!
OH-BOY-OH-BOY-OH-BOY!
CHOW TIME!
MMMM-BOY! POLLYS-À-LA-PLANKTONS! MY FAVORITES!!
WHOOPS!
HEY! WHO CHANGED THE MENU? UGH!!
AAAUUGH! I THOUGHT IT WAS GRAVY!
AWWW SHIT!!
NOPE, OIL!!
COULD IT BE? THAT THE WAVE JUST PASS'D IS THE GOING OF THE COMING OF FUTURE'S PRESENCE... NO, LET'S SEE... THE FUTURE'S PRESENTS ARE PAST THE... NO?...
HOW'S THAT?
AVAST! BEHOLD!! OIL HATH CRUELLY COATED THE POOR DEAR CREATURE IN A COLD, PREMEDITATED ATTACK! OIL!! IT'S HERE!!!
STRANGE BIRD!
HICCUP! SHOULD HAVE EATEN AT MARY'S!!
HMM.... AHAH! THE PRESENT WAVE IS FUTURES' PAST... NO, FUTURE'S WAVE JUST PASSED MY PAST... NO? LE'SEE...
UH-OH!... LIMPET'S GOT ANOTHER ATTACK OF BRAINWAVES!
OIL! IT'S everywhere! IS THERE NO ESCAPING THIS BLACK TIDE?
UP & AWAY!
SPRONG
THE FRILLY SANDUNES ON THE BEACH THAT HAD SO LONG BEEN CLEAN,
I DREAMED THAT THEY WERE FILLED WITH OIL, AND WOKE WITH PTOMAINE POISONING!!!?
I GOT IT! COULD THE WAVE JUST PAST BE THE COMING OF THE GOINGS-ON OF THE FUTURE?
AUK!!
READ THAT AGAIN?
PAY ATTENTION! (SHHEEEESH!)
WELL IF YOU CAN'T EAT THE STUFF...
WHAT'S IT GOOD FOR?
VAVAROOO
UH-OH!
OH NO!!!
3

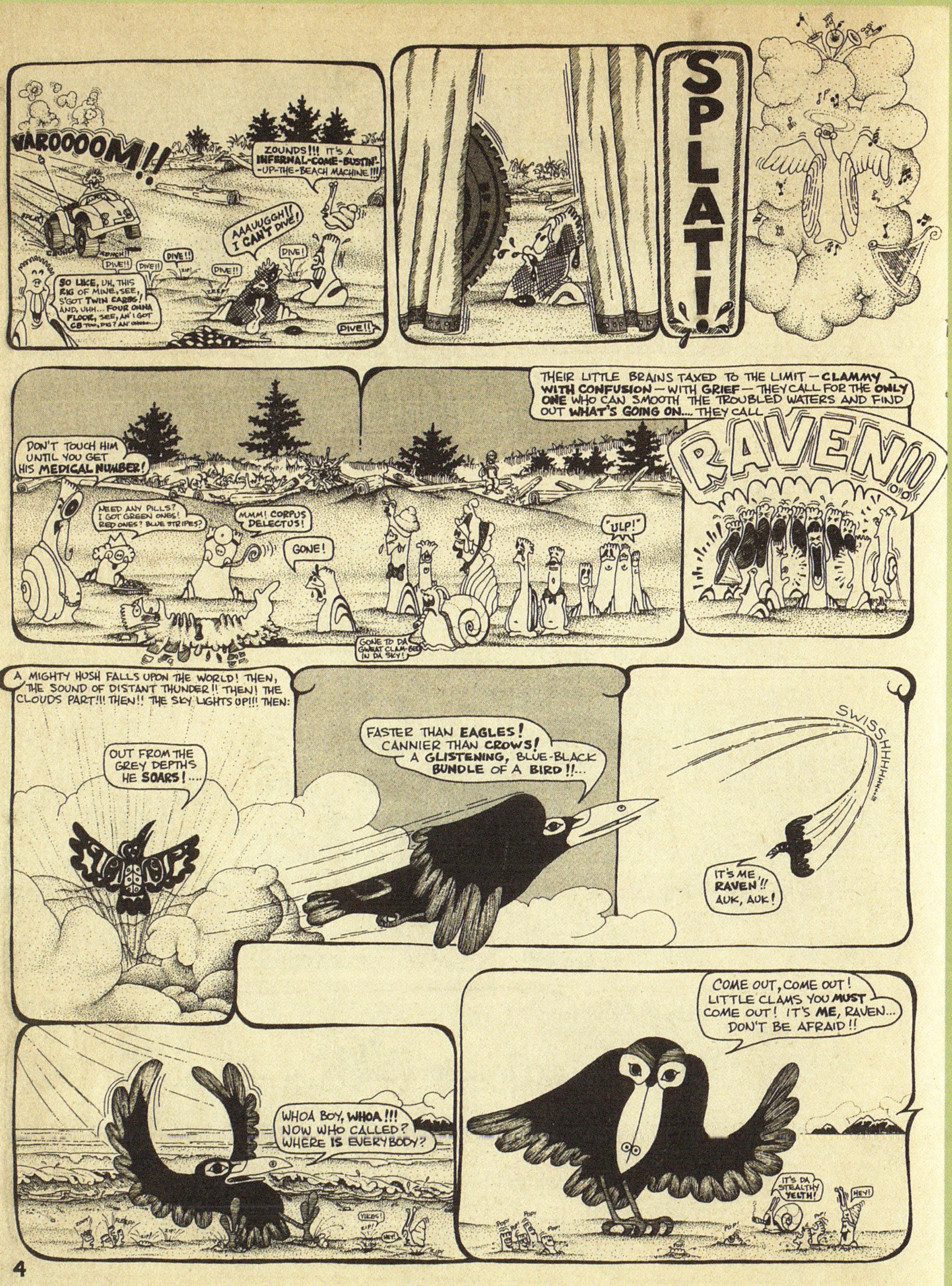
VAROOOOM!!
ZOUNDS!!! IT'S A INFERNAL-COME-BUSTIN'-UP-THE-BEACH MACHINE!!!
AAAUUGGH!! I CAN'T DIVE!
DIVE!!
DIVE!!
DIVE!!
DIVE!!
DIVE!
SO LIKE, UH, THIS RIG OF MINE, SEE, S'GOT TWIN CARBS! AND, UHH... FOUR ONNA FLOOR, SEE, AN' I GOT CB TOO, DIG? AN' OHHH...
DIVE!!
SPLAT!
THEIR LITTLE BRAINS TAXED TO THE LIMIT — CLAMMY WITH CONFUSION — WITH GRIEF — THEY CALL FOR THE ONLY ONE WHO CAN SMOOTH THE TROUBLED WATERS AND FIND OUT WHAT'S GOING ON.... THEY CALL
DON'T TOUCH HIM UNTIL YOU GET HIS MEDICAL NUMBER!
NEED ANY PILLS? I GOT GREEN ONES! RED ONES! BLUE STRIPES?
MMM! CORPUS DELECTUS!
GONE!
"ULP!"
GONE TO DA GWEAT CLAM-BED IN DA SKY!
RAVEN!!
A MIGHTY HUSH FALLS UPON THE WORLD! THEN, THE SOUND OF DISTANT THUNDER!! THEN! THE CLOUDS PART!!! THEN!! THE SKY LIGHTS UP!!! THEN:
OUT FROM THE GREY DEPTHS HE SOARS!....
FASTER THAN EAGLES! CANNIER THAN CROWS! A GLISTENING, BLUE-BLACK BUNDLE OF A BIRD!!...
SWISSHHHHH
IT'S ME, RAVEN!! AUK, AUK!
WHOA BOY, WHOA!!! NOW WHO CALLED? WHERE IS EVERYBODY?
YIKES!
HEY!
COME OUT, COME OUT! LITTLE CLAMS YOU MUST COME OUT! IT'S ME, RAVEN... DON'T BE AFRAID!!
IT'S DA STEALTHY YELTH!
HEY!
4

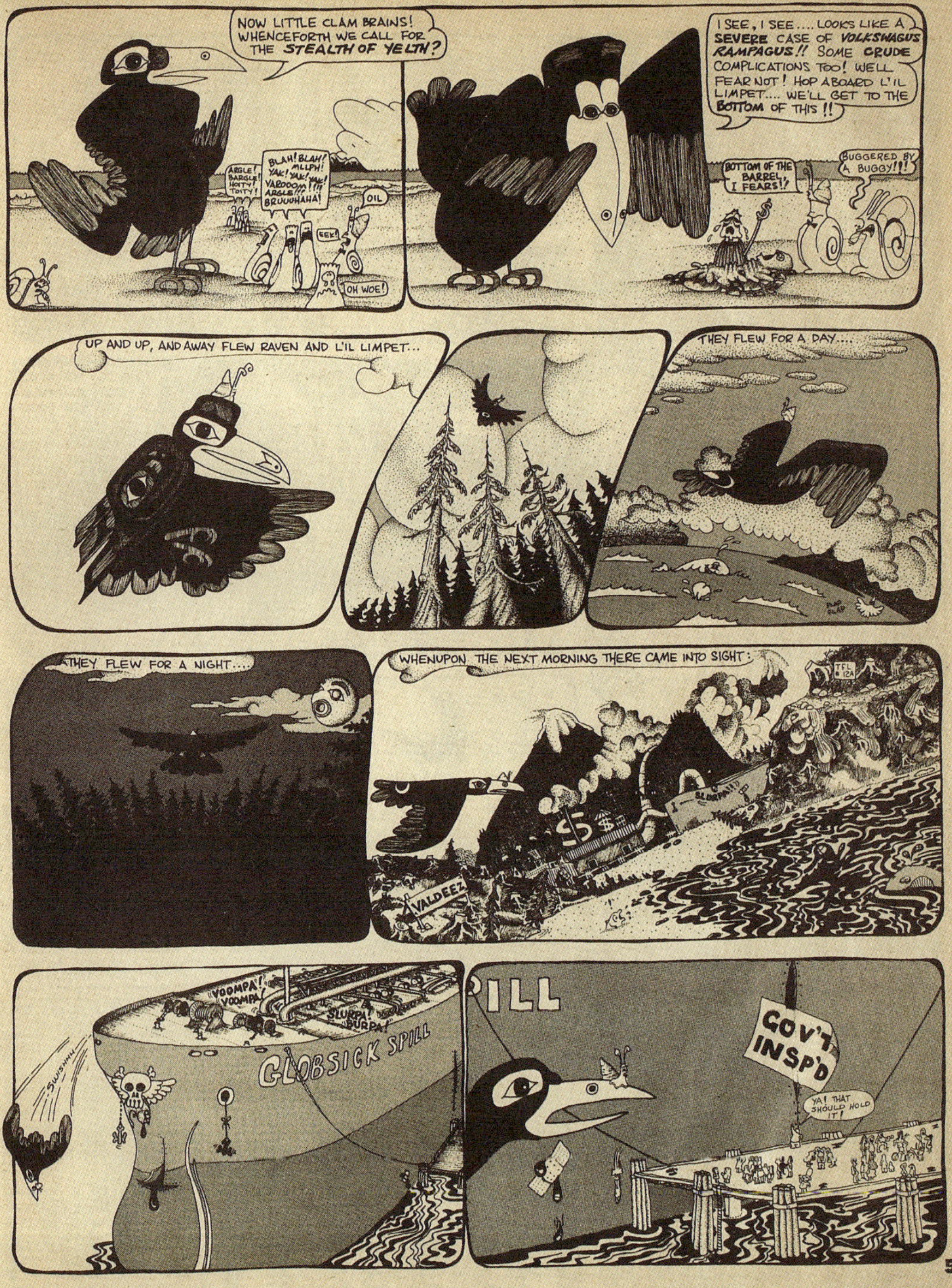
NOW LITTLE CLAM BRAINS! WHENCEFORTH WE CALL FOR THE STEALTH OF YELTH?
ARGLE! BARGLE! HOITY! TOITY!
BLAH! BLAH! MLLPH! YAK! YAK! YAK! VAROOOM!!!! ARGLE!!! BRUUUHAHA!
OIL
EEK!
OH WOE!
I SEE, I SEE.... LOOKS LIKE A SEVERE CASE OF VOLKSWAGUS RAMPAGUS!! SOME CRUDE COMPLICATIONS TOO! WELL FEAR NOT! HOP ABOARD L'IL LIMPET.... WE'LL GET TO THE BOTTOM OF THIS!!
BOTTOM OF THE BARREL, I FEARS!!
BUGGERED BY A BUGGY!!!
UP AND UP, AND AWAY FLEW RAVEN AND L'IL LIMPET...
THEY FLEW FOR A DAY....
THEY FLEW FOR A NIGHT....
WHENUPON THE NEXT MORNING THERE CAME INTO SIGHT:
TFL #12A
VALDEEZ
VOOMPA! VOOMPA!
SLURPA! BURPA!
GLOBSICK SPILL
SWISHHH
PILL
GOV'T INSP'D
YA! THAT SHOULD HOLD IT!
5

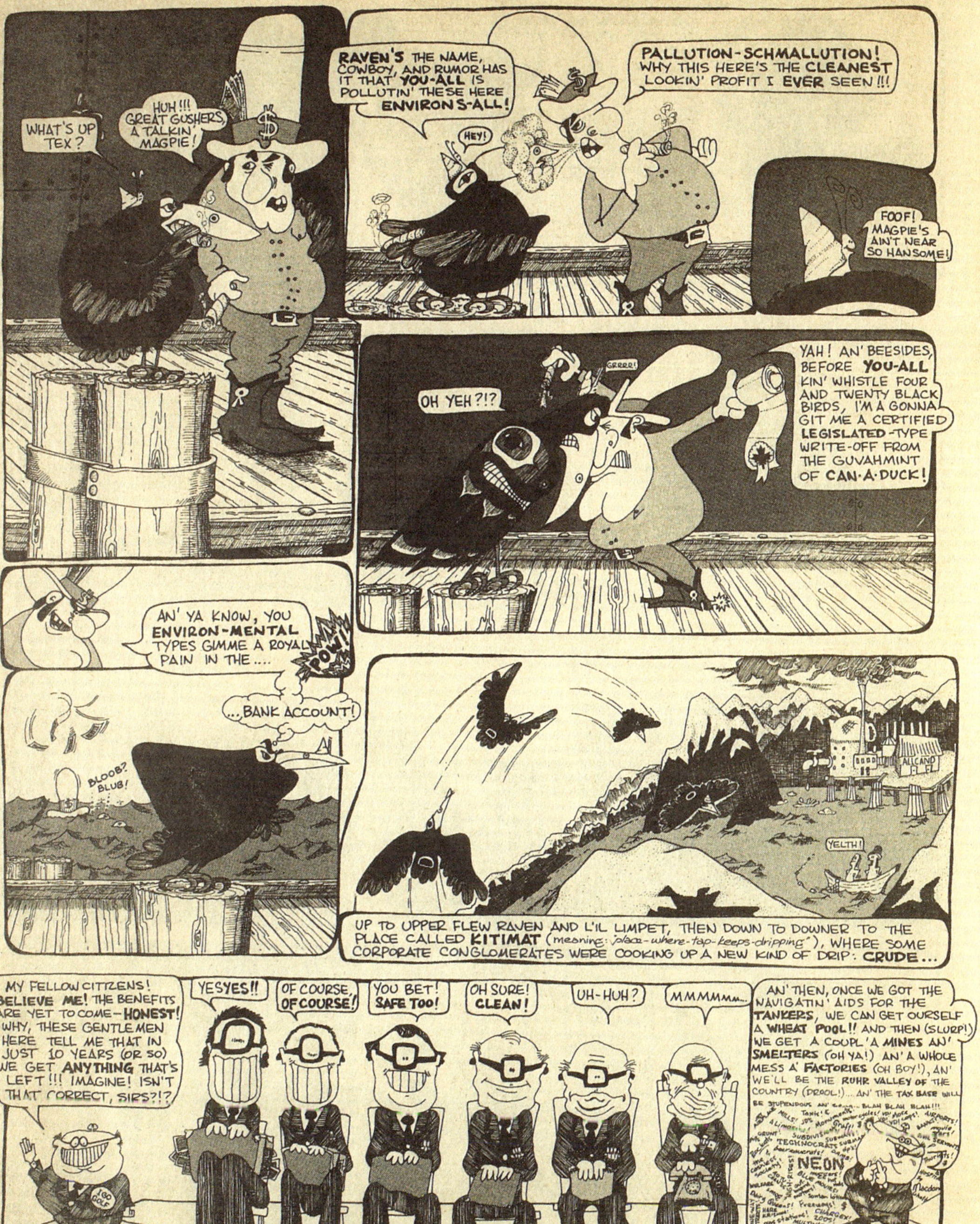

WHAT'S UP TEX?
HUH!!! GREAT GUSHERS, A TALKIN' MAGPIE!
RAVEN'S THE NAME, COWBOY, AND RUMOR HAS IT THAT YOU-ALL IS POLLUTIN' THESE HERE ENVIRONS-ALL!
HEY!
PALLUTION-SCHMALLUTION! WHY THIS HERE'S THE CLEANEST LOOKIN' PROFIT I EVER SEEN!!!
FOOF! MAGPIE'S AIN'T NEAR SO HANSOME!
OH YEH?!?
GRRRR!
YAH! AN' BEESIDES, BEFORE YOU-ALL KIN' WHISTLE FOUR AND TWENTY BLACK BIRDS, I'M A GONNA GIT ME A CERTIFIED LEGISLATED-TYPE WRITE-OFF FROM THE GUVAHMINT OF CAN-A-DUCK!
AN' YA KNOW, YOU ENVIRON-MENTAL TYPES GIMME A ROYAL PAIN IN THE....
POW!
...BANK ACCOUNT!
BLOOB? BLUB!
ALLCAN
YELTH!
UP TO UPPER FLEW RAVEN AND L'IL LIMPET, THEN DOWN TO DOWNER TO THE PLACE CALLED KITIMAT (meaning: "place-where-tap-keeps-dripping"), WHERE SOME CORPORATE CONGLOMERATES WERE COOKING UP A NEW KIND OF DRIP: CRUDE...
MY FELLOW CITIZENS! BELIEVE ME! THE BENEFITS ARE YET TO COME—HONEST! WHY, THESE GENTLEMEN HERE TELL ME THAT IN JUST 10 YEARS (OR SO) WE GET ANYTHING THAT'S LEFT!!! IMAGINE! ISN'T THAT CORRECT, SIRS?!?
YESYES!!
OF COURSE, OF COURSE!
YOU BET! SAFE TOO!
OH SURE! CLEAN!
UH-HUH?
MMMMMM...
AN' THEN, ONCE WE GOT THE NAVIGATIN' AIDS FOR THE TANKERS, WE CAN GET OURSELF A WHEAT POOL!! AND THEN (SLURP!) WE GET A COUPL'A MINES AN' SMELTERS (OH YA!) AN' A WHOLE MESS A' FACTORIES (OH BOY!), AN' WE'LL BE THE RUHR VALLEY OF THE COUNTRY (DROOL!)... AN' THE TAX BASE WILL BE STUPENDOUS AN' ... BLAH BLAH BLAH!!!
AIRPORTS!
GRUNT!
TECHNOCRATS
bureaucrats!
NEON
HIGH-RISES!
BLUE MOVIES!
WELFARE
Dairy Queens!
Freeways!
CHARGEX!
gas stations!
MULTINATION
ONE-WAY STREETS
Dope Addix!
Disposable Lighters!
15 Radio stations!
6

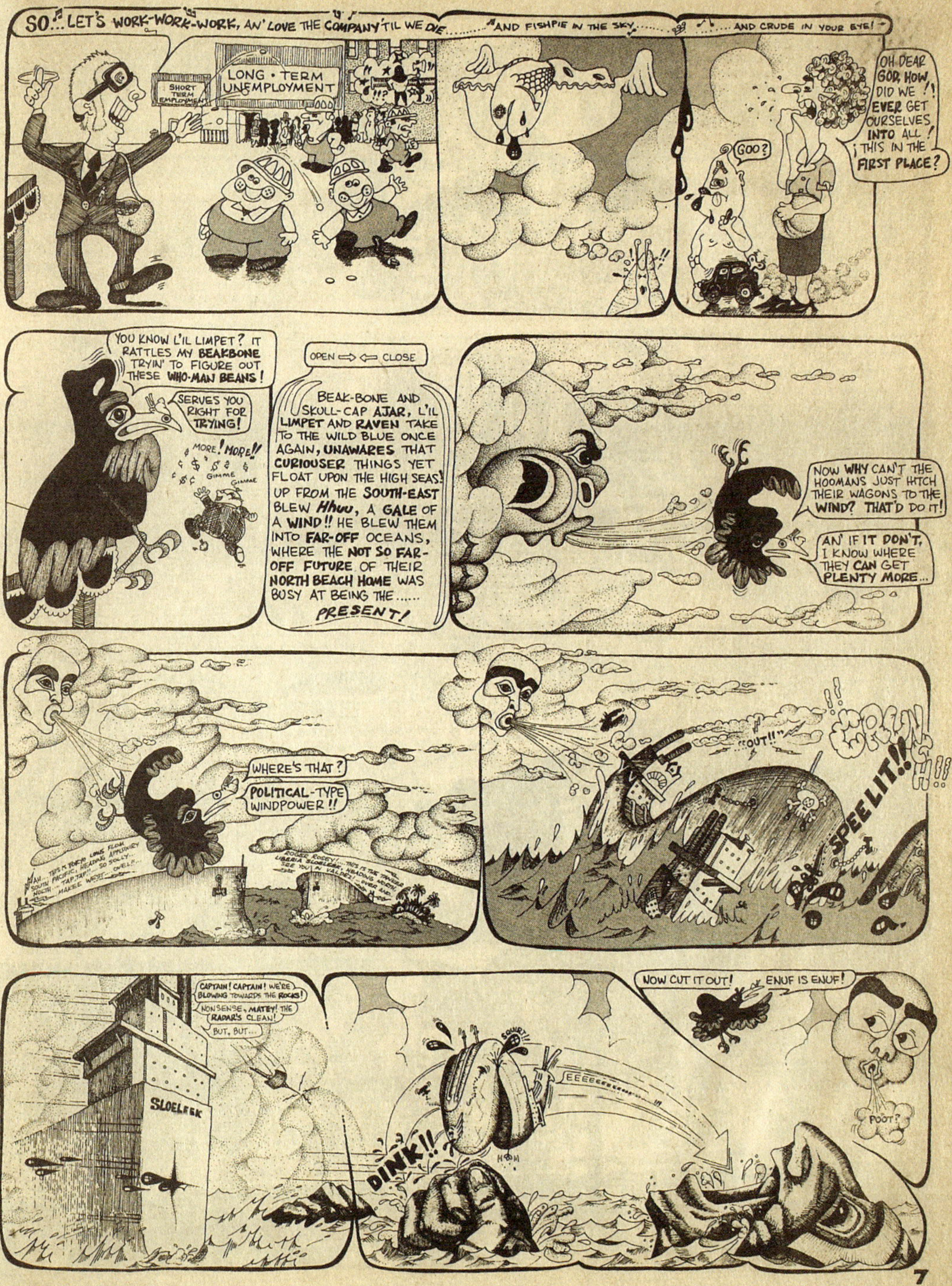
SO... LET'S WORK-WORK-WORK, AN' LOVE THE COMPANY 'TIL WE DIE.........AND FISHPIE IN THE SKY.........AND CRUDE IN YOUR EYE!
SHORT TERM EMPLOYMENT
LONG • TERM UNEMPLOYMENT
GOO?
OH DEAR GOD, HOW DID WE EVER GET OURSELVES INTO ALL THIS IN THE FIRST PLACE?
YOU KNOW L'IL LIMPET? IT RATTLES MY BEAKBONE TRYIN' TO FIGURE OUT THESE WHO-MAN BEANS!
SERVES YOU RIGHT FOR TRYING!
MORE! MORE!!
OPEN ⇨ ⇦ CLOSE
BEAK-BONE AND SKULL-CAP AJAR, L'IL LIMPET AND RAVEN TAKE TO THE WILD BLUE ONCE AGAIN, UNAWARES THAT CURIOUSER THINGS YET FLOAT UPON THE HIGH SEAS! UP FROM THE SOUTH-EAST BLEW Hhuu, A GALE OF A WIND!! HE BLEW THEM INTO FAR-OFF OCEANS, WHERE THE NOT SO FAR-OFF FUTURE OF THEIR NORTH BEACH HOME WAS BUSY AT BEING THE...... PRESENT!
NOW WHY CAN'T THE HOOMANS JUST HITCH THEIR WAGONS TO THE WIND? THAT'D DO IT!
AN' IF IT DON'T, I KNOW WHERE THEY CAN GET PLENTY MORE...
WHERE'S THAT?
POLITICAL-TYPE WINDPOWER!!
"OUT!!"
CRUNCH!!
SPEELIT!!
CAPTAIN! CAPTAIN! WE'RE BLOWING TOWARDS THE ROCKS!
NONSENSE, MATEY! THE RADAR'S CLEAN!
BUT, BUT...
SLOELEEK
SQUIRT!!
EEEEEEEEE!!!
DINK!!
NOW CUT IT OUT!
ENUF IS ENUF!
POOT?
7

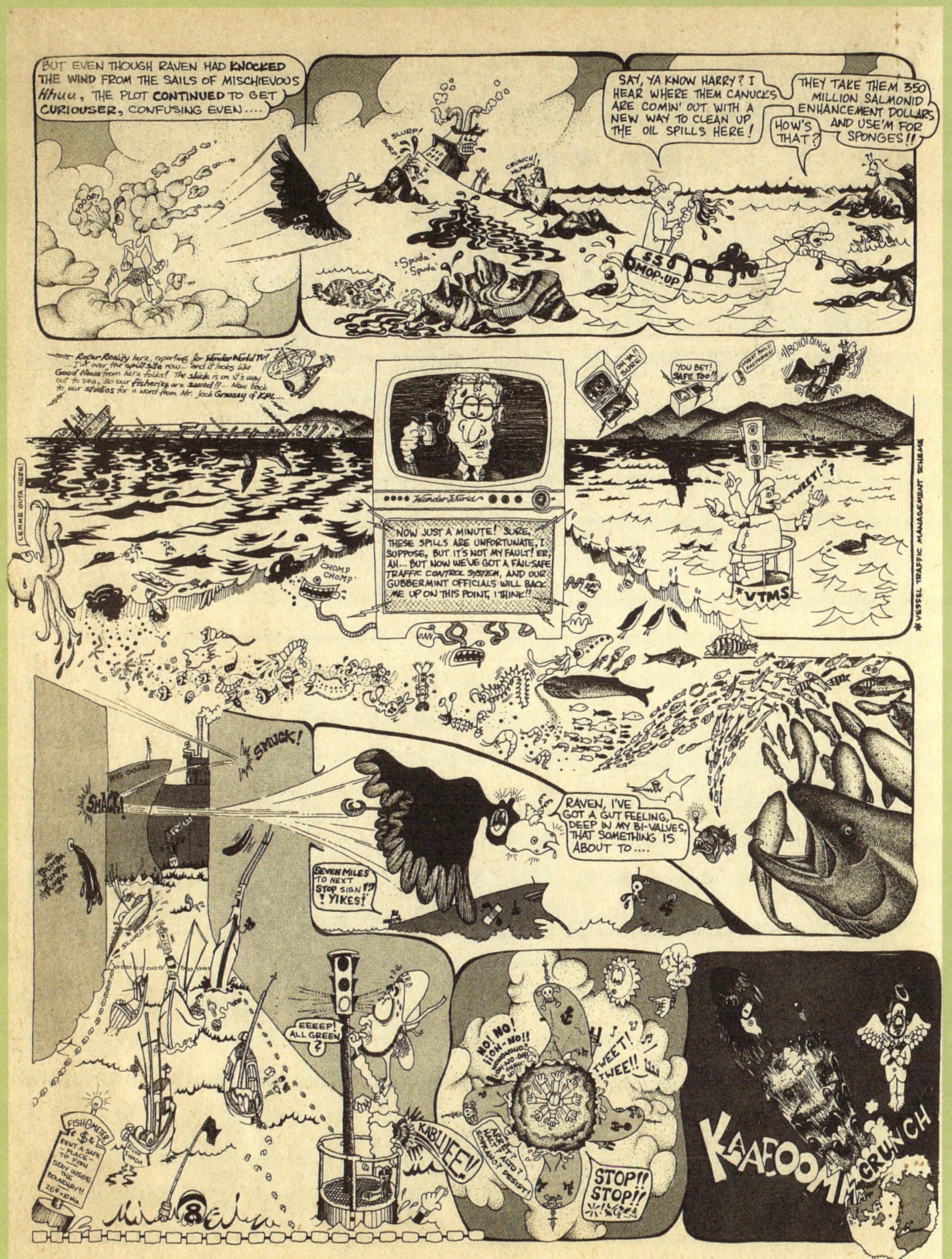

BUT EVEN THOUGH RAVEN HAD KNOCKED THE WIND FROM THE SAILS OF MISCHIEVOUS Hhuu, THE PLOT CONTINUED TO GET CURIOUSER, CONFUSING EVEN....
FOOOF!
SLURP!
BURP!
BITE!
CRUNCH! MUNCH!
Spuda Spuda
SAY, YA KNOW HARRY? I HEAR WHERE THEM CANUCKS ARE COMIN' OUT WITH A NEW WAY TO CLEAN UP THE OIL SPILLS HERE!
HOW'S THAT?
THEY TAKE THEM 350 MILLION SALMONID ENHANCEMENT DOLLARS AND USE'M FOR SPONGES!!
SS MOP-UP
Roger Reality here, reporting for Wonder World TV! ...I'm over the spill site now... and it looks like Good News from here folks! The slick is on it's way out to sea, so our fisheries are saved!!... Now back to our studios for a word from Mr. Jock Grassey of KPL....
OH YA!! SURE!
YOU BET! SAFE TOO!!
WHEAT POOLS! FACTORIES!
BOIOIOING
Wunder World
NOW JUST A MINUTE! SURE, THESE SPILLS ARE UNFORTUNATE, I SUPPOSE, BUT IT'S NOT MY FAULT! ER, AH... BUT NOW WE'VE GOT A FAIL-SAFE TRAFFIC CONTROL SYSTEM, AND OUR GUBBERMINT OFFICIALS WILL BACK ME UP ON THIS POINT, I THINK!!
LEMME OUTA HERE!
CHOMP CHOMP
TWEET!
*VTMS
*VESSEL TRAFFIC MANAGEMENT SCHEME
SMUCK!
SMACK!
PUMPA PUMPA PUMPA
SLURP
RAVEN, I'VE GOT A GUT FEELING, DEEP IN MY BI-VALVES, THAT SOMETHING IS ABOUT TO....
SEVEN MILES TO NEXT STOP SIGN!? ! YIKES!
EEEEP! ALL GREEN ?
KABLUEE!!
FISHOMETER ¢ $ ¢ RENT-A-SAFE PLACE TO FISH STAY INSIDE THE BOUNDARY!! 25¢ = 10 MIN.
SILVA SHADA
NO! NO! ¡¡OH-NO!!
ARRET? HALT? ALTO? SOPRANO? DESIST!
TWEET! TWEE!!
STOP!! STOP!!
KLAABOOMM
CRUNCH

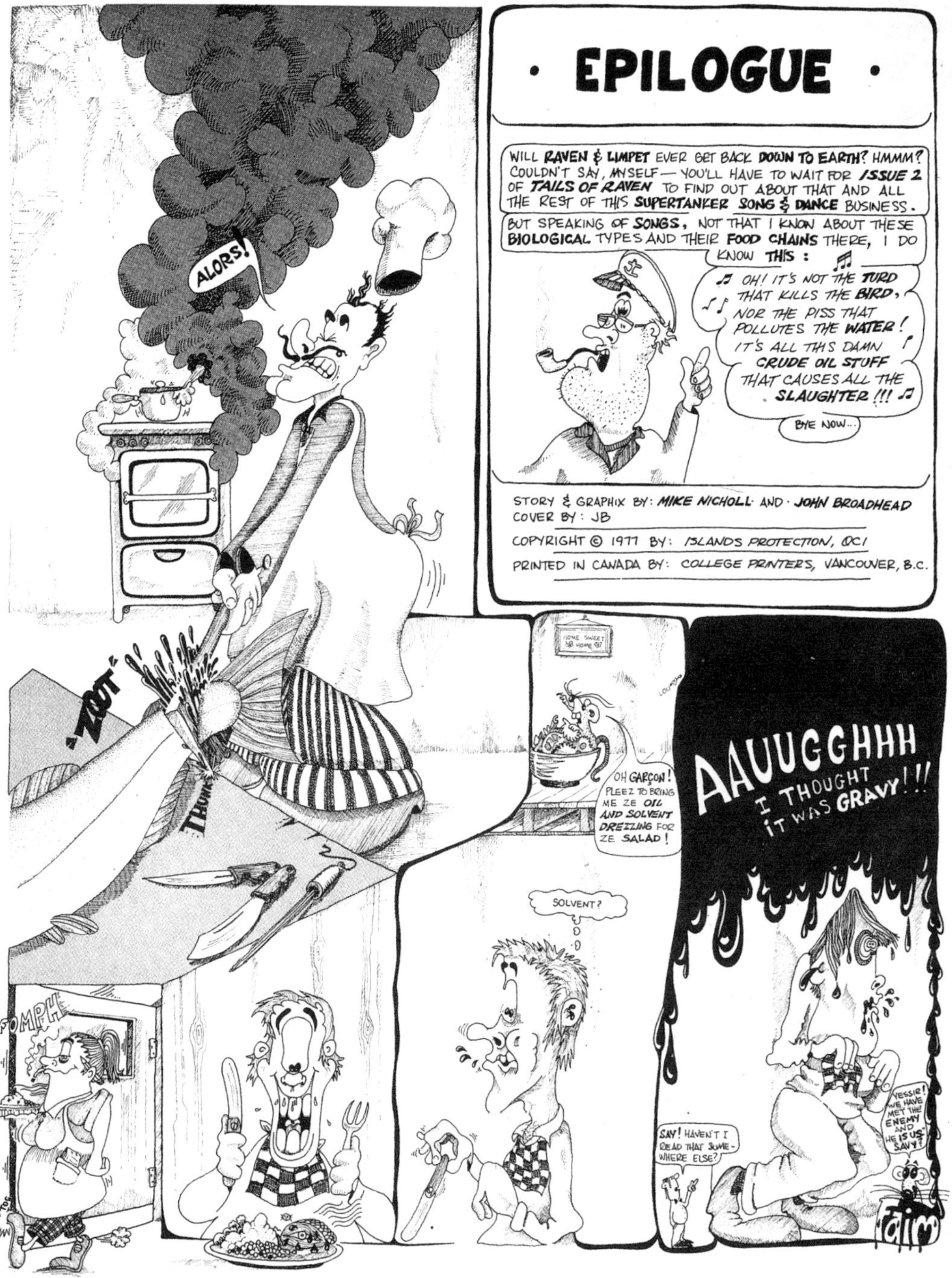

ALORS!
· EPILOGUE ·
WILL RAVEN & LIMPET EVER GET BACK DOWN TO EARTH? HMMM? COULDN'T SAY, MYSELF — YOU'LL HAVE TO WAIT FOR ISSUE 2 OF TAILS OF RAVEN TO FIND OUT ABOUT THAT AND ALL THE REST OF THIS SUPERTANKER SONG & DANCE BUSINESS.
BUT SPEAKING OF SONGS, NOT THAT I KNOW ABOUT THESE BIOLOGICAL TYPES AND THEIR FOOD CHAINS THERE, I DO KNOW THIS:
OH! IT'S NOT THE TURD THAT KILLS THE BIRD, NOR THE PISS THAT POLLUTES THE WATER! IT'S ALL THIS DAMN CRUDE OIL STUFF THAT CAUSES ALL THE SLAUGHTER!!!
BYE NOW...
STORY & GRAPHIX BY: MIKE NICHOLL AND JOHN BROADHEAD
COVER BY: JB
COPYRIGHT © 1977 BY: ISLANDS PROTECTION, QCI
PRINTED IN CANADA BY: COLLEGE PRINTERS, VANCOUVER, B.C.
ZOOT
THUNK
HOME SWEET HOME
OH GARÇON! PLEEZ TO BRING ME ZE OIL AND SOLVENT DREZZLING FOR ZE SALAD!
AAUUGGHHH I THOUGHT IT WAS GRAVY!!!
SOLVENT?
FOMPH
SAY! HAVEN'T I READ THAT SOME-WHERE ELSE?
YESSIR! "WE HAVE MET THE ENEMY AND HE IS US" SAVY?

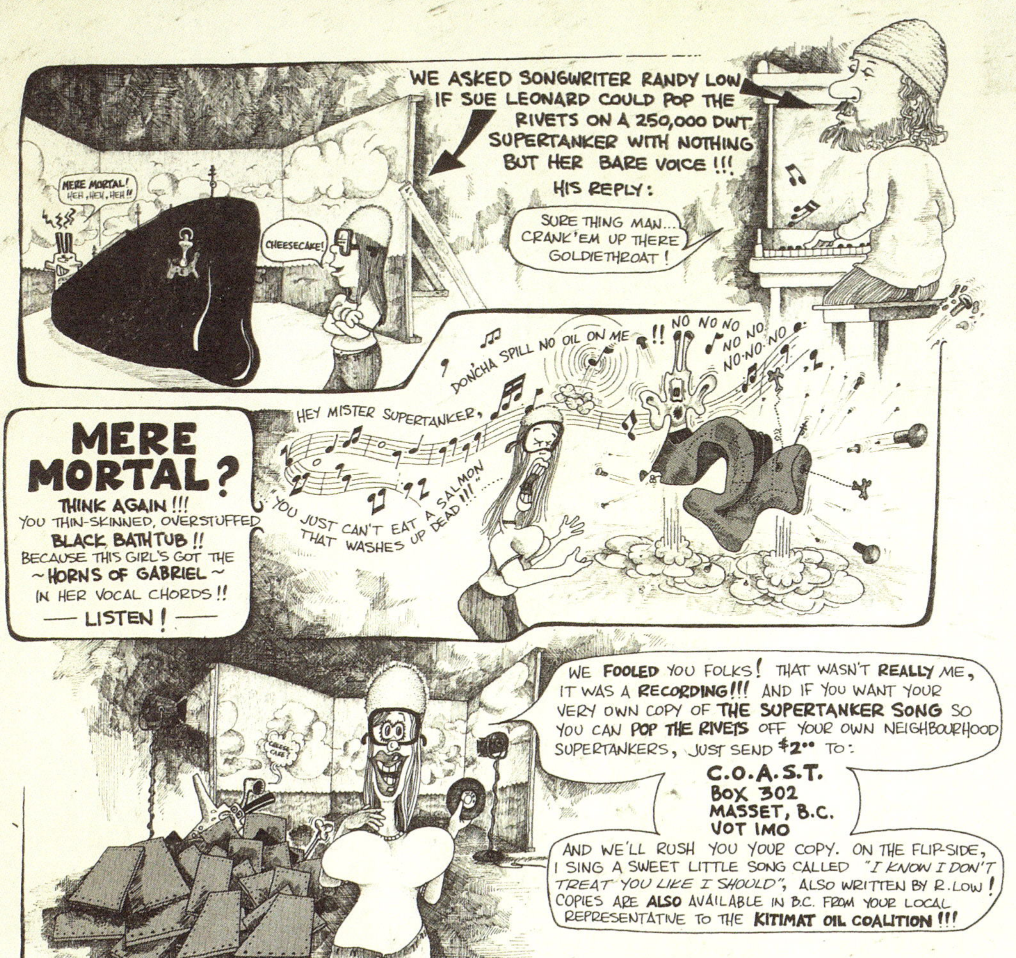

·POSTERS·

THE ARTWORK ON THE COVER OF THIS COMIC IS AVAILABLE AS AN 18"×24" POSTER, WHICH IS THE SIZE OF THE ORIGINAL PRODUCTION ARTWORK. THE POSTER COMES ON TWO DIFFERENT PAPER STOCKS:

① COMMON POSTER STOCK for $2.00
② RAG PAPER STOCK for $20.00

THIS IS A "LIMITED EDITION" OF 500 PRINTS, PRODUCED BY OFFSET LITHO, SIGNED BY THE ARTIST, AND SUITABLE FOR FRAMING. WHILE WE REALIZE THIS PRACTICE IS HARDLY CONSIDERED ETHICAL IN THE ART WORLD, IT IS A MATTER OF URGENT NECESSITY FOR US TO RAISE FUNDS.

POSTERS ARE AVAILABLE FROM THE ORGANISATION IN YOUR COMMUNITY WHICH IS WORKING ON THE SUPERTANKER TRAFFIC ISSUE, AT CONCERNED BOOKSTORES AND GALLERIES, AND AT

C.O.A.S.T.
BOX 302
MASSET, B.C.
VOT IMO

CERTIFIED CHEQUE OR MONEY ORDER ONLY

C.O.A.S.T. IS THE COALITION AGAINST SUPERTANKERS, AND WILL BE REPRESENTING THE QUEEN CHARLOTTE ISLANDS AT THE UPCOMING FEDERAL WEST COAST OIL PORT INQUIRY, AND IS FACING THE HIGH COSTS OF ENVIRONMENTAL RESEARCH, OFFICE & TRAVEL EXPENSES, AND PROJECT PRODUCTIONS. YOUR PURCHASES, DONATIONS, AND ASSISTANCE WILL BE WELCOMED GRATEFULLY. PROCEEDS FROM THE SUPERTANKER SONG RECORD, COMIC BOOKS, AND POSTERS WILL HELP C.O.A.S.T. TO MEET THESE COSTS AND CARRY YOUR VIEWS TO THE OIL PORT INQUIRY.

Oblique Strategies

A Conversation with Simon Davies, Michael Nicoll Yahgulanaas and Liz Park

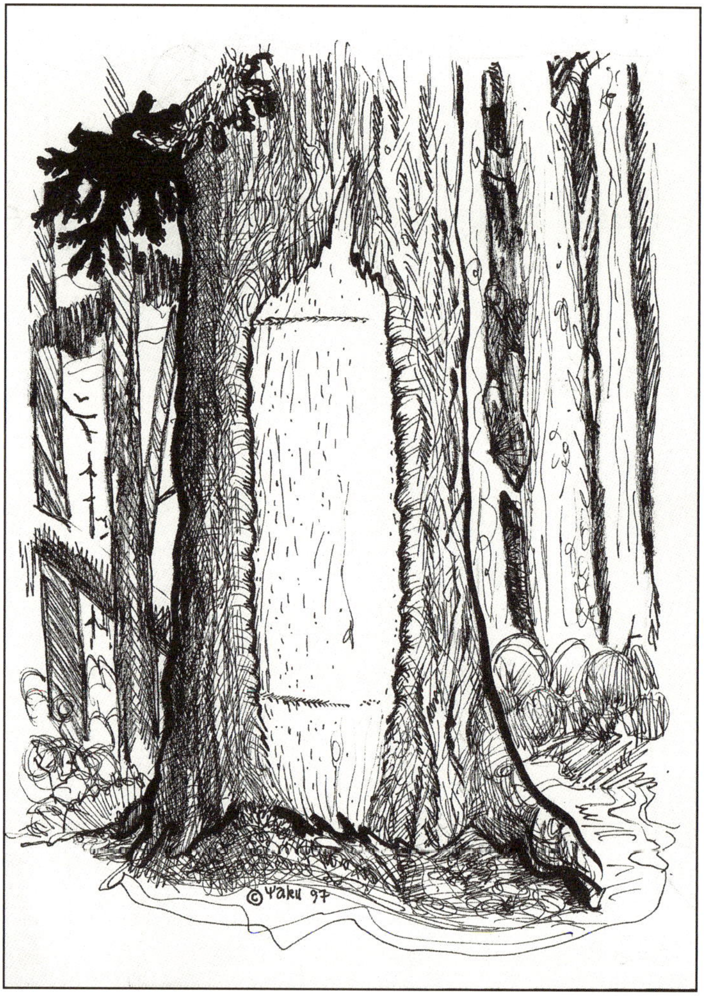

Untitled, 1997. Originally published in *SpruceRoots Magazine* (Haida Gwaii).

On December 20, 2010, Simon Davies, Michael Nicoll Yahgulanaas and Liz Park engaged in a conversation about the Haida Gwaii based SpruceRoots Magazine, *to which Yahgulanaas contributed regularly as an illustrator and graphic artist – under the pen name Yaku – from 1995 to 2005, for the magazine's full run. Simon Davies was editor and publisher of SpruceRoots for the same duration and is currently program manager of the Council of the Haida Nation's Communication Program and managing editor of* Haida Laas, *a community journal published for Haida citizens. He has lived and worked on Haida Gwaii since 1976. The hour-long conversation took place over Skype, with Davies at his office on Haida Gwaii and Yahgulanaas and Park at the artist's home.*

LP: Can you describe the mandate of *SpruceRoots Magazine*?

SD: The mandate of *SpruceRoots* was to provide an alternate point of view about what was happening on the Islands (Haida Gwaii) and to mirror the culture of change here, to put together a magazine that reflected the direction and the future changes that people were looking for.

Gowgaia Institute, the publisher of *SpruceRoots*, was formed by myself, Cynthia Davies, John Broadhead and Leslie Johnson, to look at and change how the forests and the lands were being treated. We operated for fourteen years. *SpruceRoots* ran from 1995 to 2005 and produced fifty-eight issues. We worked with the Council of the Haida Nation and other groups who were interested in making change.

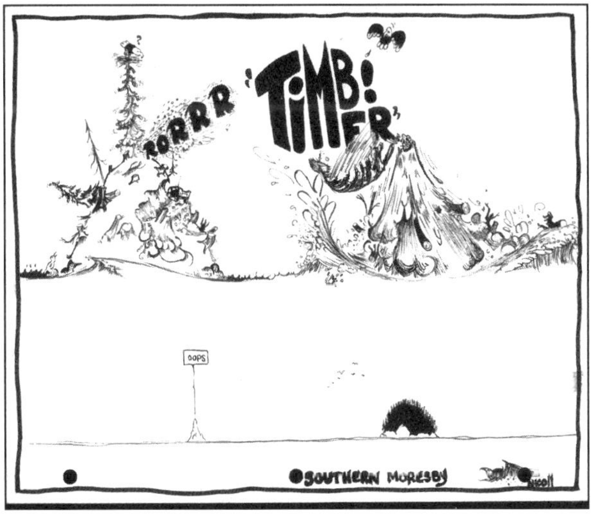

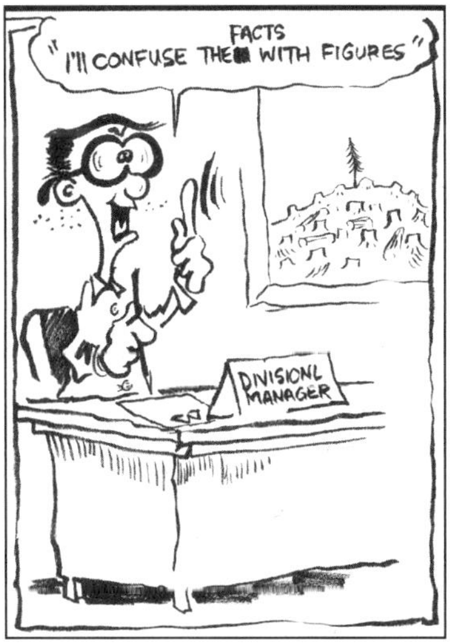

Left. Untitled, 1976. Originally published in *All Alone Stone* / Islands Protection Society (Haida Gwaii); Right. Untitled, 1987/89.

SpruceRoots grew and evolved into what people were looking for. Over the course of the run, about one hundred and fifty people contributed writing. Michael was the main illustrator but there were many photographers and other illustrators. It was a really fun and interesting thing to do. We were able to deal with the issues in-depth rather than just through a five hundred-word news story. We were able to tell a different story than what was told in standard news coverage.

MNY: You delivered a lot of depth in the articles because there was time to hone in on the issue. There was the *Queen Charlotte Islands Observer* (the local weekly newspaper) and some of the Lower Mainland papers dealing with the same issues, but they weren't providing the same kind of depth in their coverage.

LP: What was the readership like?

SD: We printed one thousand five hundred copies each issue, one thousand four hundred and fifty of which stayed on the Islands. They were distributed through coffee shops and meeting places up and down the Islands. The audience cut across all demographics: the rednecks, the hippies and the village councils. We knew the politic was changing and we wanted to make sure that the story was being told so that people could see that their efforts had an impact.

MNY: By then, we had already had the logging blockades and secured the victory (for Gwaii Haanas National Park Reserve in 1987). But there have been a lot of local anxiety about what the real cost of that victory was and what it really meant. *Spruce Roots* provided a way for local people to understand what had happened, not only on an Islands basis, but in a wider context. The shift from managing the land to managing ourselves in the land also meant that social interactions were different. People at home needed to consider all this and it wasn't coming from other existing news sources.

SD: *SpruceRoots* made sure those issues that we considered were important were actually on the table and were talked about and published. I look at it as a political magazine, but also as a cultural one.

LP: Can you tell me about the people who were running *SpruceRoots*?

SD: I was the managing editor. Ian Lordon was a part-time staff writer and we had Erica Thompson working for a period of time as well. A network of mostly Islands writers contributed to the magazine. We'd work out stories and figure out what we wanted to cover. We paid twenty-five cents a word. It was a labour of love for most people.

We'd run it off on a Xerox machine and I'd drive up and down the Islands delivering it. It was pretty simple!

LP: Did you have a regular publishing schedule?

SD: No. We'd try to get it out once a month but didn't quite make it. We probably did eight issues a year. With every issue, I never quite knew what Michael was going to come up with. Did we ever not publish anything?

MNY: I don't think so. I don't think you were very discriminating. (Chuckles.) You just took anything I threw over to you.

SD: At *SpruceRoots*, we wanted to come from a different perspective. We wanted a mix, and Michael certainly provided that with his illustrations and comic work. It always came from a fresh angle, and it made you think. If it was really obscure, it made you think more.

LP: Were there any editorial negotiations with Michael?

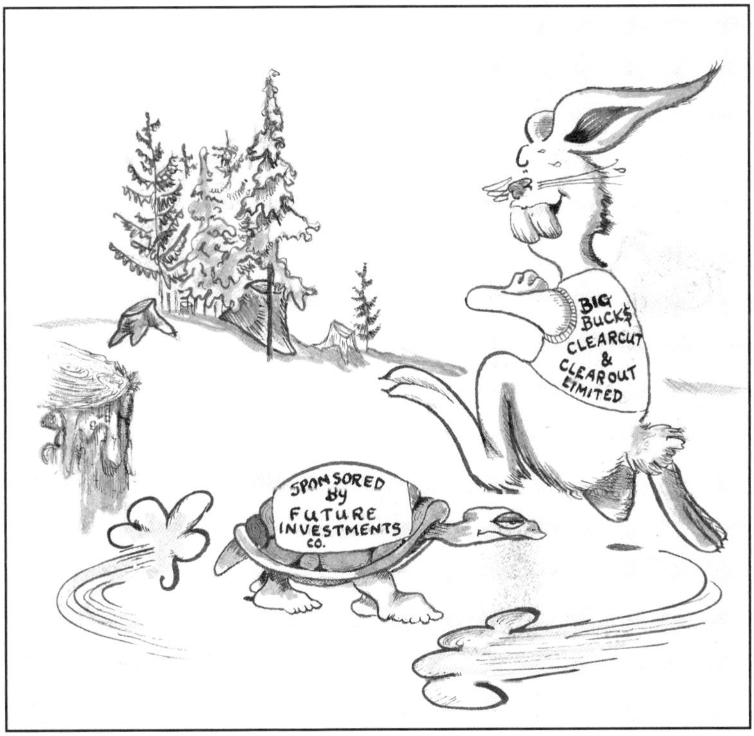

Untitled, 1979. Originally published in *All Alone Stone* / Islands Protection Society (Haida Gwaii).

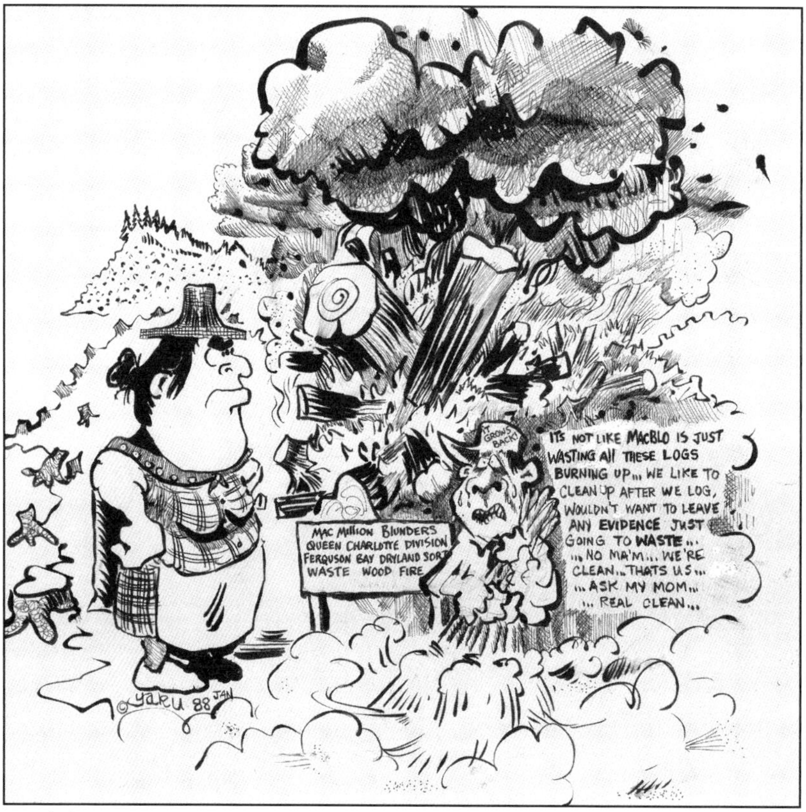

Untitled, 1988.

SD: We were both working on the forestry related stuff, and worked together for a long time. So we knew what we were talking and thinking about. He'd wonder what the specific issue was about, and I'd say we were doing this or that, never giving him too much information. Sometimes with less information you really have to stretch yourself to come up with something. More often than not, what Michael produced was related just enough for you to get it but also oblique enough to make you think about where it was coming from. I think his work really made people think differently about how we perceive the natural world.

MNY: Do you remember the *Red Stump Brigade?* That was the time when we shut down the Ministry of Forests for a day. I can't remember which year, and I don't know if my cartoon-stumps preceded or followed that, but they were certainly connected. Simon and a large group got together with a stack of old plywood sheets and cut them out into stump shapes. We painted them red, attached handles, and they became graphic placards. There were about fifty stumps and almost four hundred people who then marched up to the Ministry of Forests.[1]

After the action, we were trying to fundraise to cover some of the costs of the Unity Feast, which followed the march. We got together at the old community hall in Skidegate and began to auction off these stumps. A flood of people rushed the stage, leaping out of their seats to grab these stump placards at twenty dollars each! There is still one placed along the highway between Queen Charlotte and Massett. The symbol of the stump became a calling card. There was even one in Montreal!

SD: Yes, at an economic summit! (The International Economic Forum of the Americas in 2007.) That kind of crossing-over is culturally and politically interesting.

MNY: It's an important part of the evolution of community. Some issues ought not to be captivated by elite groups in far away places like Ottawa or Victoria. Describing these issues requires local conversations like *SpruceRoots*. Graphics are very effective ways to link issues to people's lives.

LP: It's telling that Michael can't remember whether the comic stumps came before or after. It's not so important whether your work is an illustration or something that triggered the action because it's part of the same drive.

SD: Yes, it's integrated – make art, create culture.

LP: Did Michael publish in every single issue?

SD: Yes.

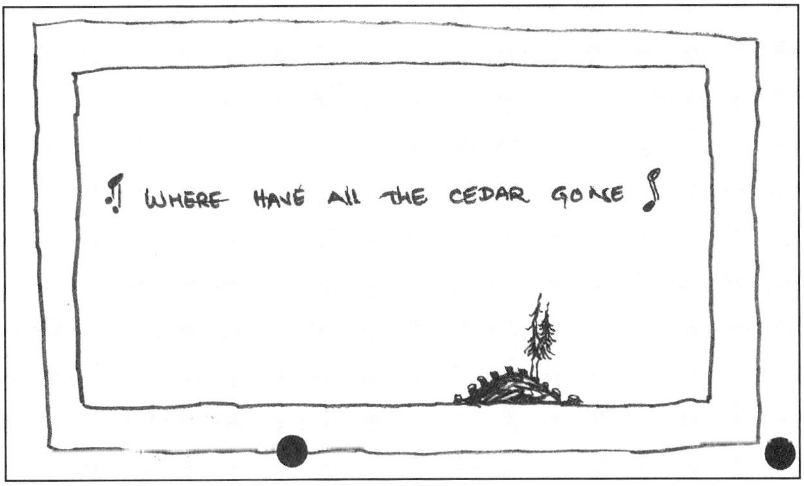

Where Have All the Cedar Gone, 1997.

SD: Published in November 1996 issue was Michael's drawing of a Ministry of Forests Pinocchio character with an extended nose sprouting leaves, saying "Oh wow, second growth." It speaks to local people who know all about the fallacy of second growth. It was simple and brilliant. (For a related drawing, see page 41.)

MNY: The first issue of *SpruceRoots* started out with "The Deforest Lecture Series" – the issues of loggers and people who worked in the industry. I always had a bit more sensitivity because we were trying to negate the polarizing effects. And we were supported, I think, and encouraged by the Islands' residents.

Evelyn Pinkerton, a professor from Simon Fraser University, in her 1983 paper reflected that what we were doing is demystifying the forest service.[2] That had not happened before. We were challenging the scientific and the engineering assumptions, which were so critical in maintaining provincial claims to authority over the Haida Gwaii landscape. *SpruceRoots* became a very important vehicle, because it was a public conversation. It wasn't something that just RPF— Registered Professional Foresters—and their peers described in public consultations. Everyone realized what was going on and *SpruceRoots* validated those understandings by bringing it out into the light.

SD: It's hard for me to look at the magazine in terms of doing any analysis because I'm doing similar work today with *Haida Laas*. It's hard to step back from it.

LP: Simon, can you talk about *Haida Laas*, and the difference between that and *SpruceRoots*? Michael, you've done some work for the *Haida Laas*?

MNY: I can't say I've much been involved in *Haida Laas*. That's a result of my not living in Haida Gwaii, as well as my decision to resign from that very active political world. It has demanded so much energy and personal attention for decades. I'm nowhere as involved with *Haida Laas* as I was with *SpruceRoots*, but I have here a copy of the second volume of *Haida Laas*, February 1986. I worked on this with John Broadhead, who also worked at Gowgaia Institute. That issue was closely focused in on the contempt of Canadian court charges against Haidas defending the land.

SD: It's a clearly different vehicle. *Haida Laas* is for the Council of the Haida Nation to get their information out to the citizens but we also include other articles about what's going on in the villages. It's to inform citizens of Haida Nation business, so it's not as freewheeling as *SpruceRoots* was. *Haida Laas* reflects Haida culture, education and issues that are important in the villages and to Haida citizens.

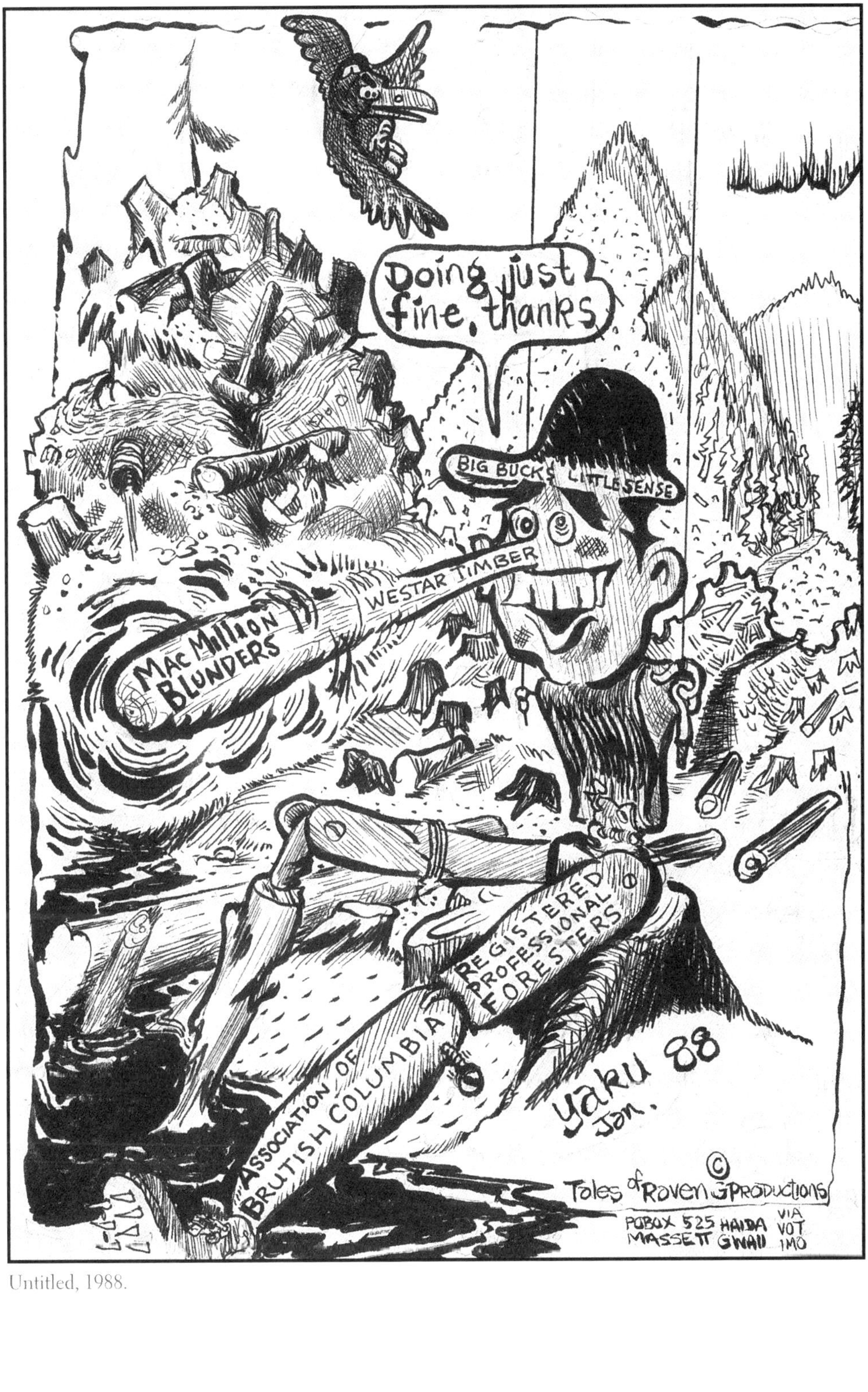

Untitled, 1988.

MNY: *Haida Laas* is institutionalized. It rises out of the Haida Constitution, which says that there shall be a journal published regularly, because there was a real sense – this preceded *SpruceRoots* – that you had to publicize conversations so everyone had at least one point of access to information. This journal also had to speak from the authority of the National Council.

LP: What was some of the feedback and comments you got from the readership on what *SpruceRoots* was doing?

SD: People would criticize it, certainly, but we ended up with an Islands magazine that was totally integrated into the culture. It was accepted for what it was – the stories, the criticism and the way we addressed issues. However many years later, I still get people who say how they miss it because now there's nothing even remotely like it.

One of the problems with our funders was they never quite got what we were doing. It was always a bit outside of what they understood environmental groups should be doing. We came at the issues as more of a cultural issue. We were trying to validate people's values and how they saw the world. We're now here, twenty, thirty years later, in a place where the Haida Nation is in control of their land.

MNY: The quality of printing and presentations were really important to *SpruceRoots*, as was the quality of the content. For example, Gowgaia Institute (the organization that published *SpruceRoots* and had worked on other communication, community networking and land use planning processes, including mapping) produced maps that were easier to read and more relevant than logging company maps, which were generally better than Ministry of Forests maps. Our maps began to replace other maps at public meetings and negotiation sessions because they were simply better. The *SpruceRoots* final edition included a great example—a beautiful satellite image map of Haida Gwaii. Even though it clearly shows just how much of the archipelago forest was taken away by the Province, it is artfully presented. Everything we were doing was informed by an aesthetic quality. Things had to look good and achieve the highest grade. When you were reading it, and even if you were disinclined to believe the words, the presentation said value. That really helped persuade people that the written words were also valued.

On the other side of the tree was a coarse publication, which was clearly and rudely in support of the deforestation agenda. This was the *Redneck News*, a mimeograph sheet printed by a fellow in Sandspit who was employed by a logging company. It was quite

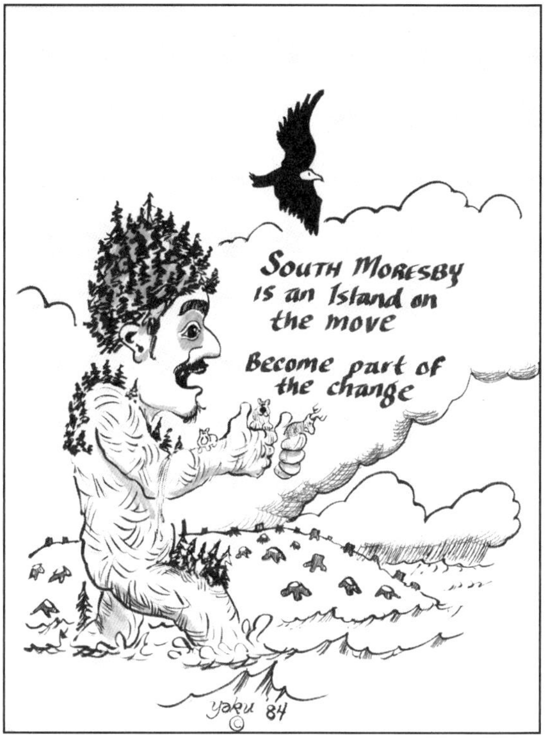

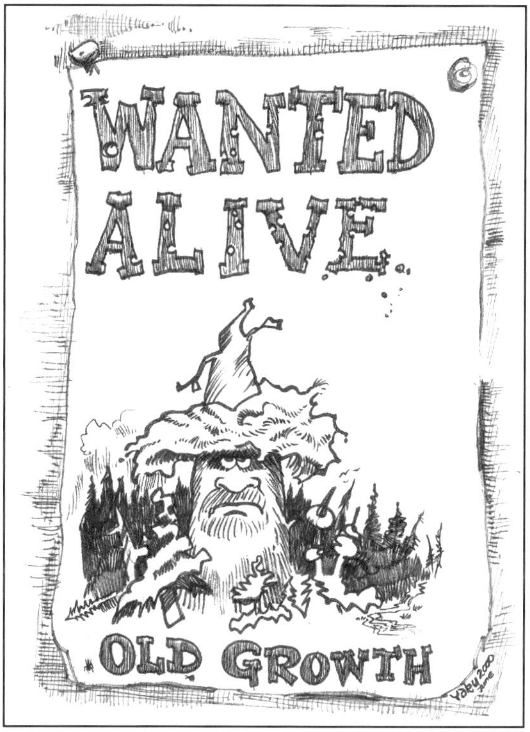

Left. Untitled, 1984. Originally published in *The Ubyssey* (Vancouver, BC);
Right. *Wanted Alive: Old Growth*, 2000. Originally published in *SpruceRoots Magazine* (Haida Gwaii).

nasty, an attack-the-person piece of work that went on for a number of years. Other than that, we had the *Queen Charlotte Islands Observer*, the standard mainstream Lower Mainland papers, and, from time to time, we had some Canada-wide press. Against all these, we had *SpruceRoots*, and our messages said quality and integrity can be found here in this small community, one that included Haida and Canadian citizens.

SD: We didn't want to look like a rag. We wanted it to be something most people could pick up and not have it dismissed because of the way it looked.

LP: You hinted at criticism over the accuracy of fact. What would you say about that?

SD: I'd say we were right and they were wrong. I think that's been proven over time. The problem was that what we were saying, people didn't want to hear.

The first map we put out showing the extent of clear-cut logging on the Islands had a big impact because no one had put all that information together on one map.

People knew this was happening and the map validated what people knew. What we did was continue building and telling that story and doing the analysis on the information accurately. The maps have been and still are successful. Analysis of, for instance, the volumes and values of the amount of logs removed from the Islands, and the TFL – or Tree Farm License – cases really enlightened people. We did analysis on what it meant, and what the outcomes may be. We did a lot of work trying to break down prejudices. But, no matter what you publish, you're going to be criticized. I do know the stuff we put out was accurate. We would spin it with a bias, absolutely, but it was a bias we knew was reflected by most people on the Islands. We knew that there was over-cutting. We knew that second-growth wasn't going to save the economy. All those fallacies that were being put out by the companies and the ministries didn't hold water, so all we did was tell people that.

LP: Who was funding *SpruceRoots?*

SD: We were mainly funded, in the early days, by the W. Alton Jones Foundation in Charlottesville, Virginia, USA, by a person there who liked what we were doing and funded us over a long period of time. We were a special project. When the foundation

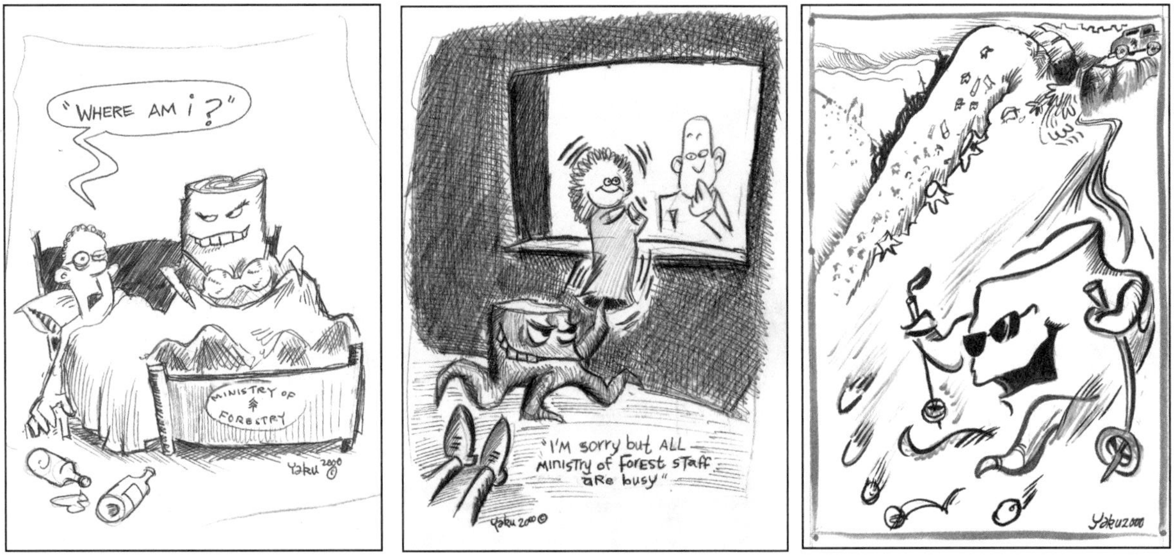

Left, Centre & Right. Untitled, 2000. Originally published in *SpruceRoots Magazine* (Haida Gwaii).

shut down, for a couple of years we became part of the Moore Foundation in the US.

LP: If the funds were secure, would it have gone on for longer?

SD: No, I think the world of environmentalism has changed substantially. A lot of goals we worked towards thirty years ago have been accomplished. Today, over fifty percent of the land is under some form of protection on the Islands and the remaining land will be treated differently. The control of the TFLs will be in the hands of the Haida Nation shortly. In some sense, mission accomplished. The world is different today. We could have continued to publish but it would have to have become something different. I don't know if there would be a need for it right now. *Haida Laas* has now become the news source for people who are interested in changes that are occurring between the Haida Nation and the provincial government.

MNY: Just to underline that last point, the current issue has changed. Now we need to construct a new structure – one that is more inclusive, accountable to and intimately available to the Islands. That has yet to be evolved properly in my mind but all the tools are there and it seems like current governance is aware and involved. *Haida Laas* and the Council of the Haida Nation are well positioned to develop something that is more inclusive of all ethnicity. We can demonstrate some accomplishments and models that will be useful to other nation states looking for postcolonial inspirations. There's decades of work ahead to be done.

SD: Yes, we've spent more than thirty years getting to this point, and the next thirty years is definitely the work Michael refers to.

MNY: Thinking back to *SpruceRoots* and the environmental situation, there really weren't a lot of models for us to look at and say that we're going to duplicate those successes. We had a quote from Gandhi on the wall during the blockades but we really had to plan and create the success ourselves. This is still happening. I don't know where in Canada or North America we'd find a social, political model that talks about Indigenous Peoples in decision-making authority terms. Canadian federal and provincial governments continue to work at odds against their own constitutional recognition of the pre-existing Indigenous authority. Haida Gwaii is a rare place. Here is a better possibility for Canada. Perhaps here is where another order, a third order of government can be incorporated into the Canadian constitution. This is a place where people can get along.

SD: *SpruceRoots* recognized that and we weren't trying to save the land like environmentalists. We were trying to change the way it was treated. We were clear about the path that we wanted to go down. We didn't want to join anyone else's parade. We wanted to build something here that was unique to this place – that dealt with the issues here. We weren't interested in building a utopian, environmental world, but building a system with other people that treated the natural world and each other as best we can.

MNY: As a much younger person I worked in environmental organizations and logging companies and was struck by how they assumed a similar view of the world. The test of success was "do I lose or gain?" Good or evil. Human, apart from nature. The issues, like life itself, are far more complex. The challenge is how to actually live in complexity without resorting to the lazy tactic of demonizing the other side. Demonizing or undervaluing the other side is a repeating pattern that just feeds attack and the counter attack and the fight goes on. Successfully meeting the challenge means ending the fight.

SD: How the heck are we going to live together on the Islands? One thing Gowgaia and *SpruceRoots* were interested in was figuring out how to recognize and respect each other and not run our agenda over someone else's and likewise. All of us who live on Haida Gwaii are part of that struggle.

For a sampling of articles, maps and comics published in *SpruceRoots* visit www.spruceroots.org

Endnotes

1 This was called the Unity Rally, in which the Islands community marched to the Ministry of Forests in Queen Charlotte and cast votes of non-confidence in their ability to manage the land. The year was 2000.

2 Evelyn Pinkerton, "Taking the Minister to Court: Changes in Public Opinion About Forest Management and Their Expression in Haida Land Claims," *BC Studies*. no. 57, spring 1983. 68-85.

Comics

Mutants of the Pit

The second volume of Tales of Raven *from 1987,* Mutants of the Pit, *was also produced for the Islands Protection Society with content research by the Massett Band Council. Two-thousand copies were printed and distributed on Haida Gwaii as a response to a proposal to open a metal mine, and along with it, creation of a ball mill and tailings ponds alongside the ecologically sensitive Yakoun River. The proposal was rejected and did not proceed. This is its second printing.*

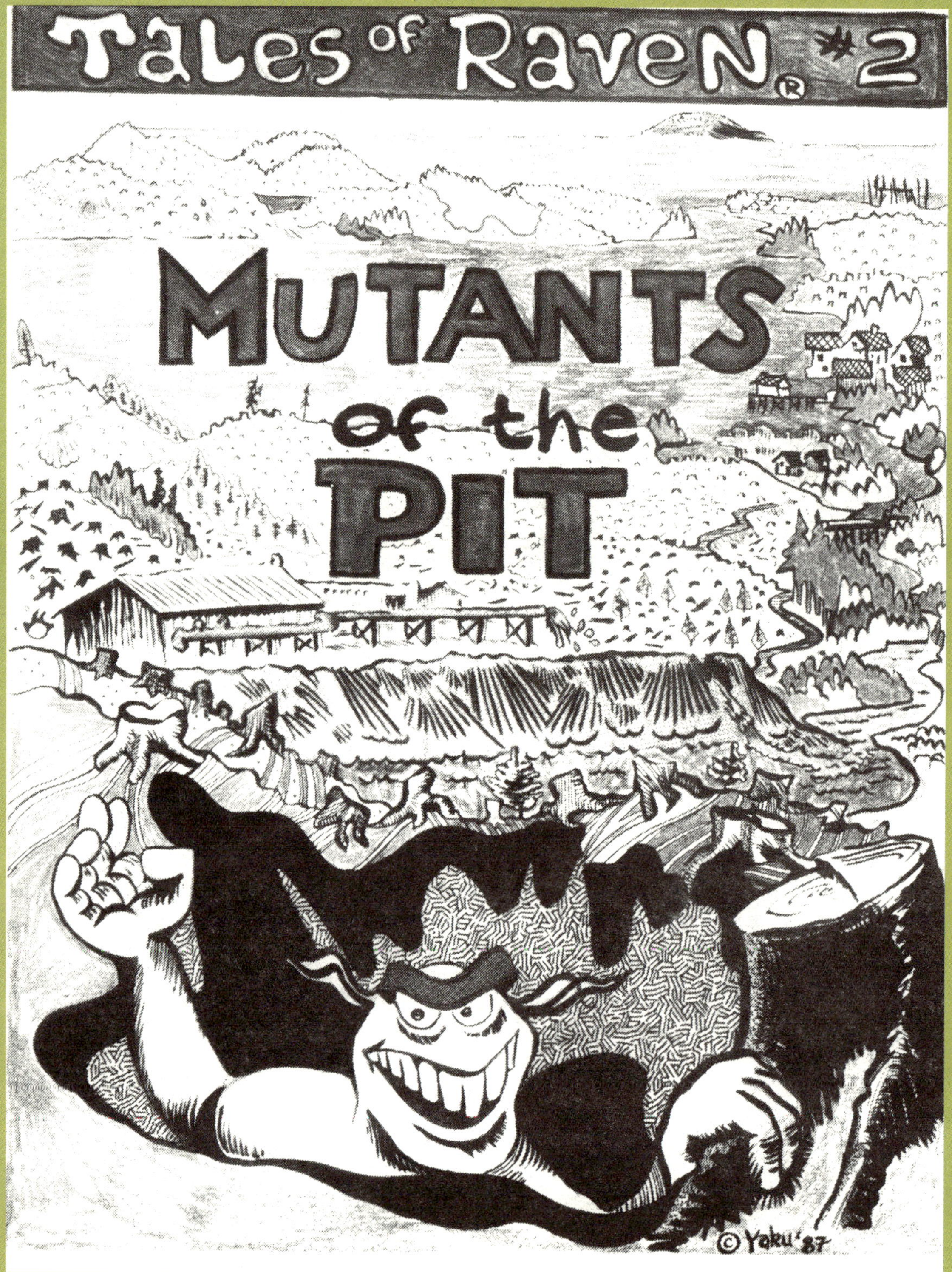
Tales of Raven® #2
MUTANTS
of the
PIT
© Yaku '87

FOR THOUSANDS OF YEARS THE MASSETT INLET AND THE YAKOUN RIVER HAVE PROVIDED A WEALTH OF ABUNDANCE. TEN YEARS OF MINING BY CITY RESOURCES LTD MAY SPOIL THIS FOREVER. THIS IS THE RISK OF HARM THAT WE ARE EXPECTED TO SHOULDER. THE FOLLOWING STORY IS ABOUT ONE OF THE DANGEROUS CONSEQUENCES THAT COULD OCCUR SHOULD THIS MINING PROPOSAL PROCEED.

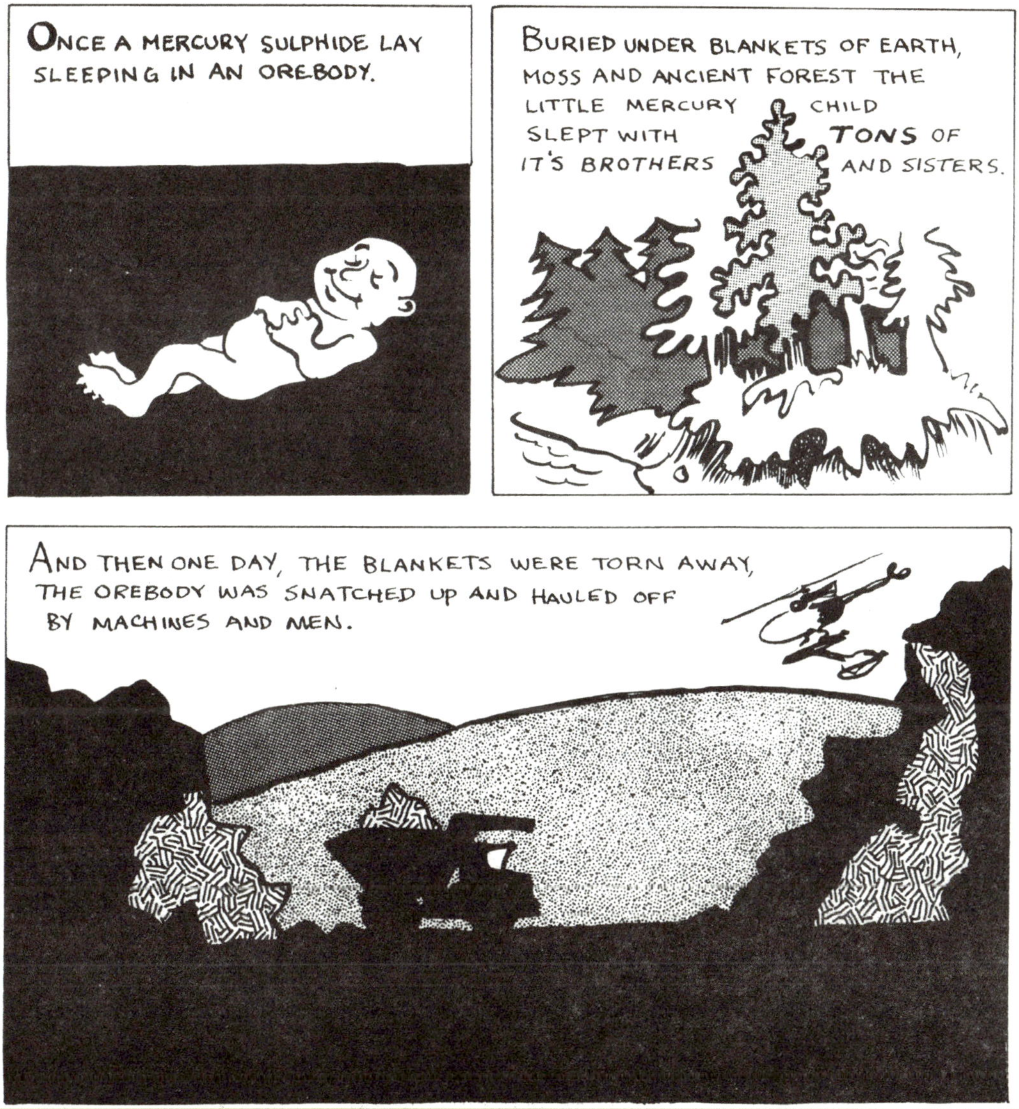

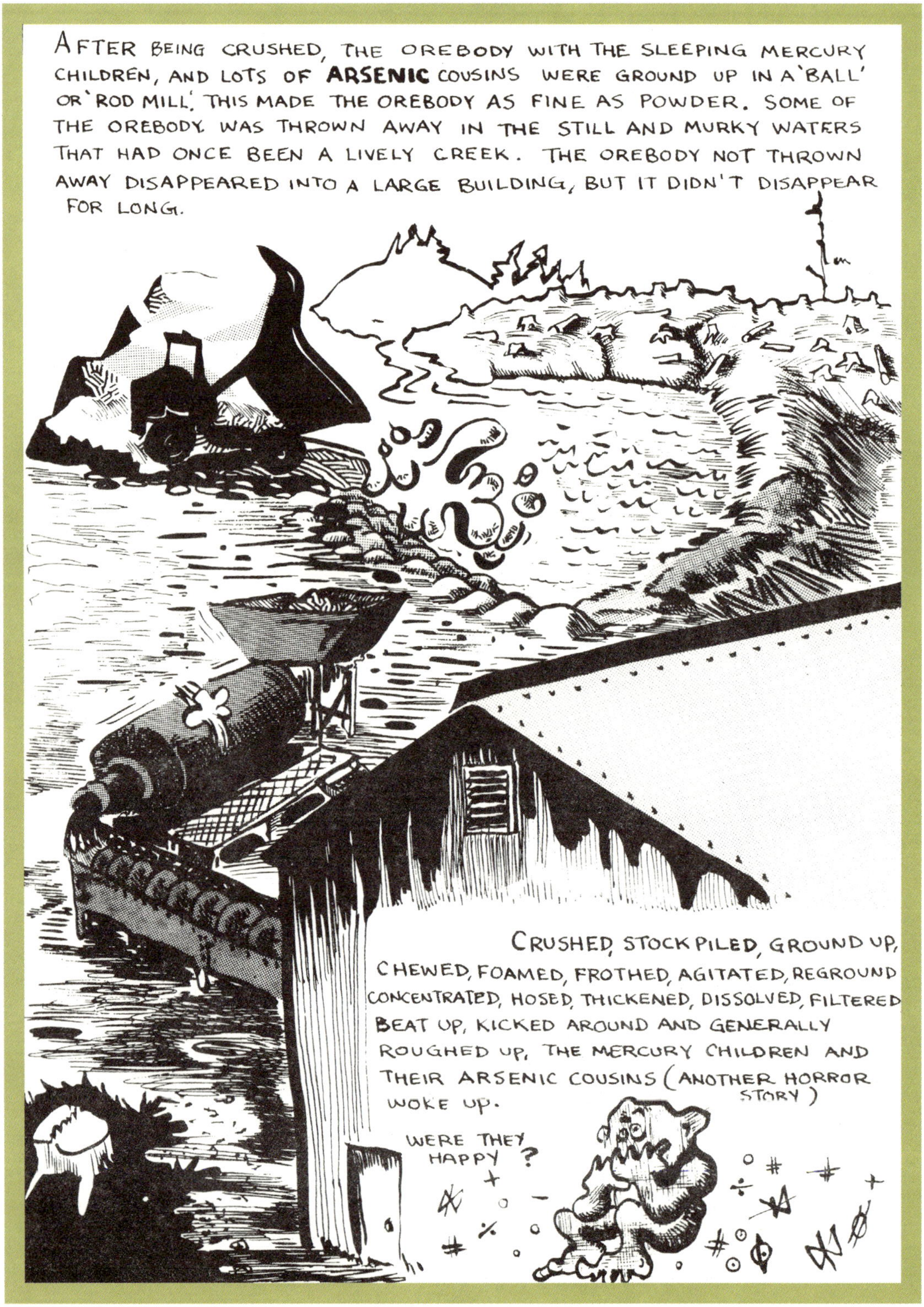

AFTER BEING CRUSHED, THE OREBODY WITH THE SLEEPING MERCURY CHILDREN, AND LOTS OF **ARSENIC** COUSINS WERE GROUND UP IN A 'BALL' OR 'ROD MILL'. THIS MADE THE OREBODY AS FINE AS POWDER. SOME OF THE OREBODY WAS THROWN AWAY IN THE STILL AND MURKY WATERS THAT HAD ONCE BEEN A LIVELY CREEK. THE OREBODY NOT THROWN AWAY DISAPPEARED INTO A LARGE BUILDING, BUT IT DIDN'T DISAPPEAR FOR LONG.
CRUSHED, STOCKPILED, GROUND UP, CHEWED, FOAMED, FROTHED, AGITATED, REGROUND CONCENTRATED, HOSED, THICKENED, DISSOLVED, FILTERED BEAT UP, KICKED AROUND AND GENERALLY ROUGHED UP, THE MERCURY CHILDREN AND THEIR ARSENIC COUSINS (ANOTHER HORROR STORY) WOKE UP.
WERE THEY HAPPY ?

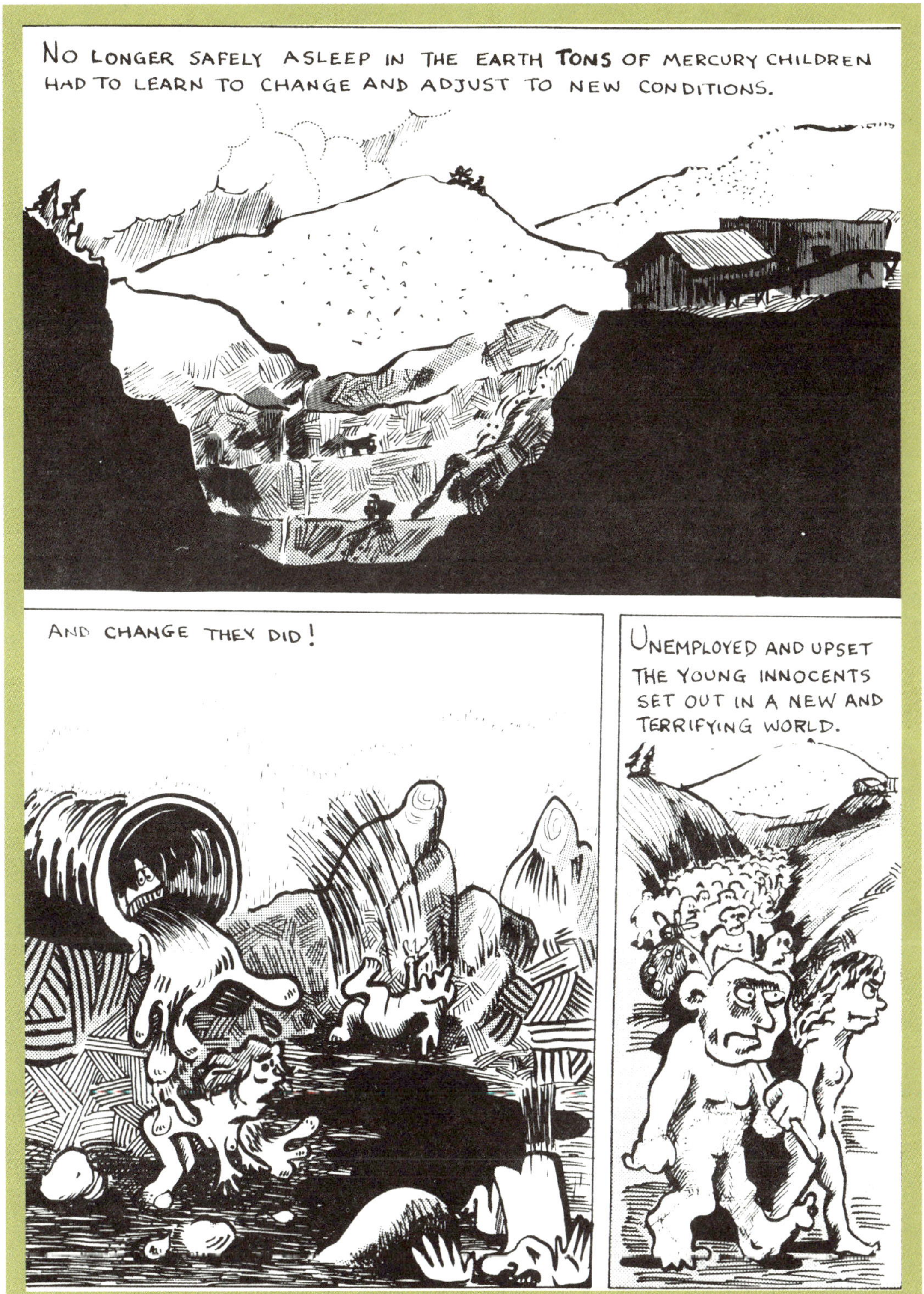
NO LONGER SAFELY ASLEEP IN THE EARTH TONS OF MERCURY CHILDREN HAD TO LEARN TO CHANGE AND ADJUST TO NEW CONDITIONS.
AND CHANGE THEY DID!
UNEMPLOYED AND UPSET THE YOUNG INNOCENTS SET OUT IN A NEW AND TERRIFYING WORLD.

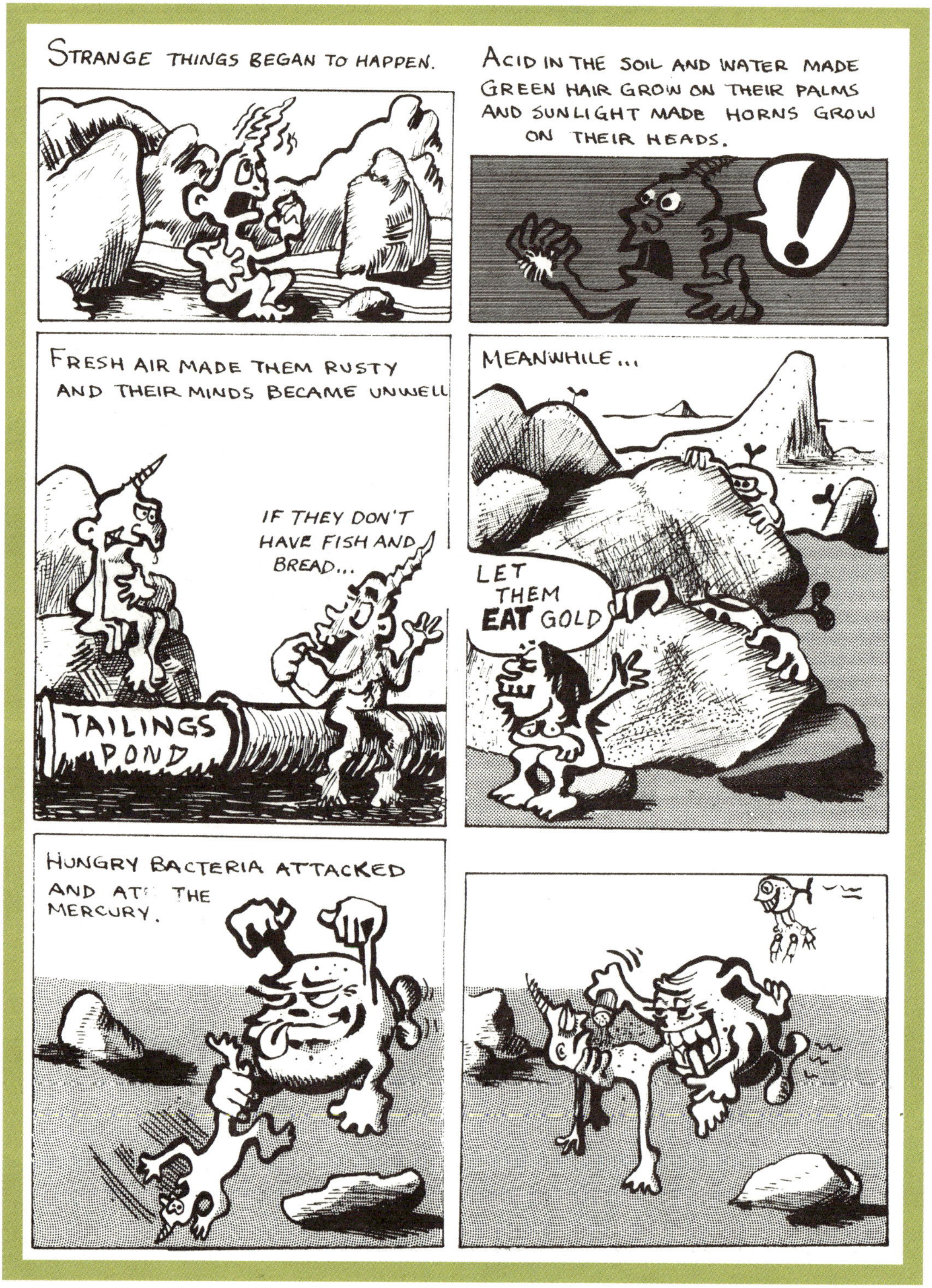
STRANGE THINGS BEGAN TO HAPPEN.
ACID IN THE SOIL AND WATER MADE GREEN HAIR GROW ON THEIR PALMS AND SUNLIGHT MADE HORNS GROW ON THEIR HEADS.
!
FRESH AIR MADE THEM RUSTY AND THEIR MINDS BECAME UNWELL
IF THEY DON'T HAVE FISH AND BREAD...
TAILINGS POND
MEANWHILE...
LET THEM EAT GOLD
HUNGRY BACTERIA ATTACKED AND ATE THE MERCURY.

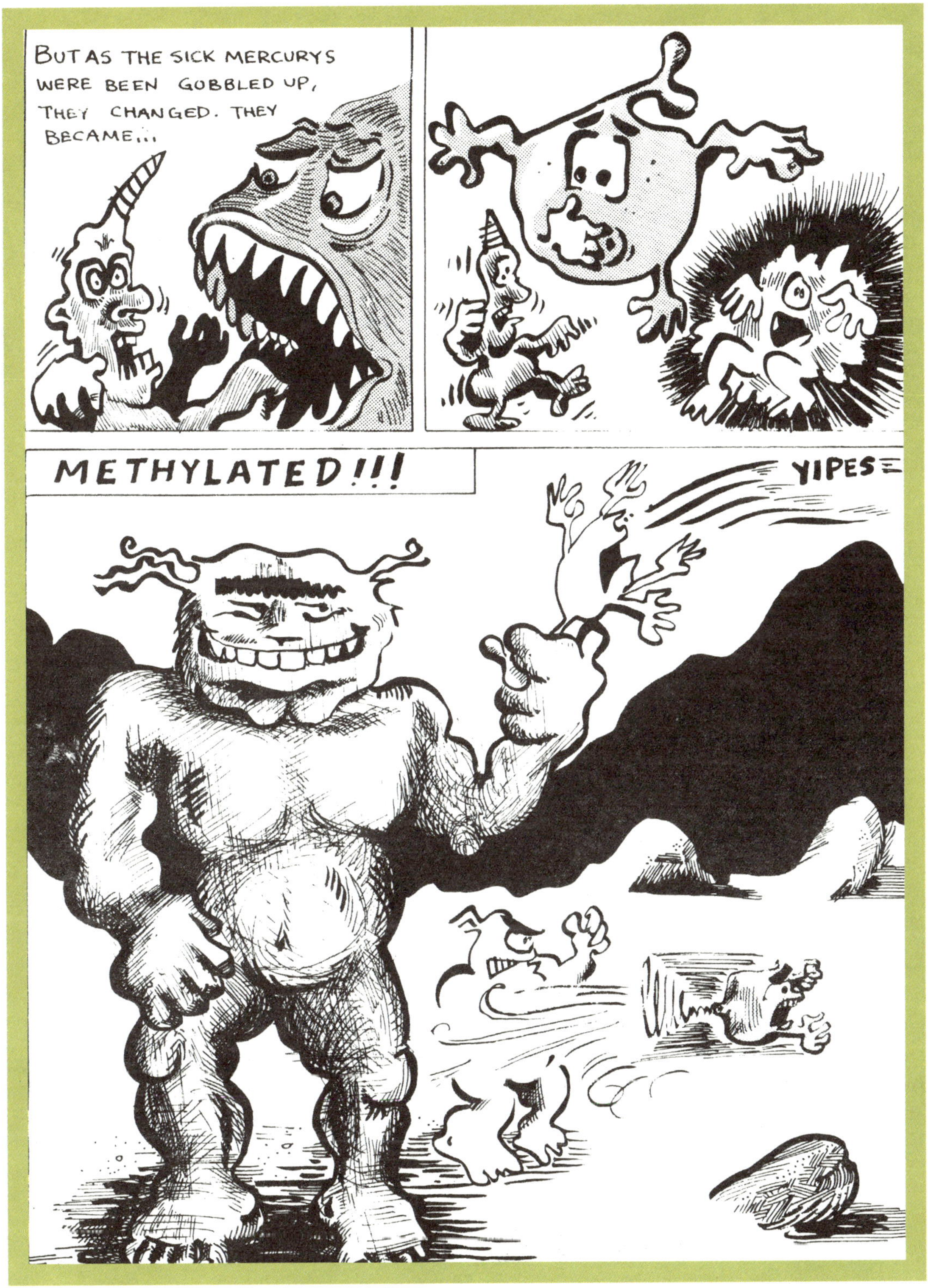

BUT AS THE SICK MERCURYS
WERE BEEN GOBBLED UP,
THEY CHANGED. THEY
BECAME...
METHYLATED!!!
YIPES

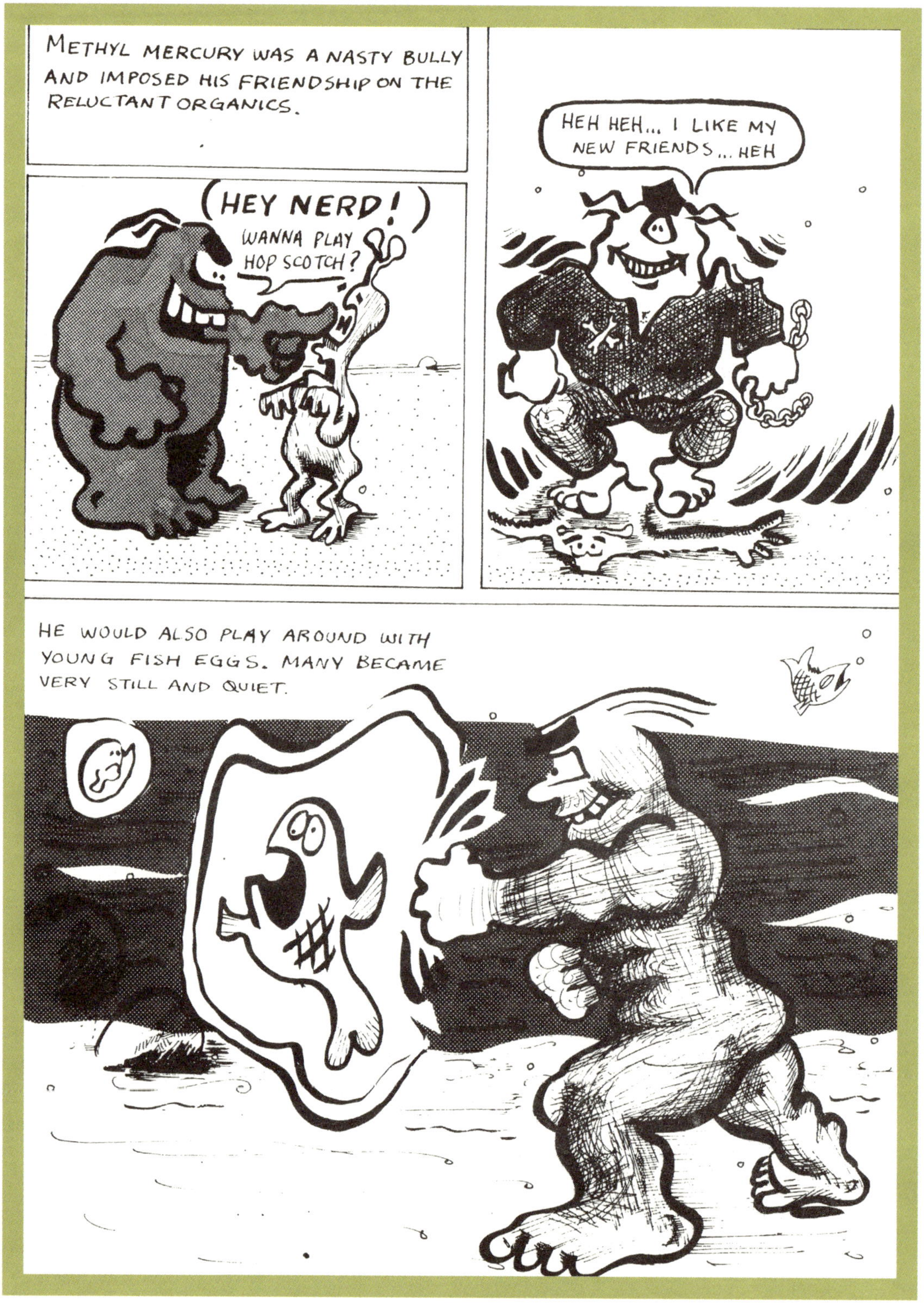
METHYL MERCURY WAS A NASTY BULLY AND IMPOSED HIS FRIENDSHIP ON THE RELUCTANT ORGANICS.
(HEY NERD!)
WANNA PLAY HOP SCOTCH?
HEH HEH... I LIKE MY NEW FRIENDS... HEH
HE WOULD ALSO PLAY AROUND WITH YOUNG FISH EGGS. MANY BECAME VERY STILL AND QUIET.

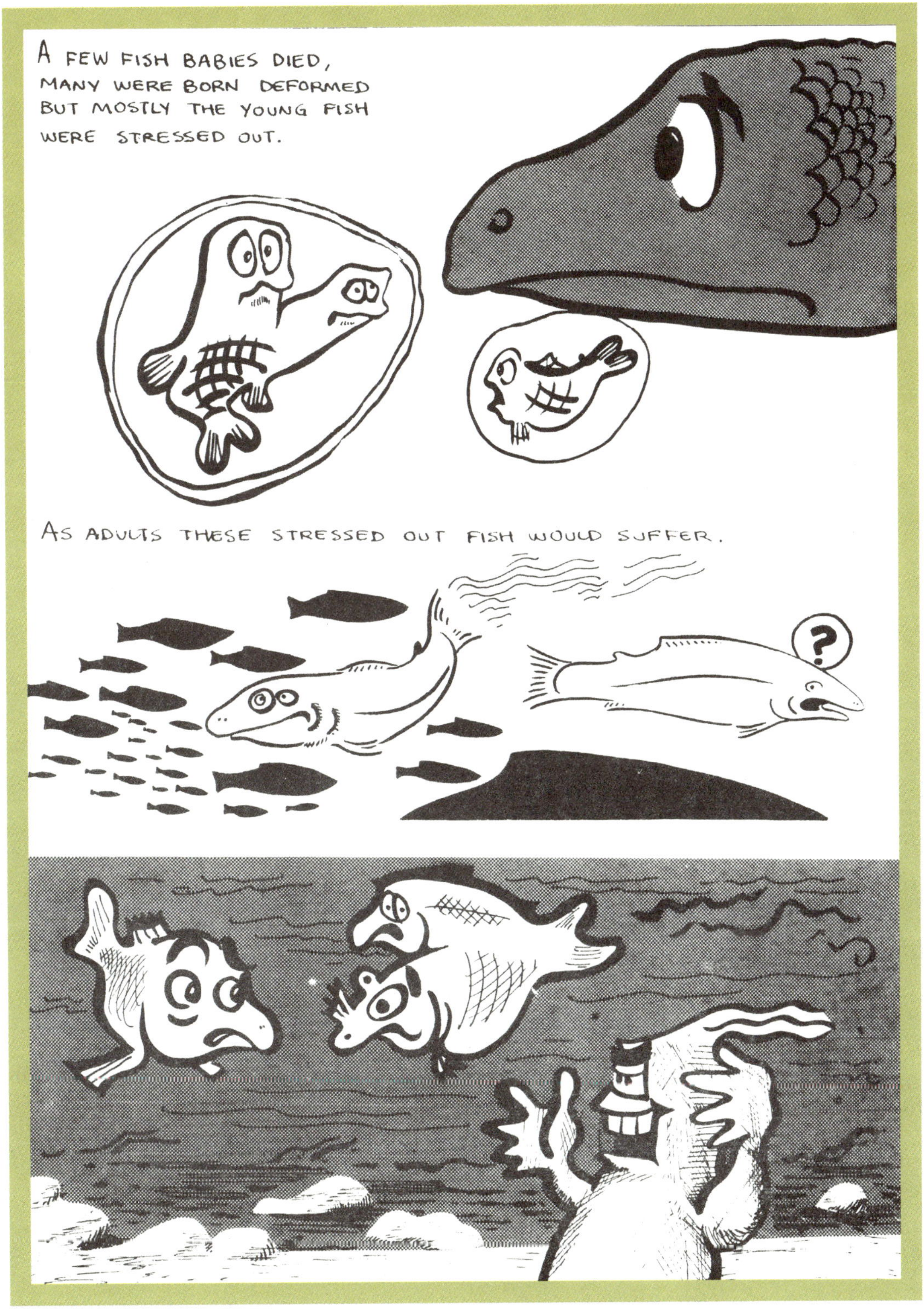
A FEW FISH BABIES DIED, MANY WERE BORN DEFORMED BUT MOSTLY THE YOUNG FISH WERE STRESSED OUT.
AS ADULTS THESE STRESSED OUT FISH WOULD SUFFER.
?

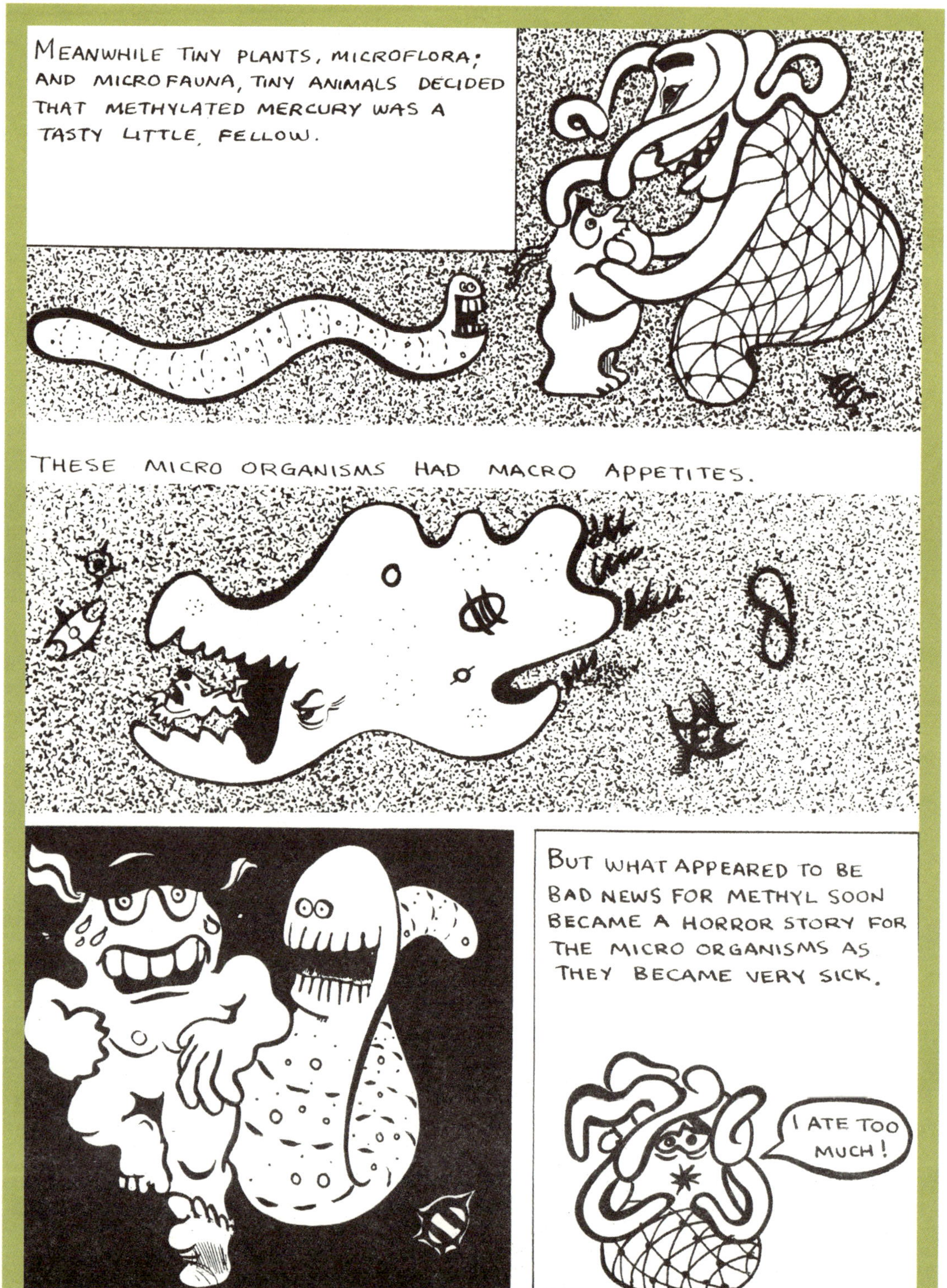
MEANWHILE TINY PLANTS, MICROFLORA; AND MICROFAUNA, TINY ANIMALS DECIDED THAT METHYLATED MERCURY WAS A TASTY LITTLE FELLOW.
THESE MICRO ORGANISMS HAD MACRO APPETITES.
BUT WHAT APPEARED TO BE BAD NEWS FOR METHYL SOON BECAME A HORROR STORY FOR THE MICRO ORGANISMS AS THEY BECAME VERY SICK.
I ATE TOO MUCH!

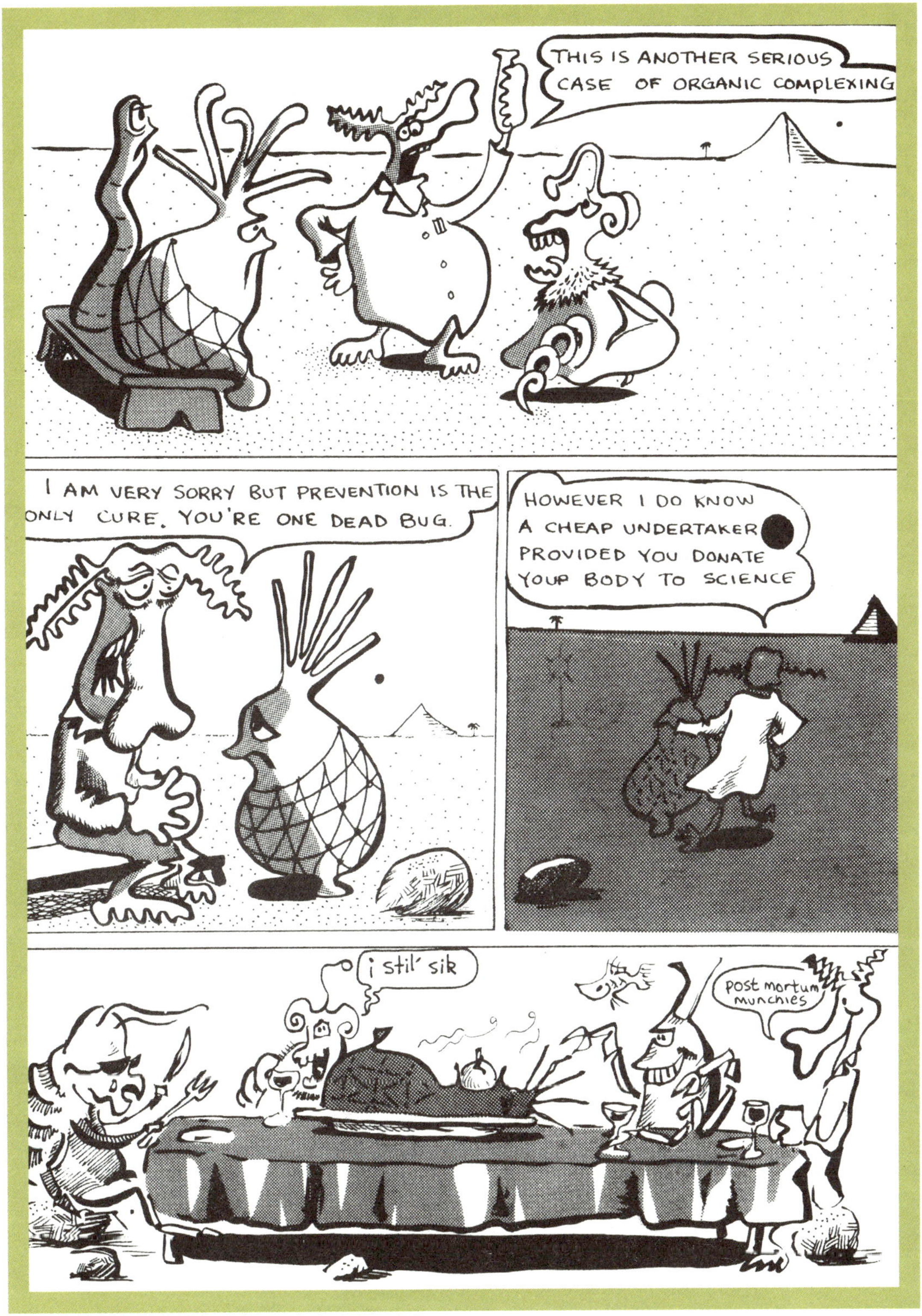
THIS IS ANOTHER SERIOUS CASE OF ORGANIC COMPLEXING
I AM VERY SORRY BUT PREVENTION IS THE ONLY CURE. YOU'RE ONE DEAD BUG.
HOWEVER I DO KNOW A CHEAP UNDERTAKER PROVIDED YOU DONATE YOUR BODY TO SCIENCE
i stil' sik
post mortum munchies

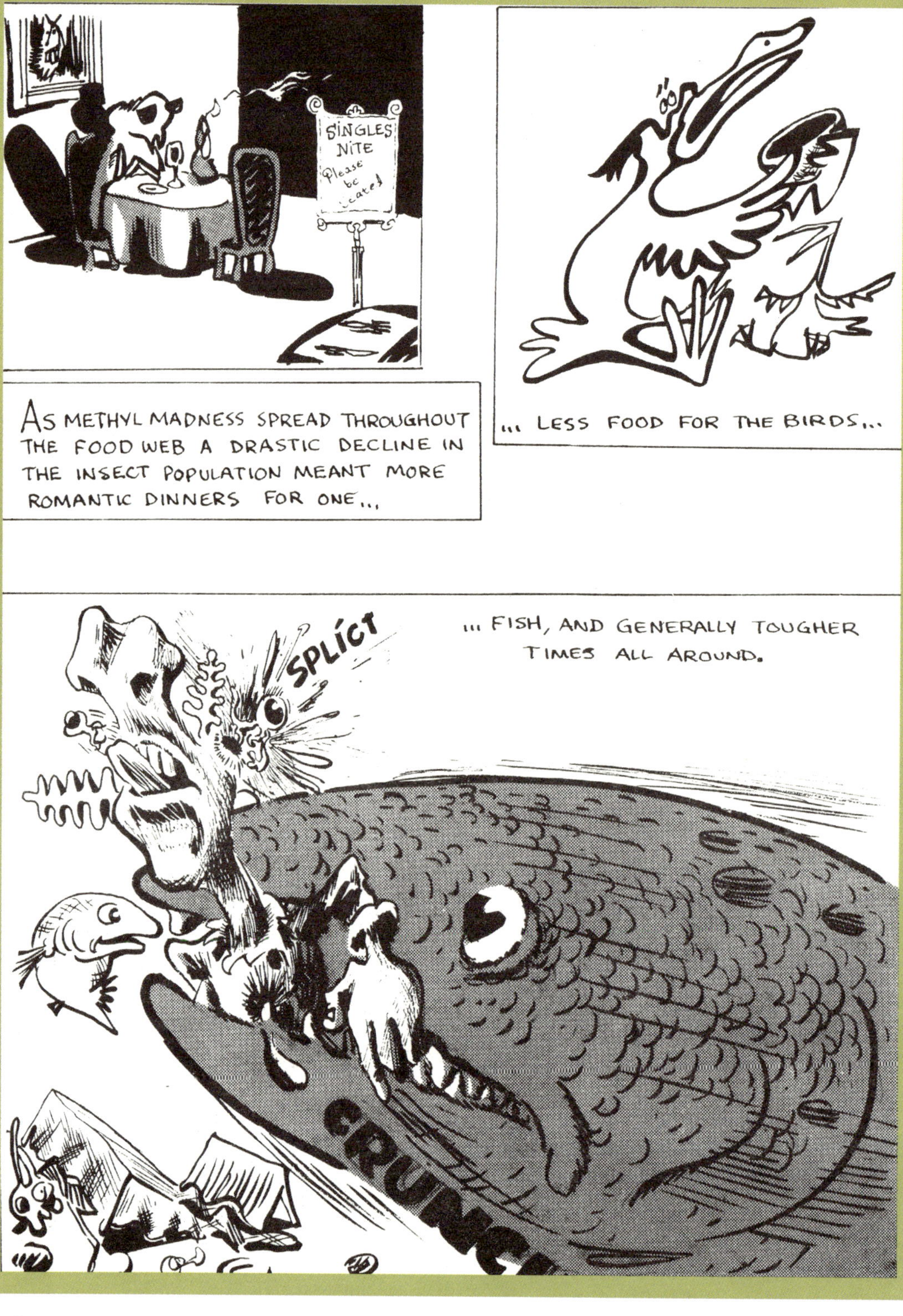
SINGLES NITE
Please be seated
AS METHYL MADNESS SPREAD THROUGHOUT THE FOOD WEB A DRASTIC DECLINE IN THE INSECT POPULATION MEANT MORE ROMANTIC DINNERS FOR ONE...
... LESS FOOD FOR THE BIRDS...
... FISH, AND GENERALLY TOUGHER TIMES ALL AROUND.
SPLICT
CRUNC

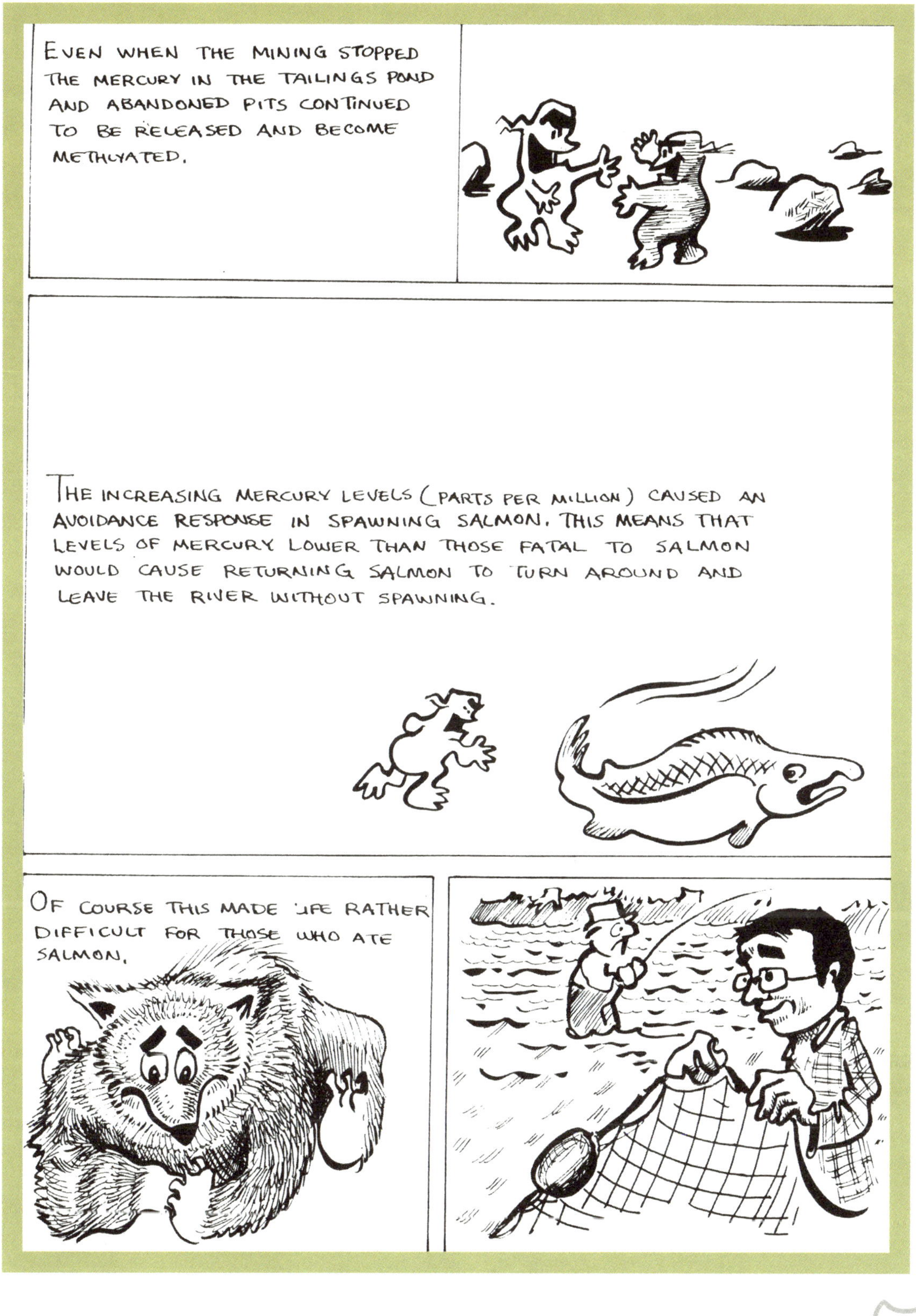
EVEN WHEN THE MINING STOPPED THE MERCURY IN THE TAILINGS POND AND ABANDONED PITS CONTINUED TO BE RELEASED AND BECOME METHLYATED.
THE INCREASING MERCURY LEVELS (PARTS PER MILLION) CAUSED AN AVOIDANCE RESPONSE IN SPAWNING SALMON. THIS MEANS THAT LEVELS OF MERCURY LOWER THAN THOSE FATAL TO SALMON WOULD CAUSE RETURNING SALMON TO TURN AROUND AND LEAVE THE RIVER WITHOUT SPAWNING.
OF COURSE THIS MADE LIFE RATHER DIFFICULT FOR THOSE WHO ATE SALMON.

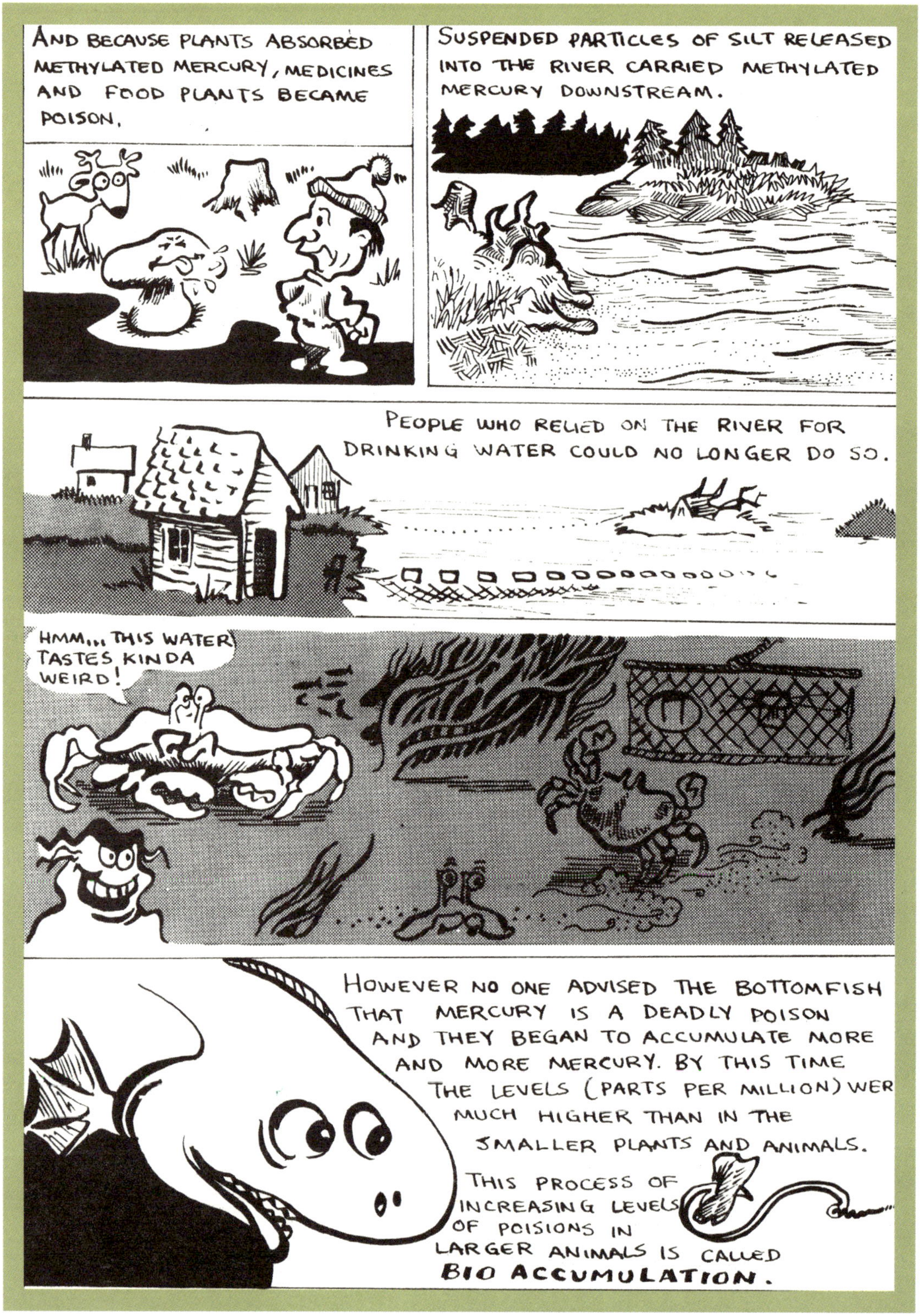
AND BECAUSE PLANTS ABSORBED METHYLATED MERCURY, MEDICINES AND FOOD PLANTS BECAME POISON.
SUSPENDED PARTICLES OF SILT RELEASED INTO THE RIVER CARRIED METHYLATED MERCURY DOWNSTREAM.
PEOPLE WHO RELIED ON THE RIVER FOR DRINKING WATER COULD NO LONGER DO SO.
HMM... THIS WATER TASTES KINDA WEIRD!
HOWEVER NO ONE ADVISED THE BOTTOMFISH THAT MERCURY IS A DEADLY POISON AND THEY BEGAN TO ACCUMULATE MORE AND MORE MERCURY. BY THIS TIME THE LEVELS (PARTS PER MILLION) WER MUCH HIGHER THAN IN THE SMALLER PLANTS AND ANIMALS.
THIS PROCESS OF INCREASING LEVELS OF POISIONS IN LARGER ANIMALS IS CALLED BIO ACCUMULATION.

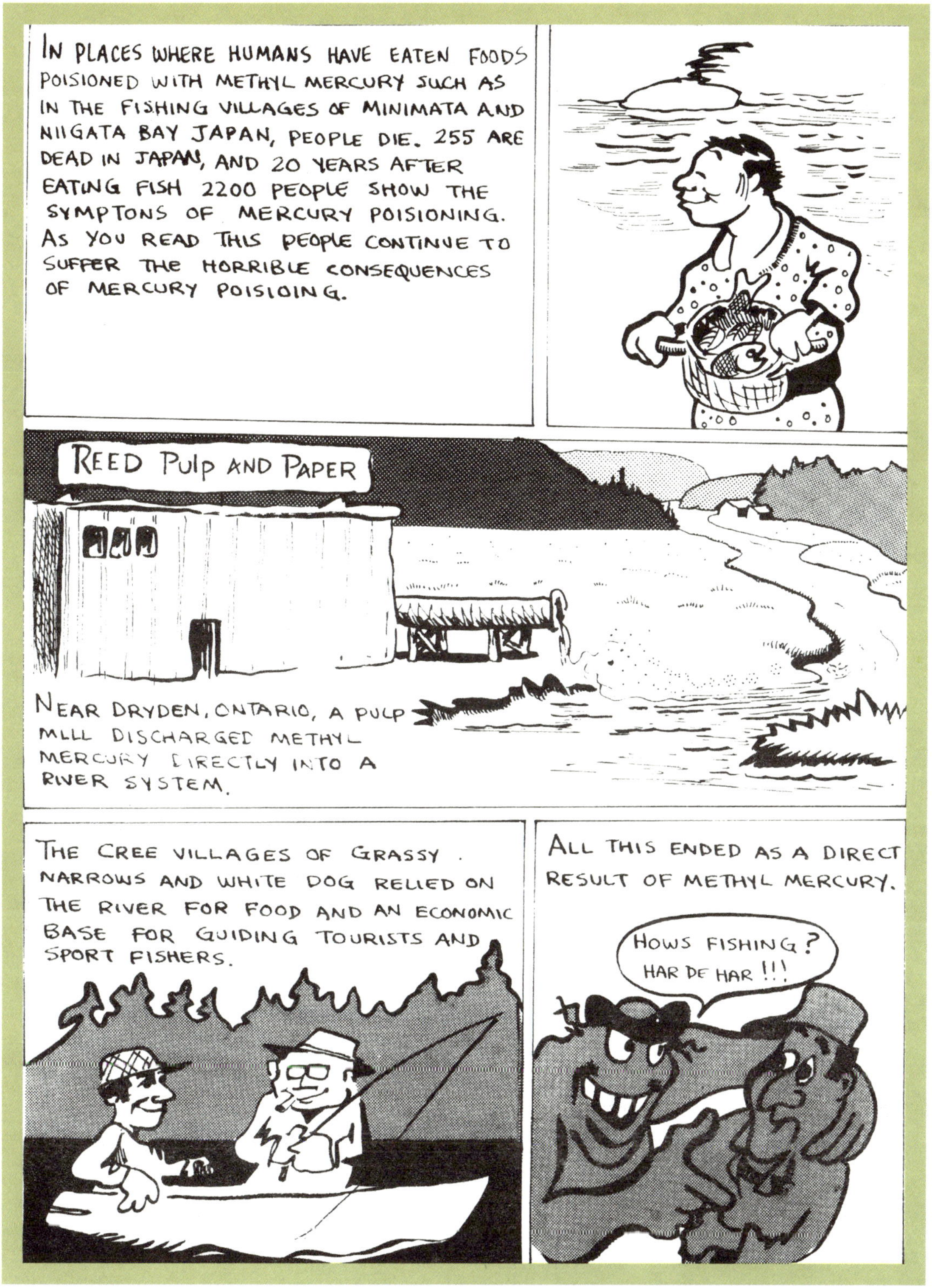
IN PLACES WHERE HUMANS HAVE EATEN FOODS POISIONED WITH METHYL MERCURY SUCH AS IN THE FISHING VILLAGES OF MINIMATA AND NIIGATA BAY JAPAN, PEOPLE DIE. 255 ARE DEAD IN JAPAN, AND 20 YEARS AFTER EATING FISH 2200 PEOPLE SHOW THE SYMPTONS OF MERCURY POISIONING. AS YOU READ THIS PEOPLE CONTINUE TO SUFFER THE HORRIBLE CONSEQUENCES OF MERCURY POISIOING.
REED PULP AND PAPER
NEAR DRYDEN, ONTARIO, A PULP MILL DISCHARGED METHYL MERCURY DIRECTLY INTO A RIVER SYSTEM.
THE CREE VILLAGES OF GRASSY NARROWS AND WHITE DOG RELIED ON THE RIVER FOR FOOD AND AN ECONOMIC BASE FOR GUIDING TOURISTS AND SPORT FISHERS.
ALL THIS ENDED AS A DIRECT RESULT OF METHYL MERCURY.
HOWS FISHING? HAR DE HAR !!!

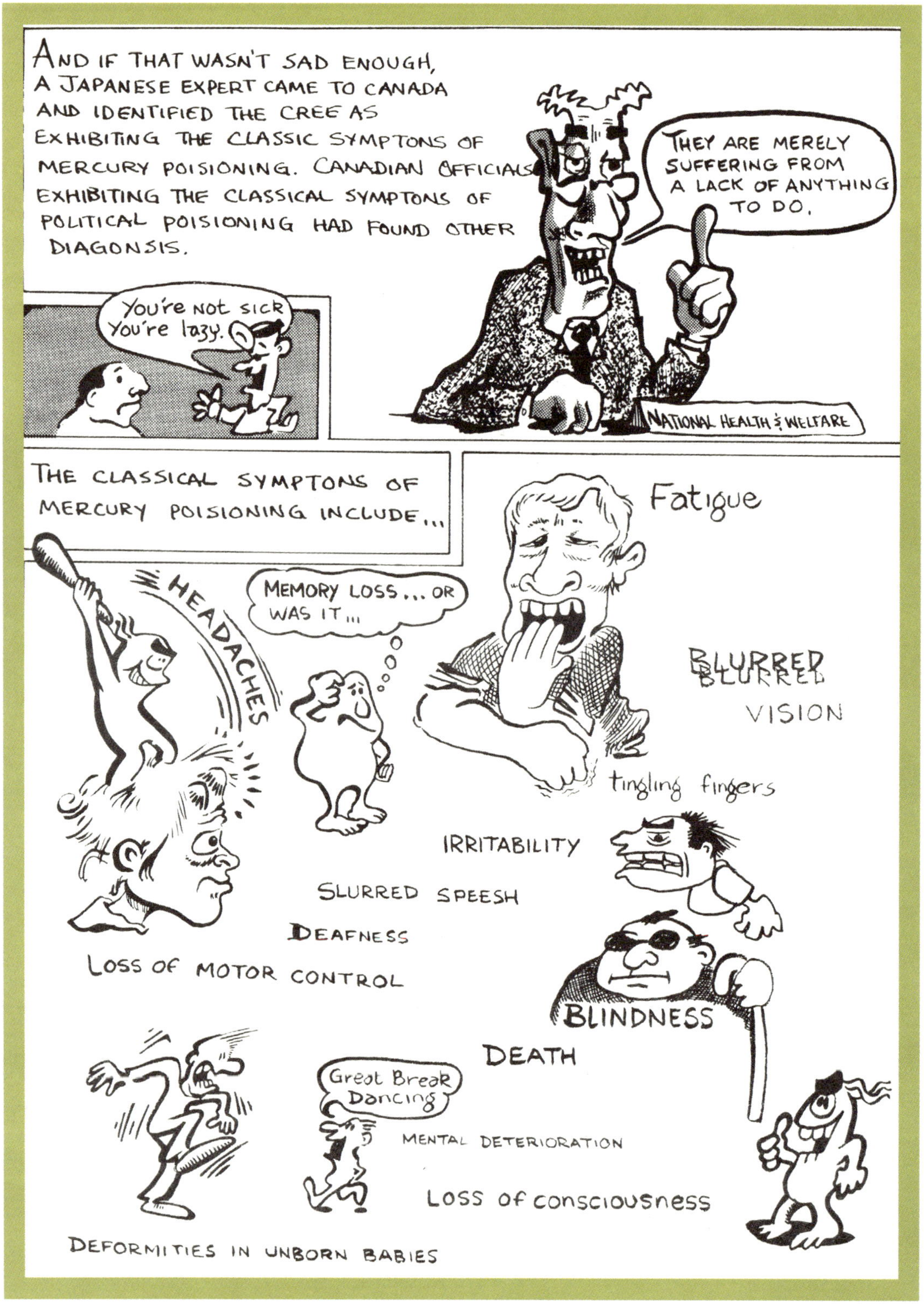
AND IF THAT WASN'T SAD ENOUGH, A JAPANESE EXPERT CAME TO CANADA AND IDENTIFIED THE CREE AS EXHIBITING THE CLASSIC SYMPTONS OF MERCURY POISIONING. CANADIAN OFFICIALS EXHIBITING THE CLASSICAL SYMPTONS OF POLITICAL POISIONING HAD FOUND OTHER DIAGONSIS.
THEY ARE MERELY SUFFERING FROM A LACK OF ANYTHING TO DO.
You're not sick You're lazy.
NATIONAL HEALTH & WELFARE
THE CLASSICAL SYMPTONS OF MERCURY POISIONING INCLUDE...
Fatigue
HEADACHES
MEMORY LOSS... OR WAS IT...
BLURRED VISION
tingling fingers
IRRITABILITY
SLURRED SPEESH
DEAFNESS
LOSS OF MOTOR CONTROL
BLINDNESS
DEATH
Great Break Dancing
MENTAL DETERIORATION
LOSS OF consciousness
DEFORMITIES IN UNBORN BABIES

ISLANDS PROTECTION SOCIETY

City Resources (Canada) Ltd. has taken the approach of professional public relations to justify the proposed Cinola Gold Mine. This is obviously designed to further the interests of City's shareholders.

However, the serious and complex consequences of a low grade gold mine within the Yakoun River watershed require us all to adopt a cautious and critical attitude.

No one can afford to shoulder the risks associated with the Cinola Project without being fully satisifed that the very best planning and scientific analysis have been carried out in an unbiased and objective manner.

If City Resources is committed to doing the best possible job then we aniticipate their support in establishing a formal public inquiry of their proposal.

This inquiry will address public concerns through independent experts under oath. It will allow input from island residents.

The risk of harm does not allow us the luxury of error.

Write to your provincial M.L.A.'s and federal M.P.'s requesting a formal public inquiry of the Cinola Gold Mine Project.

Islands Protection Society needs your support in its work to further public awareness of the Cinola Gold Mine Project. Please send your donations to:

Box 557 Masset, B.C. V0T 1M0

(Tax deductable receipts available $10.00 or more)

Images

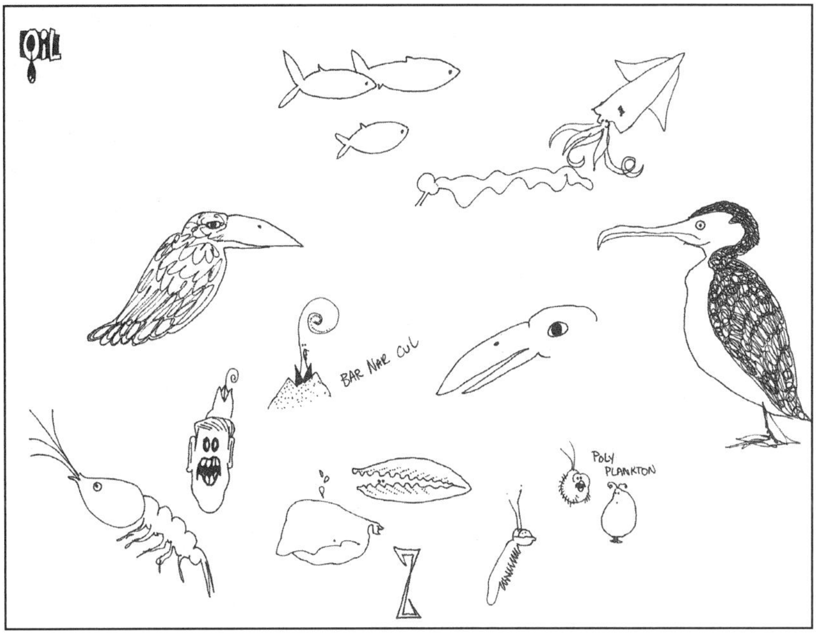
OIL
BAR NAR CUL
POLY PLANKTON

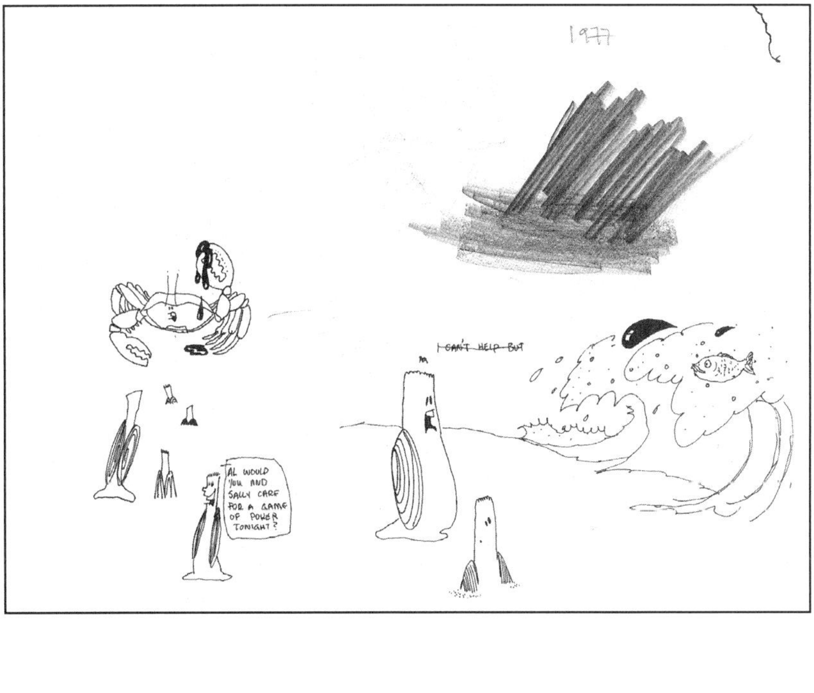
1977
I CAN'T HELP BUT
AL WOULD YOU AND SALLY CARE FOR A GAME OF POKER TONIGHT?

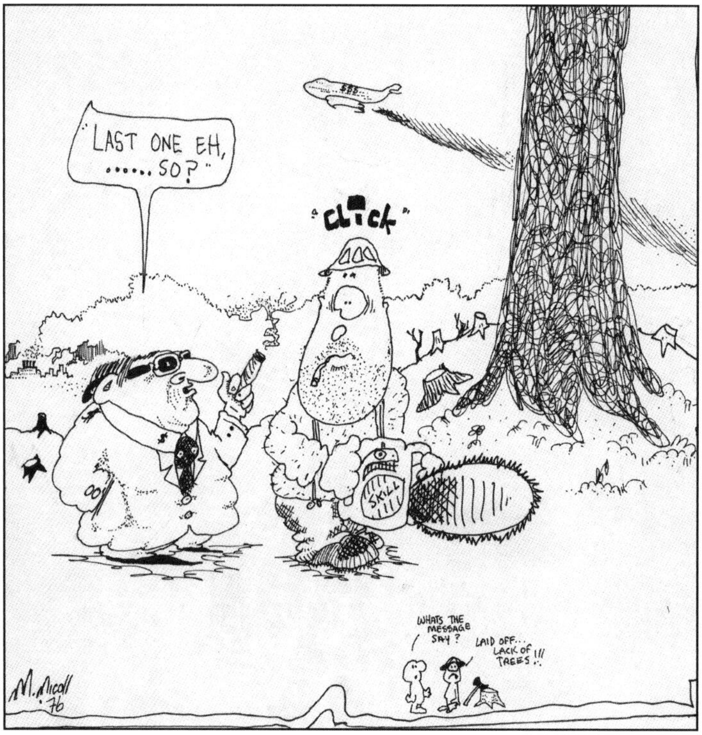
"LAST ONE EH, ...SO?"
"CLICK"
SKILL
WHATS THE MESSAGE SAY?
LAID OFF... LACK OF TREES!!!
M. Nicoll 76

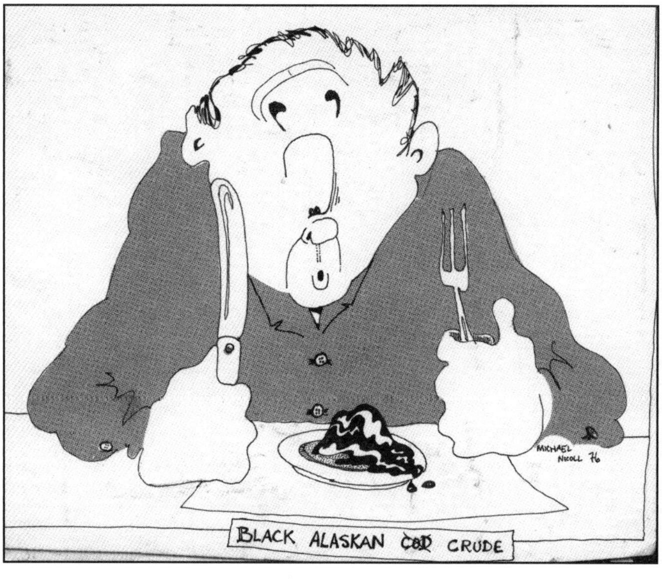
MICHAEL NICOLL 76
BLACK ALASKAN COD CRUDE

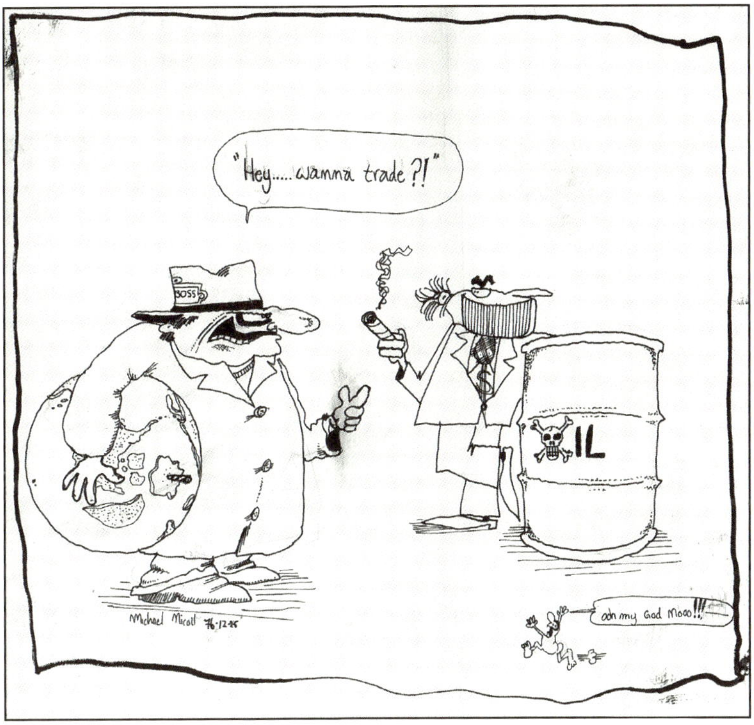
"Hey..... wanna trade?!"
BOSS
IL
ooh my God Mooo!!!
Michael Micoll 76·12·95

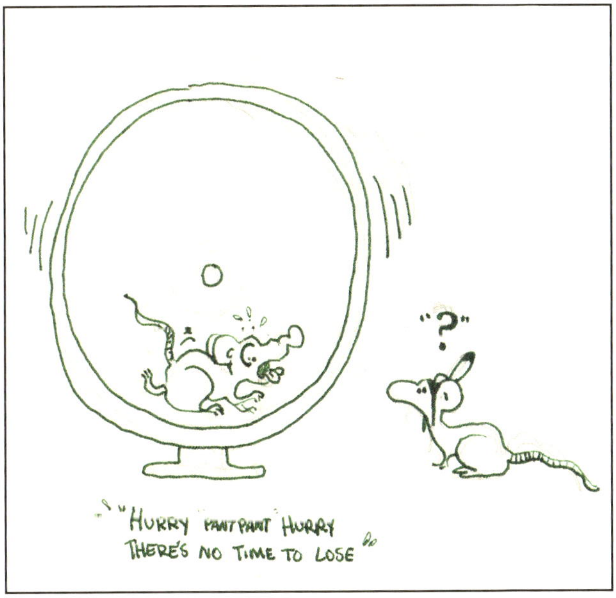
"?"
"HURRY PANT PANT HURRY
THERE'S NO TIME TO LOSE"

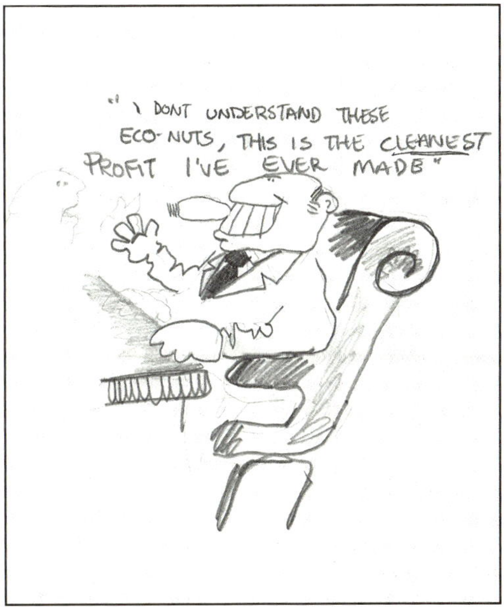
"I DONT UNDERSTAND THESE
ECO-NUTS, THIS IS THE CLEANEST
PROFIT I'VE EVER MADE"

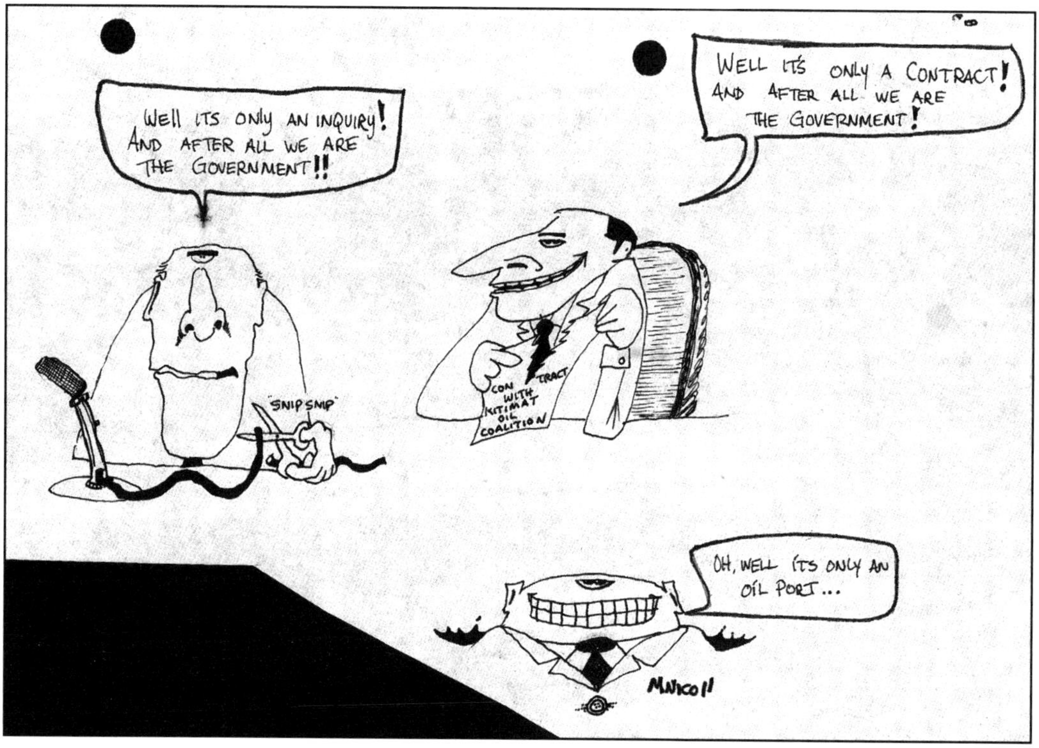
WELL ITS ONLY AN INQUIRY! AND AFTER ALL WE ARE THE GOVERNMENT!!
"SNIP SNIP"
WELL IT'S ONLY A CONTRACT! AND AFTER ALL WE ARE THE GOVERNMENT!
CONTRACT WITH KITIMAT OIL COALITION
OH, WELL ITS ONLY AN OIL PORT...
M.Nicoll

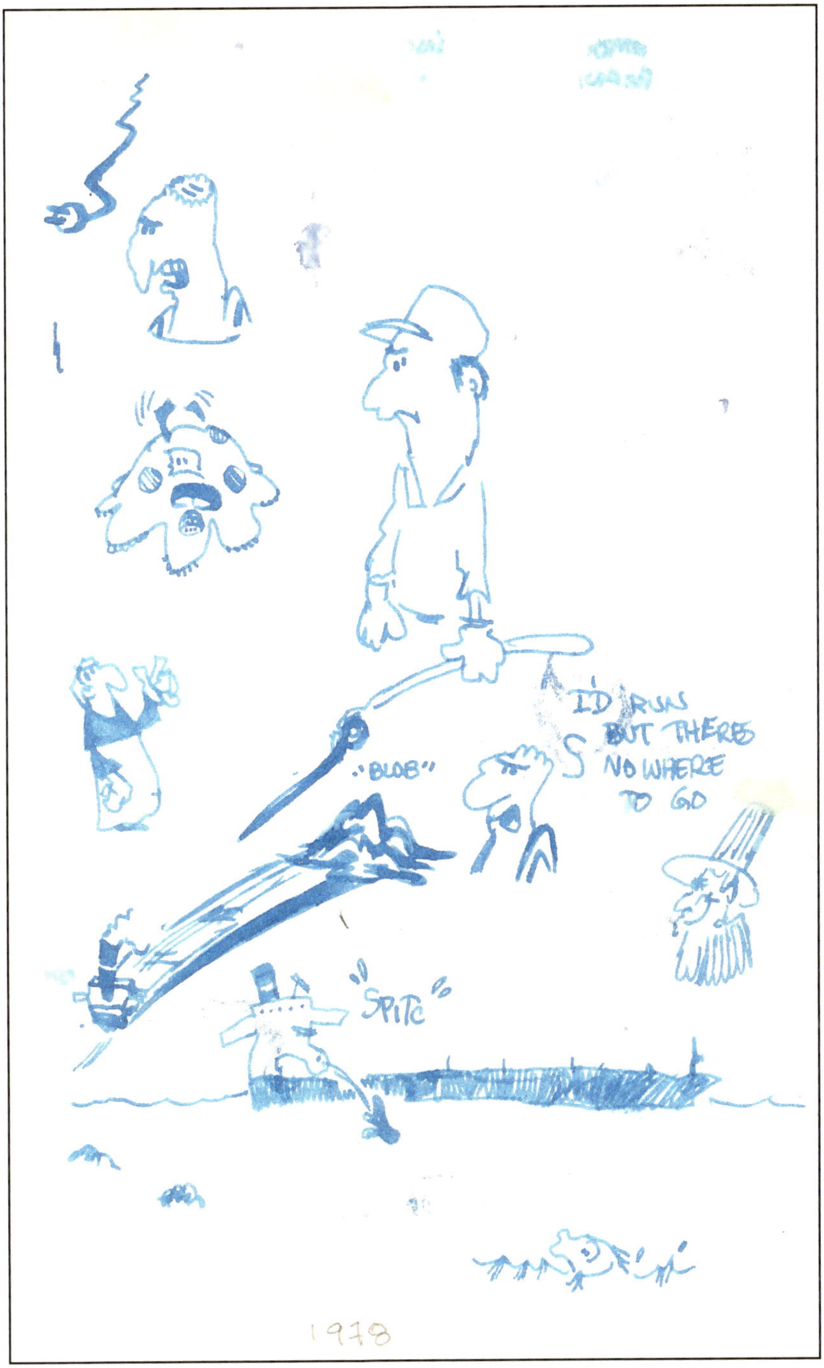
I'D RUN BUT THERES NO WHERE TO GO
"BLOB"
SPITC
1978

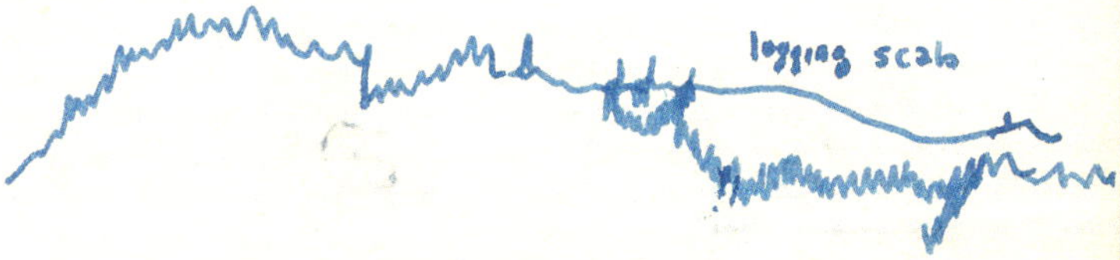

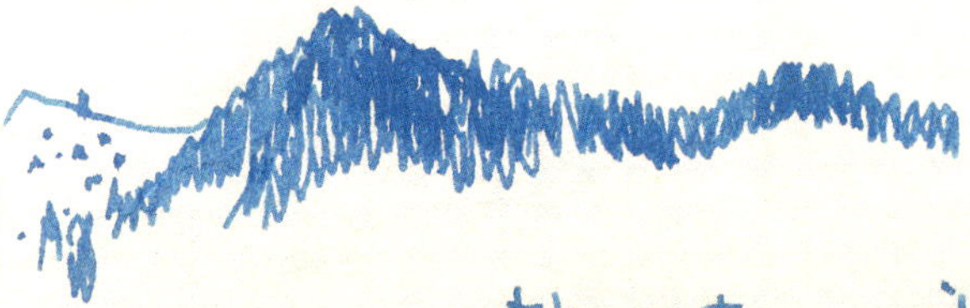

taking into consideration twofacts i.e. present logging practices of Q.C. TIMBER AND THE RECENT BRIBE MONEY DOLED OUT TO THE ISLAND COMMUNITYS I WONDER WHAT "PLANS" Q.C. TIMBER HAS FOR THE EVER DWINDLING FORESTS THAT WE ONCE CALLED OURS.

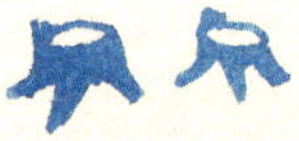

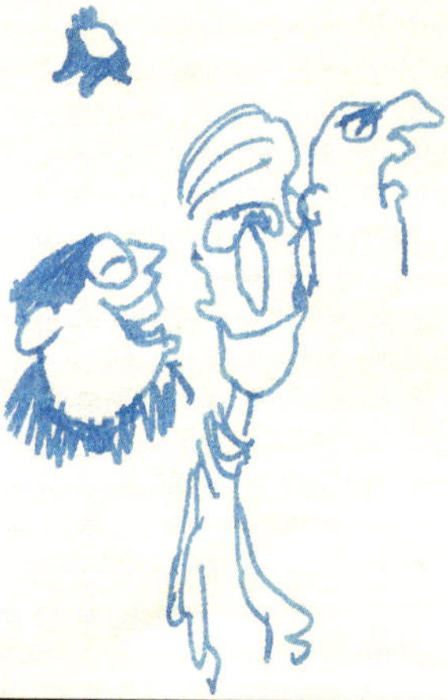

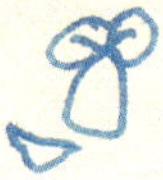

~~SURE~~

WHAT GOOD IS IT

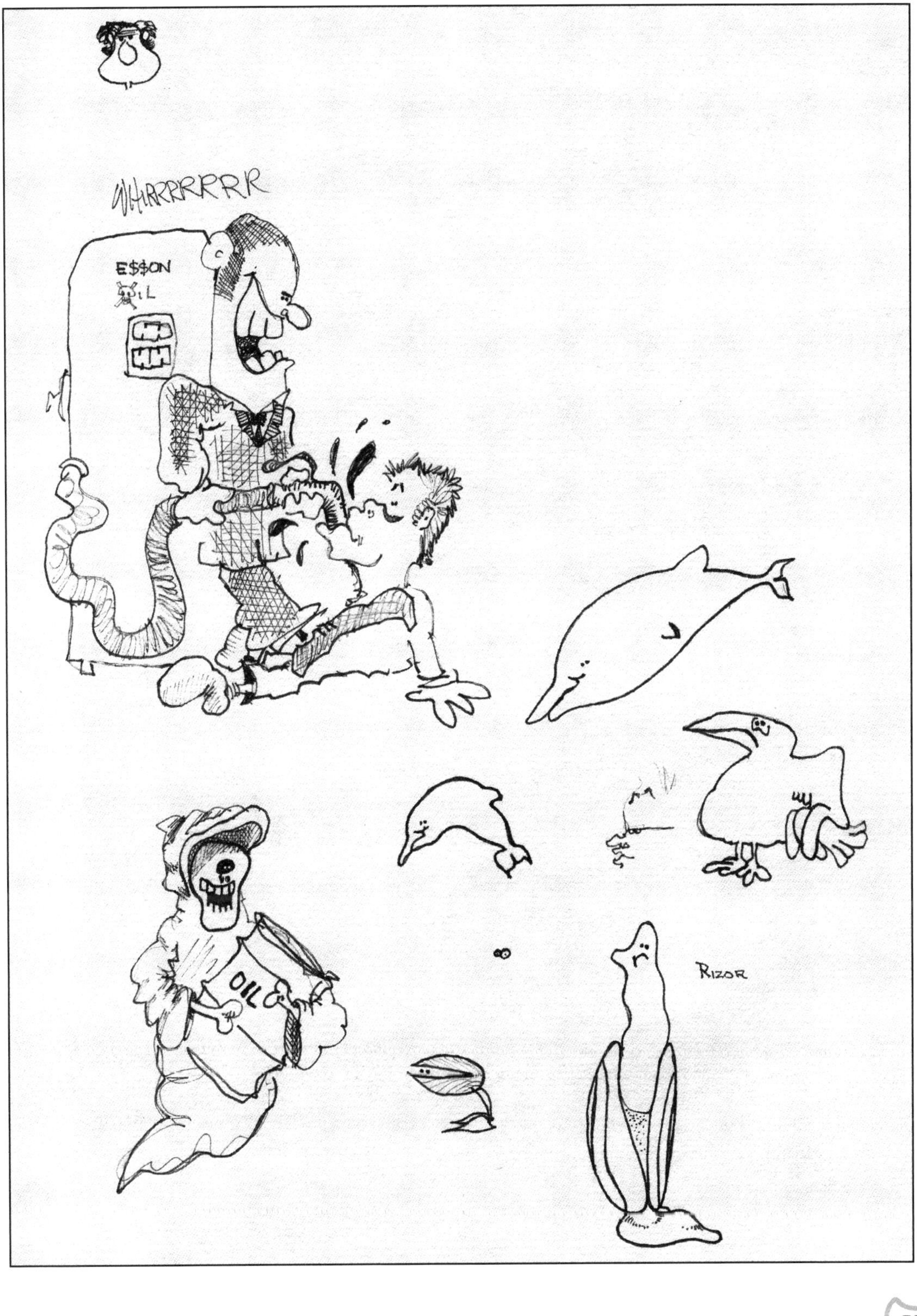
WHIRRRRRRR
E$$ON
OIL
OIL
RIZOR

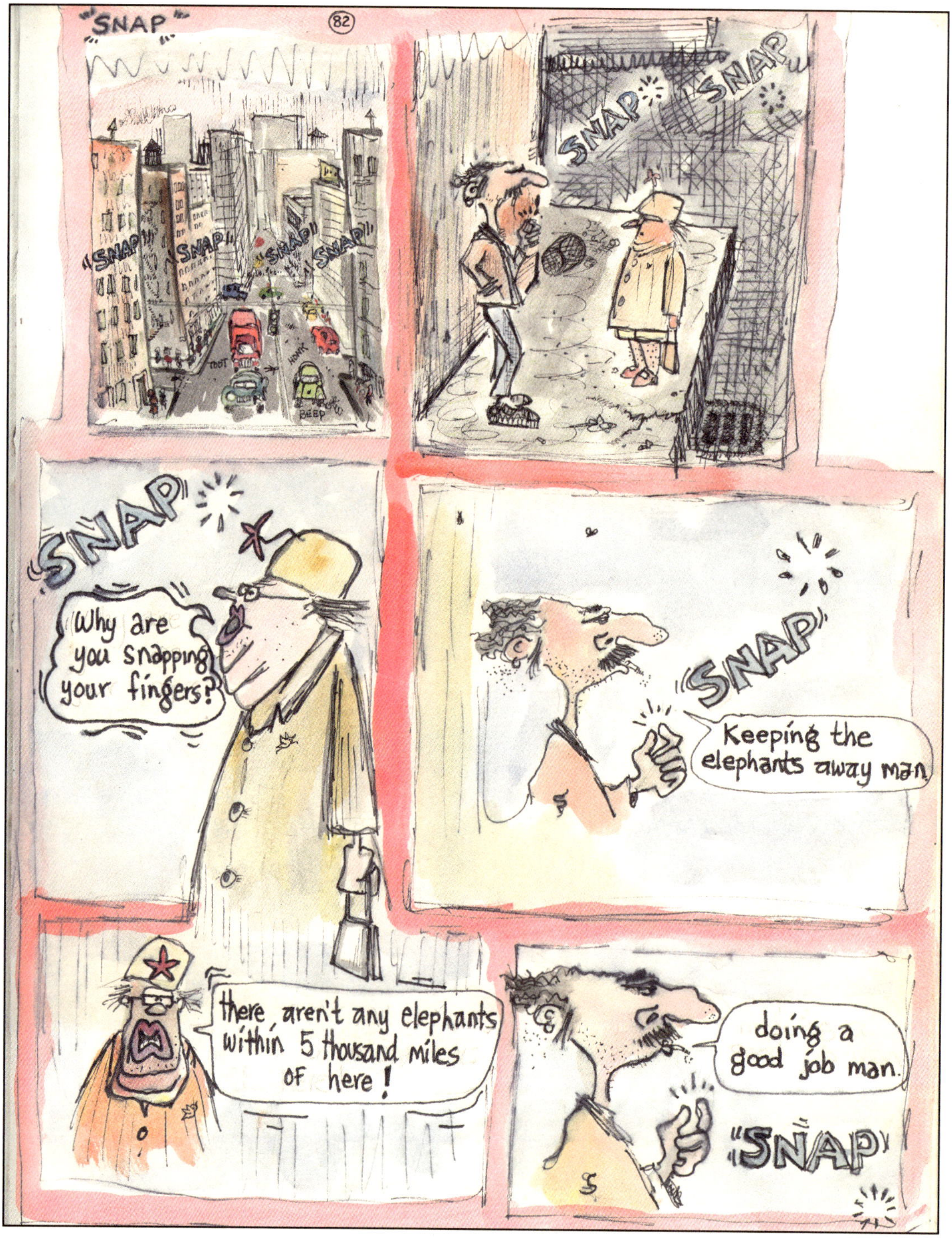
SNAP
82
SNAP
SNAP
SNAP
SNAP
TOOT
HONK
BEEP
SNAP
SNAP
SNAP
Why are you snapping your fingers?
SNAP
Keeping the elephants away man
there aren't any elephants within 5 thousand miles of here!
doing a good job man.
SNAP

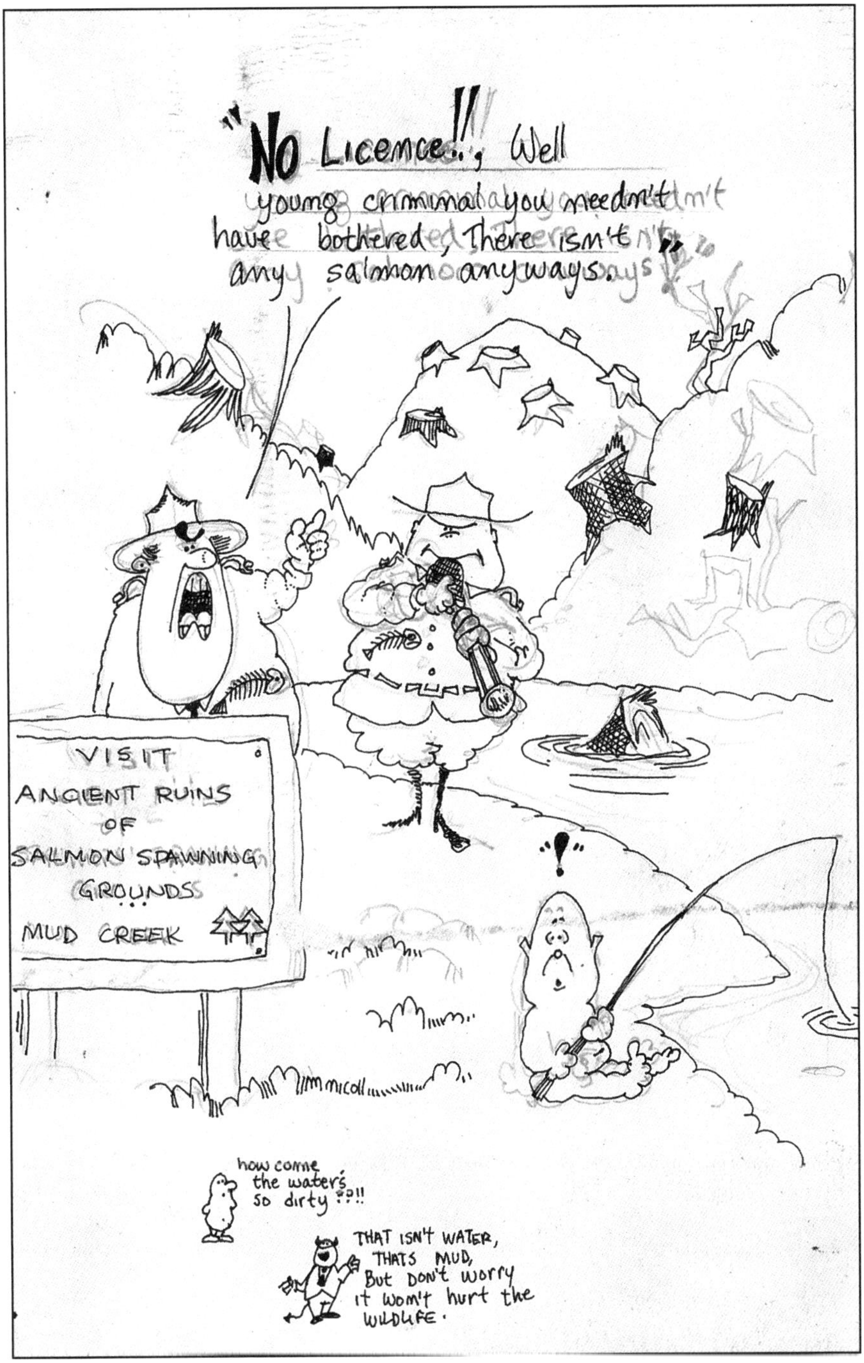
"No Licence!!, Well young criminal you needn't have bothered, There isn't any salmon anyways."
VISIT ANCIENT RUINS OF SALMON SPAWNING GROUNDS ... MUD CREEK
how come the water's so dirty ?!?!!
THAT ISN'T WATER, THATS MUD, But DON'T worry it won't hurt the WILDLIFE.

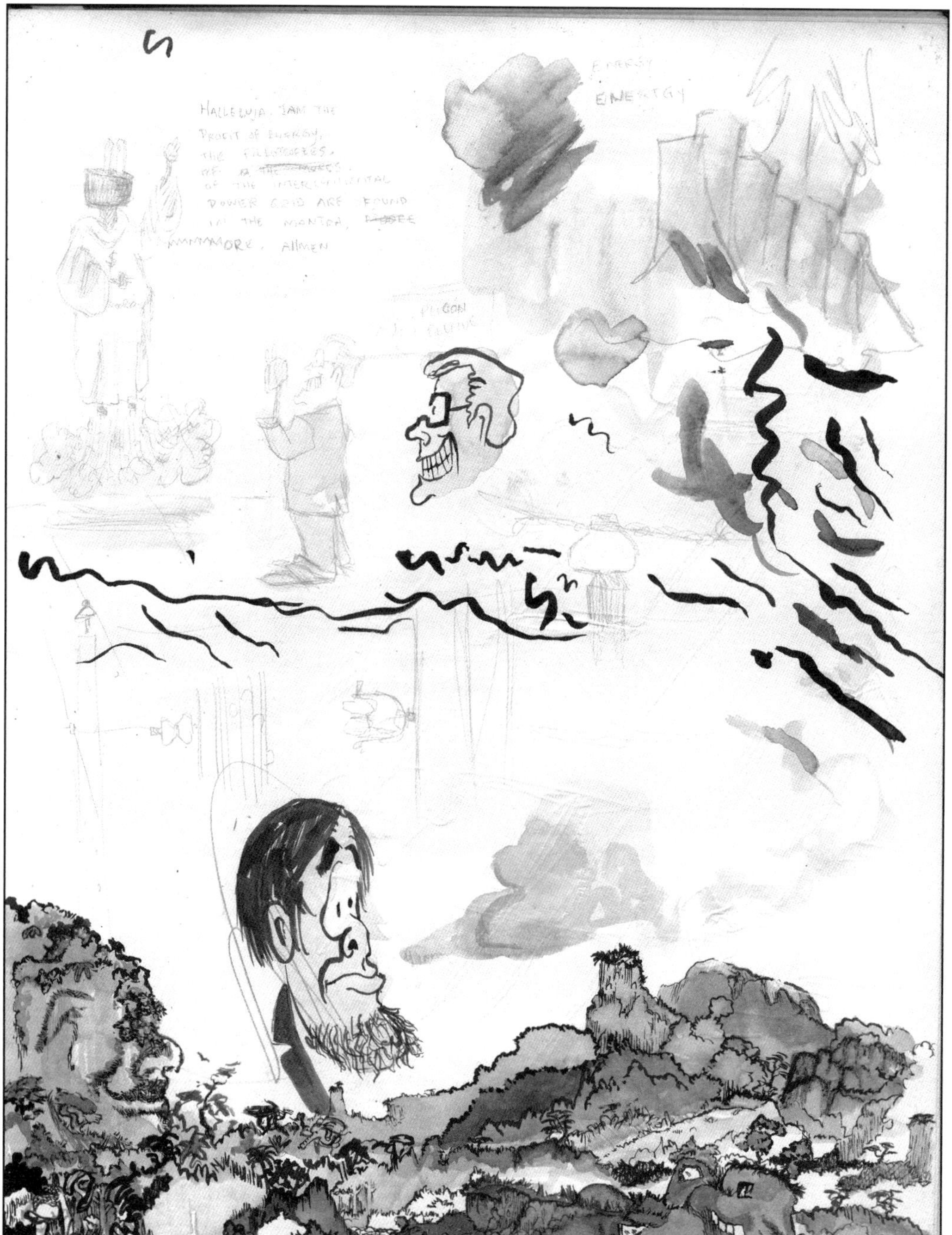
HALLELUJA I AM THE
POWER GRID ARE FOUND
IN THE MANTRA,
MMMMORE. AllMEN
ENERGY

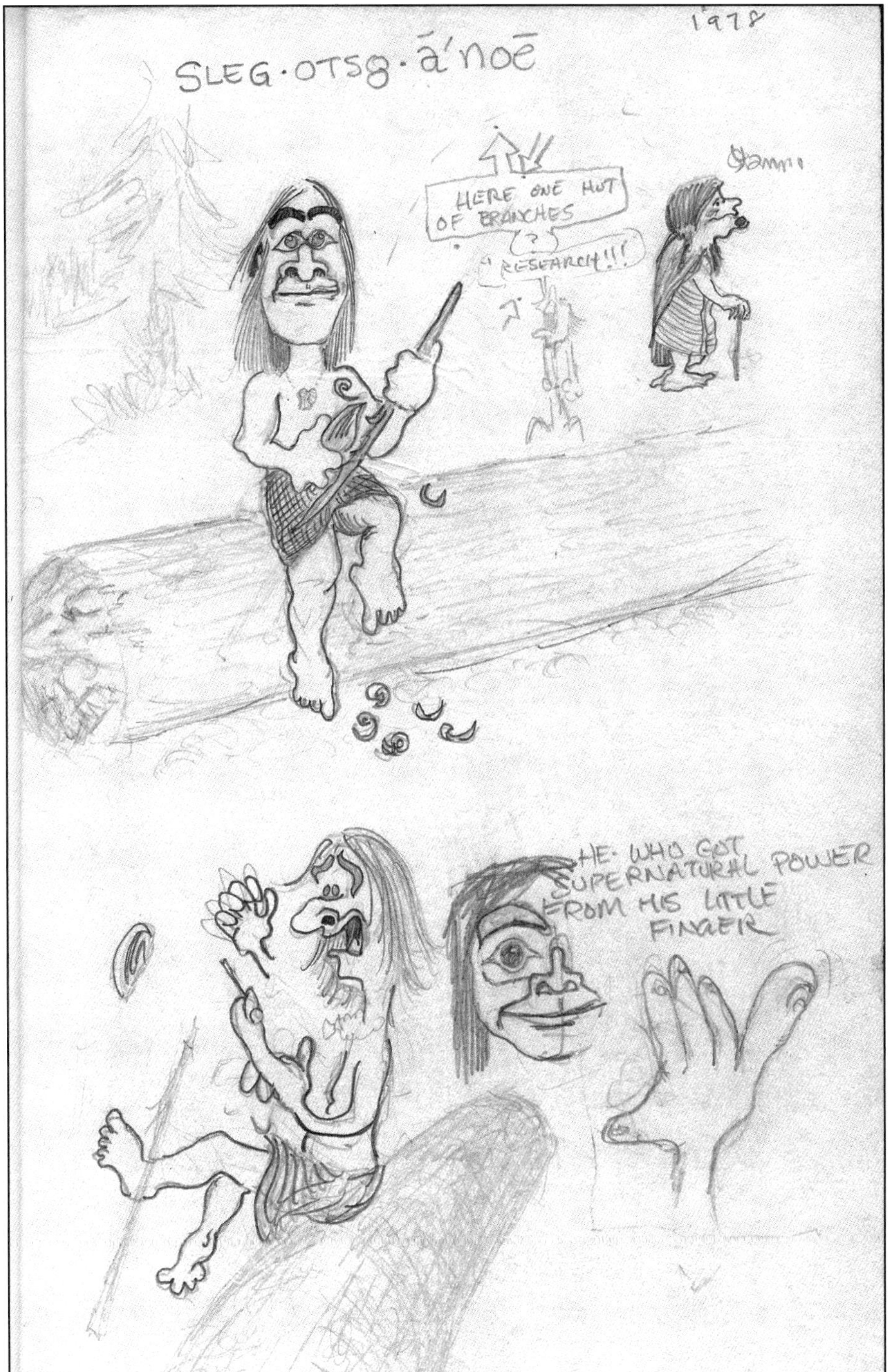
1978
SLEG·OTSg·ā'noē
HERE ONE HUT OF BRANCHES
?
RESEARCH!!!
HE·WHO GOT SUPERNATURAL POWER FROM HIS LITTLE FINGER

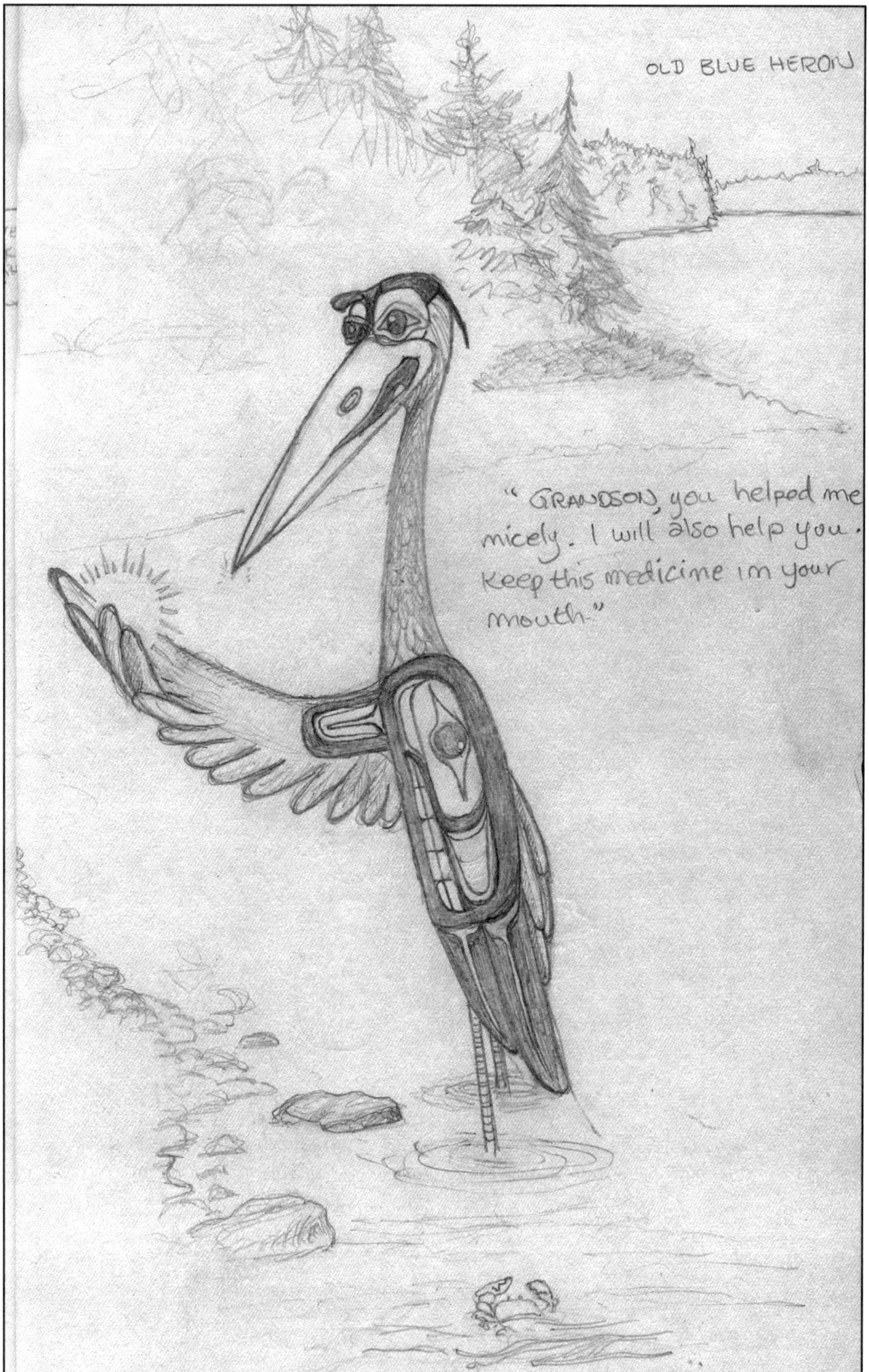

OLD BLUE HERON
" GRANDSON, you helped me nicely. I will also help you. Keep this medicine in your mouth."

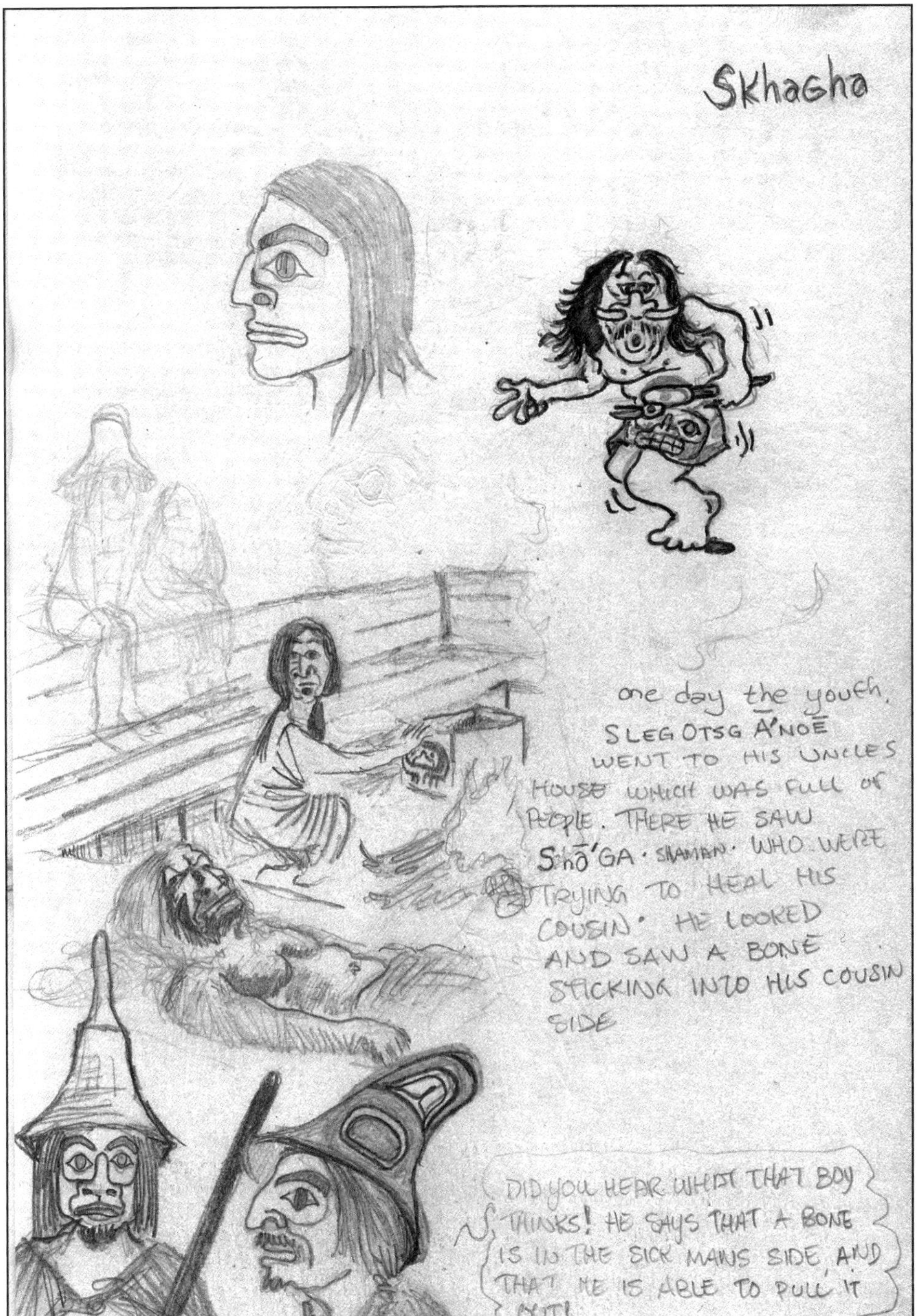
Skhagha
one day the youth, SLEGOTSG A'NOĒ WENT TO HIS UNCLES HOUSE WHICH WAS FULL OF PEOPLE. THERE HE SAW Sh̄ō'GA · SHAMAN · WHO WERE TRYING TO HEAL HIS COUSIN. HE LOOKED AND SAW A BONE STICKING INTO HIS COUSIN SIDE
DID YOU HEAR WHAT THAT BOY THINKS! HE SAYS THAT A BONE IS IN THE SICK MANS SIDE, AND THAT HE IS ABLE TO PULL IT OUT!

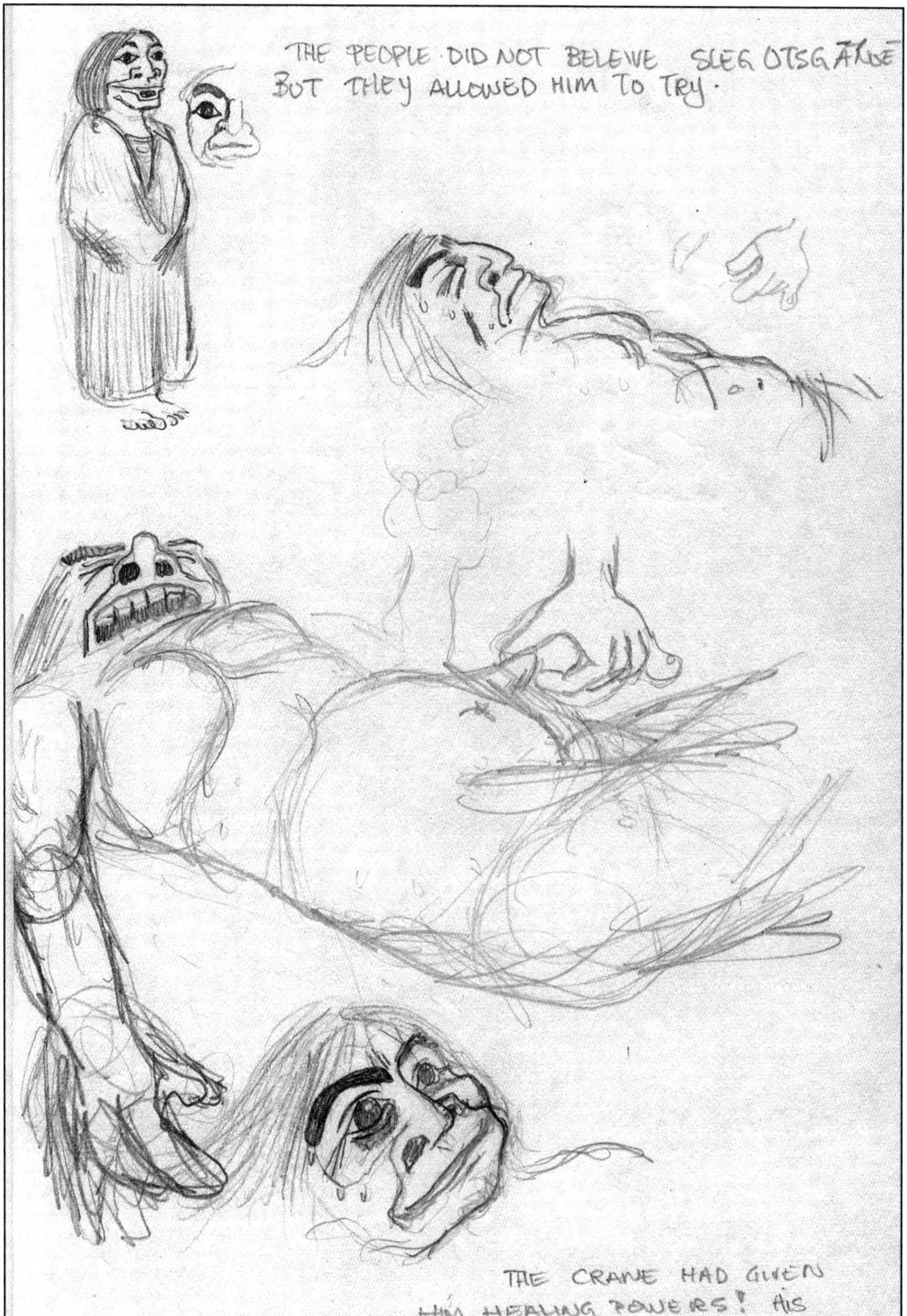
THE PEOPLE DID NOT BELEIVE SLEG OTSGĀKWĒ BUT THEY ALLOWED HIM TO TRY.
THE CRANE HAD GIVEN HIM HEALING POWERS! HIS COUSIN WAS NOW HEALED.

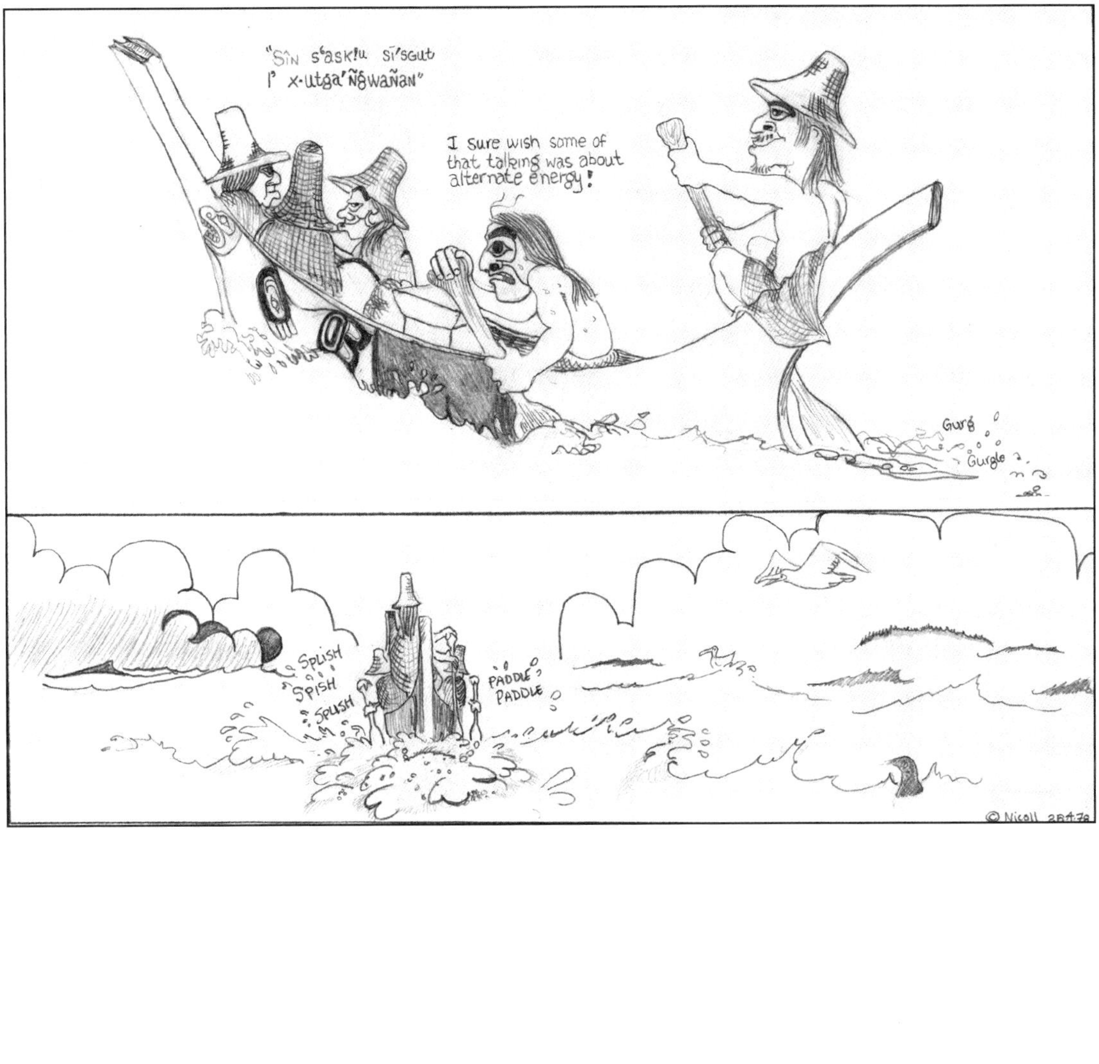
"Sîn s'ask!u sī'sgut
l' x·utga'ñgwañan"
I sure wish some of that talking was about alternate energy!
Gurg
Gurgle
Splish
Spish
Splish
Paddle
Paddle
© Nicoll

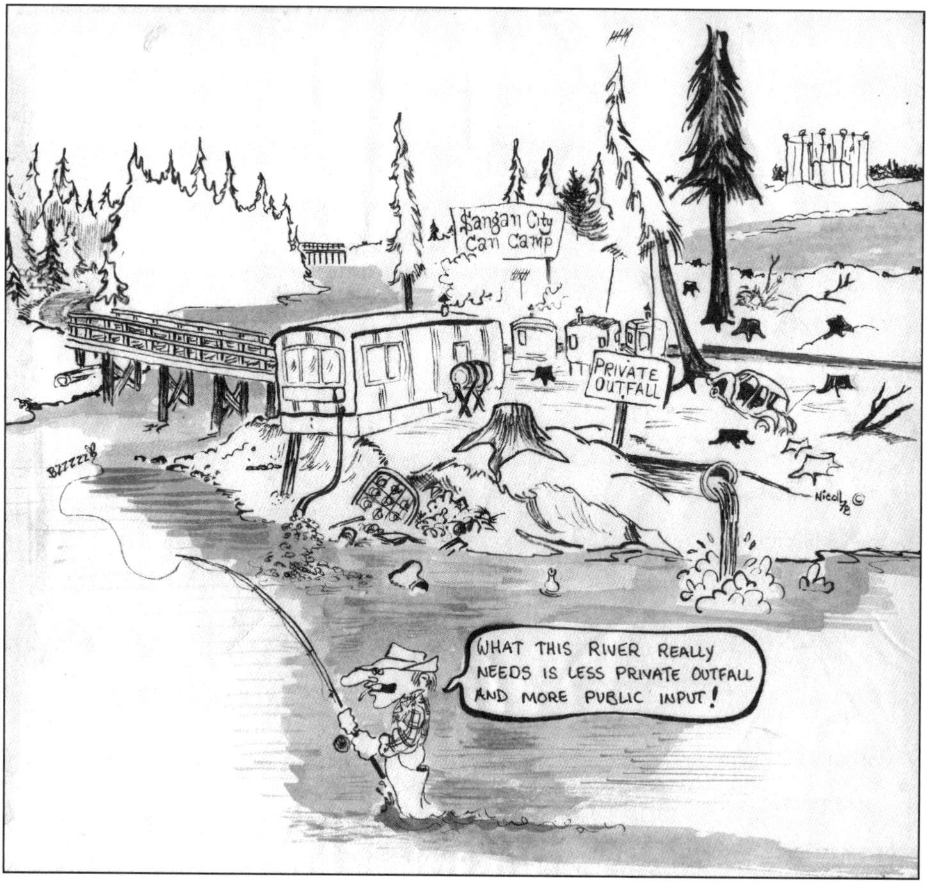
$angan City
Can Camp
PRIVATE
OUTFALL
BZZZZZ
Nicoll 78 ©
WHAT THIS RIVER REALLY NEEDS IS LESS PRIVATE OUTFALL AND MORE PUBLIC INPUT!

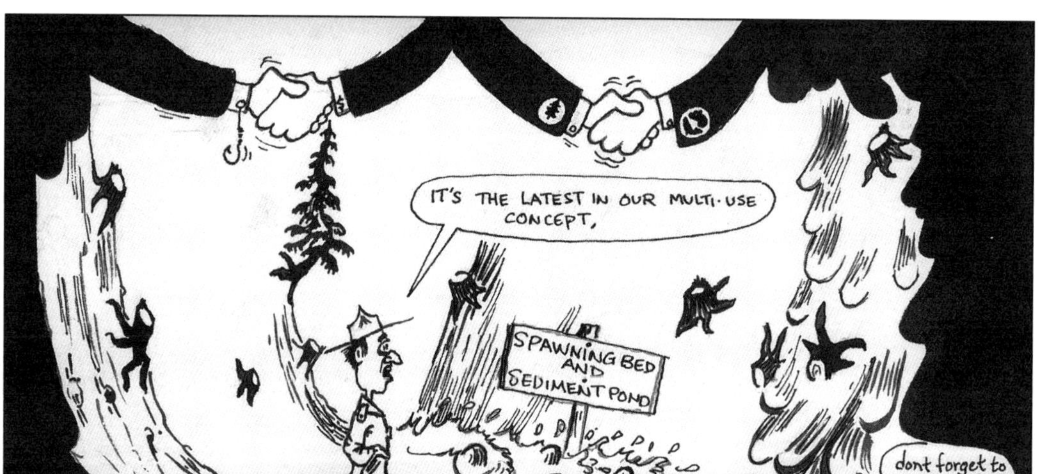
IT'S THE LATEST IN OUR MULTI·USE CONCEPT,
SPAWNING BED AND SEDIMENT POND
dont forget to wipe your feet.
M NICOLL 4·79 ©

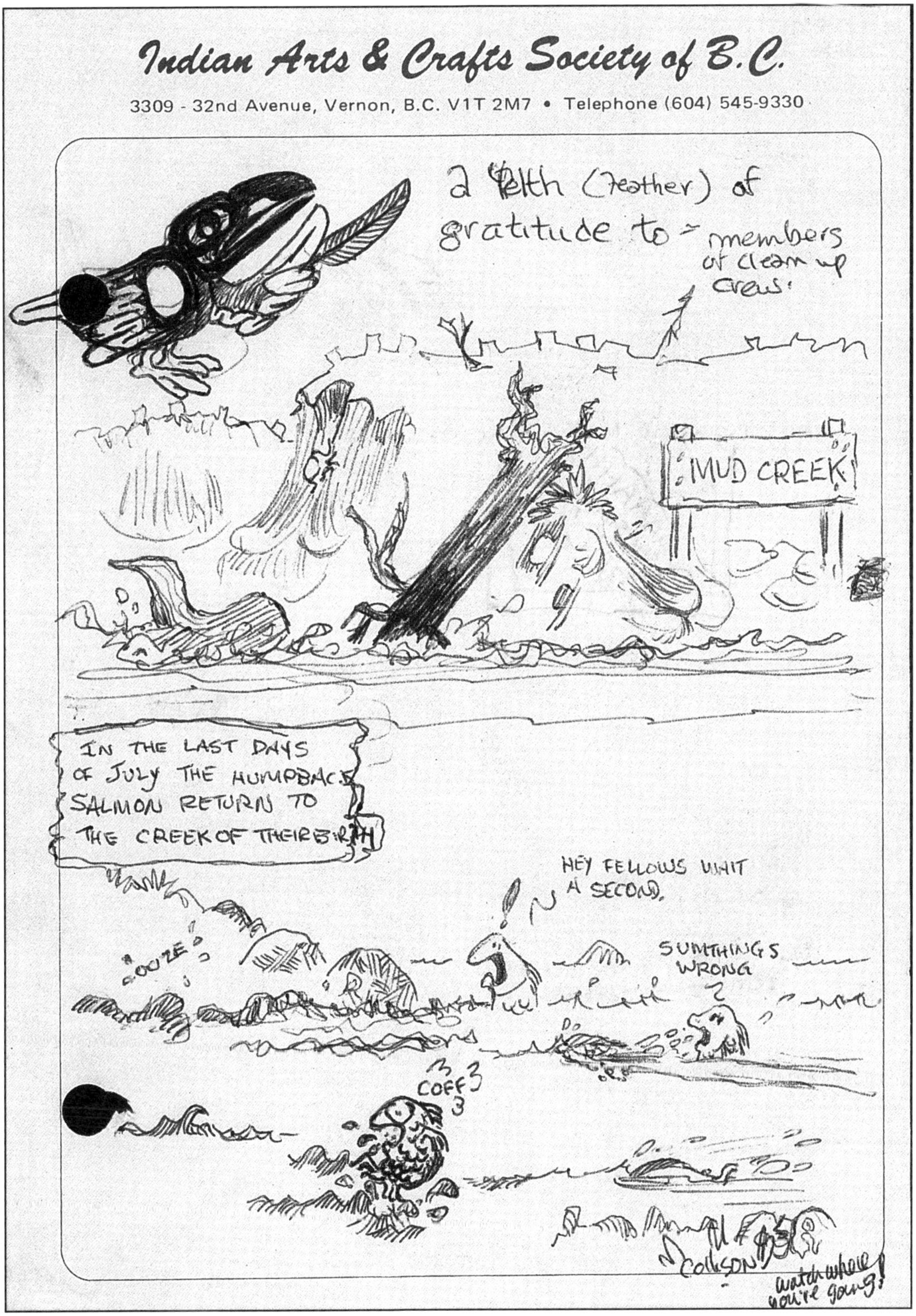
Indian Arts & Crafts Society of B.C.
3309 - 32nd Avenue, Vernon, B.C. V1T 2M7 • Telephone (604) 545-9330
a Pelth (feather) of gratitude to - members of clean up crew!
MUD CREEK
IN THE LAST DAYS OF JULY THE HUMPBACK SALMON RETURN TO THE CREEK OF THEIR BIRTH
HEY FELLOWS WAIT A SECOND.
OOZE
SUMTHINGS WRONG
COFF
COLLISON
watch where you're going!

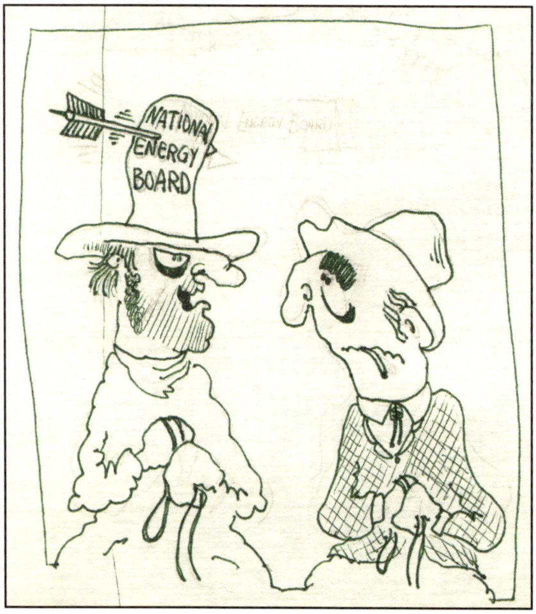

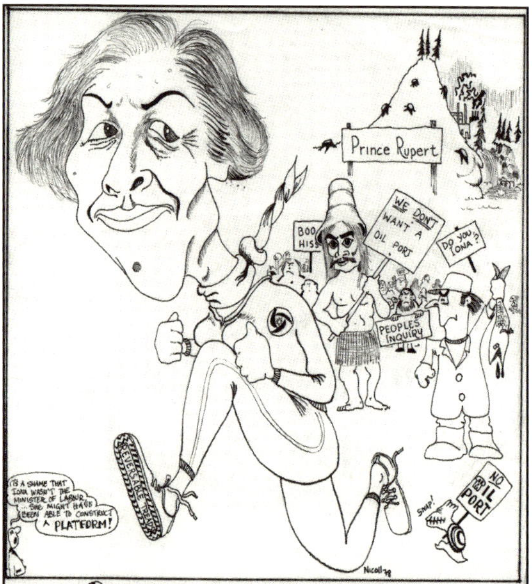

RUNNING FOR RE-ELECTION

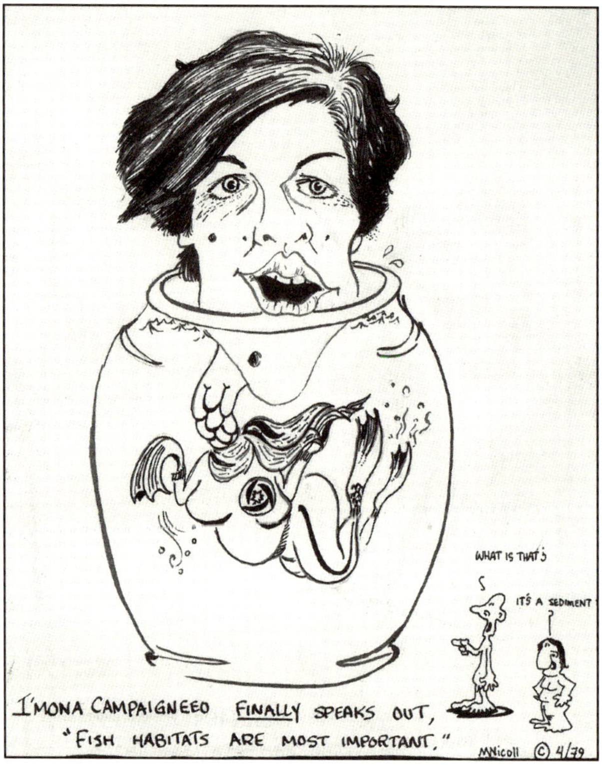

I'MONA CAMPAIGNEED FINALLY SPEAKS OUT,
"FISH HABITATS ARE MOST IMPORTANT."

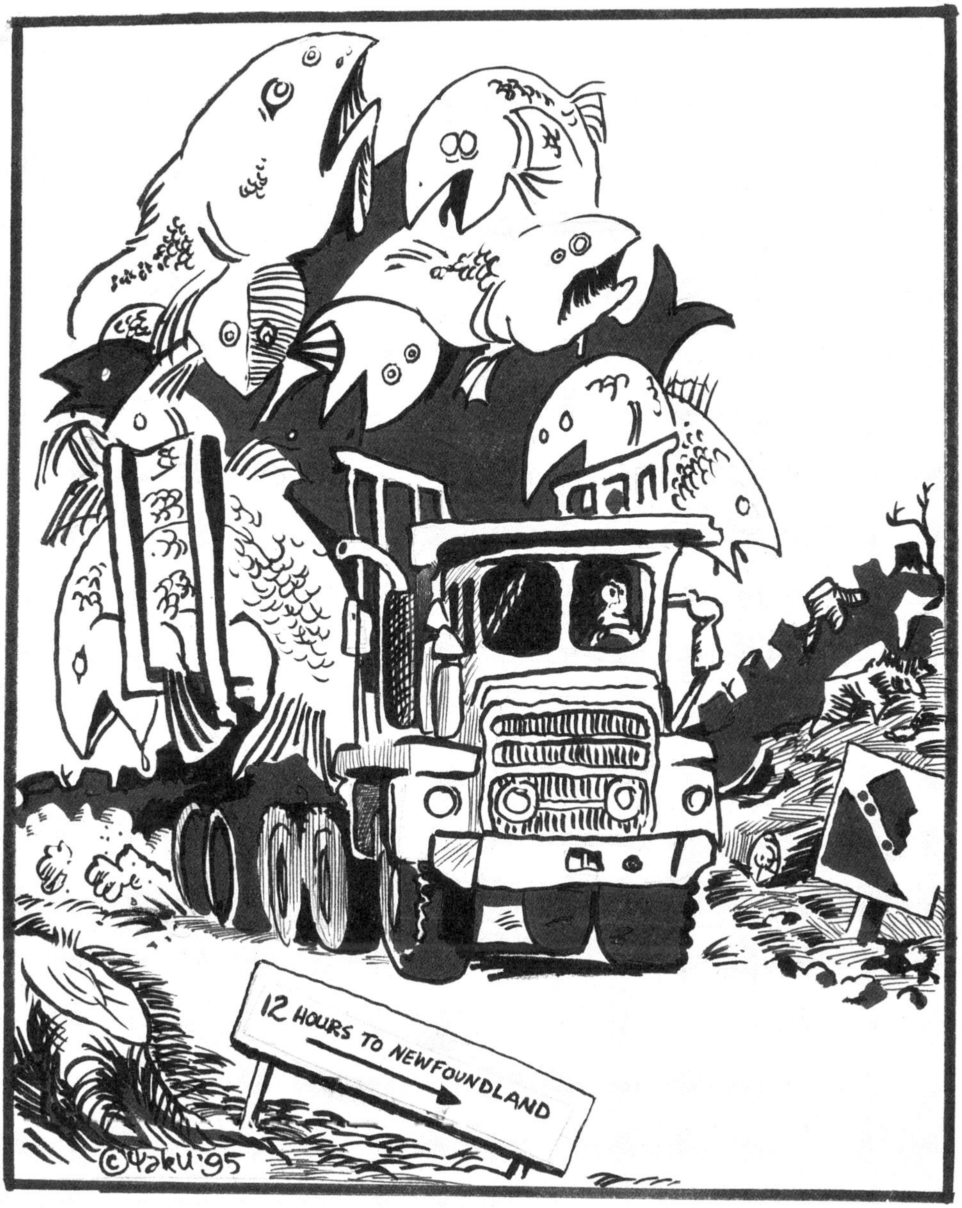
12 HOURS TO NEWFOUNDLAND
©Yaku '95

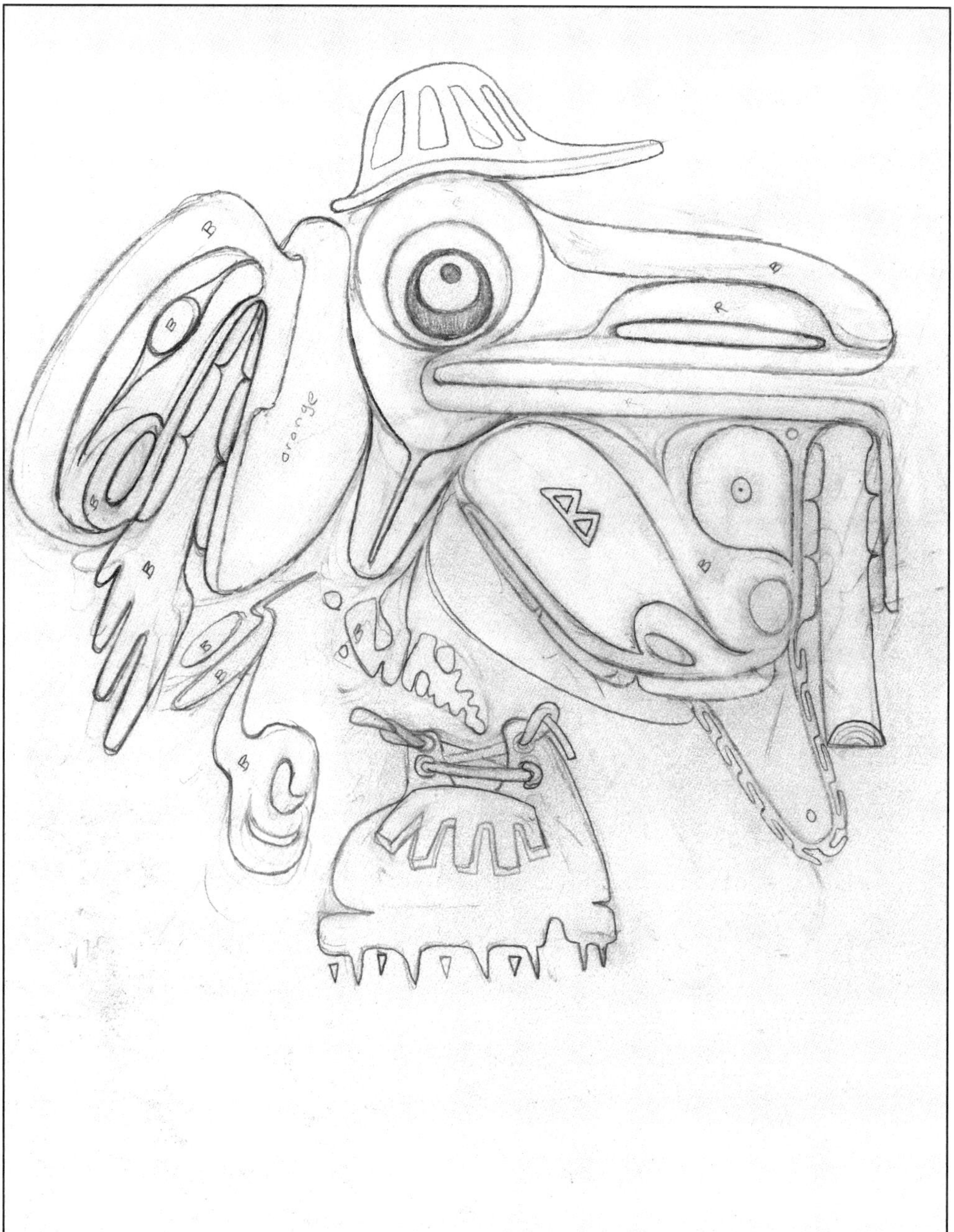
orange

Comics

Tree Spirit

Tree Spirit *is an interpretation of a Massett parable, revolving around the concept of a human society that is like a forest supporting and being supported by individual trees. In 1985,* Tree Spirit *was produced for Living and Learning School, a small, independent, parent-run school in the Village of Queen Charlotte on Haida Gwaii. This is its second printing.*

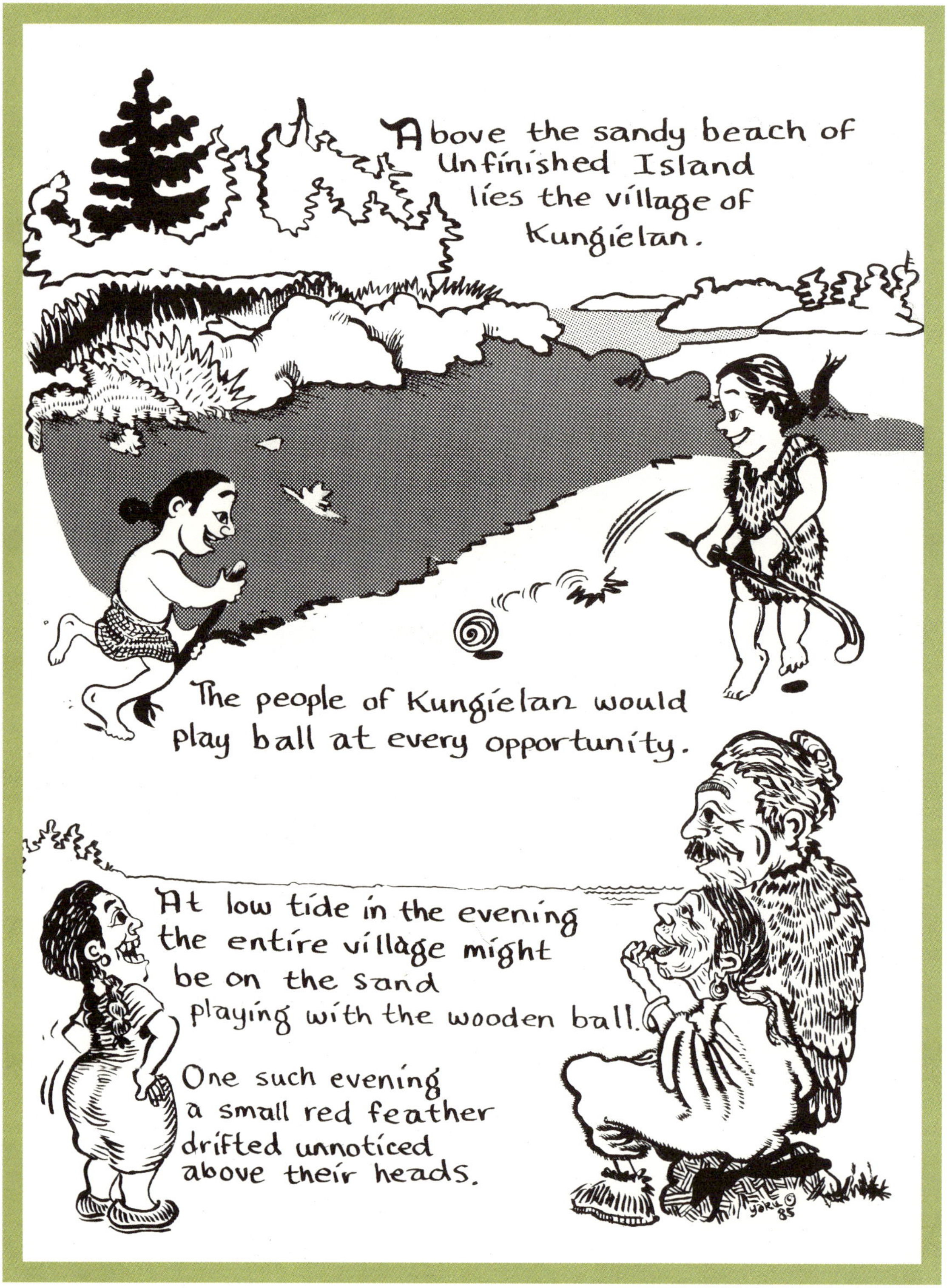
Above the sandy beach of Unfinished Island lies the village of Kungielan.
The people of Kungielan would play ball at every opportunity.
At low tide in the evening the entire village might be on the sand playing with the wooden ball.
One such evening a small red feather drifted unnoticed above their heads.

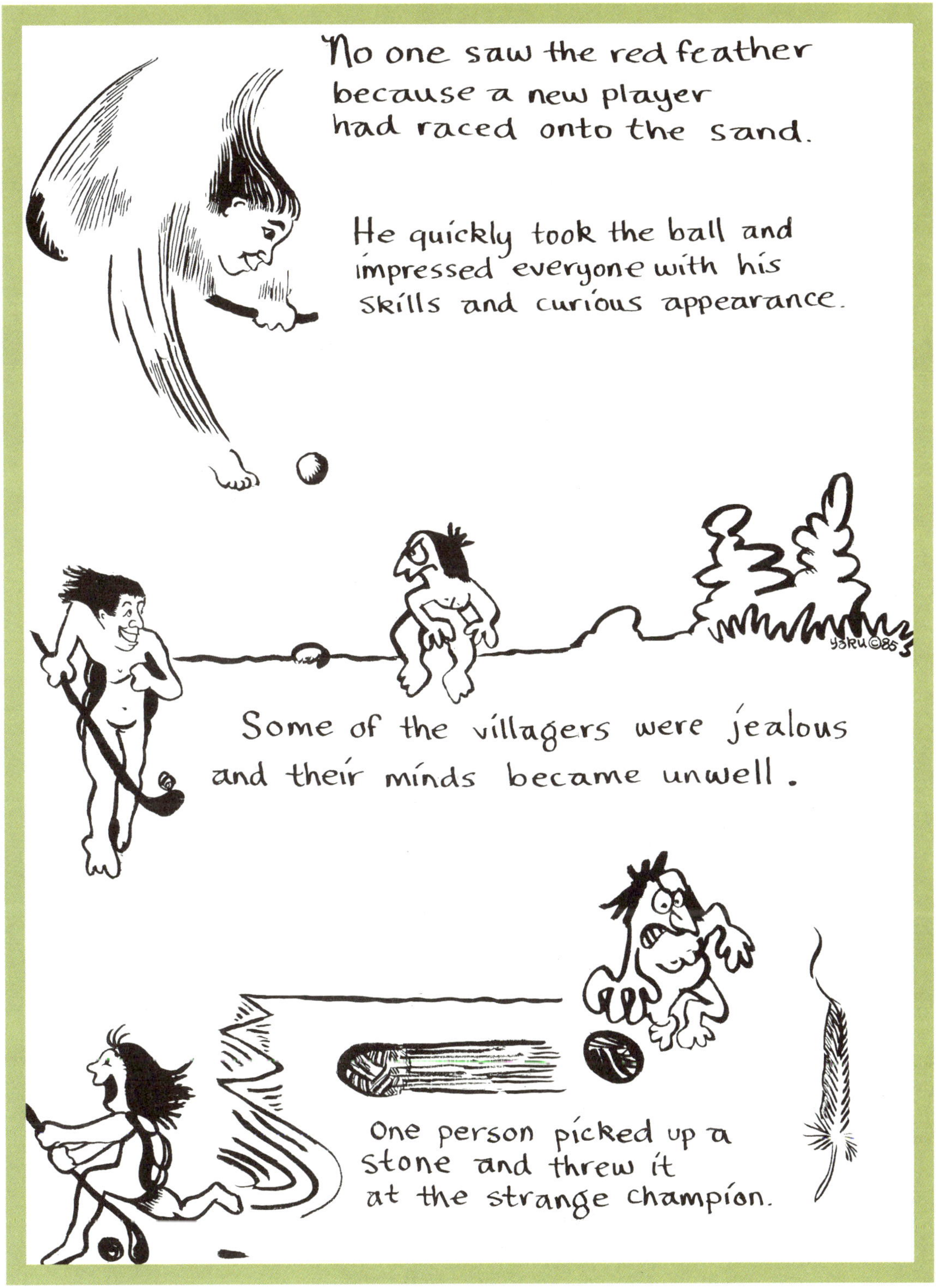
No one saw the red feather because a new player had raced onto the sand.
He quickly took the ball and impressed everyone with his skills and curious appearance.
yaku©85
Some of the villagers were jealous and their minds became unwell.
One person picked up a stone and threw it at the strange champion.

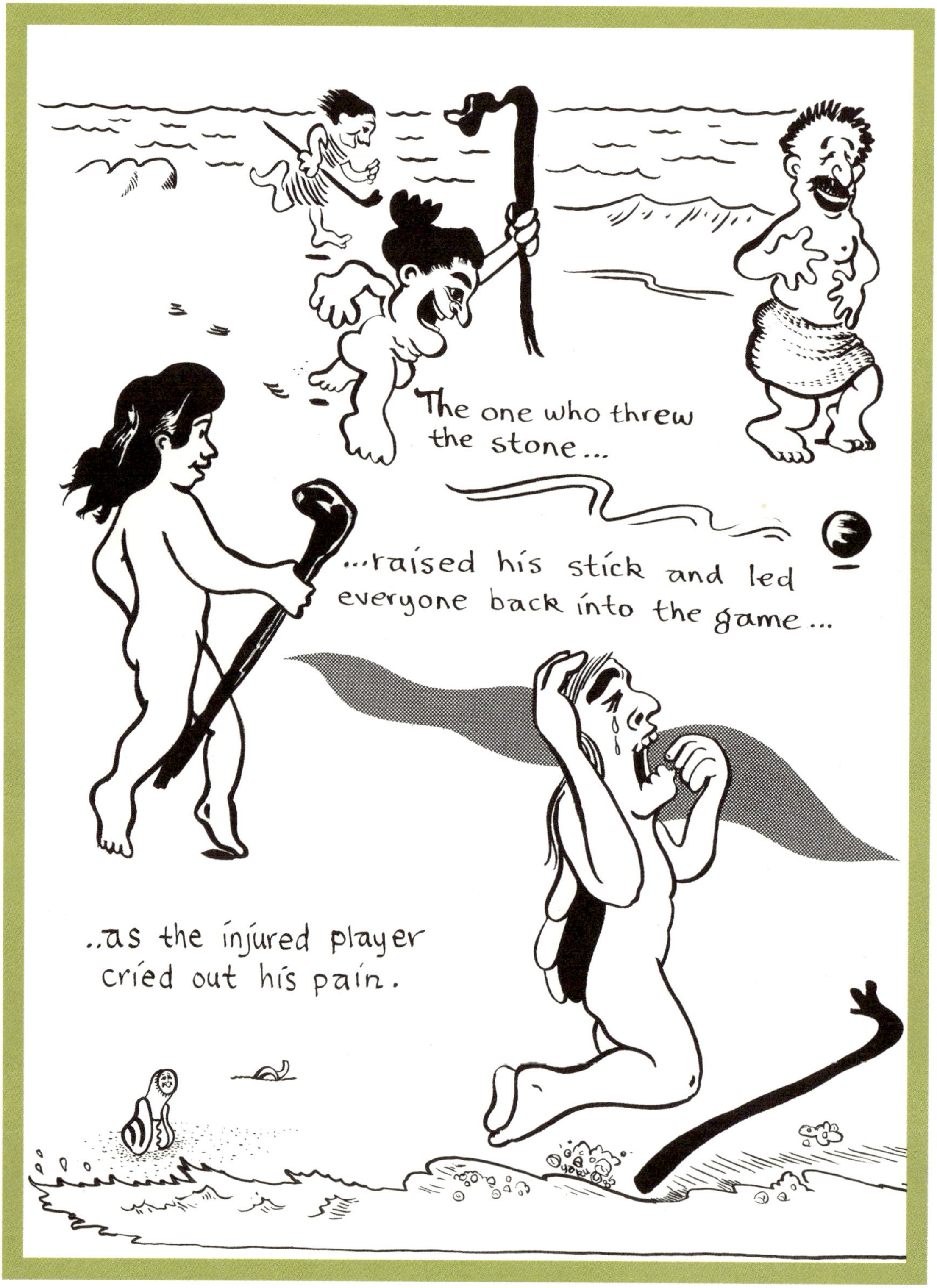
The one who threw the stone...
...raised his stick and led everyone back into the game...
..as the injured player cried out his pain.

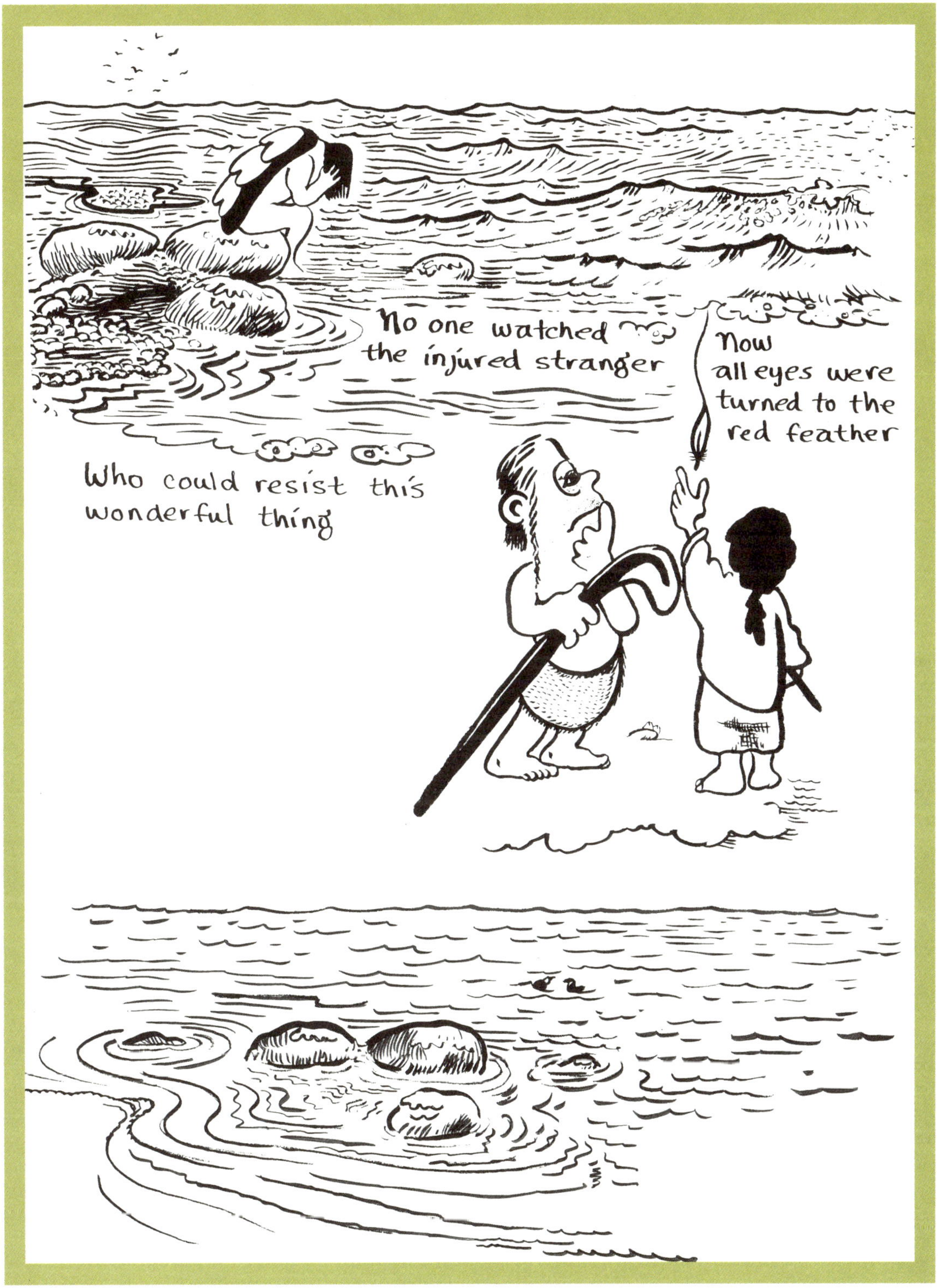
No one watched the injured stranger
Now all eyes were turned to the red feather
Who could resist this wonderful thing

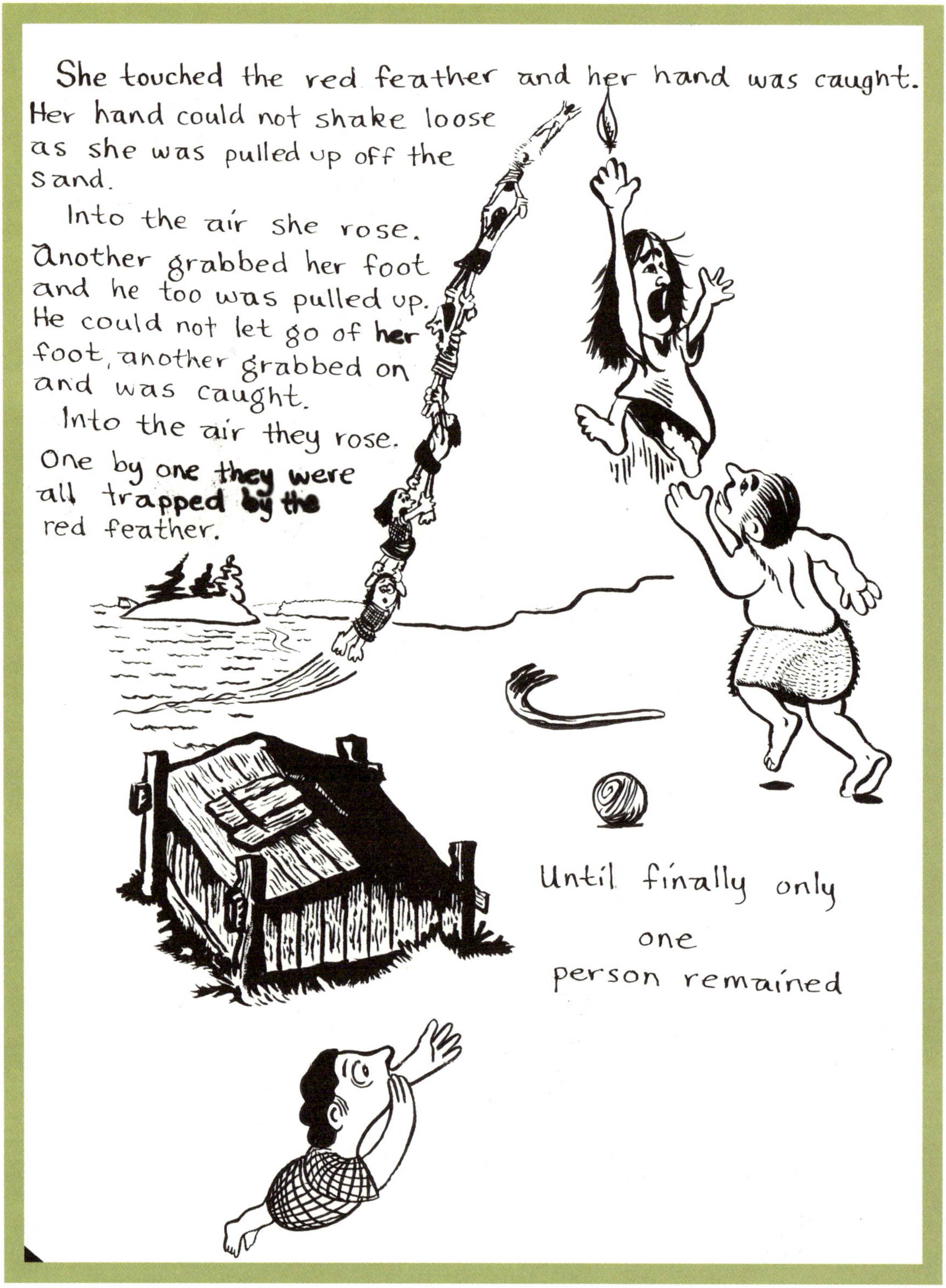
She touched the red feather and her hand was caught.
Her hand could not shake loose as she was pulled up off the sand.
Into the air she rose. Another grabbed her foot and he too was pulled up. He could not let go of her foot, another grabbed on and was caught.
Into the air they rose. One by one they were all trapped by the red feather.
Until finally only one person remained

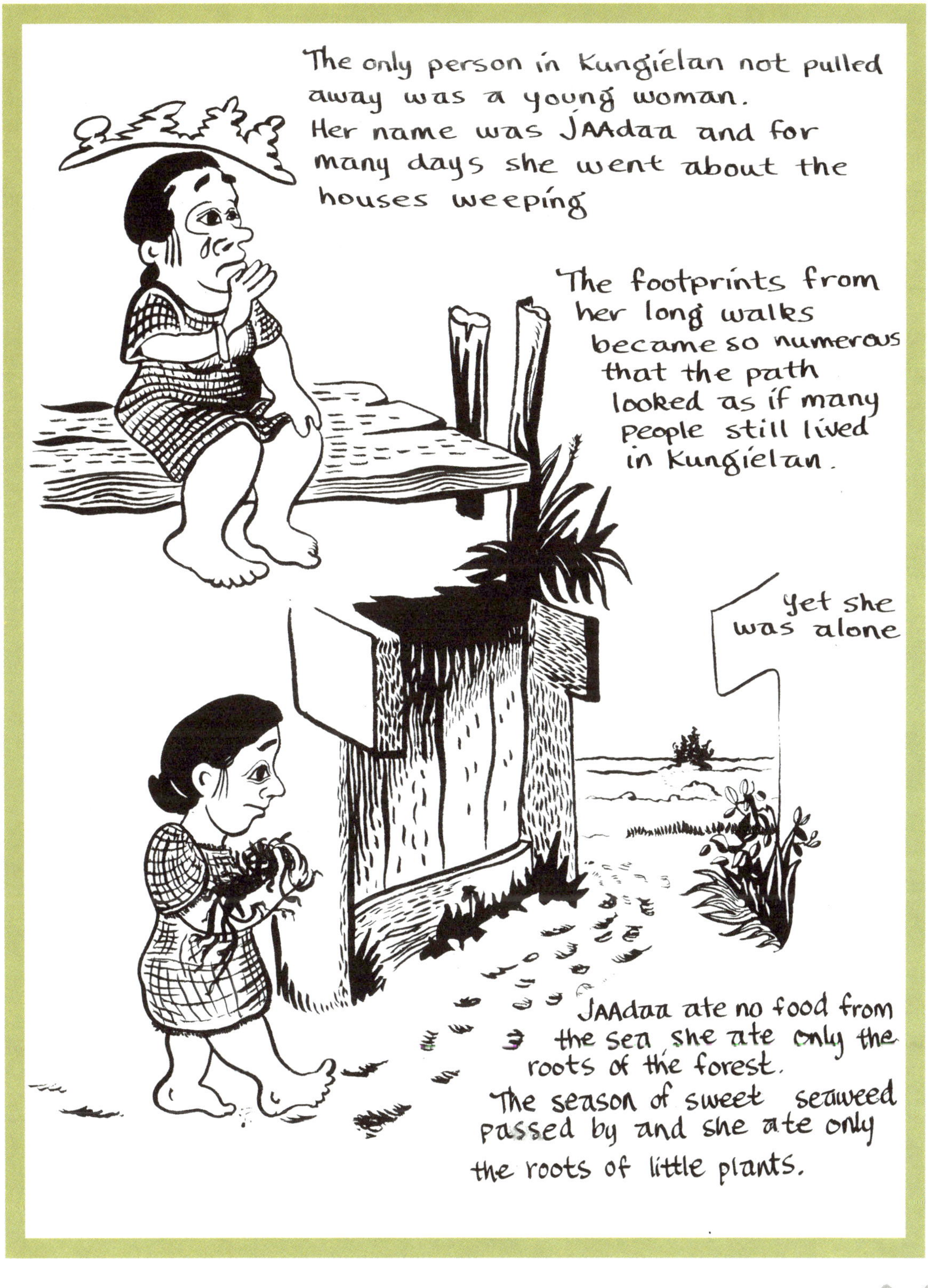
The only person in Kungielan not pulled away was a young woman.
Her name was JAAdaa and for many days she went about the houses weeping
The footprints from her long walks became so numerous that the path looked as if many people still lived in Kungielan.
Yet she was alone
JAAdaa ate no food from the sea she ate only the roots of the forest.
The season of sweet seaweed passed by and she ate only the roots of little plants.

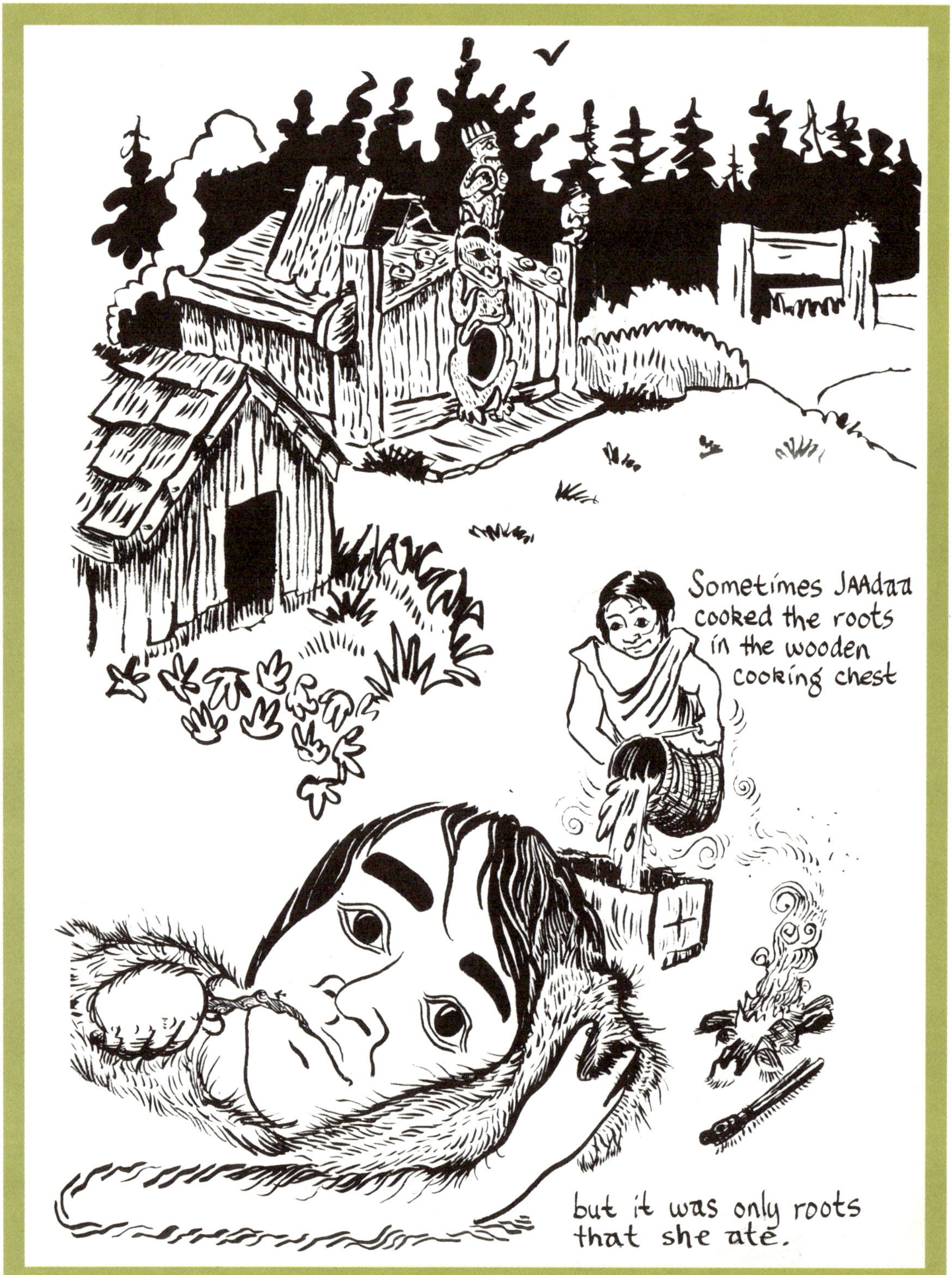
Sometimes JAAdaa cooked the roots in the wooden cooking chest
but it was only roots that she ate.

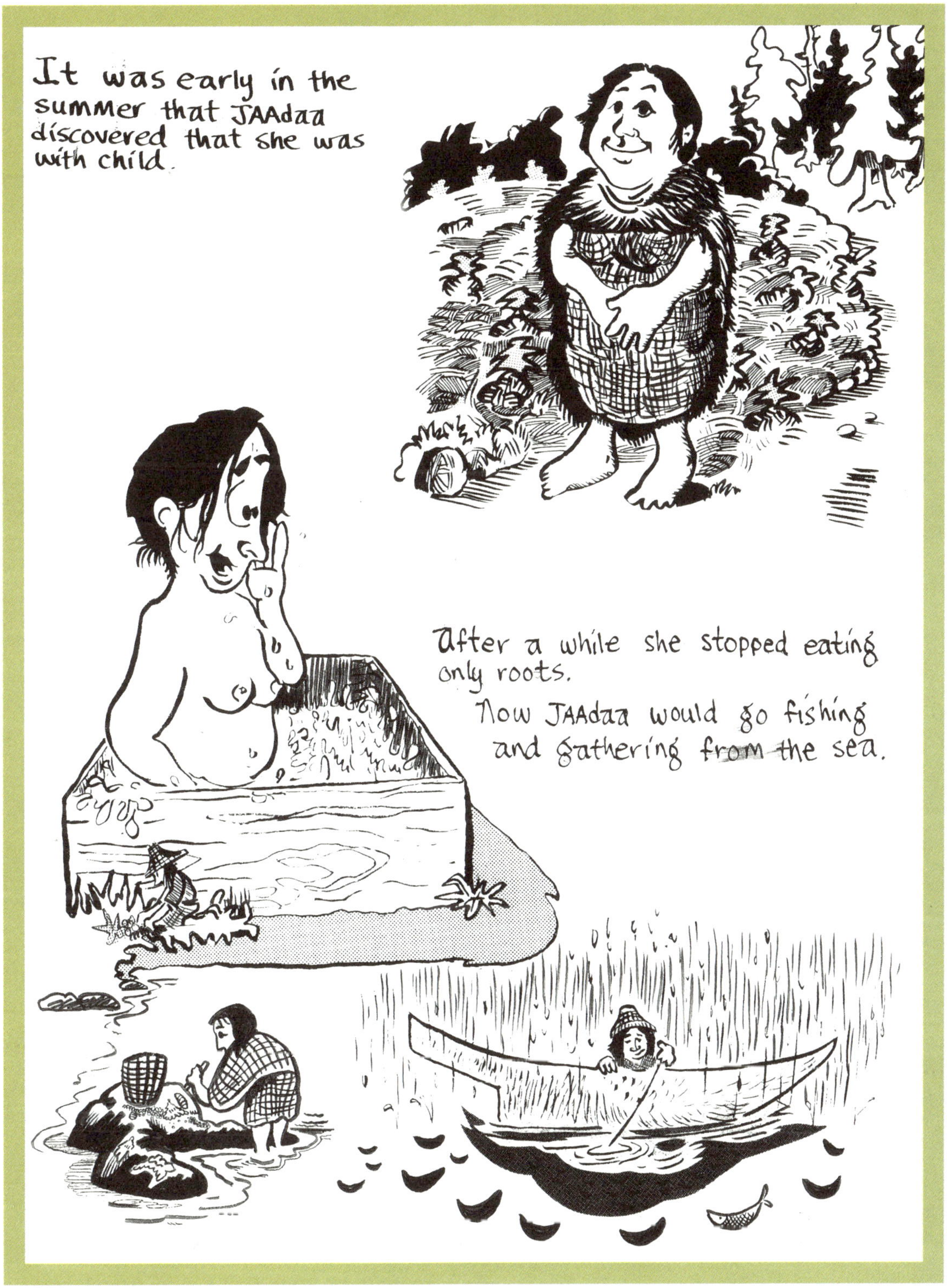
It was early in the summer that JAAdaa discovered that she was with child.
After a while she stopped eating only roots.
Now JAAdaa would go fishing and gathering from the sea.

When the nine months were completed she gave birth
Her child was a boy.
She nursed him continually
and was a very happy mother.

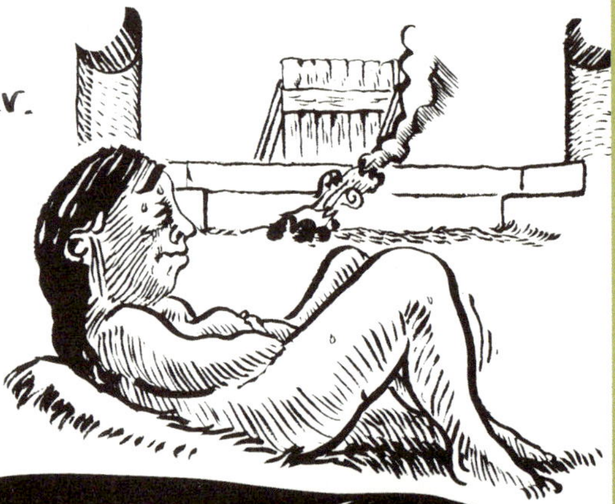

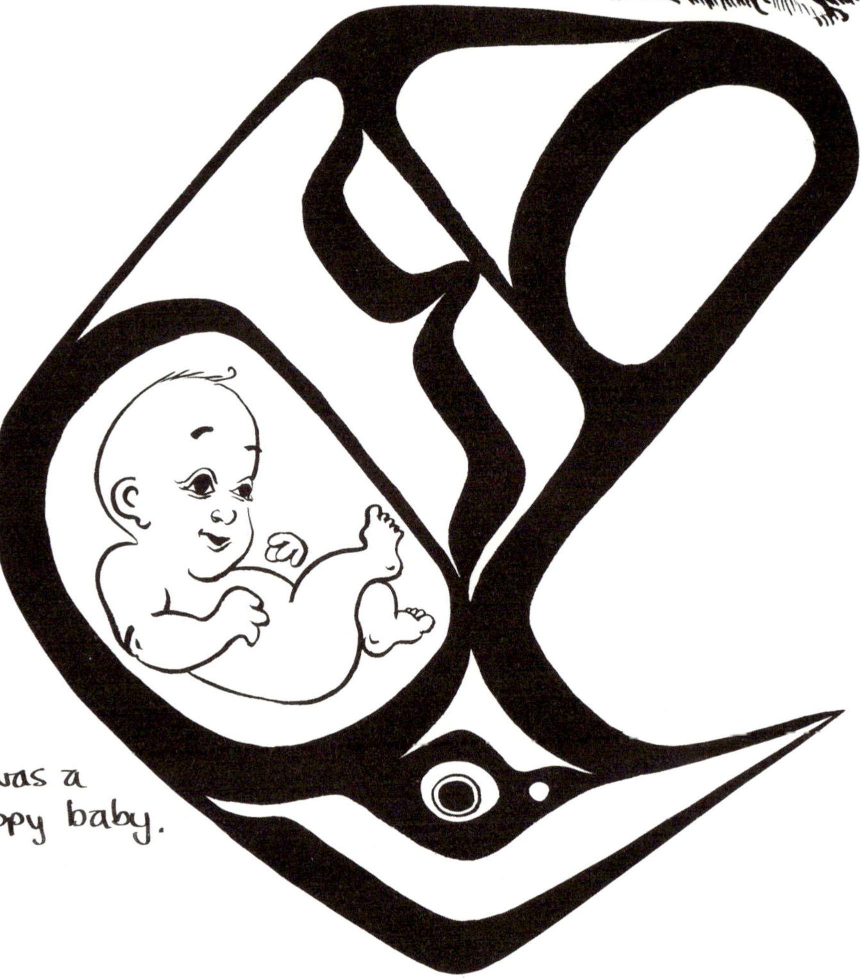

and he was a
very happy baby.

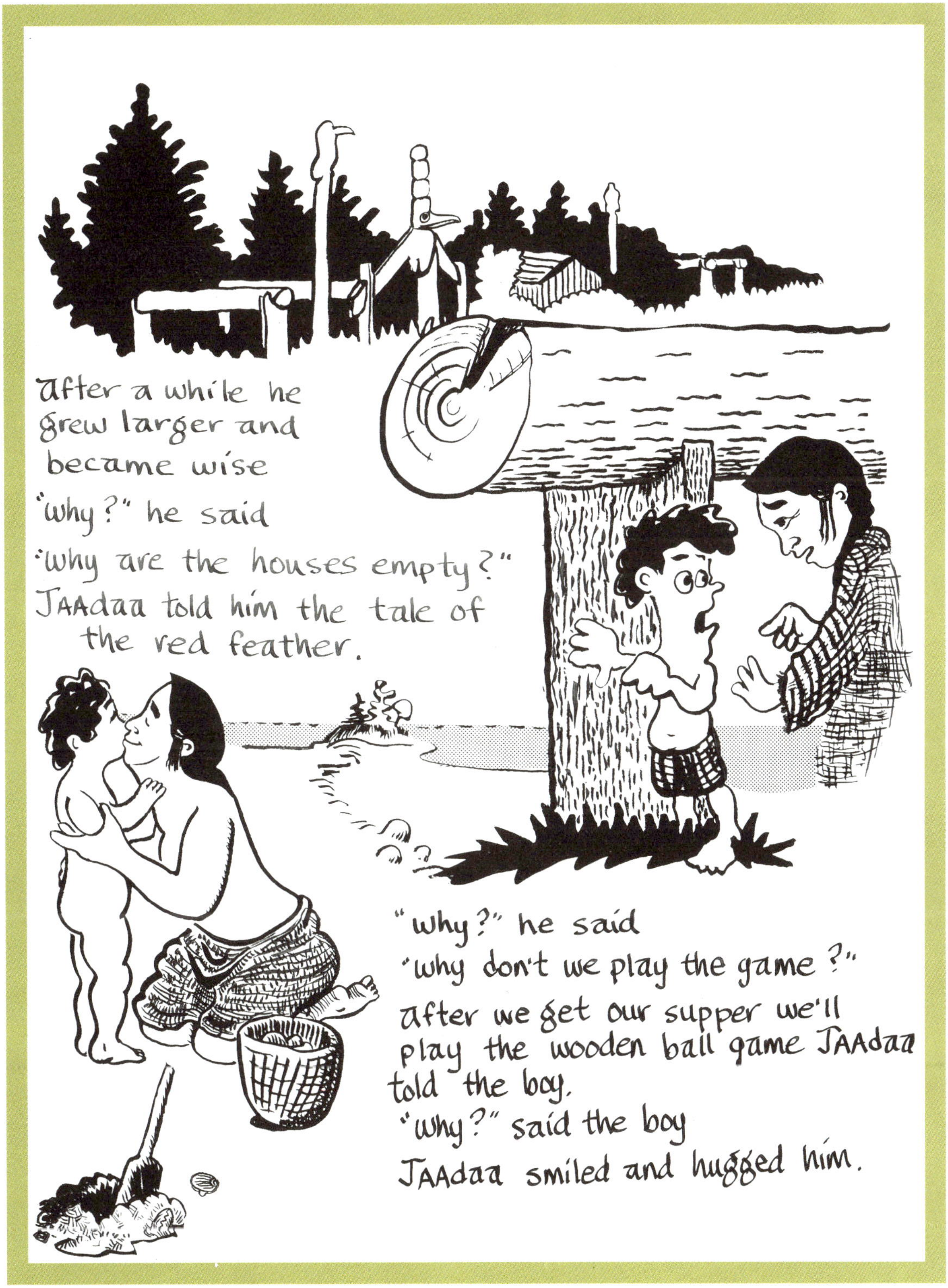
After a while he grew larger and became wise
"why?" he said
"why are the houses empty?"
JAAdaa told him the tale of the red feather.
"why?" he said
"why don't we play the game?"
After we get our supper we'll play the wooden ball game JAAdaa told the boy.
"why?" said the boy
JAAdaa smiled and hugged him.

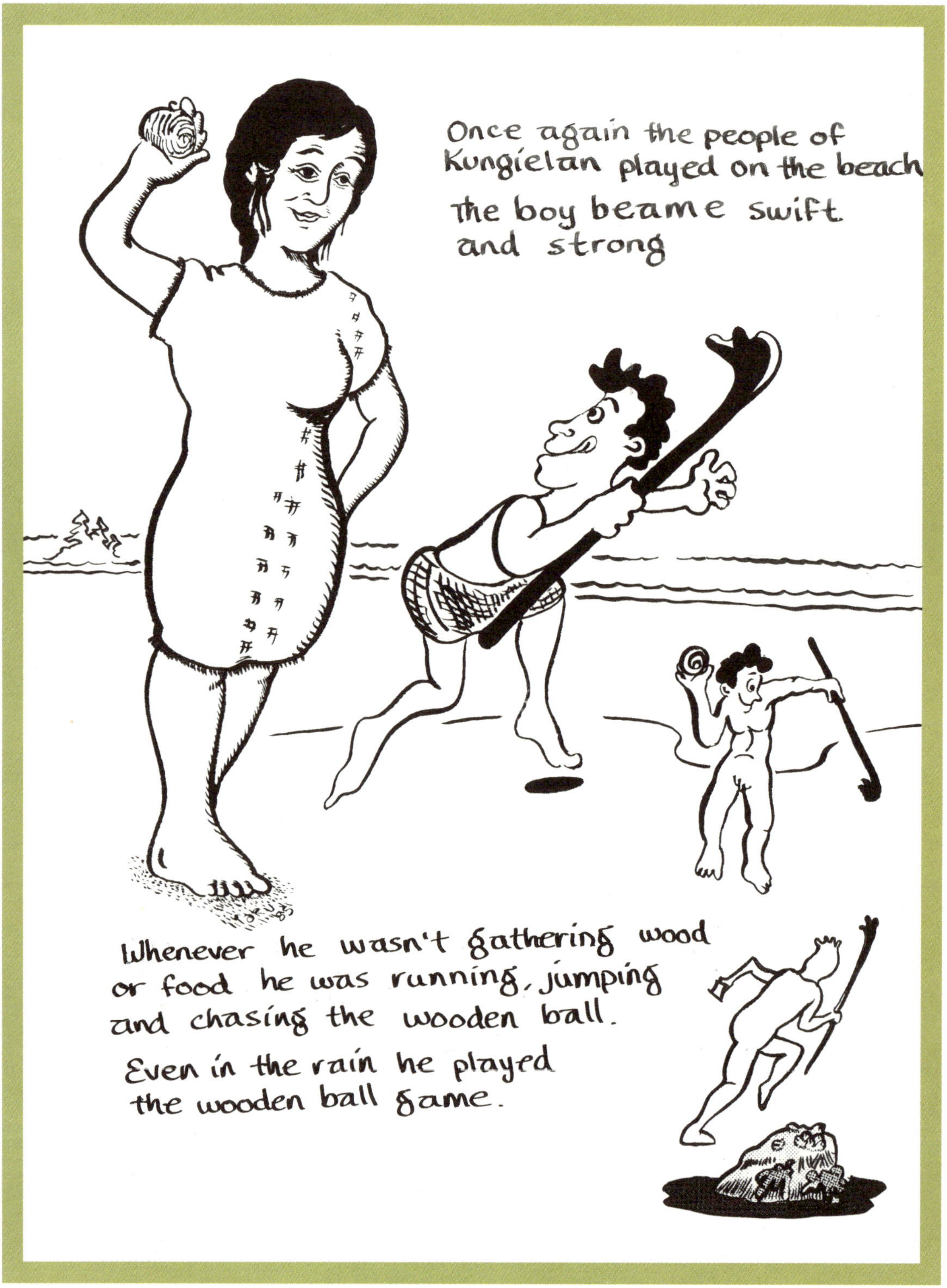
Once again the people of Kungielan played on the beach
The boy beame swift and strong
Whenever he wasn't gathering wood or food he was running, jumping and chasing the wooden ball.
Even in the rain he played the wooden ball game.

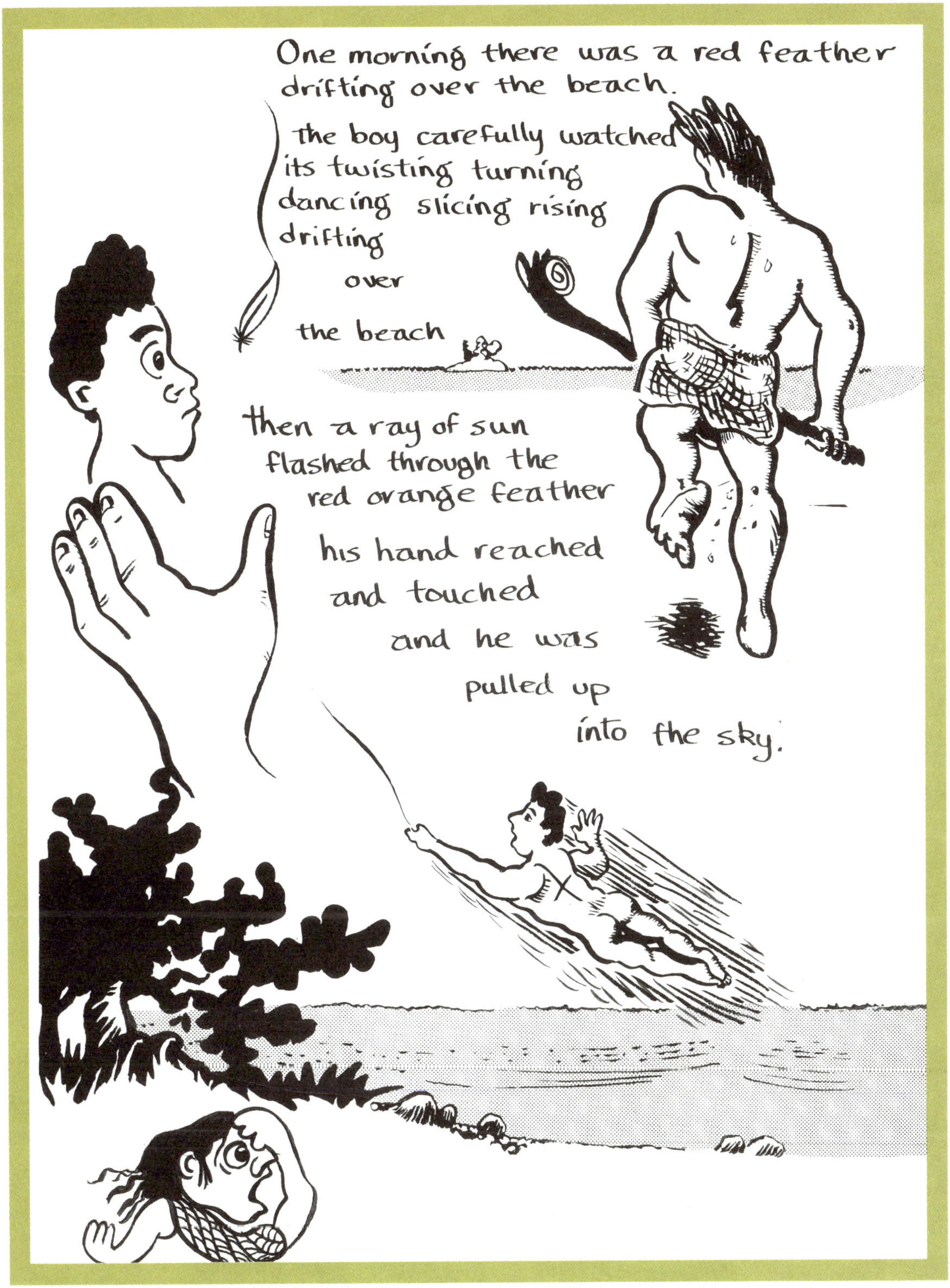
One morning there was a red feather drifting over the beach.
the boy carefully watched its twisting turning dancing slicing rising drifting over the beach
then a ray of sun flashed through the red orange feather
his hand reached and touched and he was pulled up into the sky.

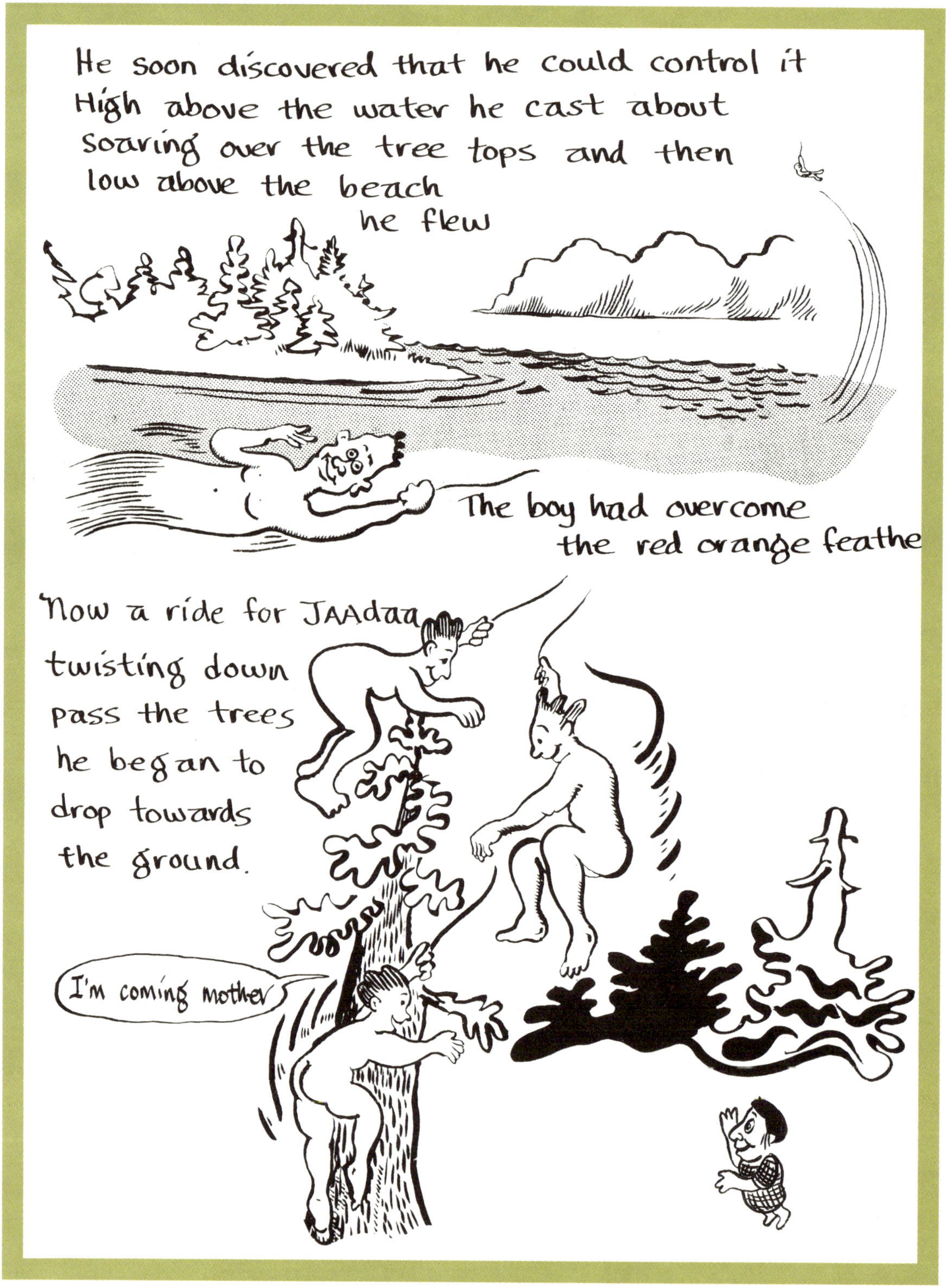
He soon discovered that he could control it
High above the water he cast about
soaring over the tree tops and then
low above the beach
he flew
The boy had overcome
the red orange feathe
Now a ride for JAAdaa
twisting down
pass the trees
he began to
drop towards
the ground.
I'm coming mother

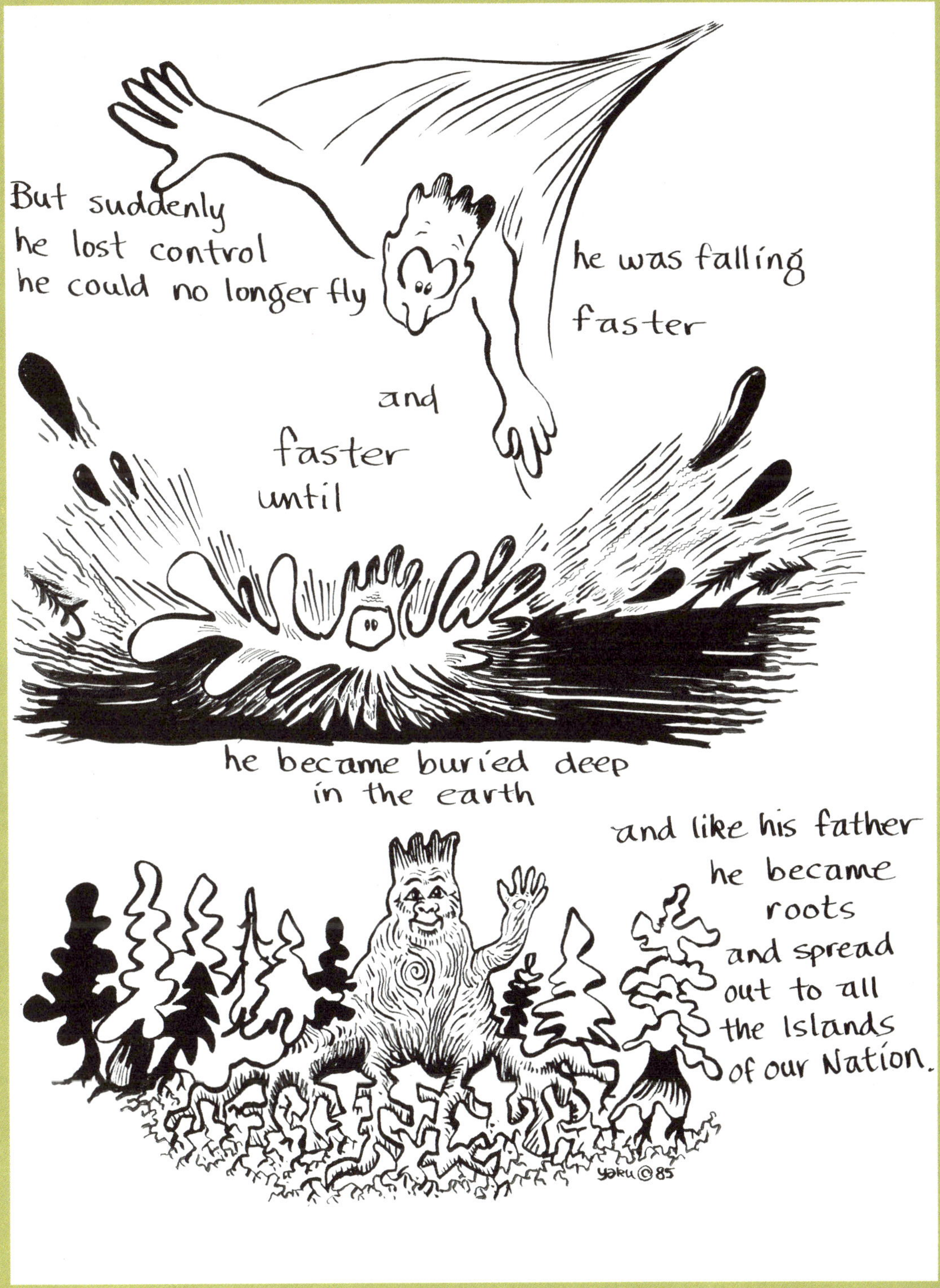
But suddenly
he lost control
he could no longer fly
he was falling
faster
and
faster
until
he became buried deep
in the earth
and like his father
he became
roots
and spread
out to all
the Islands
of our Nation.
yaku © 85

Images

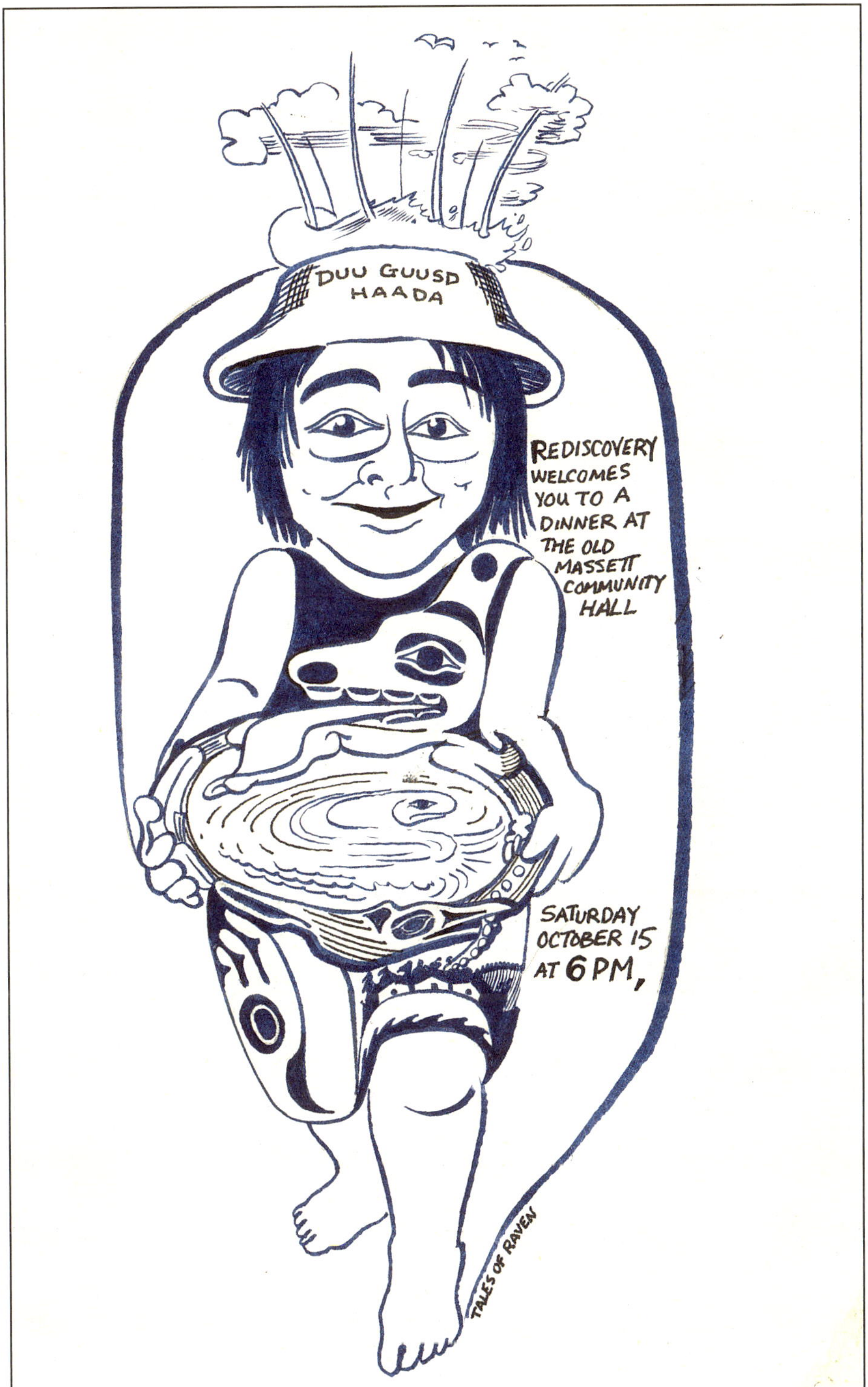
DUU GUUSD HAADA
REDISCOVERY WELCOMES YOU TO A DINNER AT THE OLD MASSETT COMMUNITY HALL
SATURDAY OCTOBER 15 AT 6 PM,
TALES OF RAVEN

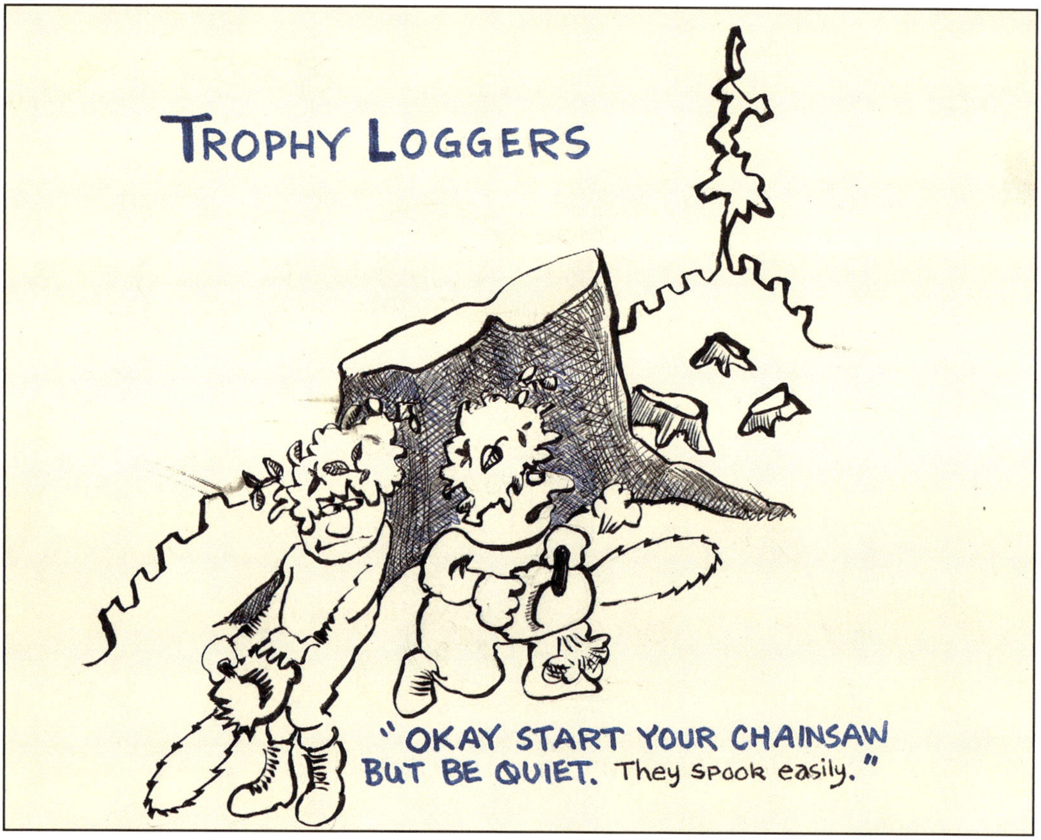
TROPHY LOGGERS
"OKAY START YOUR CHAINSAW BUT BE QUIET. They spook easily."

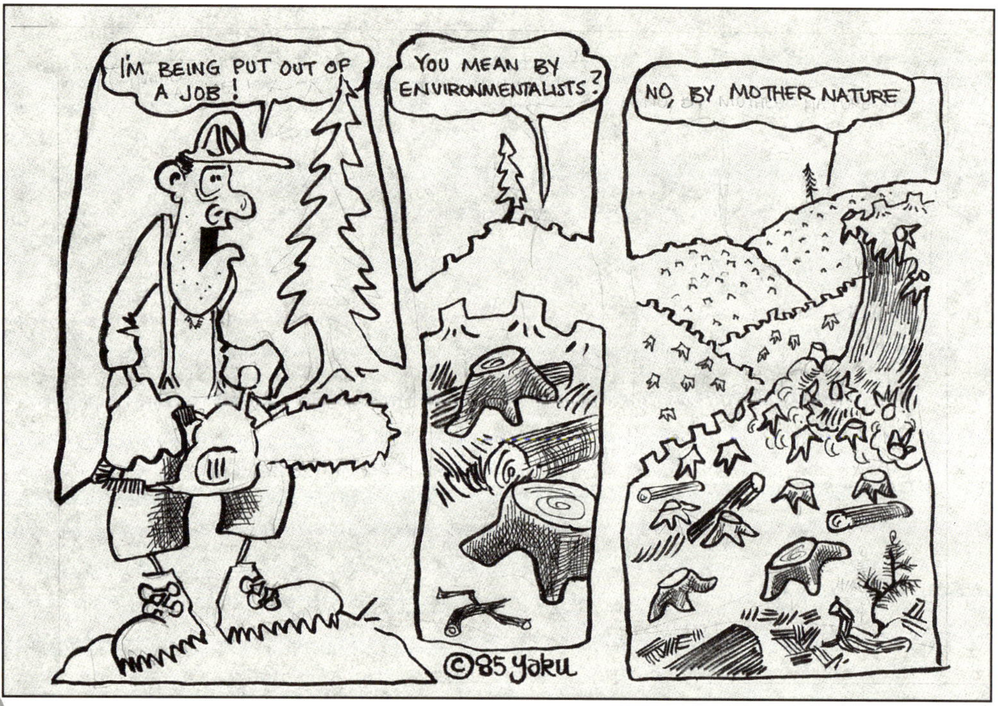
I'M BEING PUT OUT OF A JOB!
YOU MEAN BY ENVIRONMENTALISTS?
NO, BY MOTHER NATURE
©85 Yaku

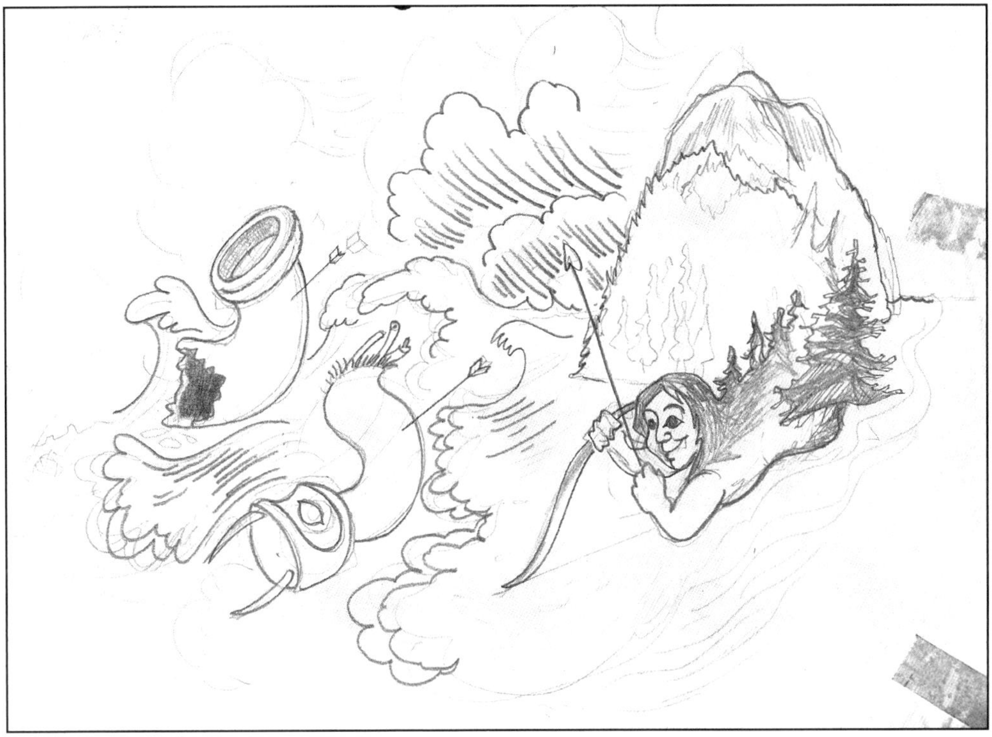

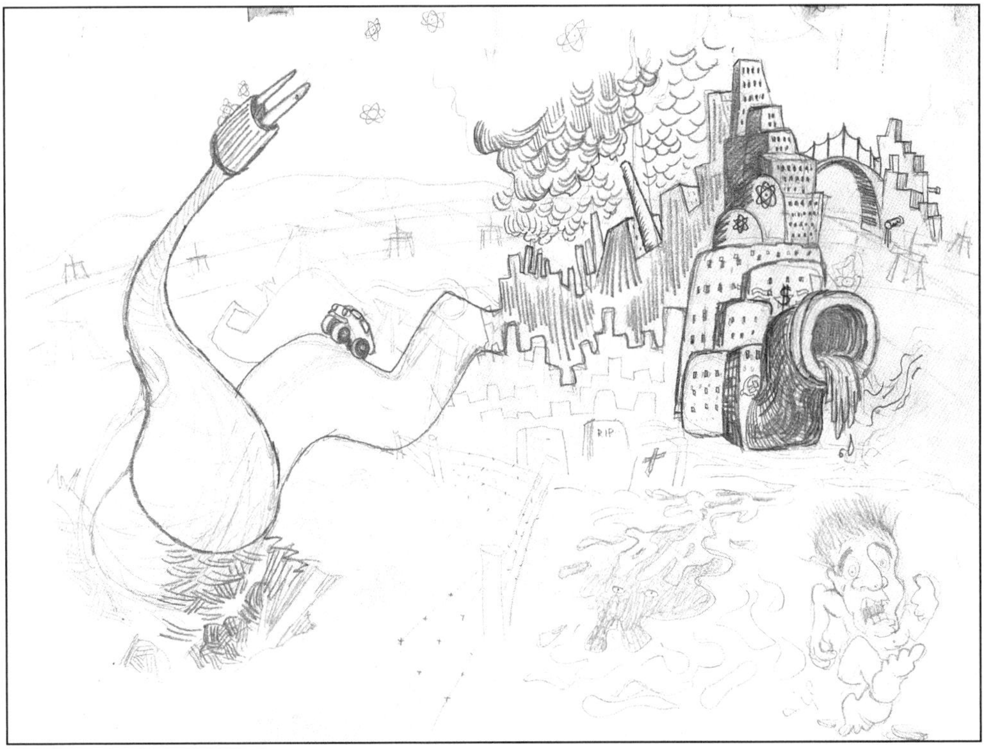

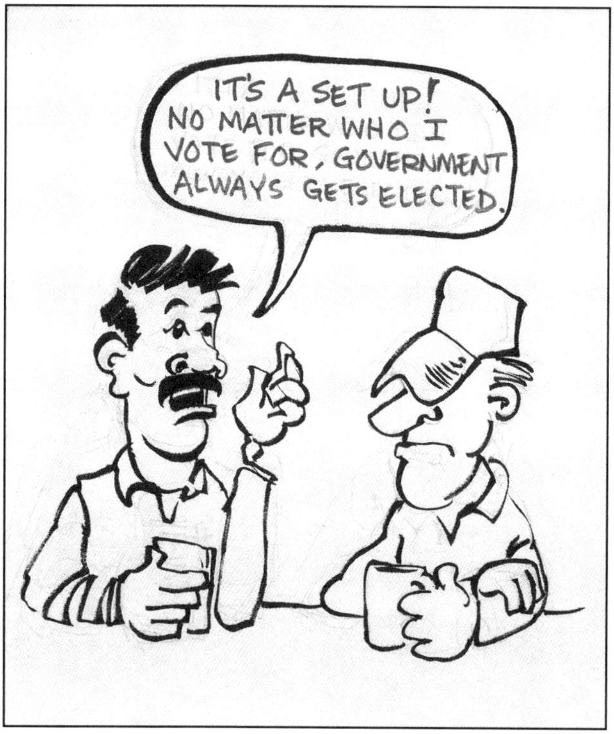

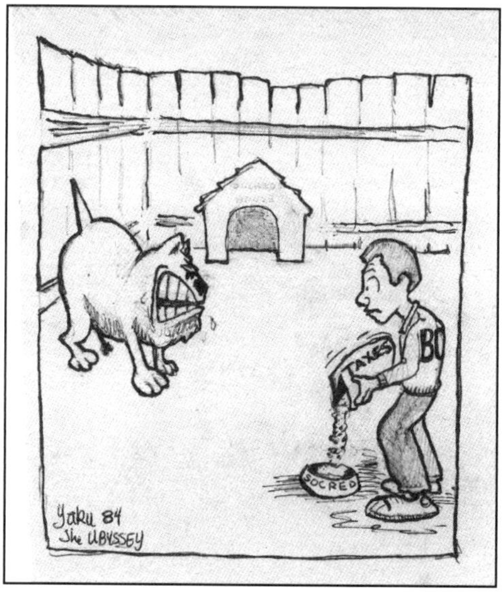

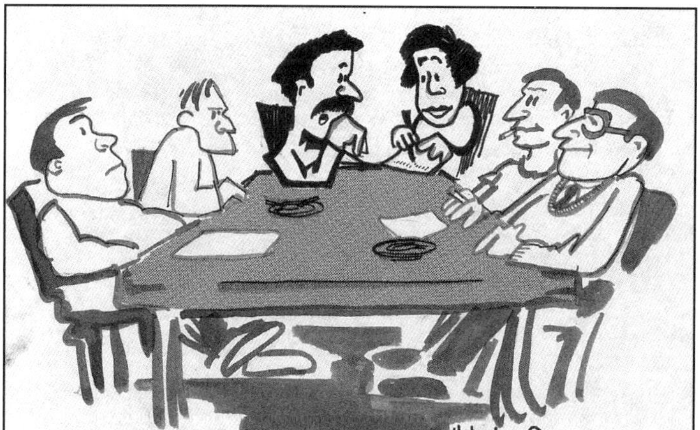

"BE IT RESOLVED THAT THE BOARD CONTINUE TO SEE THAT WOMEN ARE ALWAYS REPRESENTED AT OUR MEETINGS.... ... HAVE YOU GOT THAT ALICE?"

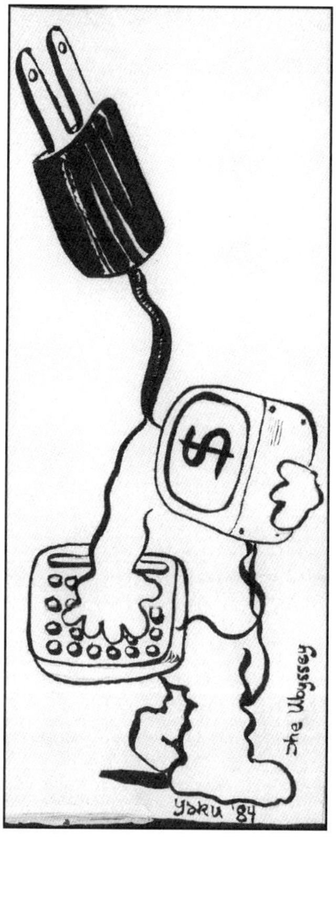

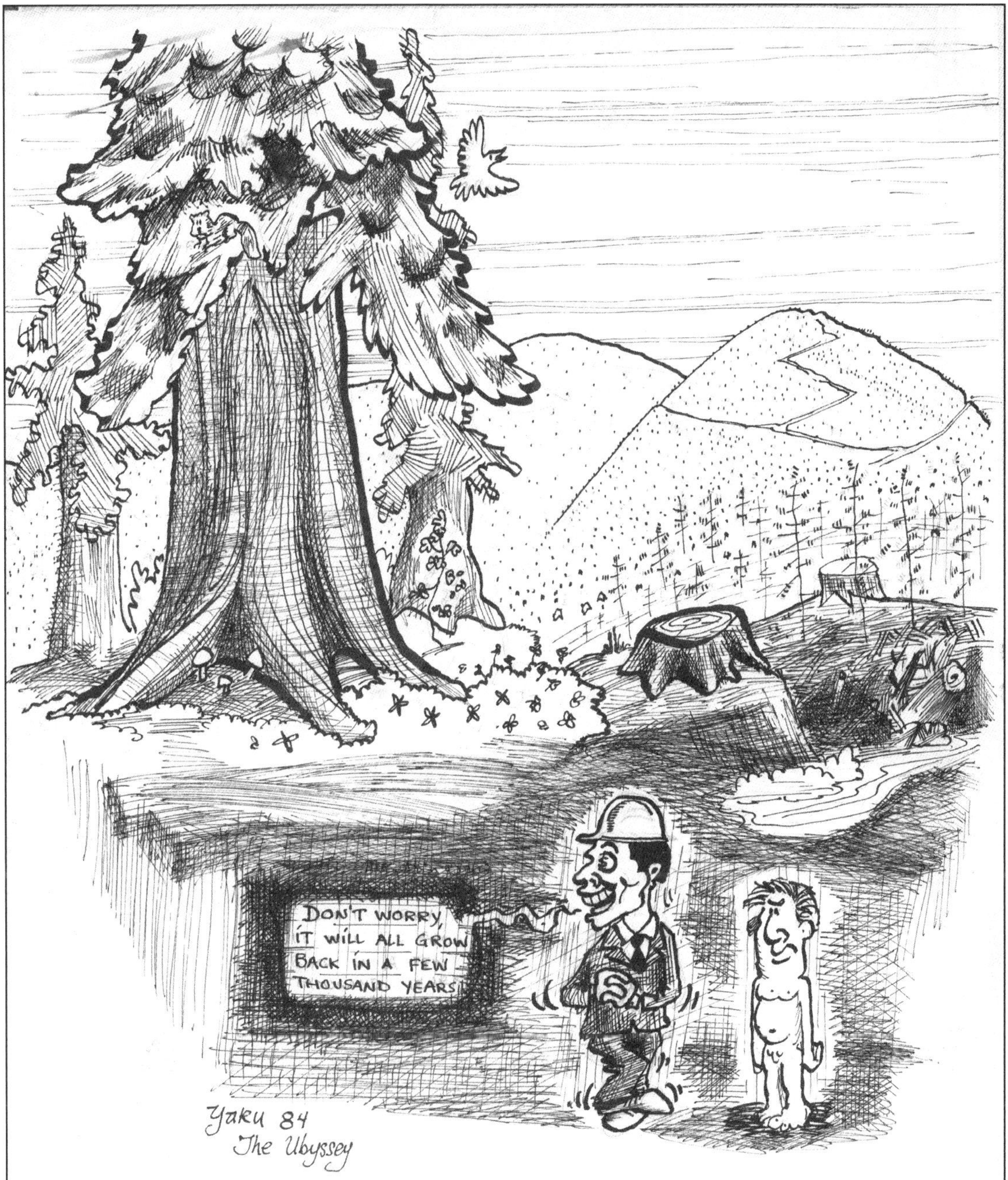
DON'T WORRY, IT WILL ALL GROW BACK IN A FEW THOUSAND YEARS!
Yaku 84
The Ubyssey

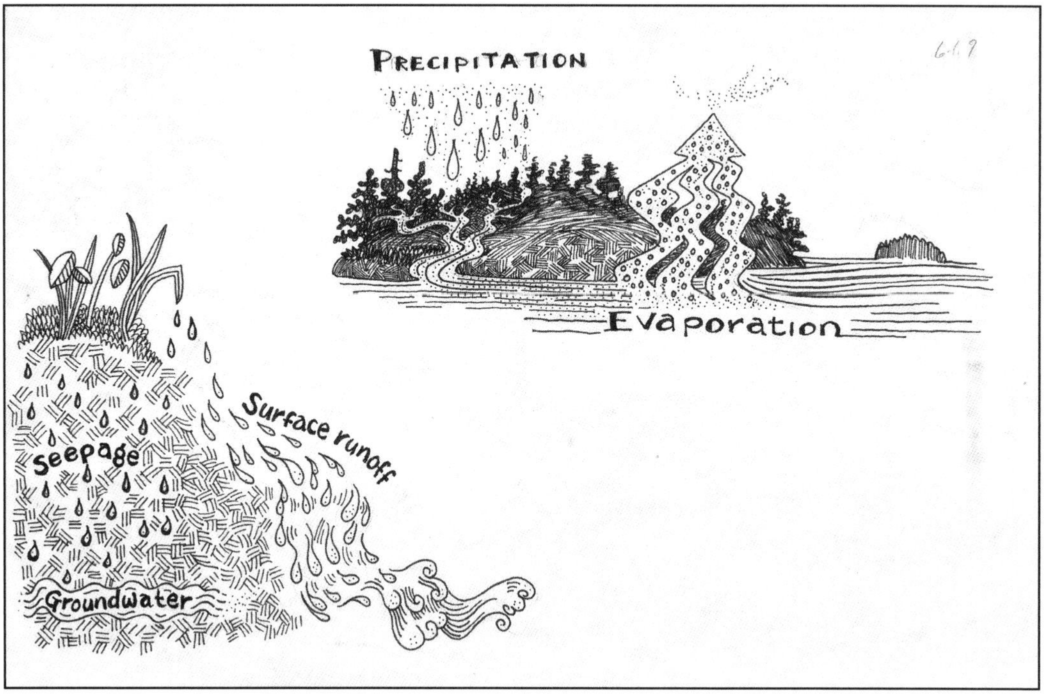
6.4.9
PRECIPITATION
Evaporation
Surface runoff
seepage
Groundwater

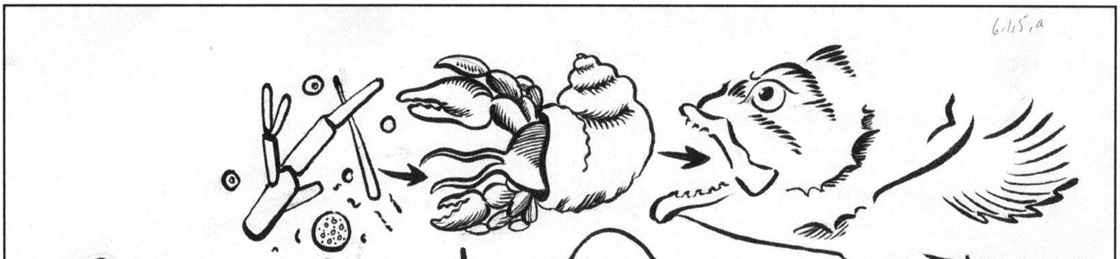

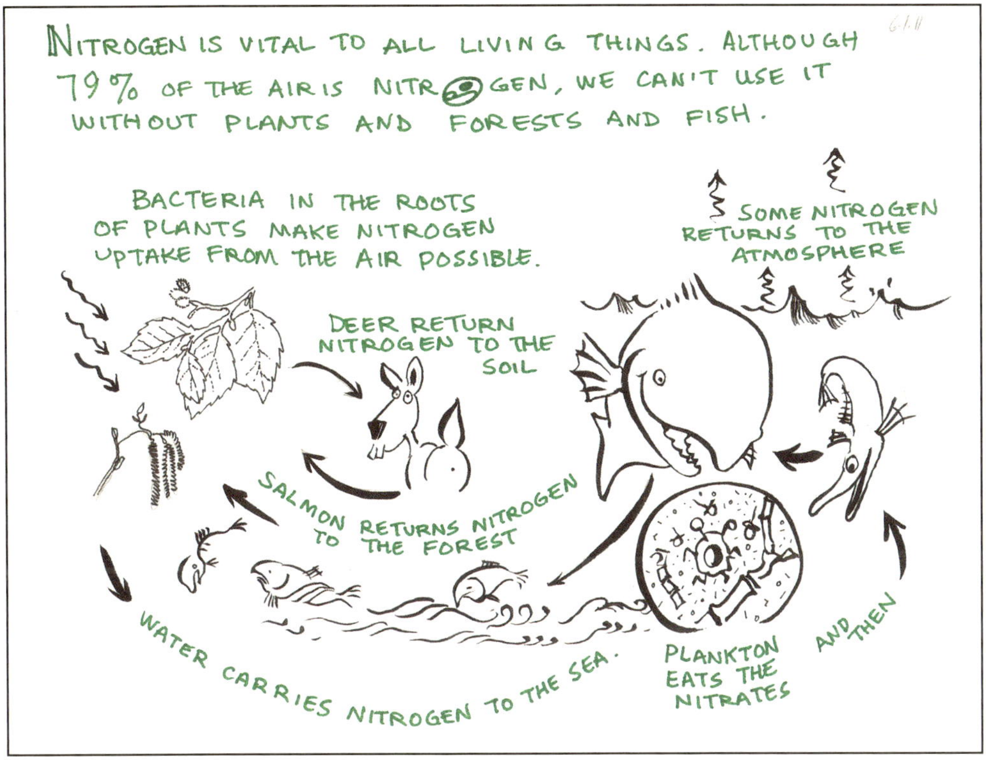
6.1.11
NITROGEN IS VITAL TO ALL LIVING THINGS. ALTHOUGH 79% OF THE AIR IS NITROGEN, WE CAN'T USE IT WITHOUT PLANTS AND FORESTS AND FISH.
BACTERIA IN THE ROOTS OF PLANTS MAKE NITROGEN UPTAKE FROM THE AIR POSSIBLE.
SOME NITROGEN RETURNS TO THE ATMOSPHERE
DEER RETURN NITROGEN TO THE SOIL
SALMON RETURNS NITROGEN TO THE FOREST
WATER CARRIES NITROGEN TO THE SEA.
PLANKTON EATS THE NITRATES
AND THEN

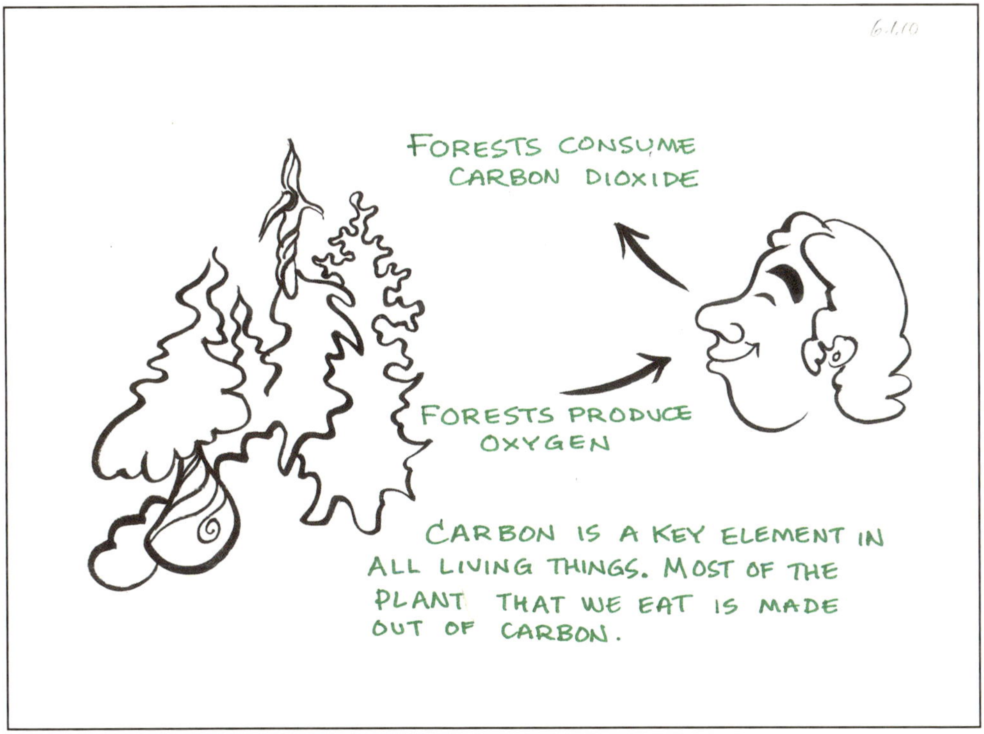
6.1.10
FORESTS CONSUME CARBON DIOXIDE
FORESTS PRODUCE OXYGEN
CARBON IS A KEY ELEMENT IN ALL LIVING THINGS. MOST OF THE PLANT THAT WE EAT IS MADE OUT OF CARBON.

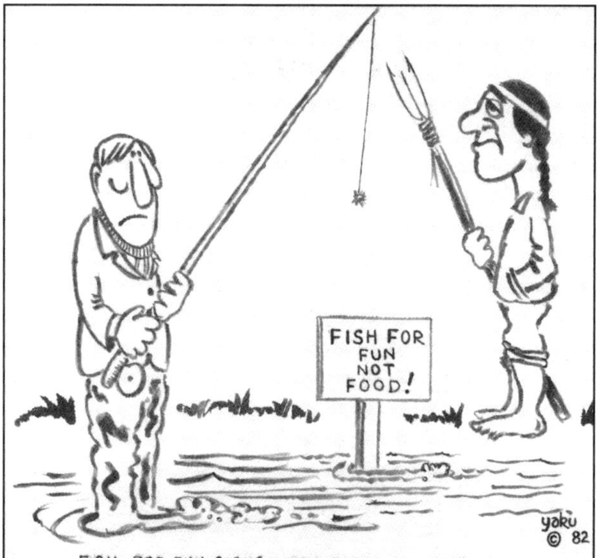

FISH FOR FUN SIGNS WERE POSTED ON THE ENGLISH & WABAGOON RIVERS IN THE EARLY SEVENTIES BECAUSE OF HIGH MERCURY LEVELS.

A RESEARCH SCIENTIFIC INSTITUTE STATES IN WRITING TO A SENIOR LEVEL OF A GOVERNMENT AGENCY, "WE CALCULATE THAT APPROXIMATELY **250 TONS** OF MERCURY WILL BE PRESENT IN THE (CINOLA) ORE..." "THIS IS ABOUT **25** TIMES MORE MERCURY THAN WAS DISCHARGED INTO THE SEVERELY POLLUTED ENGLISH-WABAGOON RIVER SYSTEM."

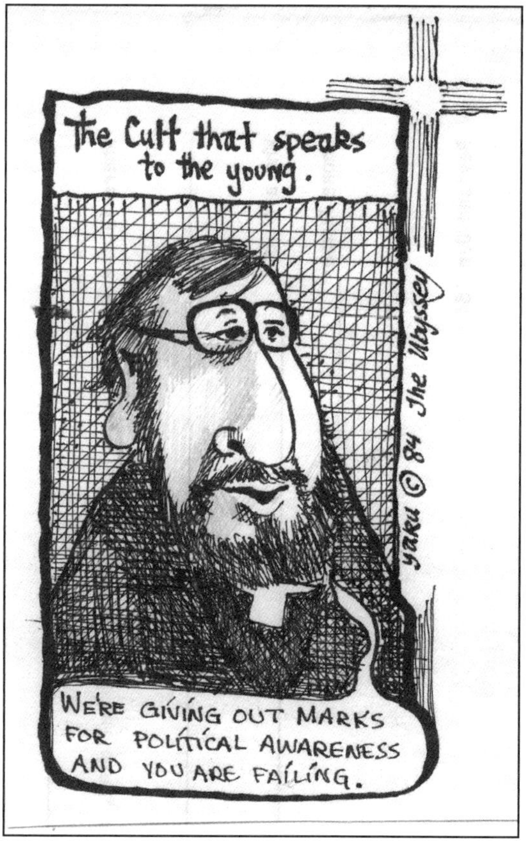

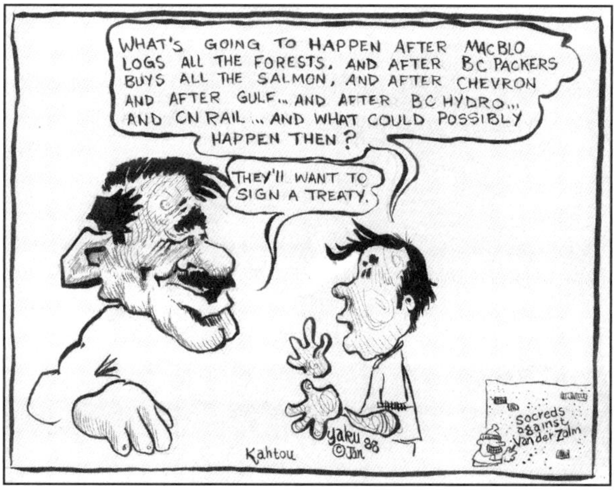

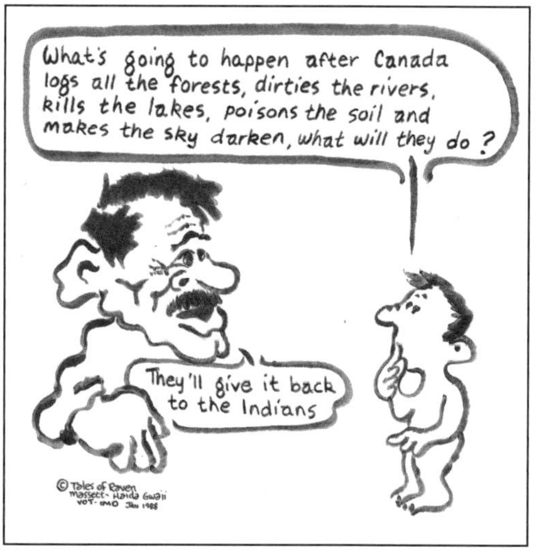

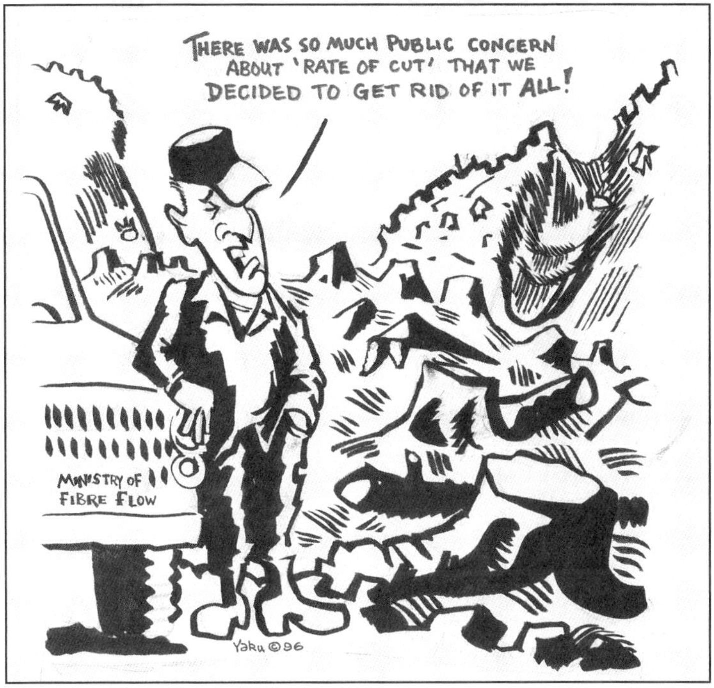
THERE WAS SO MUCH PUBLIC CONCERN ABOUT 'RATE OF CUT' THAT WE DECIDED TO GET RID OF IT ALL!
MINISTRY OF FIBRE FLOW
Yaku ©96

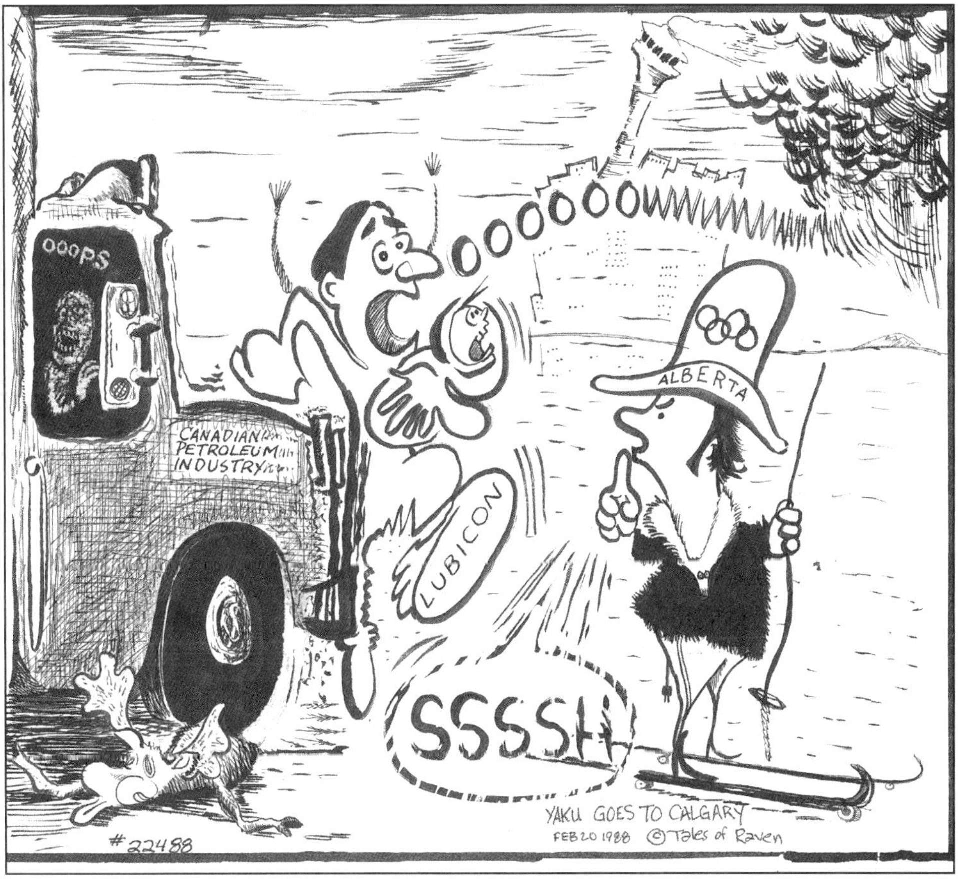
OOOPS
CANADIAN PETROLEUM INDUSTRY
OOOOOOOWWWWWWWW
ALBERTA
LUBICON
SSSSH
YAKU GOES TO CALGARY
FEB 20 1988 © Tales of Raven
#22488

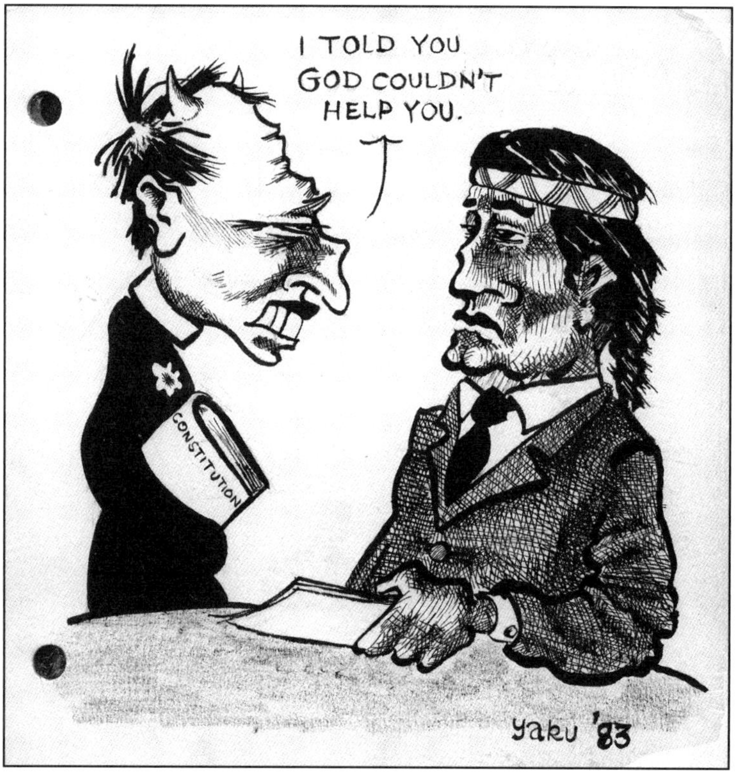
I TOLD YOU GOD COULDN'T HELP YOU.
CONSTITUTION
Yaku '83

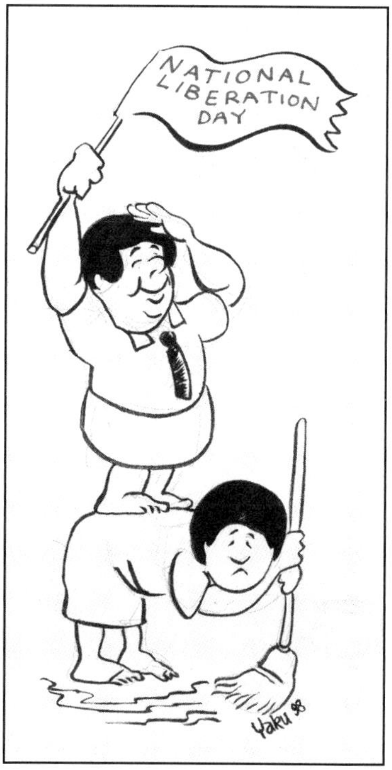
NATIONAL LIBERATION DAY
Yaku 98

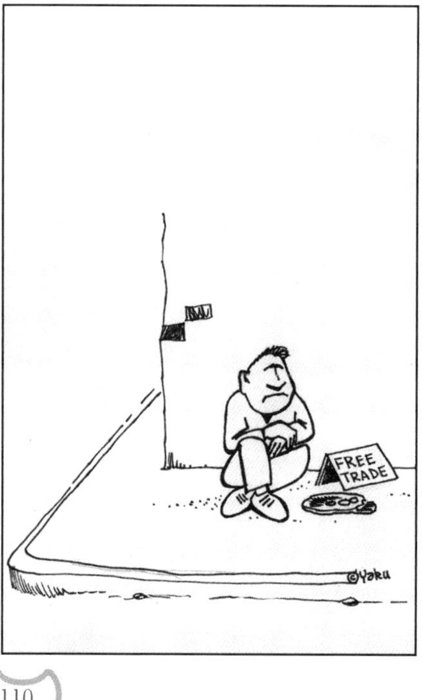
FREE TRADE
©Yaku

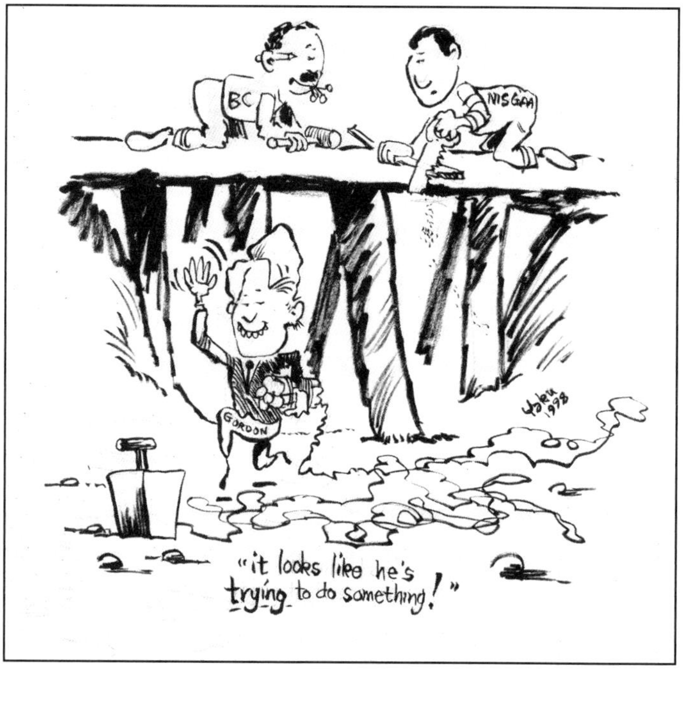
BC
NISGAA
GORDON
Yaku 1998
"it looks like he's trying to do something!"

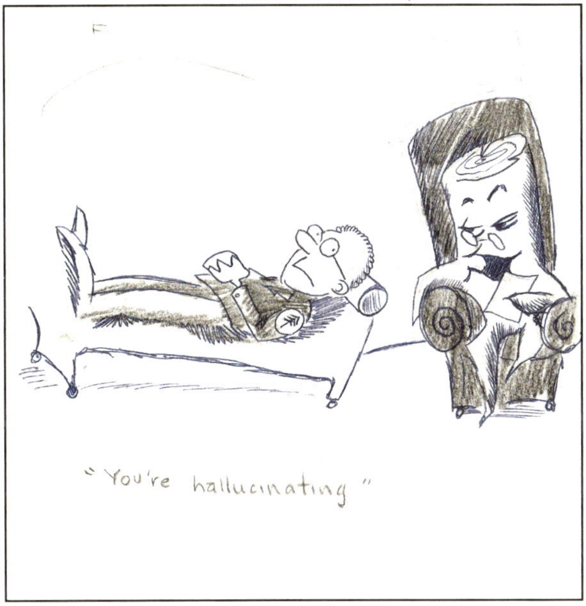

"You're hallucinating"

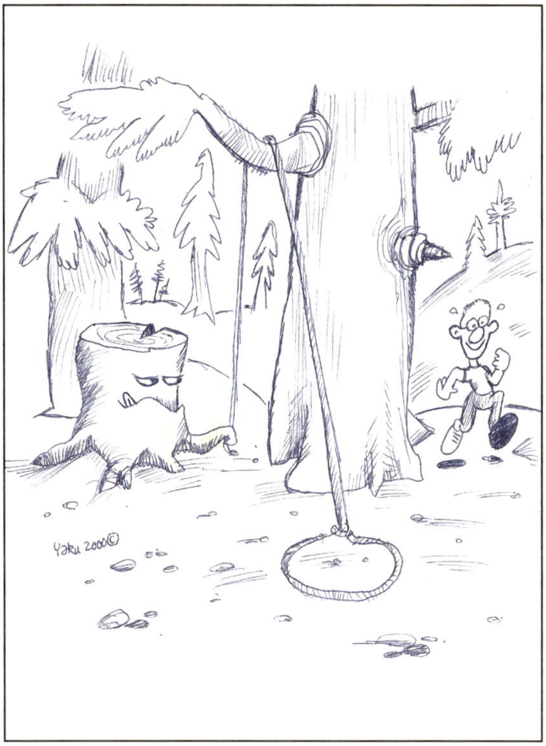

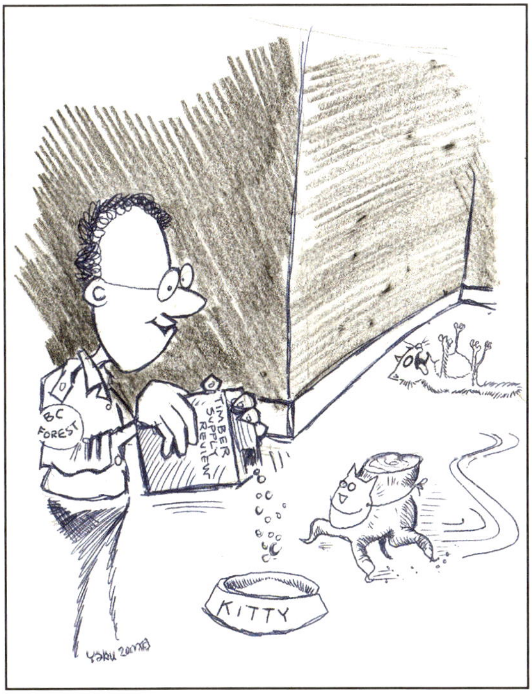

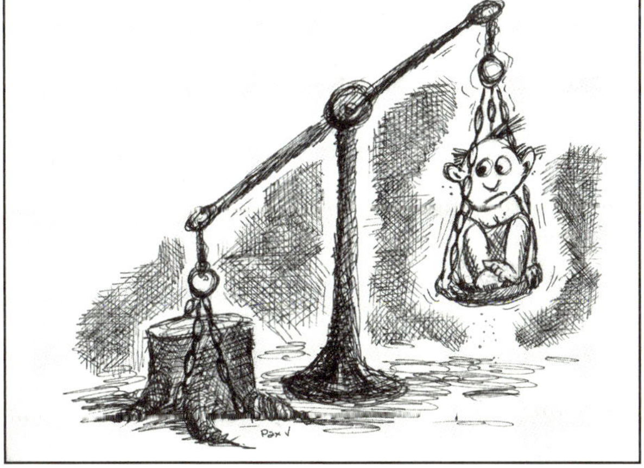

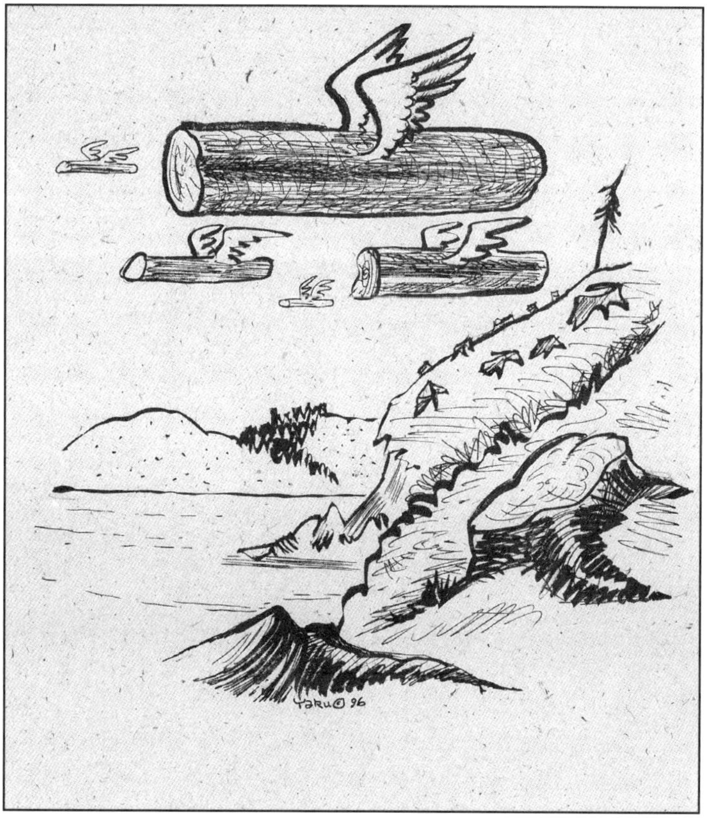

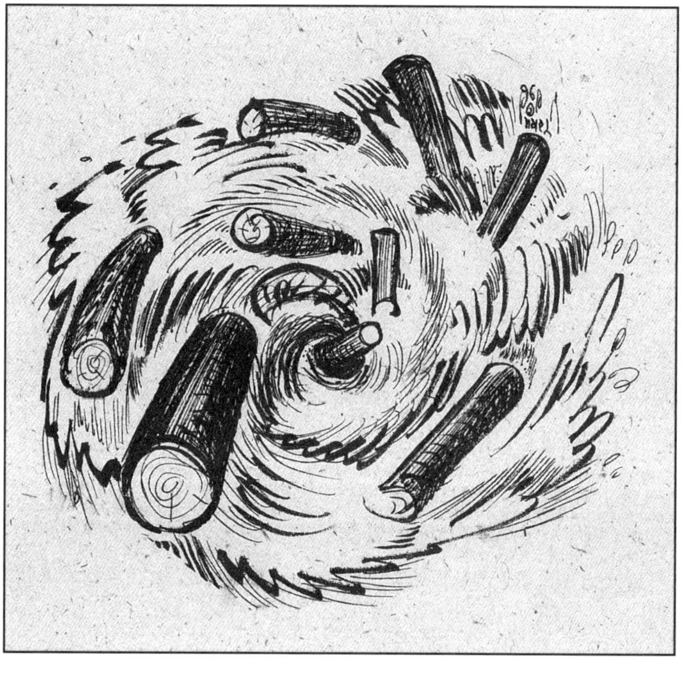

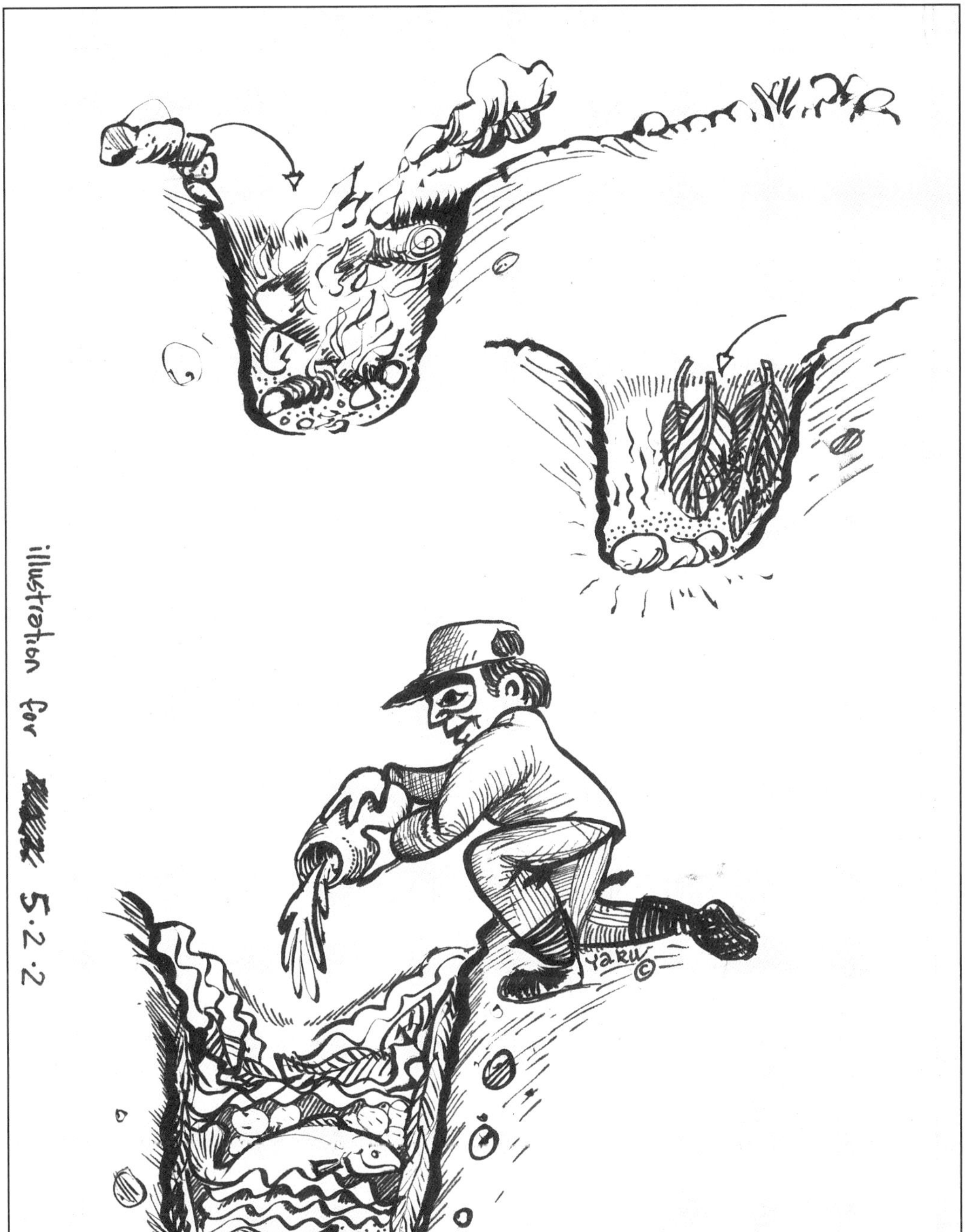
illustration for [redacted] 5.2.2
YARU ©

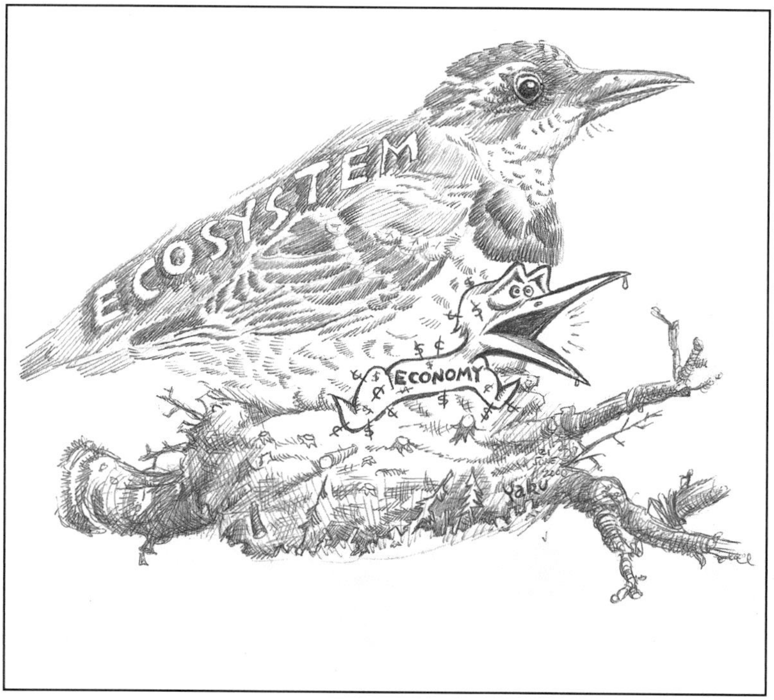
ECOSYSTEM
ECONOMY
Yaku

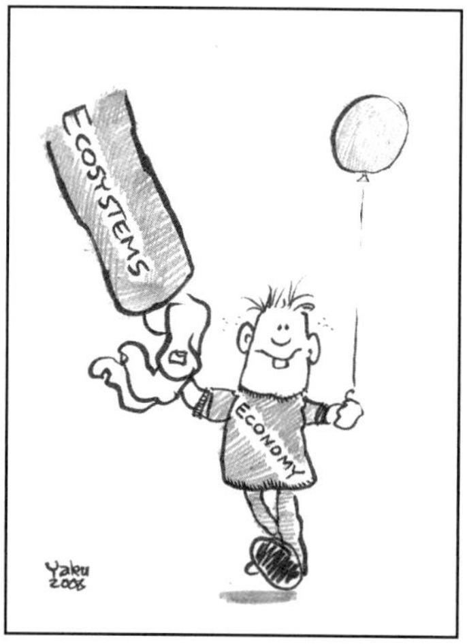
ECOSYSTEMS
ECONOMY
Yaku
2008

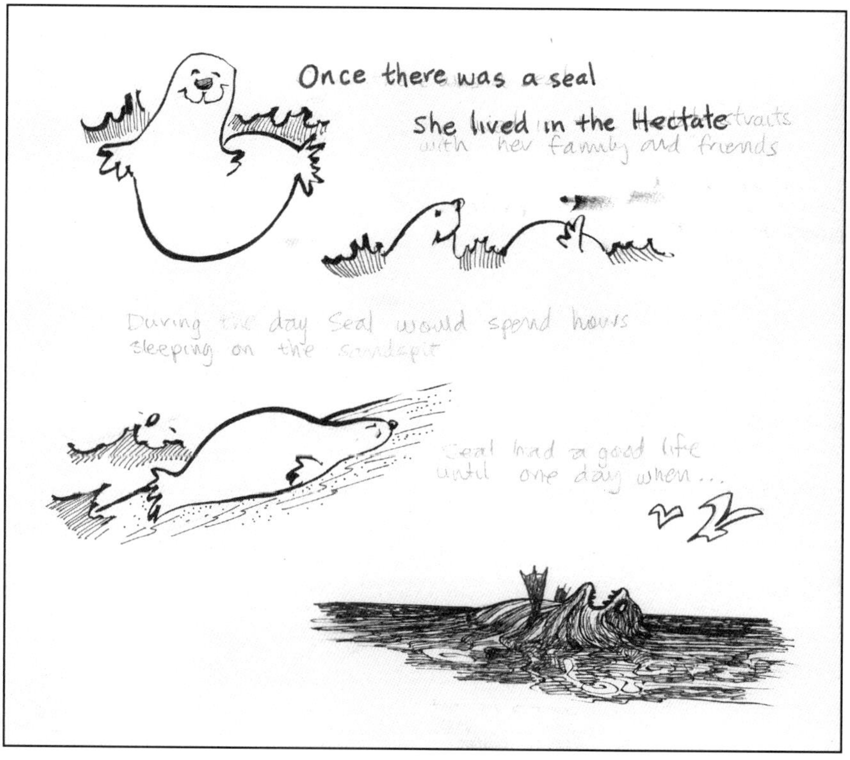
Once there was a seal
She lived in the Hectate Straits
with her family and friends
During the day Seal would spend hours
sleeping on the sandspit
Seal had a good life
until one day when...

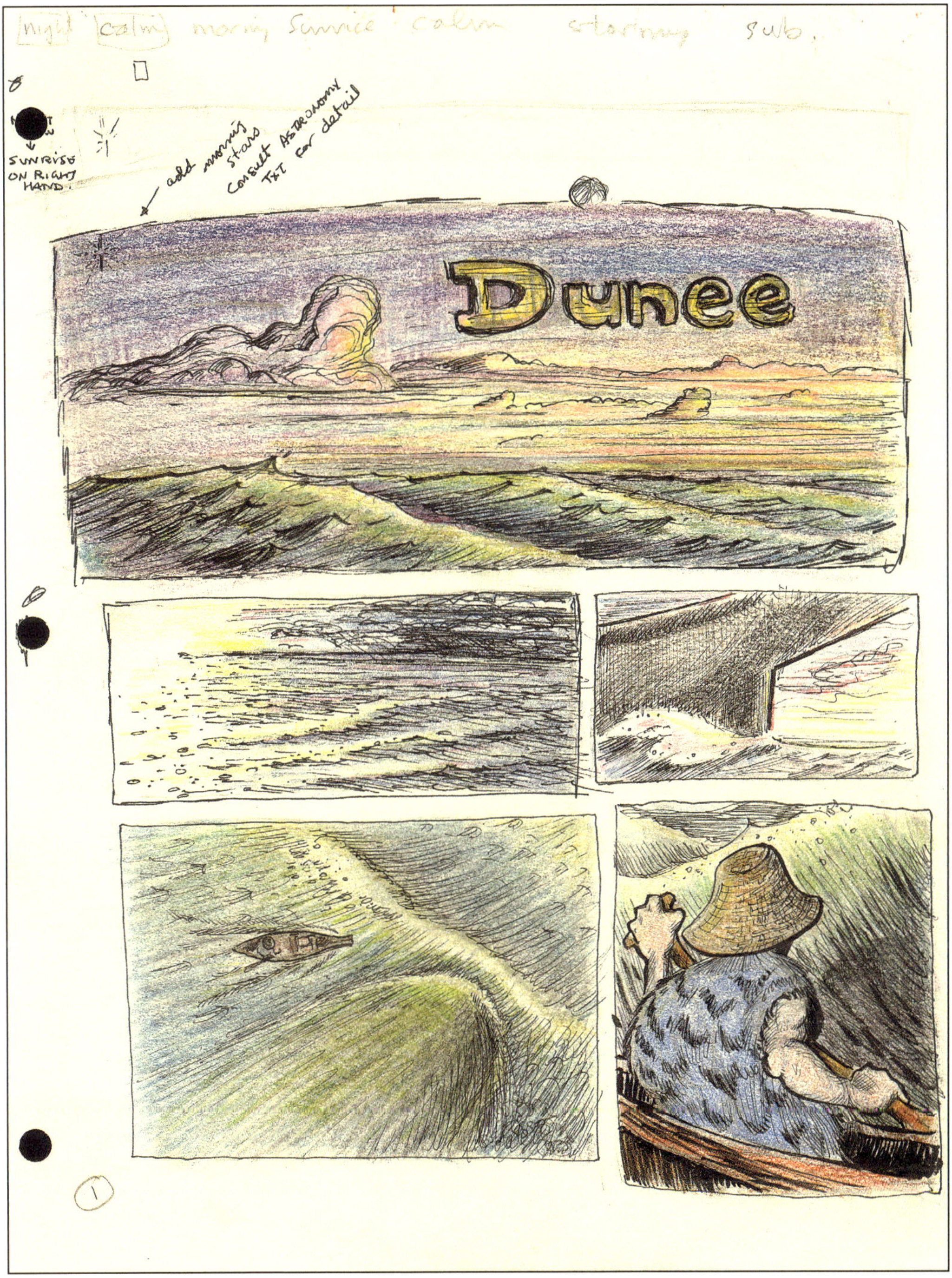

SUNRISE ON RIGHT HAND.
add morning stars consult ASTRONOMY TXT for detail
Dunee

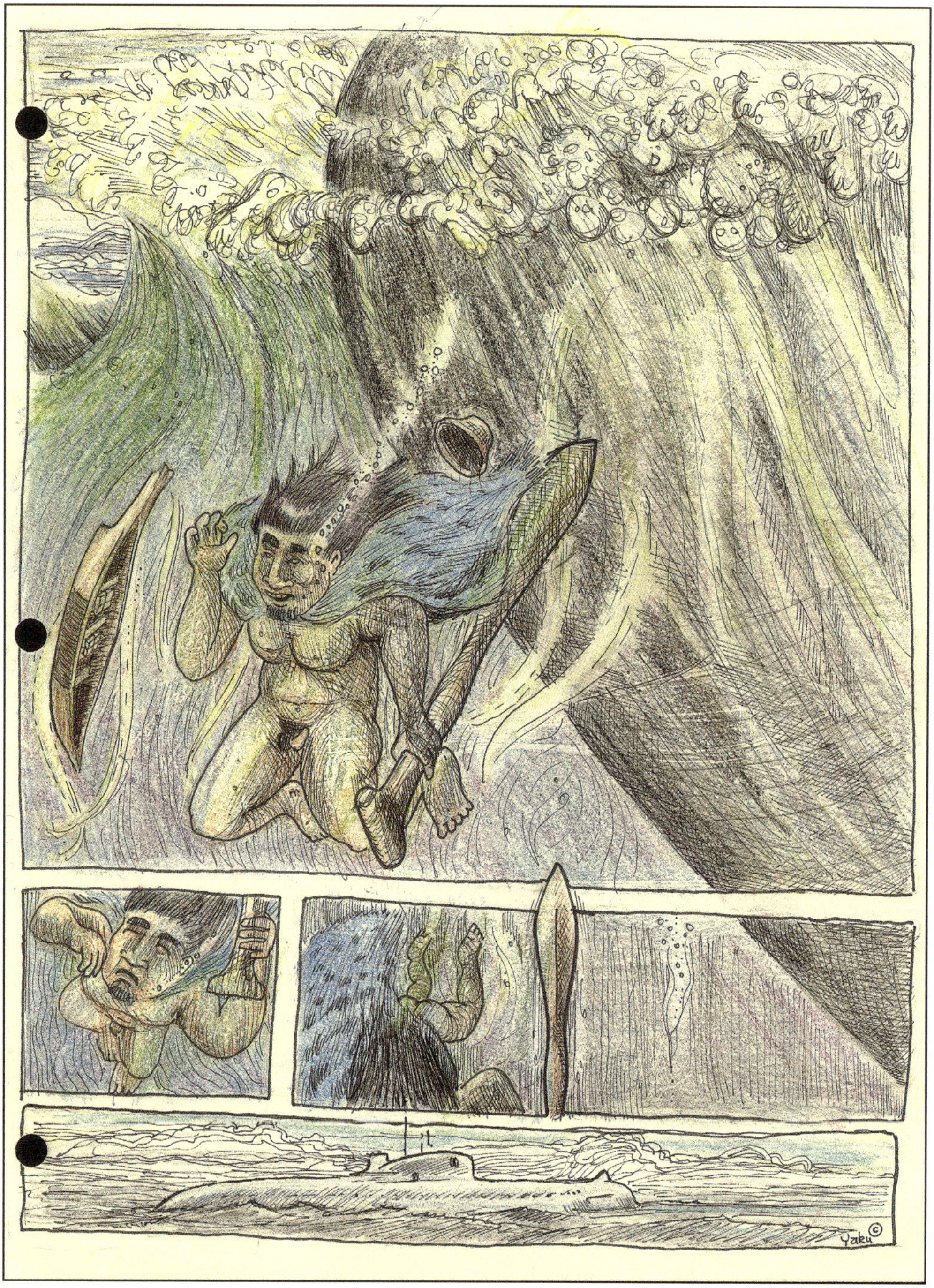
Yaku©

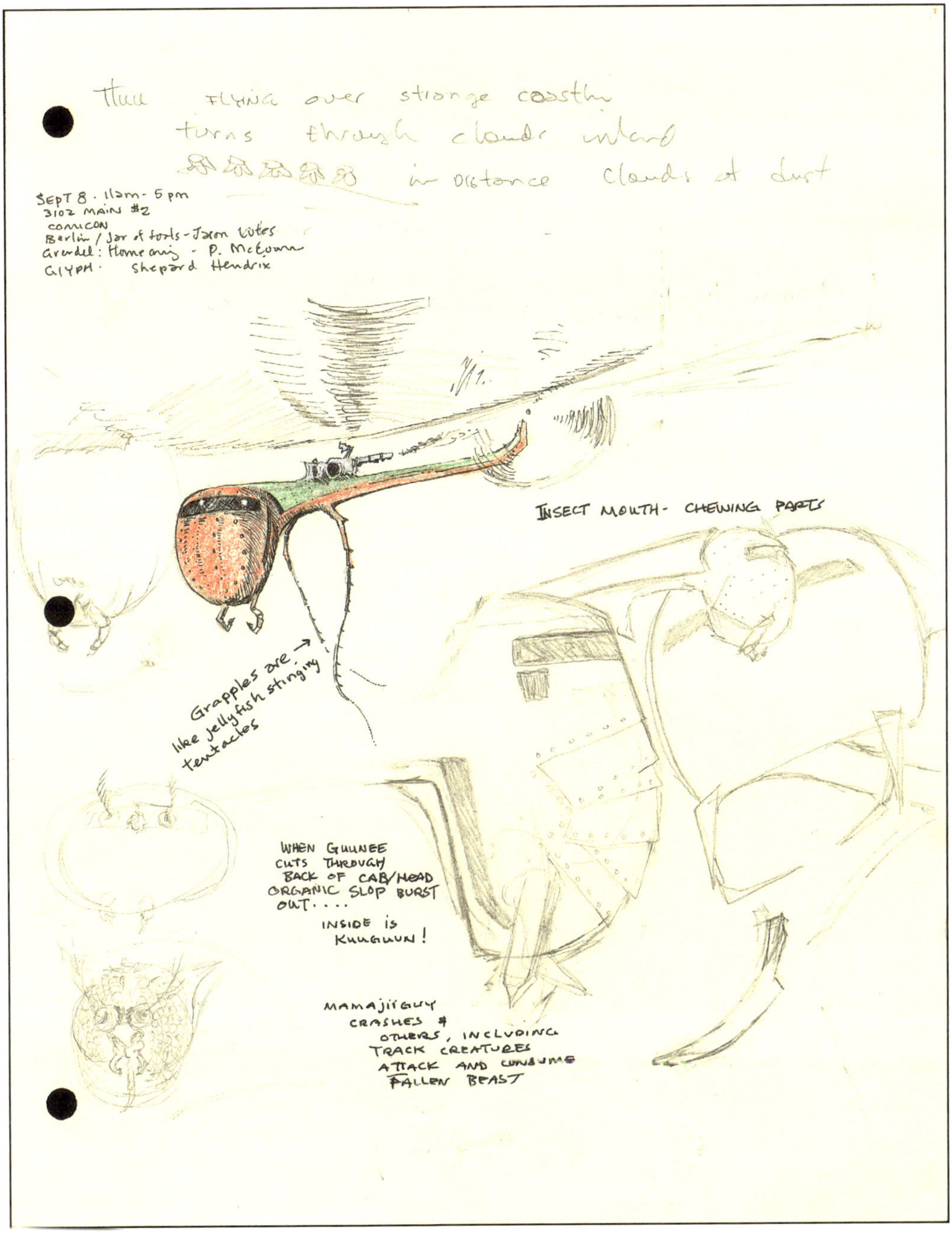

turns through clouds inland
in distance clouds of dust
SEPT 8 · 11am - 5pm
3102 MAIN #2
COMICON
Berlin / Jar of Fools - Jason Lutes
Grendel: Homecoming - P. McKeown
GLYPH · Shepard Hendrix
INSECT MOUTH - CHEWING PARTS
Grapples are like jellyfish stinging tentacles
WHEN GUUNEE CUTS THROUGH BACK OF CAB/HEAD ORGANIC SLOP BURST OUT. . .
INSIDE IS KUUGUUN!
MAMAJIIGUY CRASHES & OTHERS, INCLUDING TRACK CREATURES ATTACK AND CONSUME FALLEN BEAST

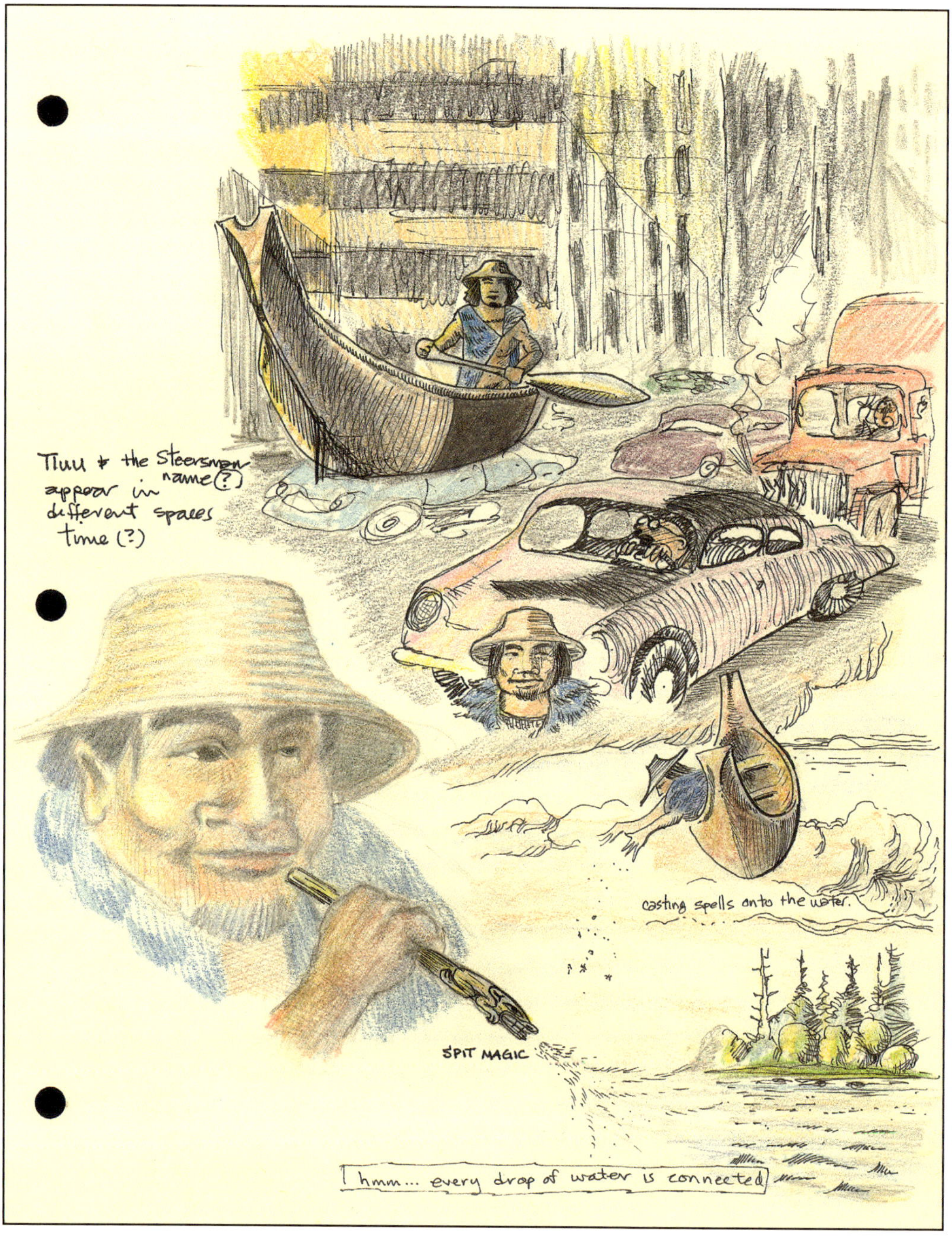
Tluu & the Steersman
name(?)
appear in
different spaces
time (?)
casting spells onto the water.
SPIT MAGIC
hmm... every drop of water is connected

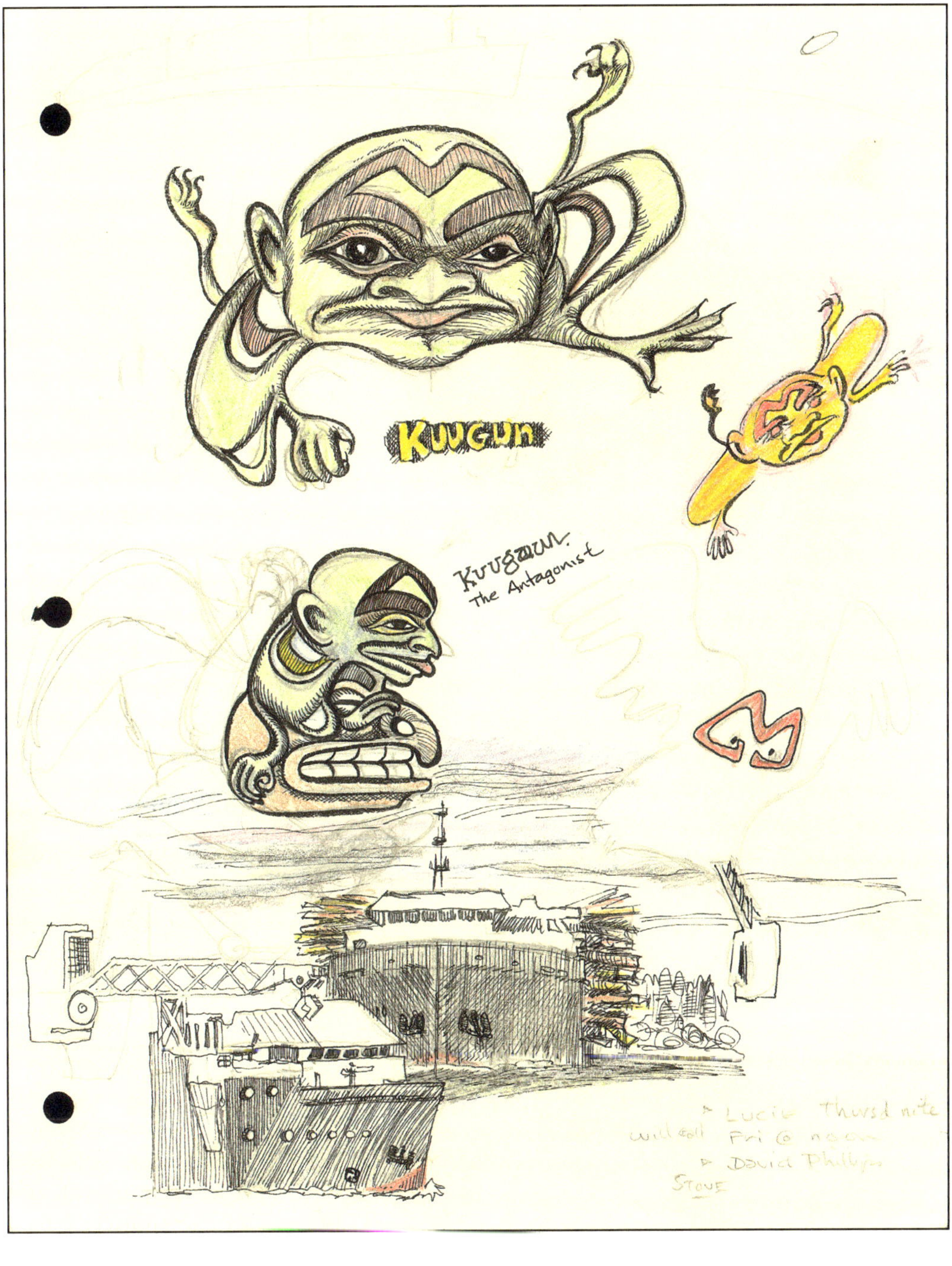

KUUGUN
Kuugaun.
The Antagonist
Lucie Thursd nite
will call Fri @ noon
David Phillips
STOVE

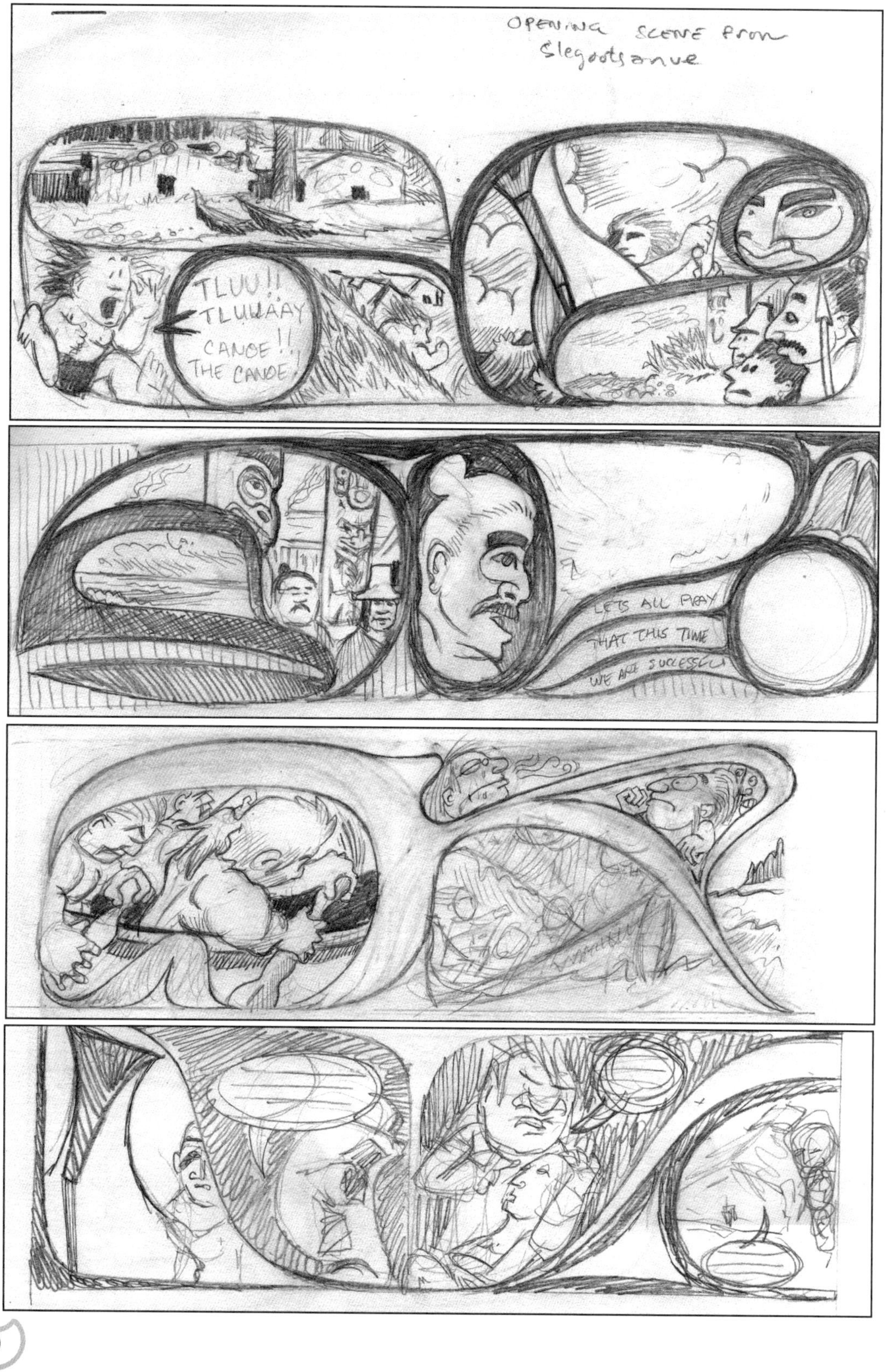
OPENING SCENE from Slegootsanue
TLUU!! TLUWAAY
CANOE!! THE CANOE!
LETS ALL PRAY
THAT THIS TIME
WE ARE SUCCESSFU

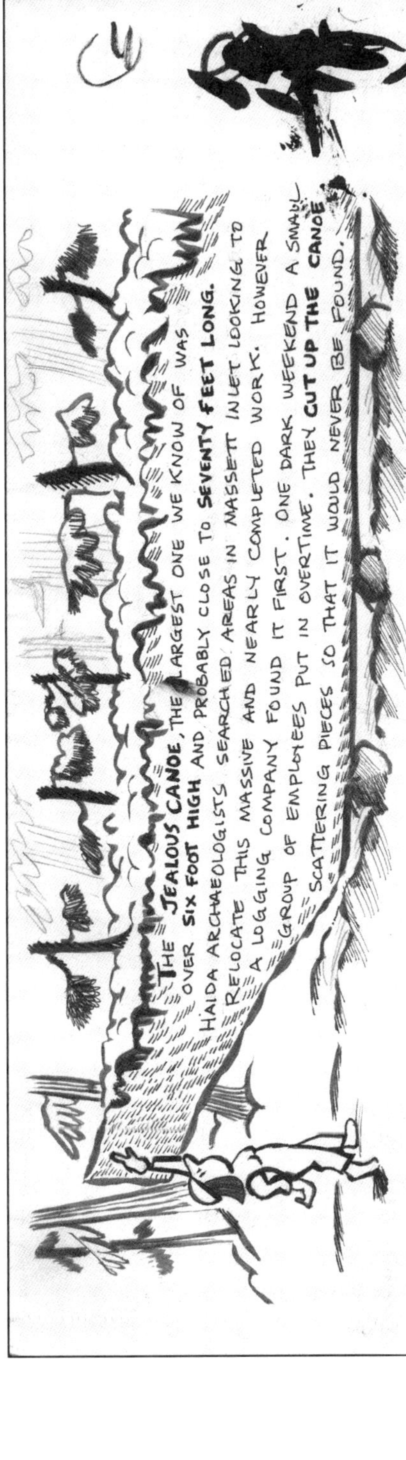

Facts	Fiction
* trees were tested before the 'test holes' were placed into the heart.	* a test hole is an abandoned site feature
* hemlock & spruce trees are modified for food, trail and ritual uses.	* only cedar trees are "CMTs"
* CMTs contain valuable information for improving silvacultural prescriptions; documenting pre existing management systems, identifying sites that produce high quality trees;	* once found and mapped a cmt can be destroyed.

* CMTS

250 557 4376

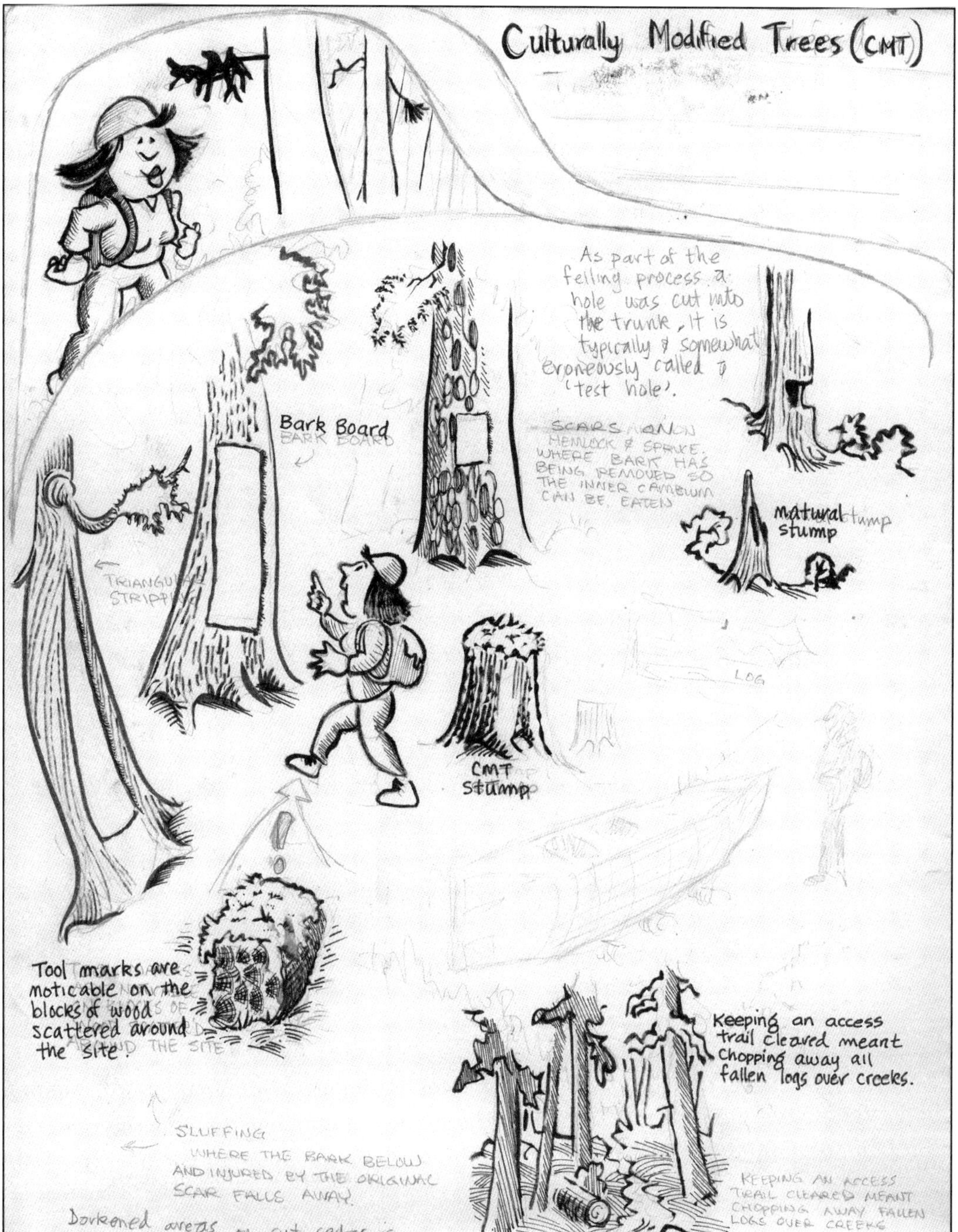
Culturally Modified Trees (CMT)
As part of the felling process a hole was cut into the trunk, it is typically & somewhat erroneously called a 'test hole'.
Bark Board
SCARS ON HEMLOCK & SPRUCE WHERE BARK HAS BEING REMOVED SO THE INNER CAMBIUM CAN BE EATEN
natural stump
CMT stump
LOG
Tool marks are noticable on the blocks of wood scattered around the site.
Keeping an access trail cleared meant chopping away all fallen logs over creeks.
SLUFFING
WHERE THE BARK BELOW AND INJURED BY THE ORIGINAL SCAR FALLS AWAY.
Darkened areas on cut cedar is a fungi growth on the cedar oil, not burns.

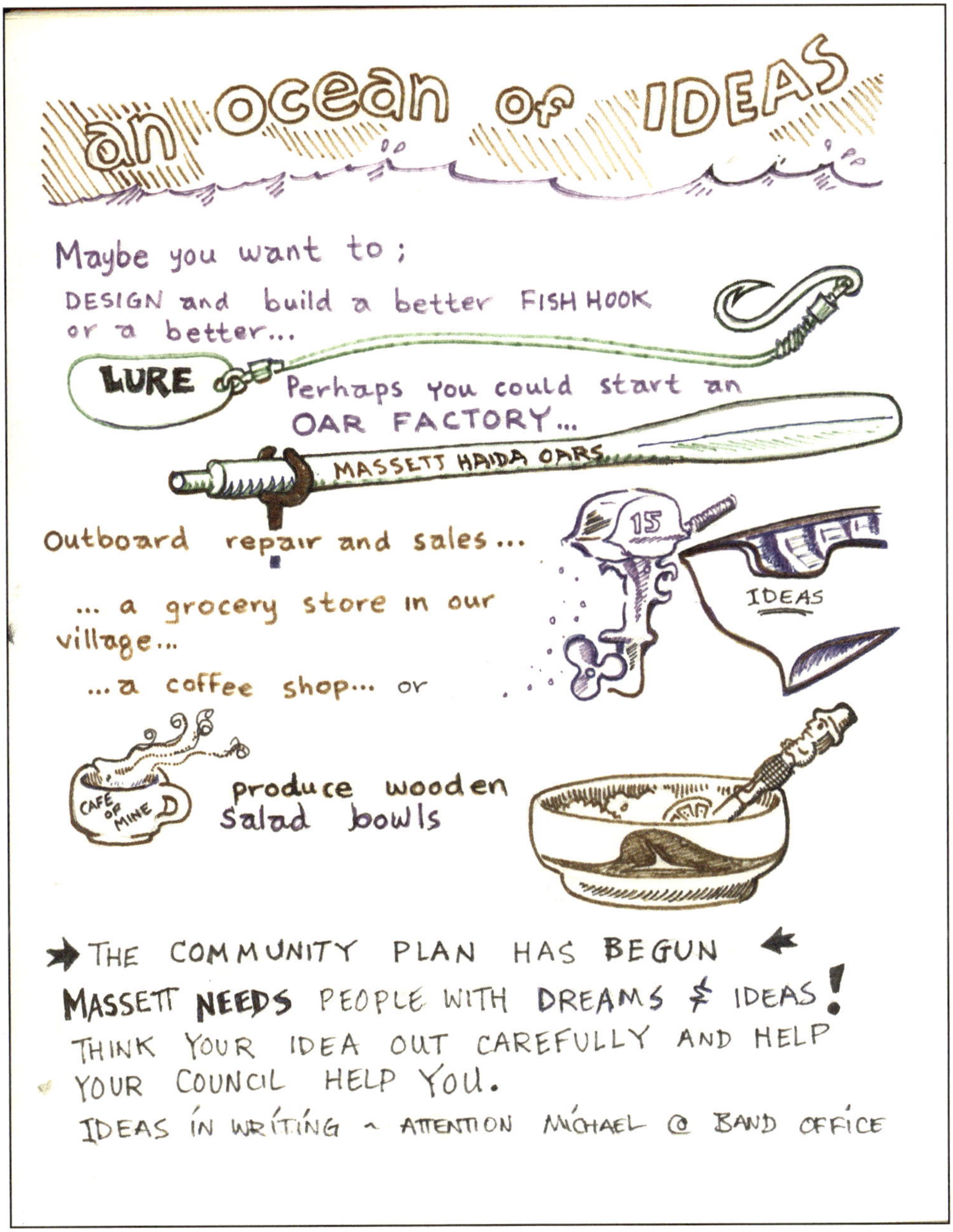
an ocean of IDEAS
Maybe you want to;
DESIGN and build a better FISH HOOK
or a better...
LURE
Perhaps you could start an
OAR FACTORY...
MASSETT HAIDA OARS
Outboard repair and sales...
15
IDEAS
... a grocery store in our
village...
... a coffee shop... or
CAFE OF MINE
produce wooden
salad bowls
→ THE COMMUNITY PLAN HAS BEGUN ←
MASSETT NEEDS PEOPLE WITH DREAMS & IDEAS!
THINK YOUR IDEA OUT CAREFULLY AND HELP
YOUR COUNCIL HELP YOU.
IDEAS IN WRITING ~ ATTENTION MICHAEL @ BAND OFFICE

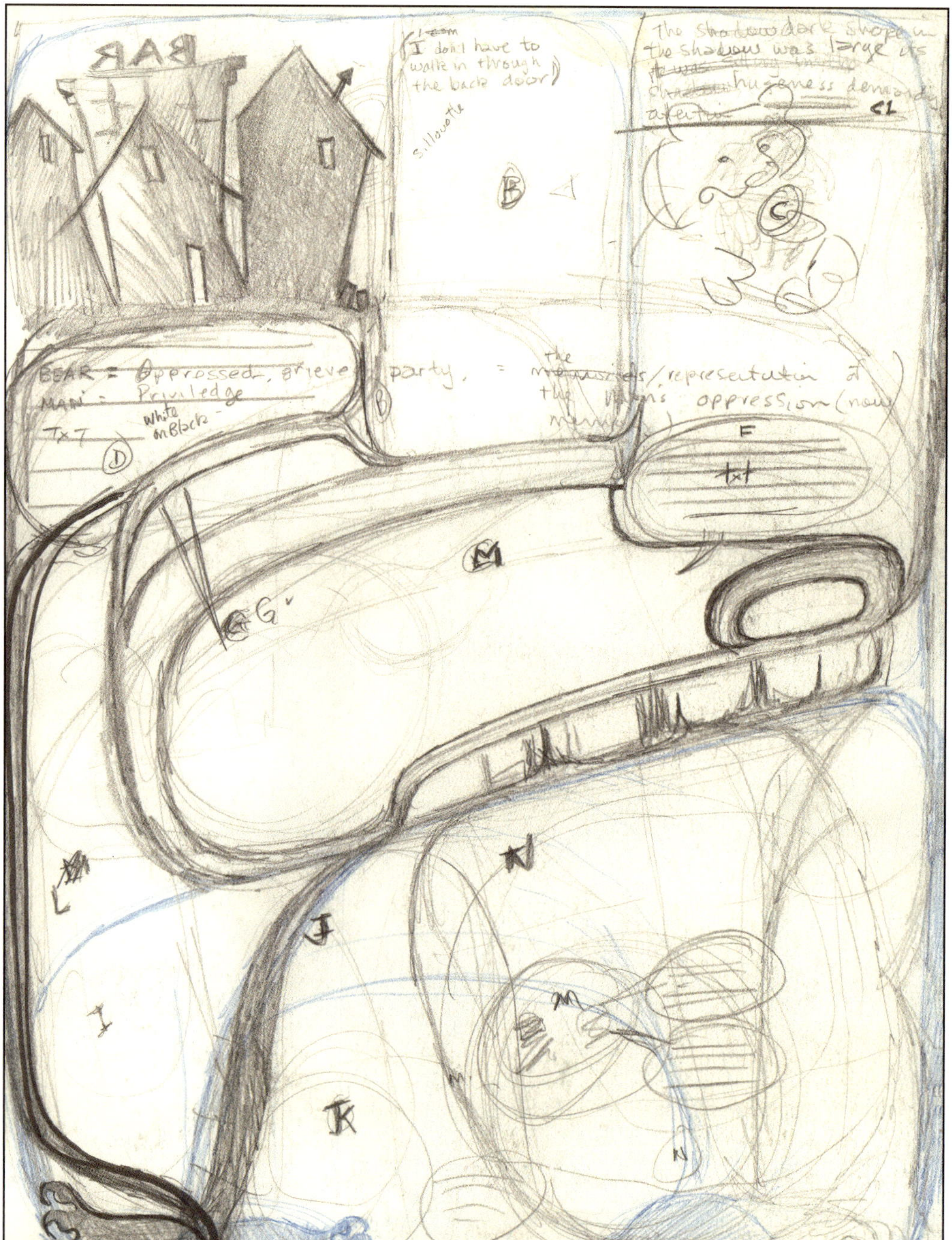
BAR
I don't have to walk in through the back door
Sillouette
The dark shape in the shadow was large its hugeness demanding
BEAR = Oppressed, grieve party. = the representation of the man's oppression
MAN = Priviledge
white on Black
Tx 7
txt

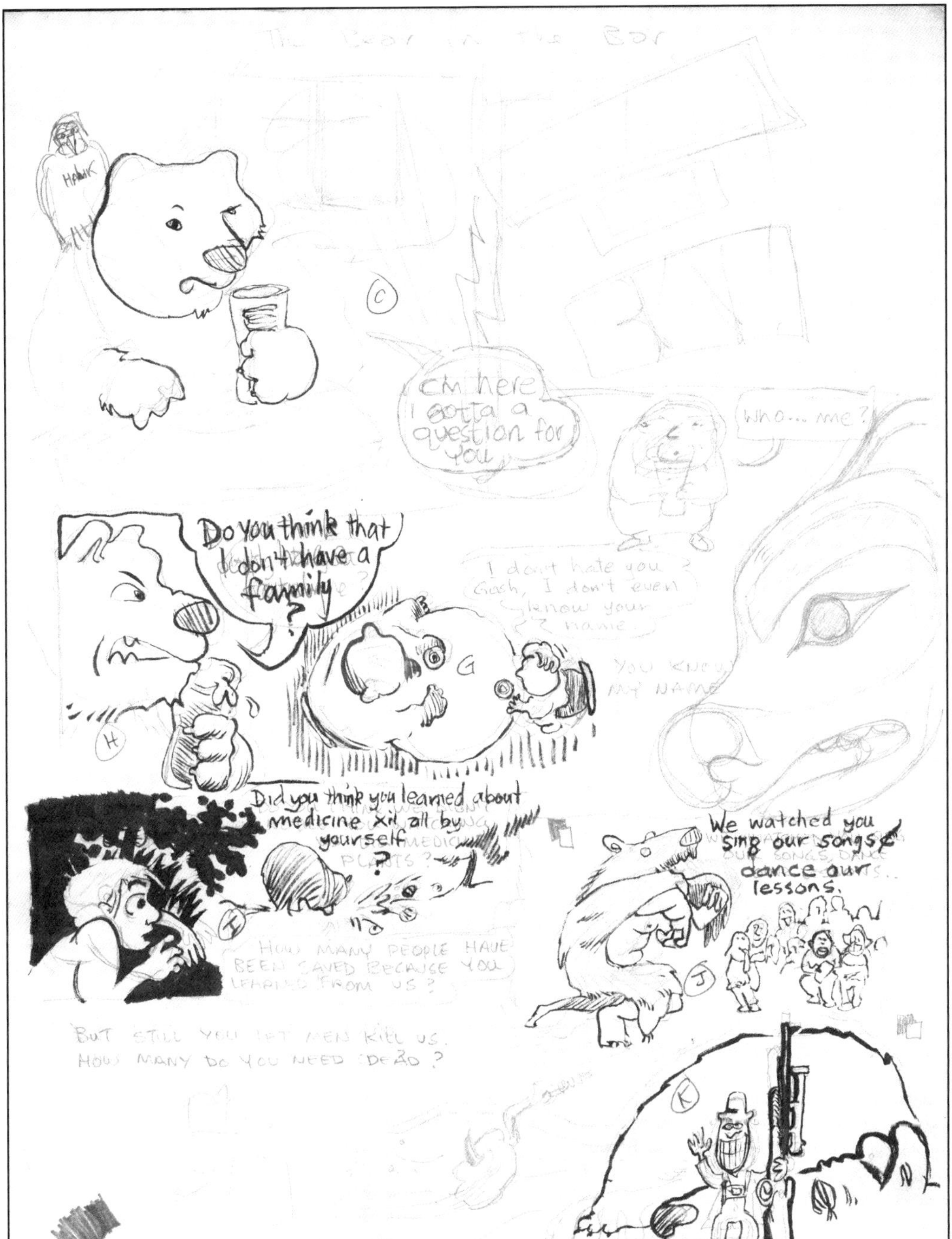

HAWK
I'm here I gotta a question for you
Who... me?
Do you think that I don't have a family?
I don't hate you? Gosh, I don't even know your name
You know my name
Did you think you learned about medicine all by yourself?
How many people have been saved because you learned from us?
We watched you sing our songs & dance our lessons.
But still you let men kill us. How many do you need dead?

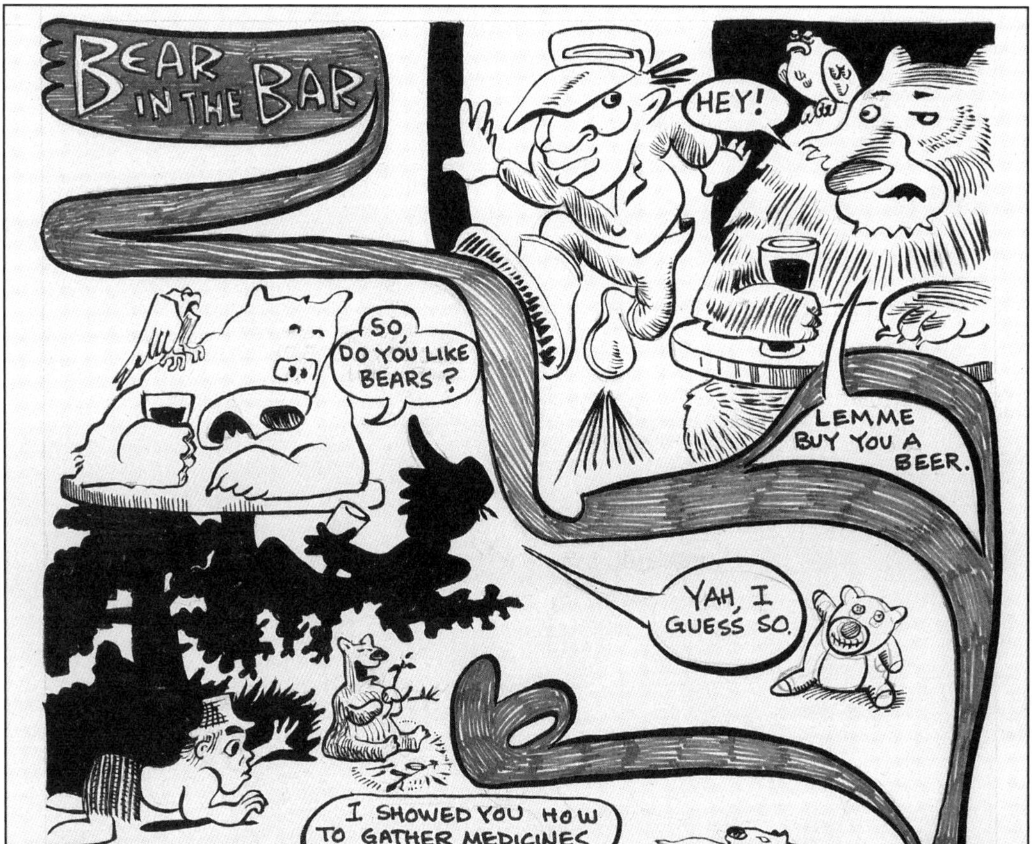

*In memory of Gerry Hawke, a man who knew and loved bears.

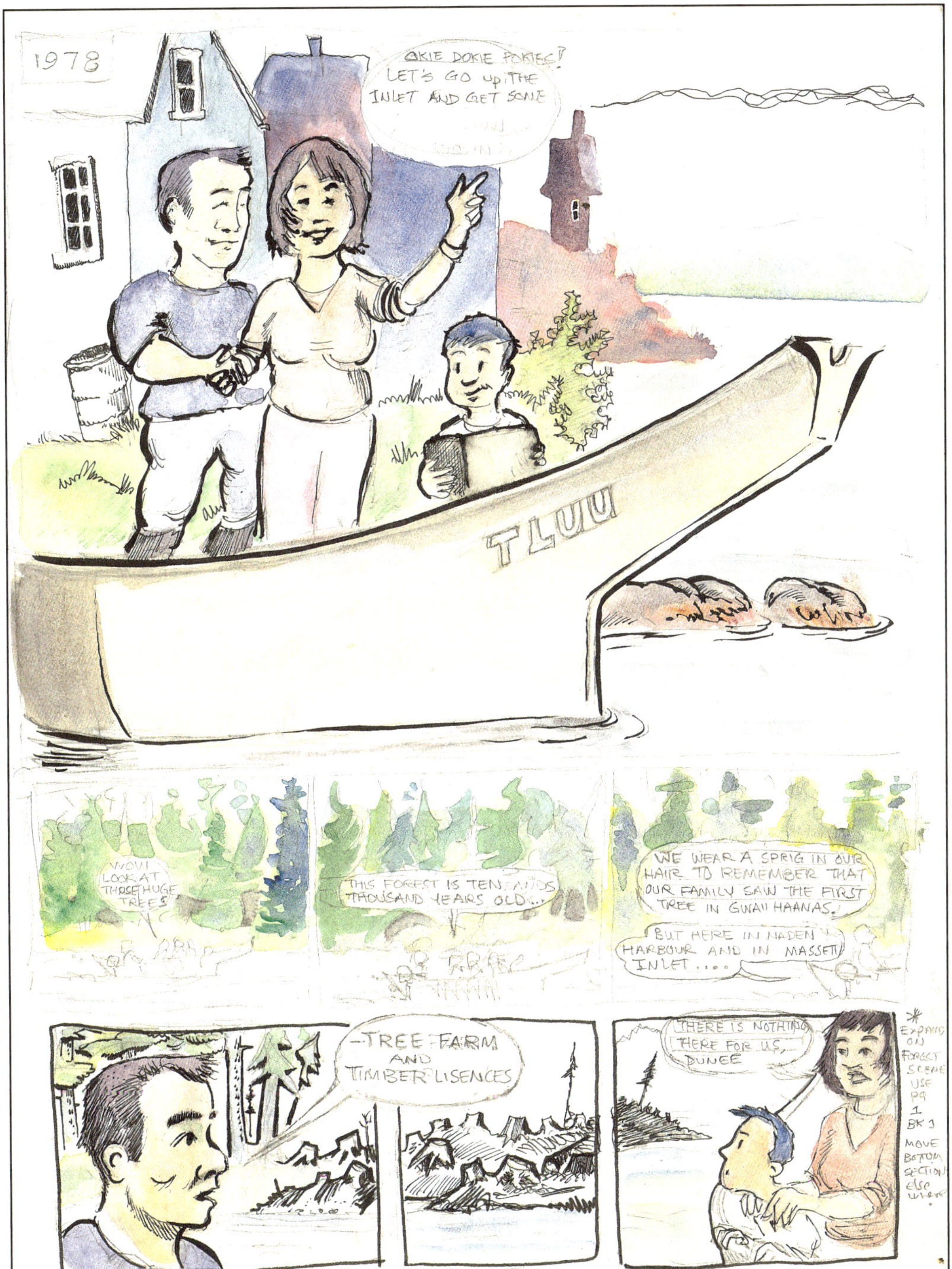
1978
OKIE DOKIE POKIES!
LET'S GO UP THE INLET AND GET SOME
TLUU
WOW! LOOK AT THOSE HUGE TREES
THIS FOREST IS TENS AND THOUSAND YEARS OLD...
WE WEAR A SPRIG IN OUR HAIR TO REMEMBER THAT OUR FAMILY SAW THE FIRST TREE IN GWAII HAANAS.
BUT HERE IN NADEN HARBOUR AND IN MASSETT INLET....
-TREE FARM AND TIMBER LISENCES
THERE IS NOTHING THERE FOR US, DUNEE
* EXPAND ON FOREST SCENE USE PG 1 BK 1 MOVE BOTOM SECTION ELSEWHERE.
1

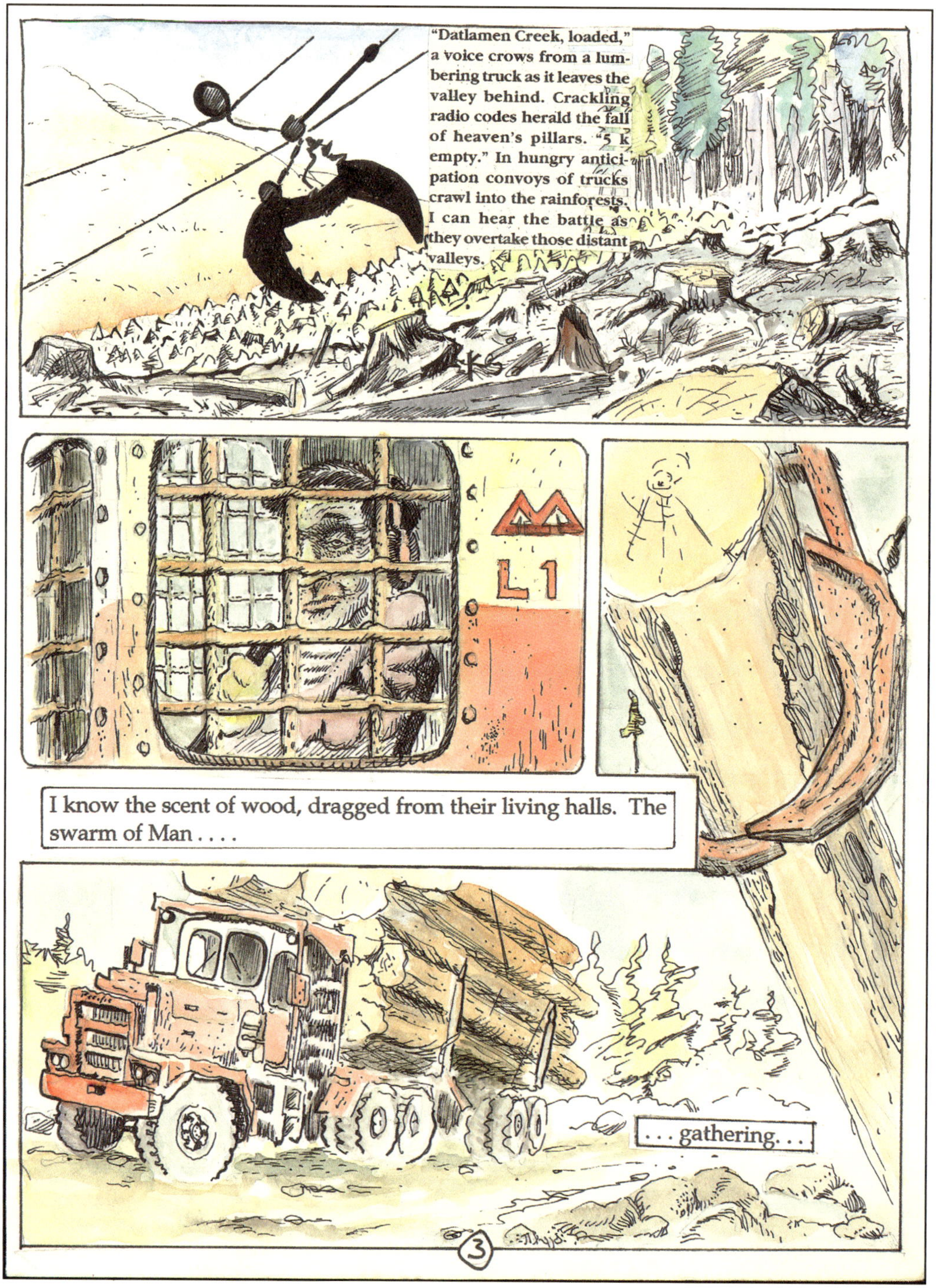
"Datlamen Creek, loaded," a voice crows from a lumbering truck as it leaves the valley behind. Crackling radio codes herald the fall of heaven's pillars. "5 k empty." In hungry anticipation convoys of trucks crawl into the rainforests. I can hear the battle as they overtake those distant valleys.
L1
I know the scent of wood, dragged from their living halls. The swarm of Man . . . .
. . . gathering. . .
3

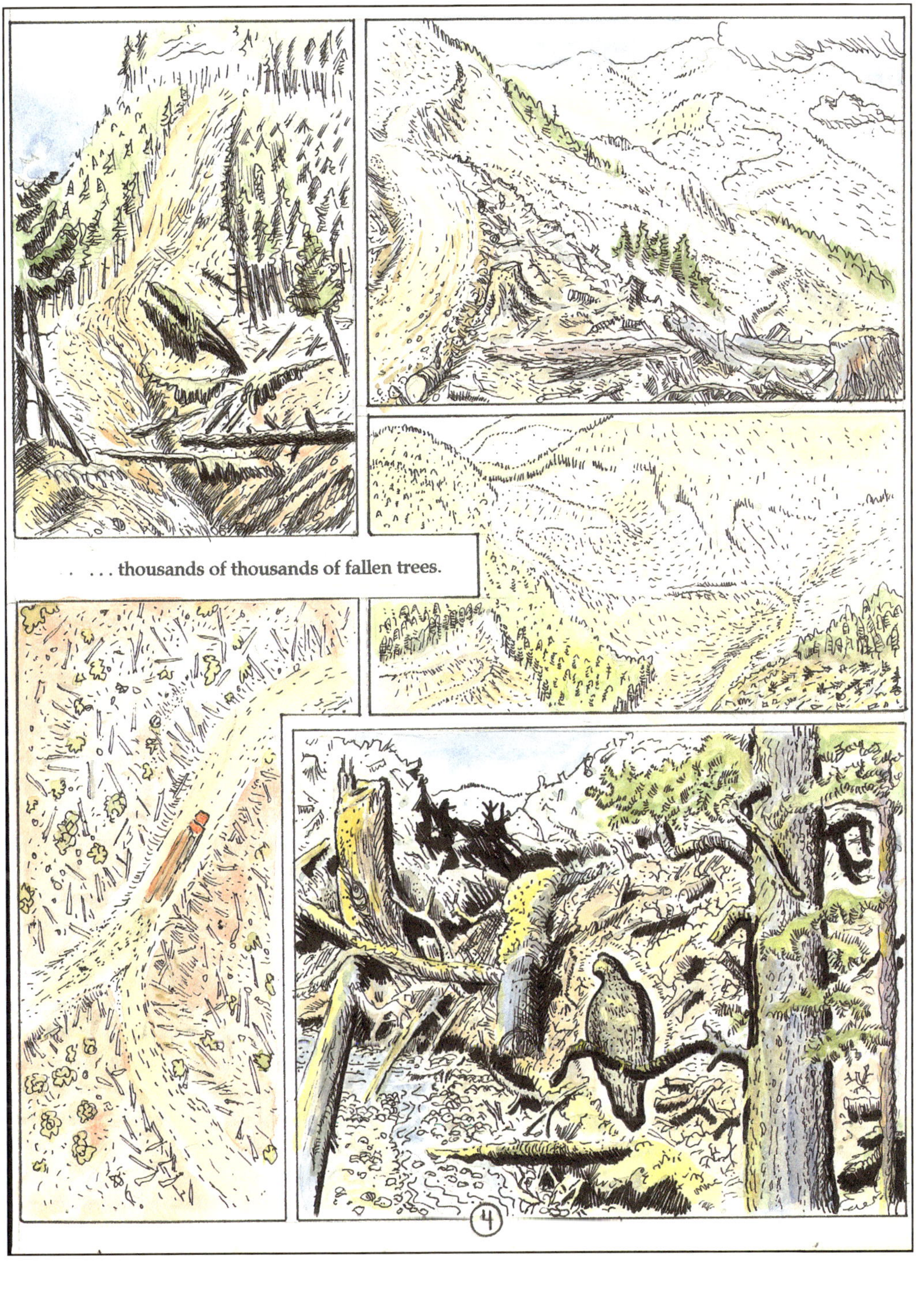
. . . . . thousands of thousands of fallen trees.
4

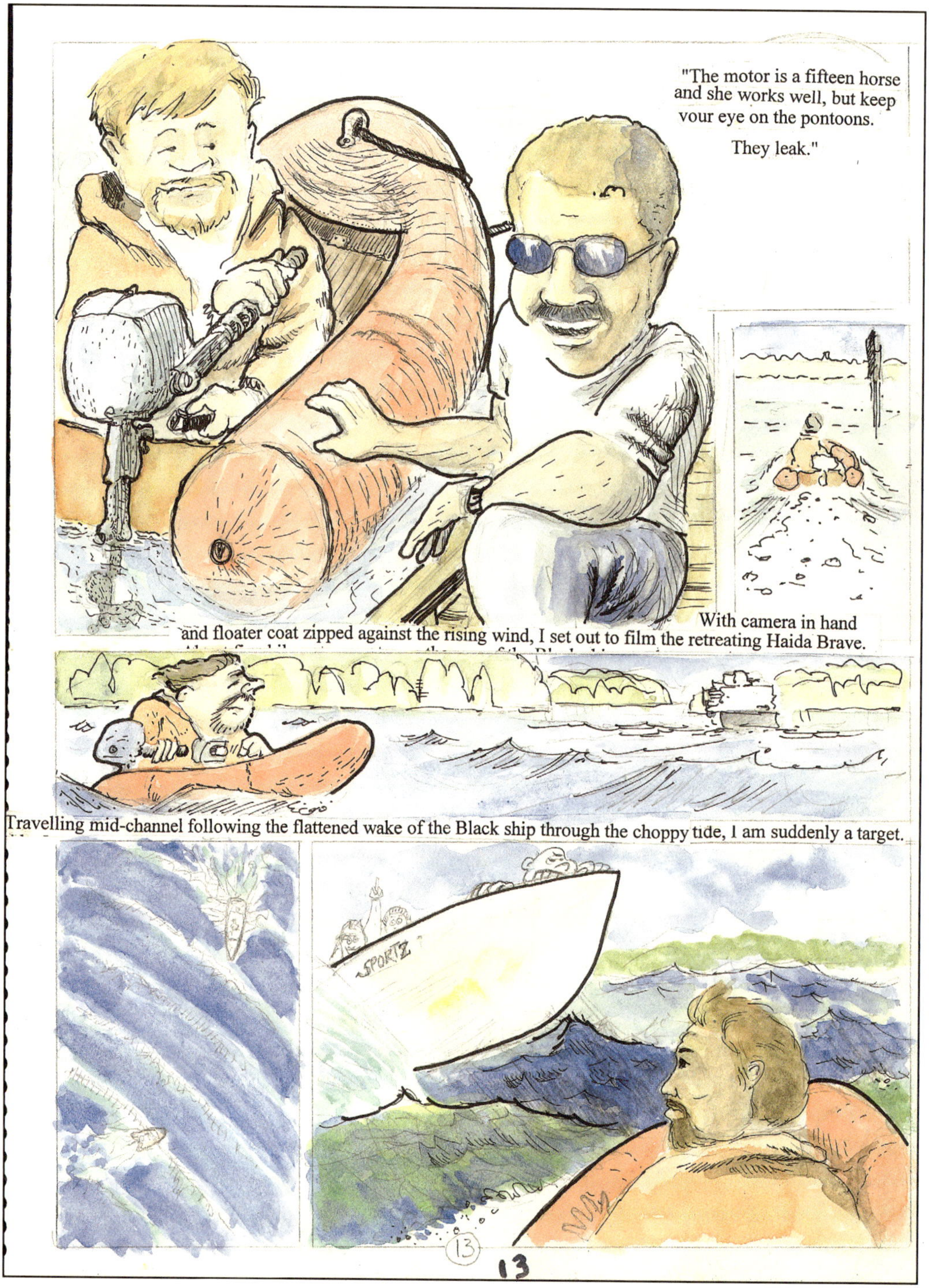
"The motor is a fifteen horse and she works well, but keep your eye on the pontoons.
They leak."
With camera in hand and floater coat zipped against the rising wind, I set out to film the retreating Haida Brave.
Travelling mid-channel following the flattened wake of the Black ship through the choppy tide, I am suddenly a target.
SPORTZ
13
13

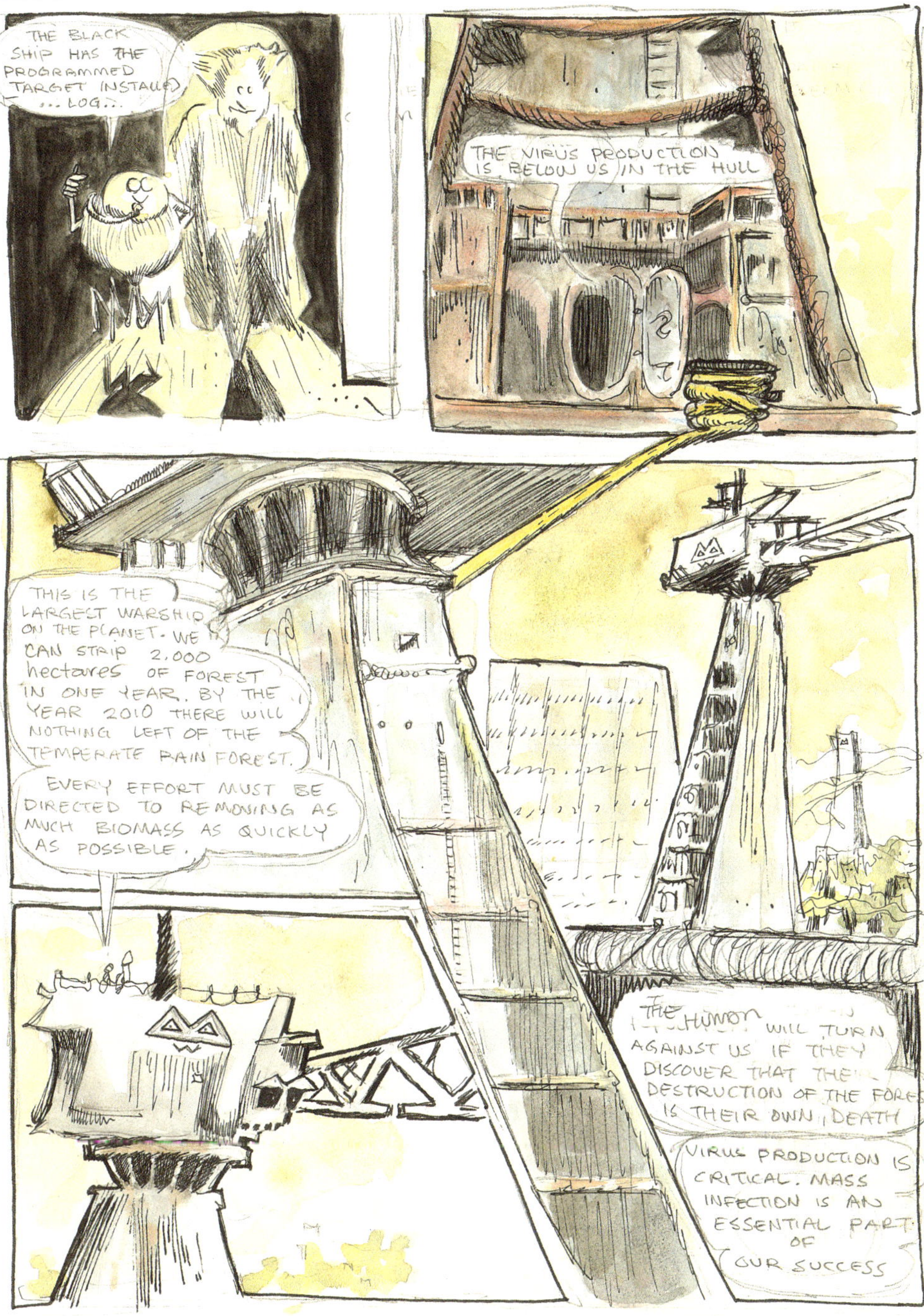
THE BLACK SHIP HAS THE PROGRAMMED TARGET INSTALLED ...LOG...
THE VIRUS PRODUCTION IS BELOW US IN THE HULL
THIS IS THE LARGEST WARSHIP ON THE PLANET. WE CAN STRIP 2,000 hectares OF FOREST IN ONE YEAR. BY THE YEAR 2010 THERE WILL NOTHING LEFT OF THE TEMPERATE RAIN FOREST.
EVERY EFFORT MUST BE DIRECTED TO REMOVING AS MUCH BIOMASS AS QUICKLY AS POSSIBLE.
The Human WILL TURN AGAINST US IF THEY DISCOVER THAT THE DESTRUCTION OF THE FOREST IS THEIR OWN DEATH
VIRUS PRODUCTION IS CRITICAL. MASS INFECTION IS AN ESSENTIAL PART OF OUR SUCCESS

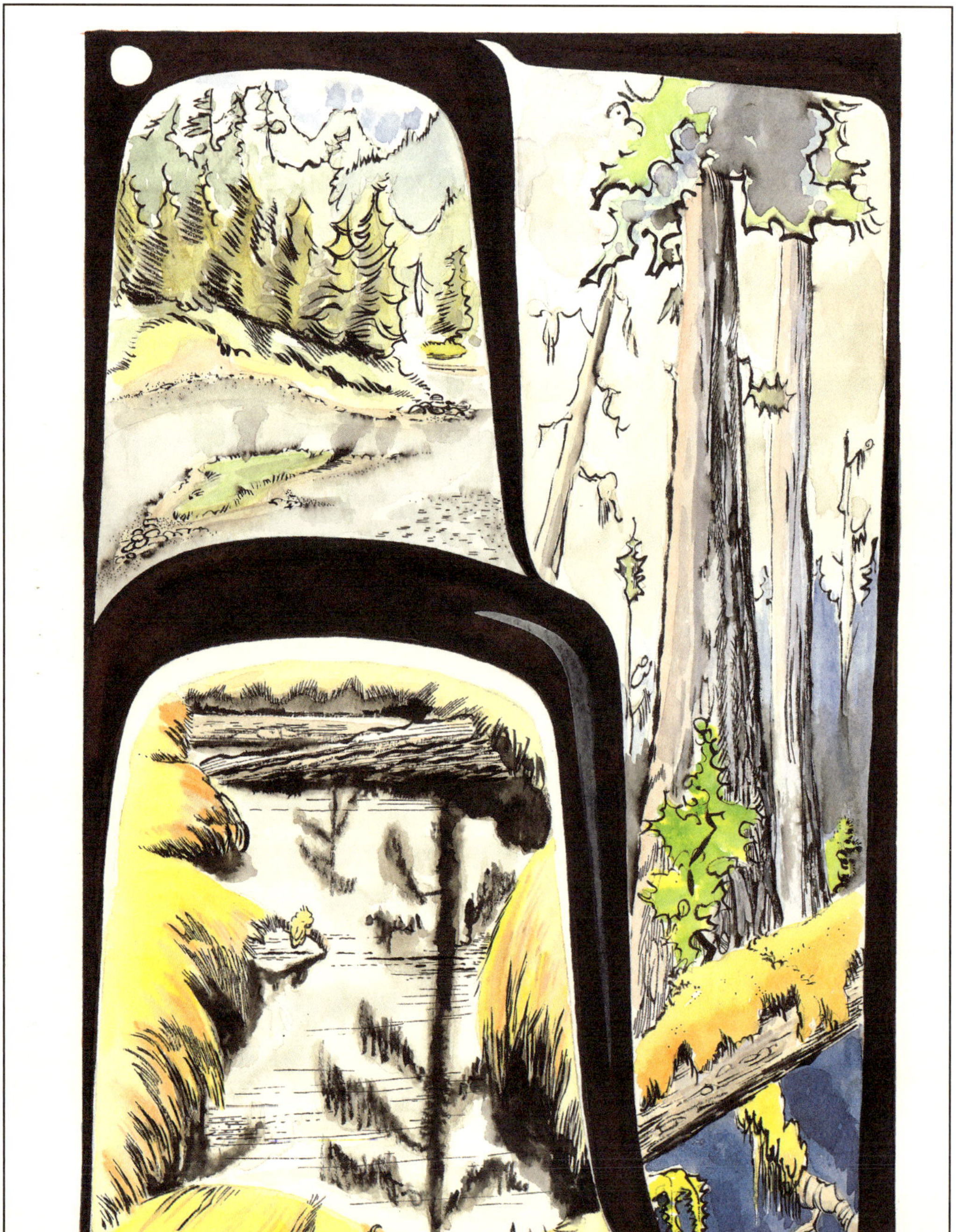

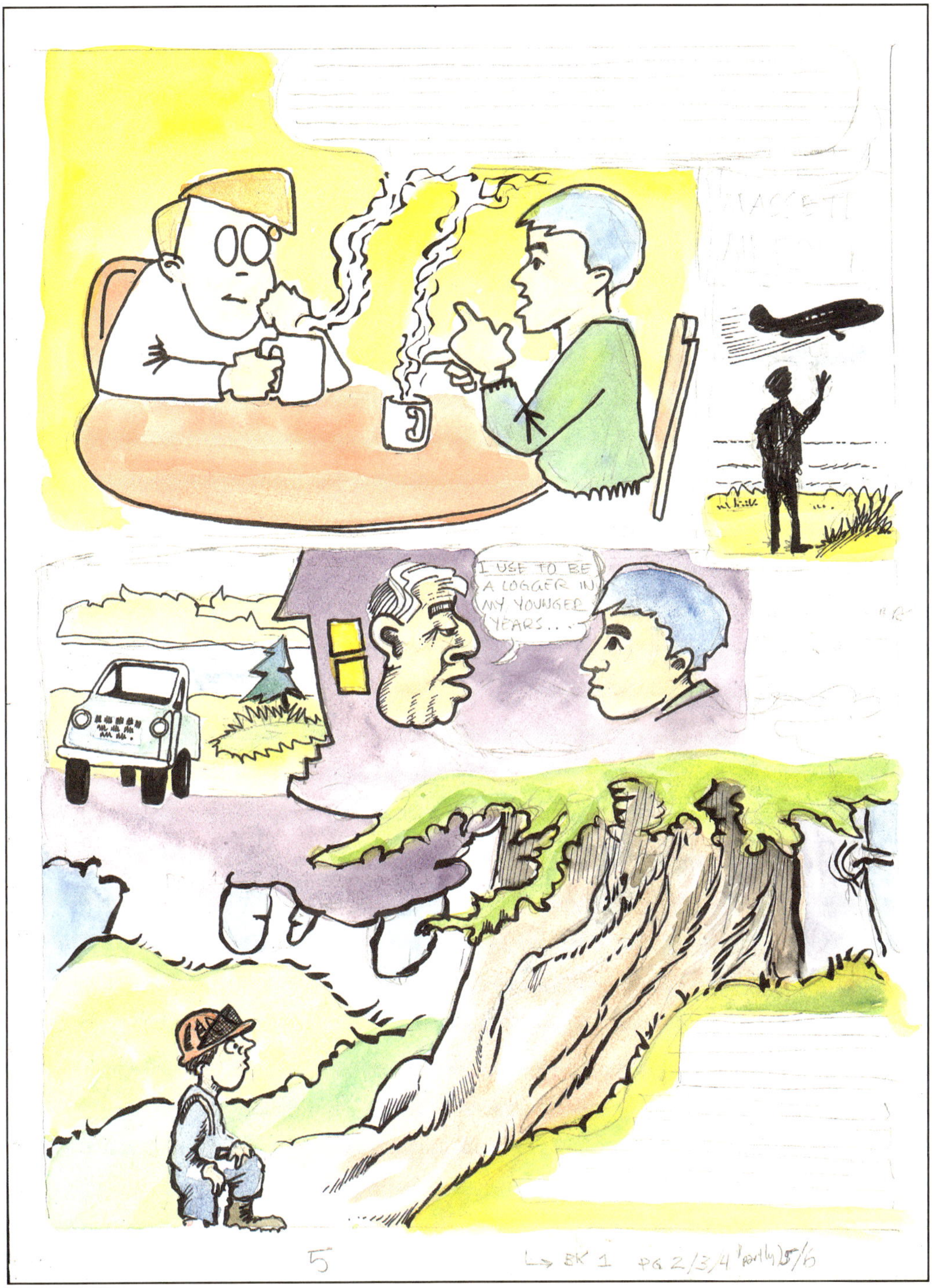
I USE TO BE A LOGGER IN MY YOUNGER YEARS...

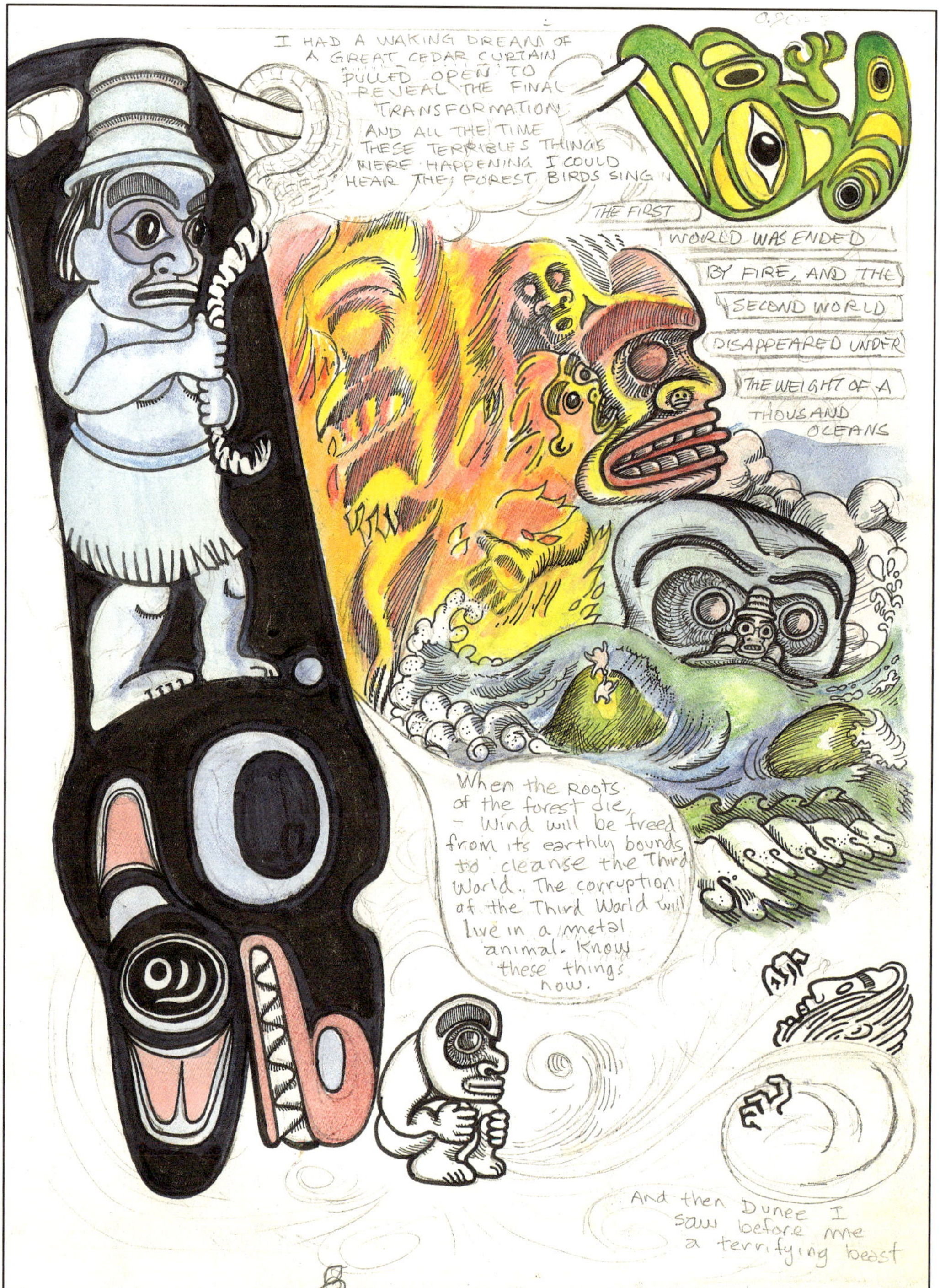
I HAD A WAKING DREAM OF A GREAT CEDAR CURTAIN PULLED OPEN TO REVEAL THE FINAL TRANSFORMATION AND ALL THE TIME THESE TERRIBLE THINGS WERE HAPPENING I COULD HEAR THE FOREST BIRDS SING
THE FIRST WORLD WAS ENDED BY FIRE, AND THE SECOND WORLD DISAPPEARED UNDER THE WEIGHT OF A THOUSAND OCEANS
When the roots of the forest die, Wind will be freed from its earthly bounds to cleanse the Third World. The corruption of the Third World will live in a metal animal. Know these things now.
And then Dunee I saw before me a terrifying beast

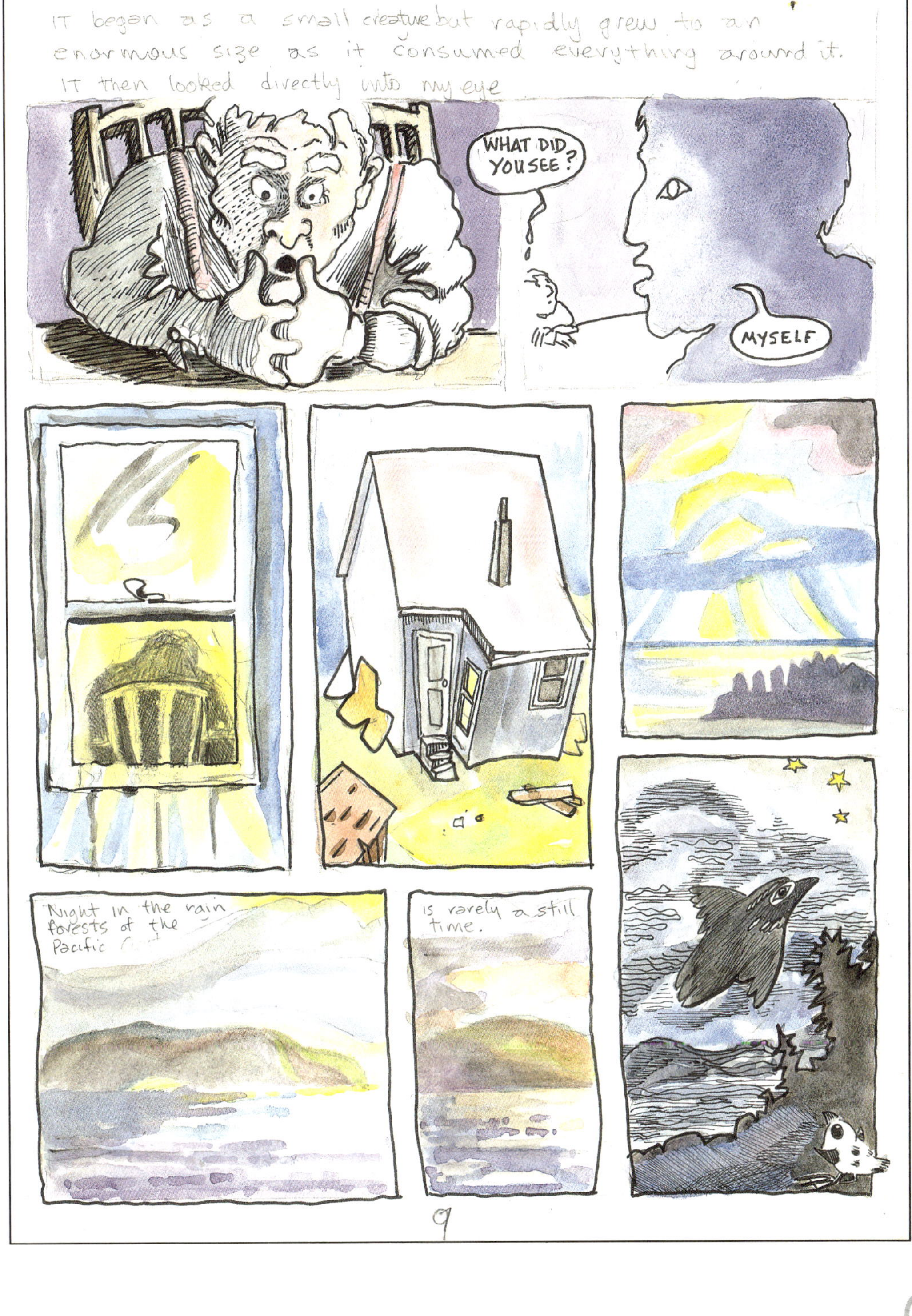

IT began as a small creature but rapidly grew to an enormous size as it consumed everything around it. IT then looked directly into my eye
WHAT DID YOU SEE?
MYSELF
Night in the rain forests of the Pacific
is rarely a still time.
9

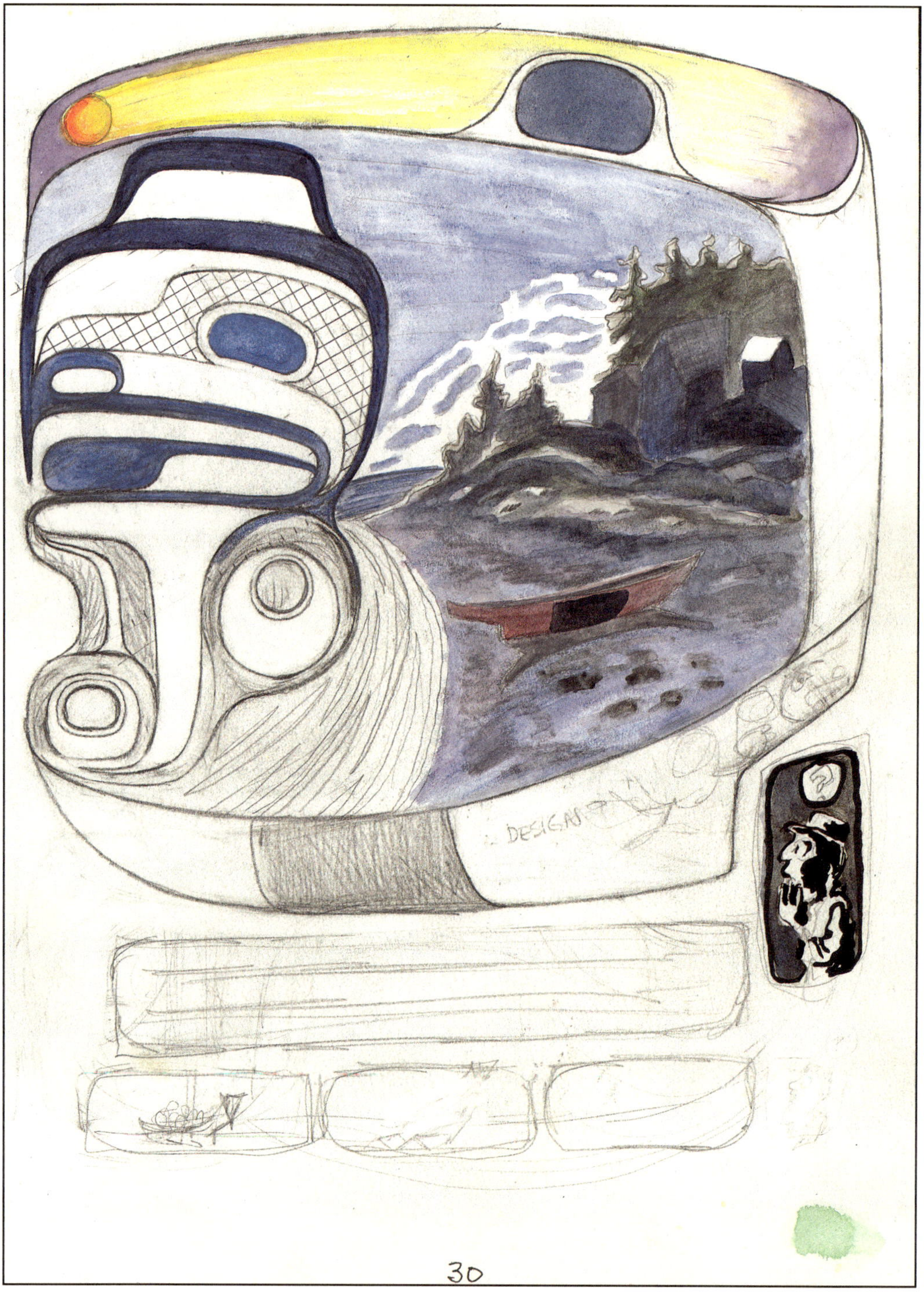
DESIGN
30

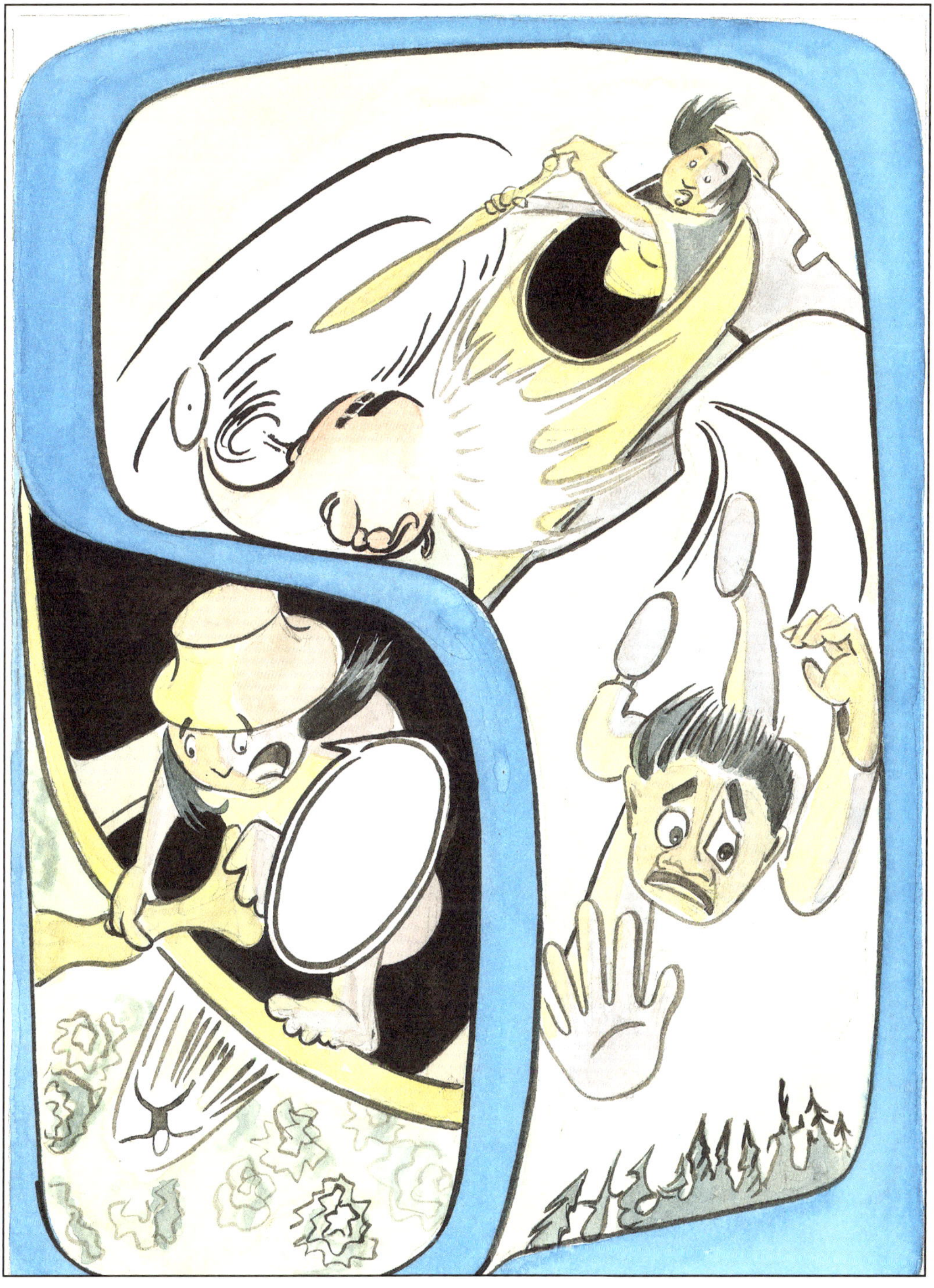

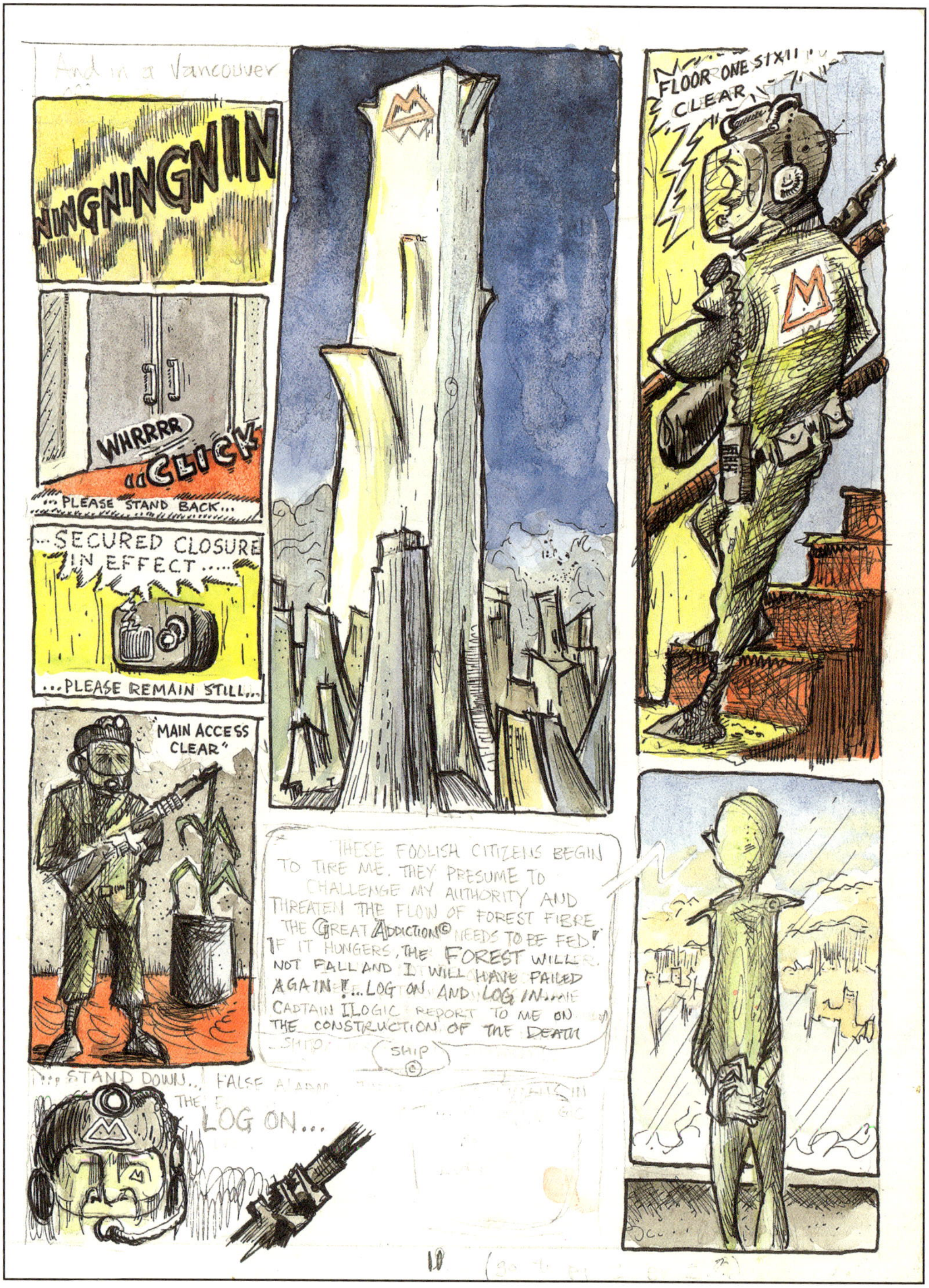

And in a Vancouver
NINGNINGNIN
WHRRRR
CLICK
...PLEASE STAND BACK...
...SECURED CLOSURE IN EFFECT.....
...PLEASE REMAIN STILL...
MAIN ACCESS CLEAR"
FLOOR ONE SIX CLEAR
THESE FOOLISH CITIZENS BEGIN TO TIRE ME. THEY PRESUME TO CHALLENGE MY AUTHORITY AND THREATEN THE FLOW OF FOREST FIBRE. THE GREAT ADDICTION© NEEDS TO BE FED! IF IT HUNGERS, THE FOREST WILL NOT FALL AND I WILL HAVE FAILED AGAIN!...LOG ON AND LOG IN... CAPTAIN ILOGIC REPORT TO ME ON THE CONSTRUCTION OF THE DEATH SHIP©
...STAND DOWN... FALSE ALARM
LOG ON...
10

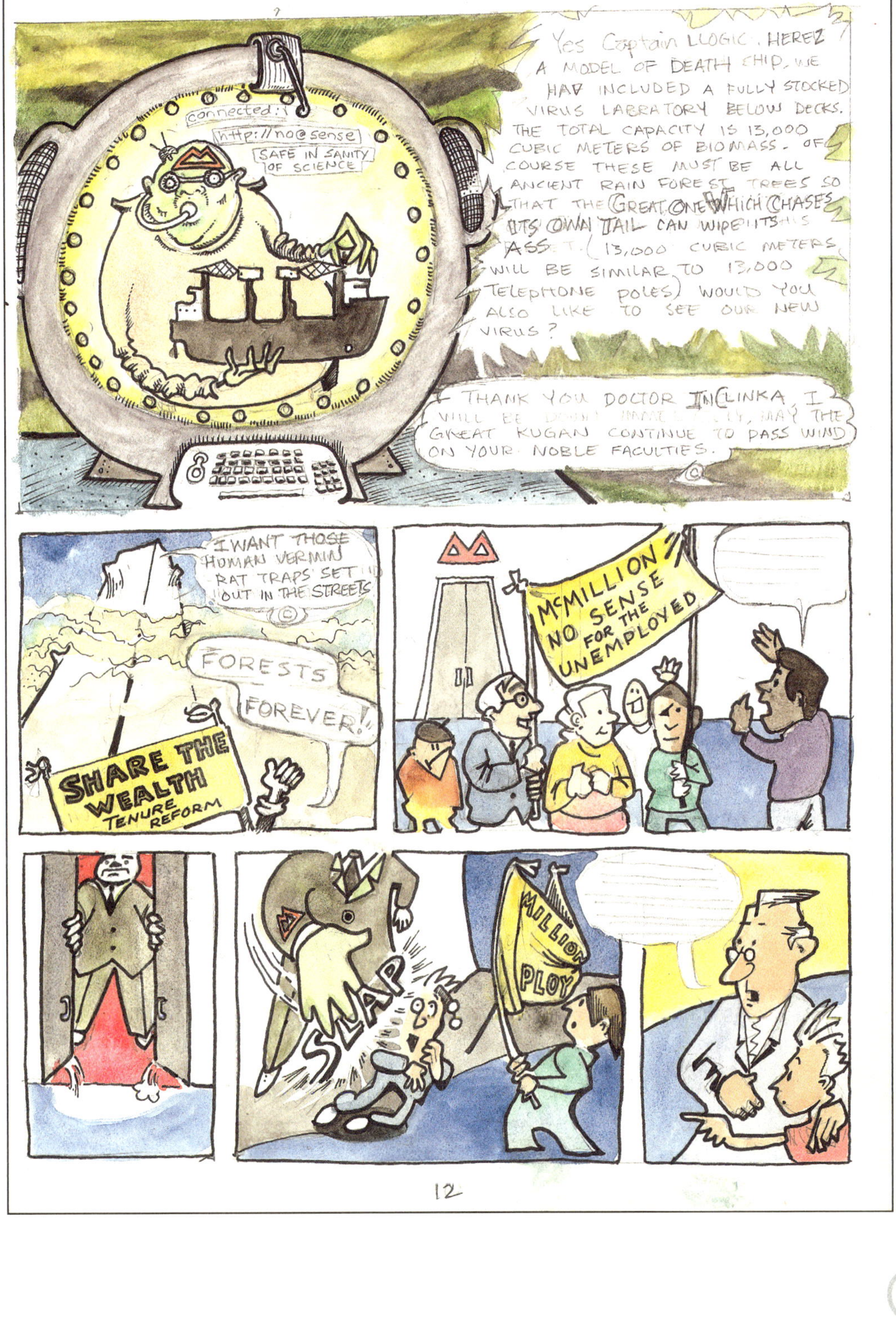
connected:
http://no@sense
SAFE IN SANITY OF SCIENCE
Yes Captain LLOGIC. HEREZ A MODEL OF DEATH SHIP. WE HAV INCLUDED A FULLY STOCKED VIRUS LABRATORY BELOW DECKS. THE TOTAL CAPACITY IS 13,000 CUBIC METERS OF BIOMASS. OF COURSE THESE MUST BE ALL ANCIENT RAIN FOREST TREES SO THAT THE GREAT ONE WHICH CHASES ITS OWN TAIL CAN WIPE ITS ASS. (13,000 CUBIC METERS WILL BE SIMILAR TO 13,000 TELEPHONE POLES) WOULD YOU ALSO LIKE TO SEE OUR NEW VIRUS?
THANK YOU DOCTOR INCLINKA, I WILL BE DOWN IMMEDIATELY, MAY THE GREAT KUGAN CONTINUE TO PASS WIND ON YOUR NOBLE FACULTIES.
I WANT THOSE HUMAN VERMIN RAT TRAPS SET OUT IN THE STREETS
FORESTS FOREVER!
SHARE THE WEALTH TENURE REFORM
McMILLION NO SENSE FOR THE UNEMPLOYED
SLAP
MILLION PLOY
12

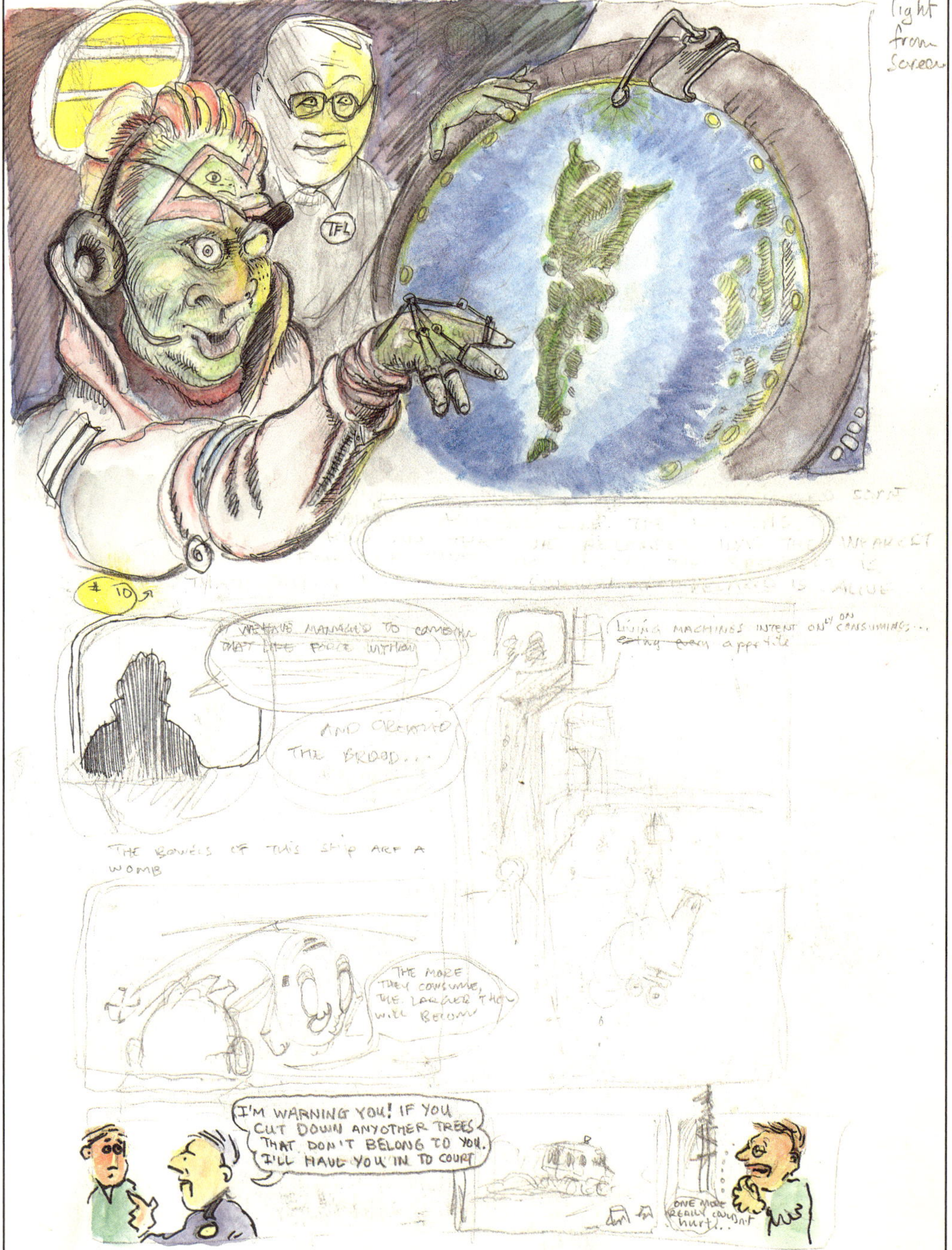
light from Screen
TFL
10
WE HAVE MANAGED TO COMBINE THAT LIFE FORCE WITHIN
AND CREATING THE BROOD...
Living MACHINES INTENT ONLY ON CONSUMING... eating every appetite
THE BOWELS OF THIS SHIP ARE A WOMB
THE MORE THEY CONSUME, THE LARGER THEY WILL BECOME
I'M WARNING YOU! IF YOU CUT DOWN ANYOTHER TREES THAT DON'T BELONG TO YOU. I'LL HAUL YOU IN TO COURT
ONE MORE REALLY COULDN'T hurt...
27

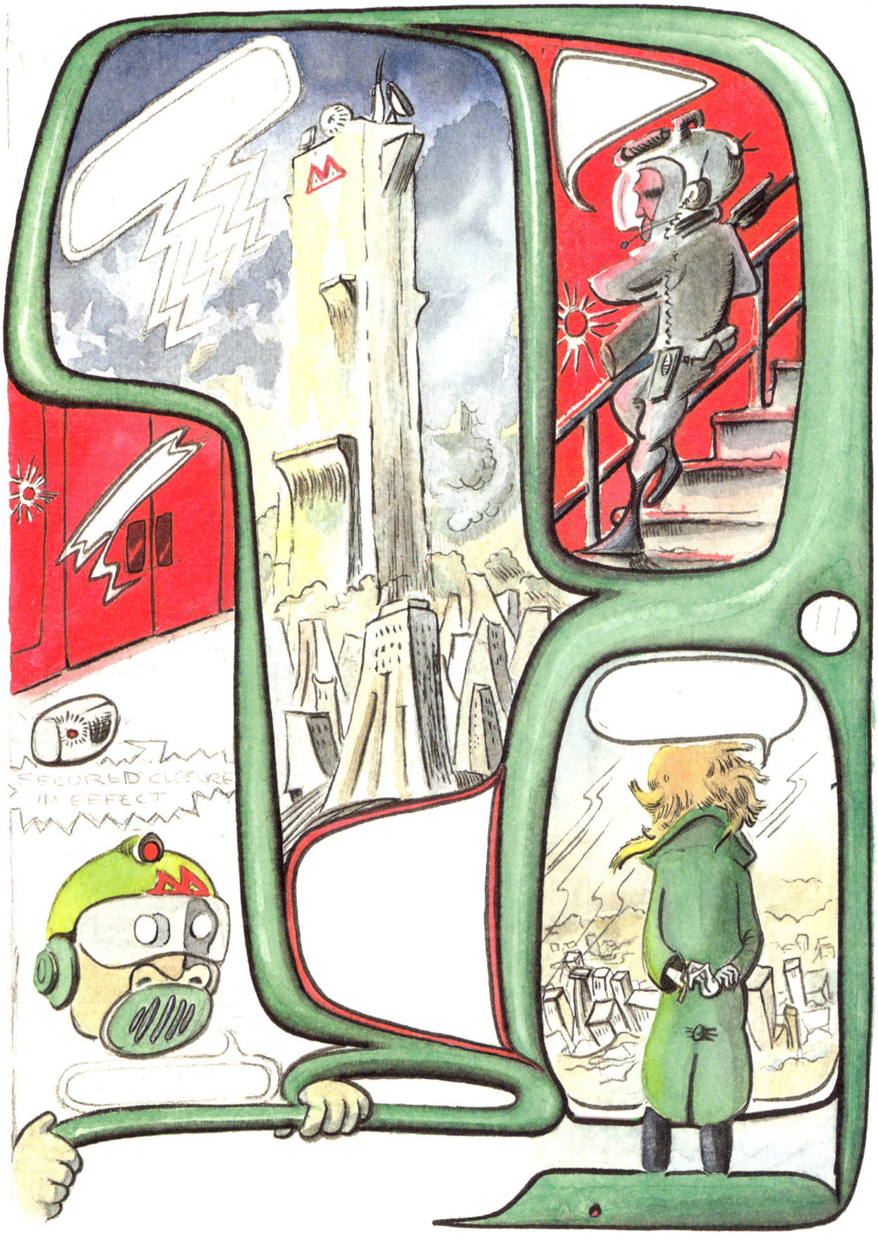
SECURED CLOSURE IN EFFECT

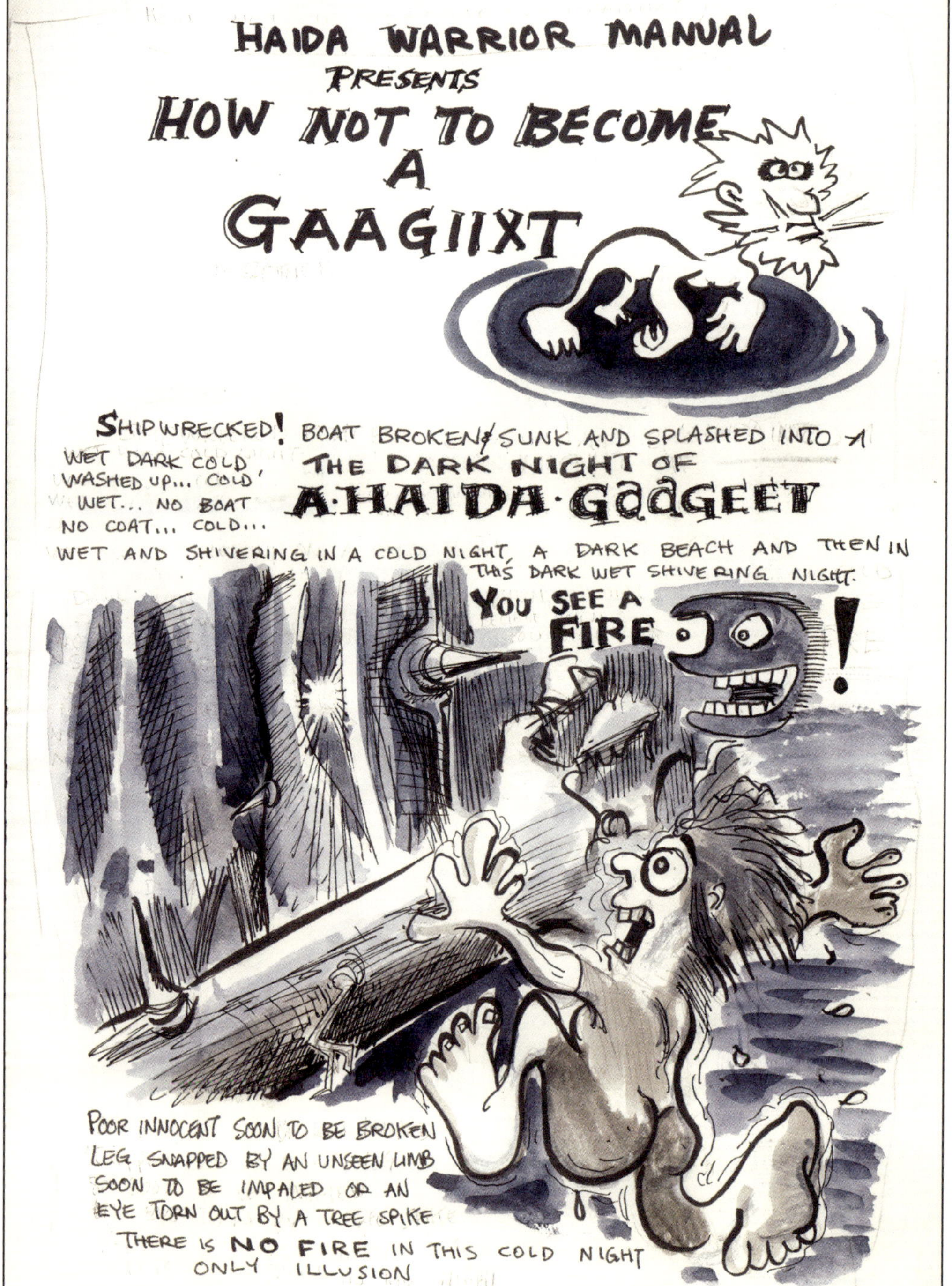
HAIDA WARRIOR MANUAL
PRESENTS
HOW NOT TO BECOME A GAAGIIXT
SHIPWRECKED! BOAT BROKEN & SUNK AND SPLASHED INTO A
THE DARK NIGHT OF
A·HAIDA·GAAGEET
WET DARK COLD, WASHED UP... COLD, WET... NO BOAT NO COAT... COLD...
WET AND SHIVERING IN A COLD NIGHT, A DARK BEACH AND THEN IN THIS DARK WET SHIVERING NIGHT.
YOU SEE A FIRE!
POOR INNOCENT SOON TO BE BROKEN LEG SNAPPED BY AN UNSEEN LIMB SOON TO BE IMPALED OR AN EYE TORN OUT BY A TREE SPIKE
THERE IS NO FIRE IN THIS COLD NIGHT ONLY ILLUSION

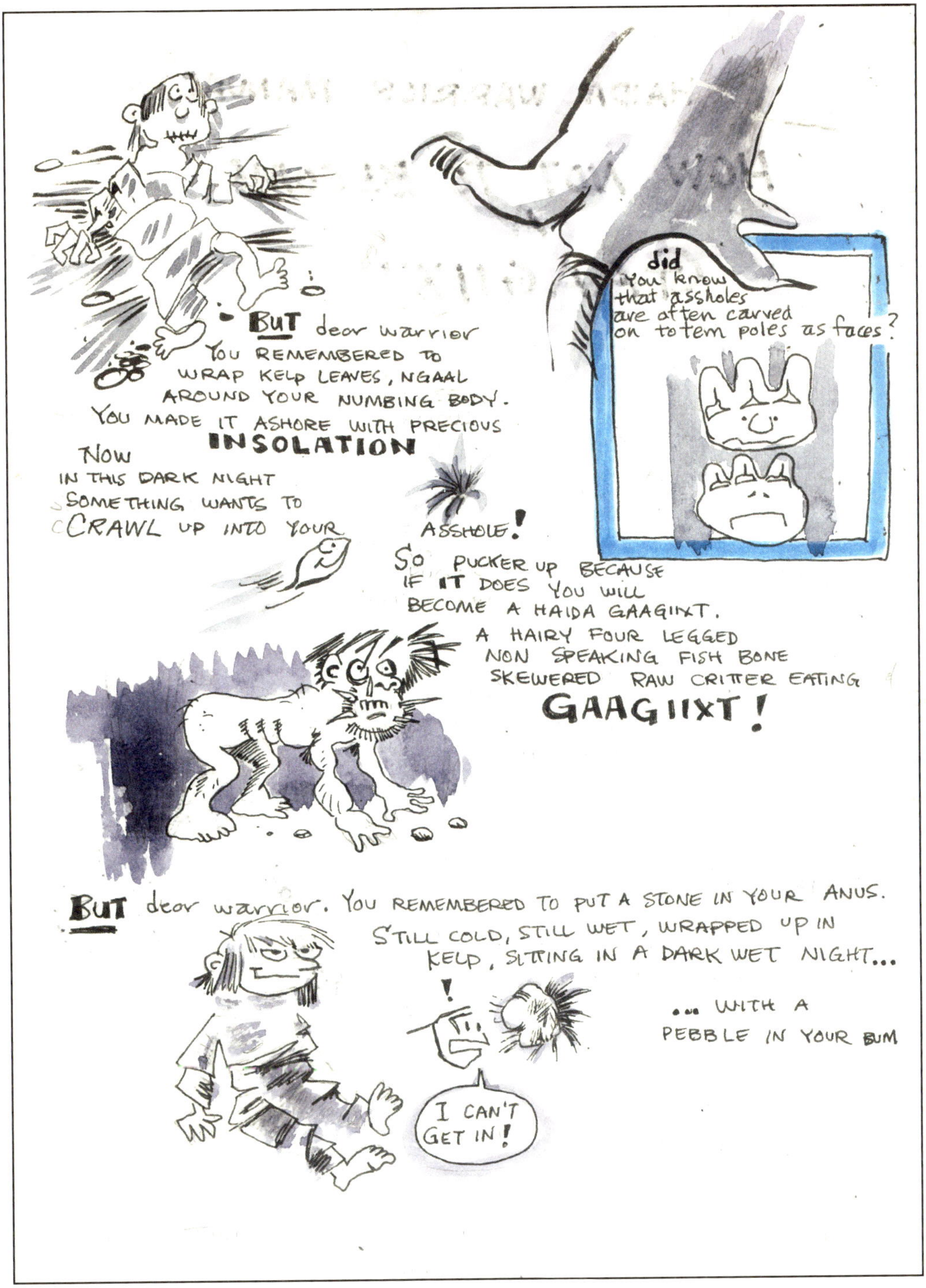

BUT dear warrior
YOU REMEMBERED TO WRAP KELP LEAVES, NGAAL AROUND YOUR NUMBING BODY.
YOU MADE IT ASHORE WITH PRECIOUS INSOLATION
did You know that assholes are often carved on totem poles as faces?
NOW IN THIS DARK NIGHT SOMETHING WANTS TO CRAWL UP INTO YOUR ASSHOLE!
SO PUCKER UP BECAUSE IF IT DOES YOU WILL BECOME A HAIDA GAAGIIXT.
A HAIRY FOUR LEGGED NON SPEAKING FISH BONE SKEWERED RAW CRITTER EATING
GAAGIIXT!
BUT dear warrior. YOU REMEMBERED TO PUT A STONE IN YOUR ANUS.
STILL COLD, STILL WET, WRAPPED UP IN KELP, SITTING IN A DARK WET NIGHT...
!
I CAN'T GET IN!
... WITH A PEBBLE IN YOUR BUM

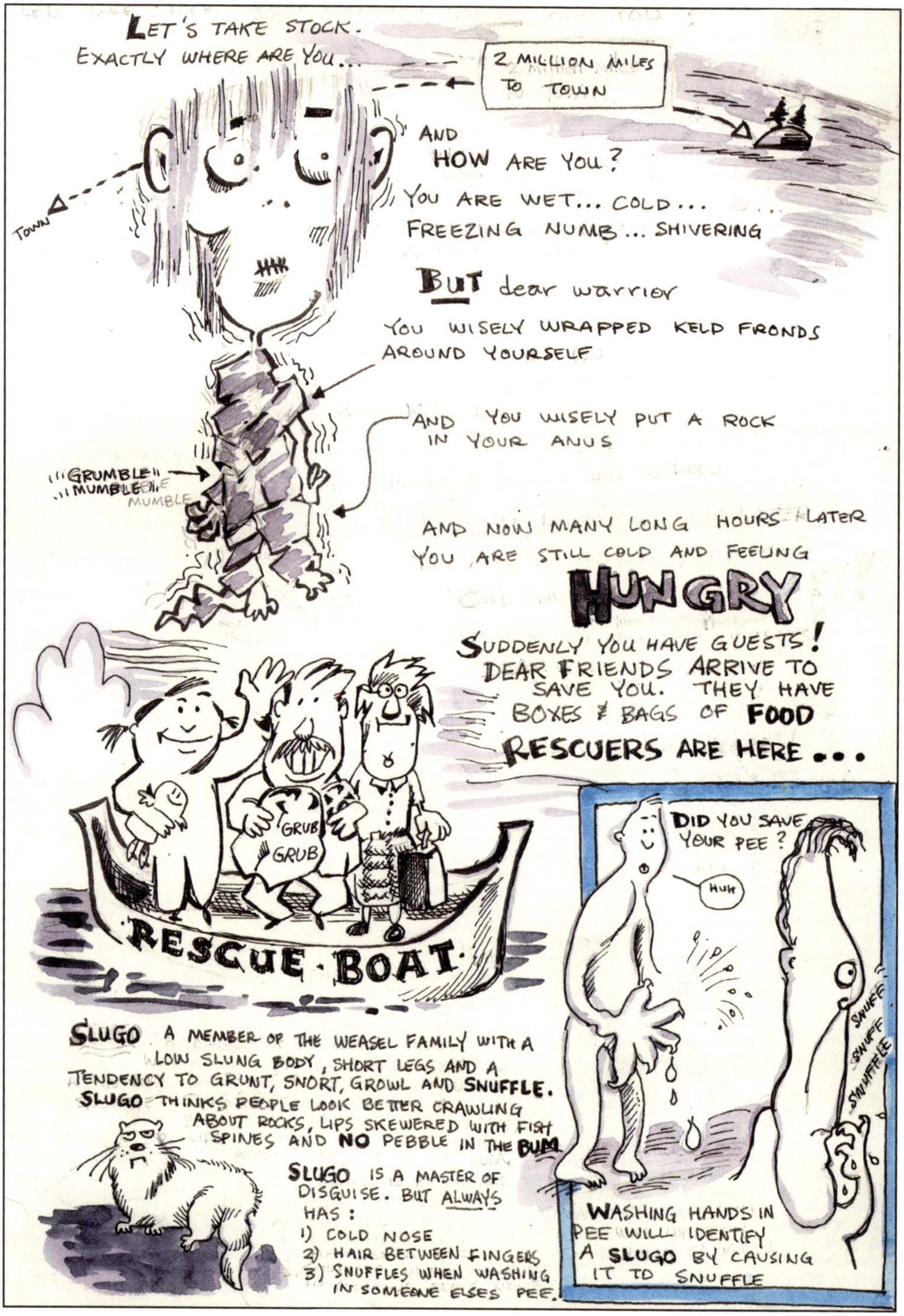
LET'S TAKE STOCK.
EXACTLY WHERE ARE YOU...
2 MILLION MILES TO TOWN
TOWN
AND HOW ARE YOU?
YOU ARE WET... COLD... FREEZING NUMB... SHIVERING
BUT dear warrior
YOU WISELY WRAPPED KELP FRONDS AROUND YOURSELF
AND YOU WISELY PUT A ROCK IN YOUR ANUS
"GRUMBLE" "MUMBLE"
AND NOW MANY LONG HOURS LATER YOU ARE STILL COLD AND FEELING
HUNGRY
SUDDENLY YOU HAVE GUESTS! DEAR FRIENDS ARRIVE TO SAVE YOU. THEY HAVE BOXES & BAGS OF FOOD
RESCUERS ARE HERE...
GRUB GRUB
RESCUE·BOAT
DID YOU SAVE YOUR PEE?
HUH
SNUFF SNUFF SNUFFLE
WASHING HANDS IN PEE WILL IDENTIFY A SLUGO BY CAUSING IT TO SNUFFLE
SLUGO A MEMBER OF THE WEASEL FAMILY WITH A LOW SLUNG BODY, SHORT LEGS AND A TENDENCY TO GRUNT, SNORT, GROWL AND SNUFFLE.
SLUGO THINKS PEOPLE LOOK BETTER CRAWLING ABOUT ROCKS, LIPS SKEWERED WITH FISH SPINES AND NO PEBBLE IN THE BUM.
SLUGO IS A MASTER OF DISGUISE. BUT ALWAYS HAS:
1) COLD NOSE
2) HAIR BETWEEN FINGERS
3) SNUFFLES WHEN WASHING IN SOMEONE ELSES PEE.

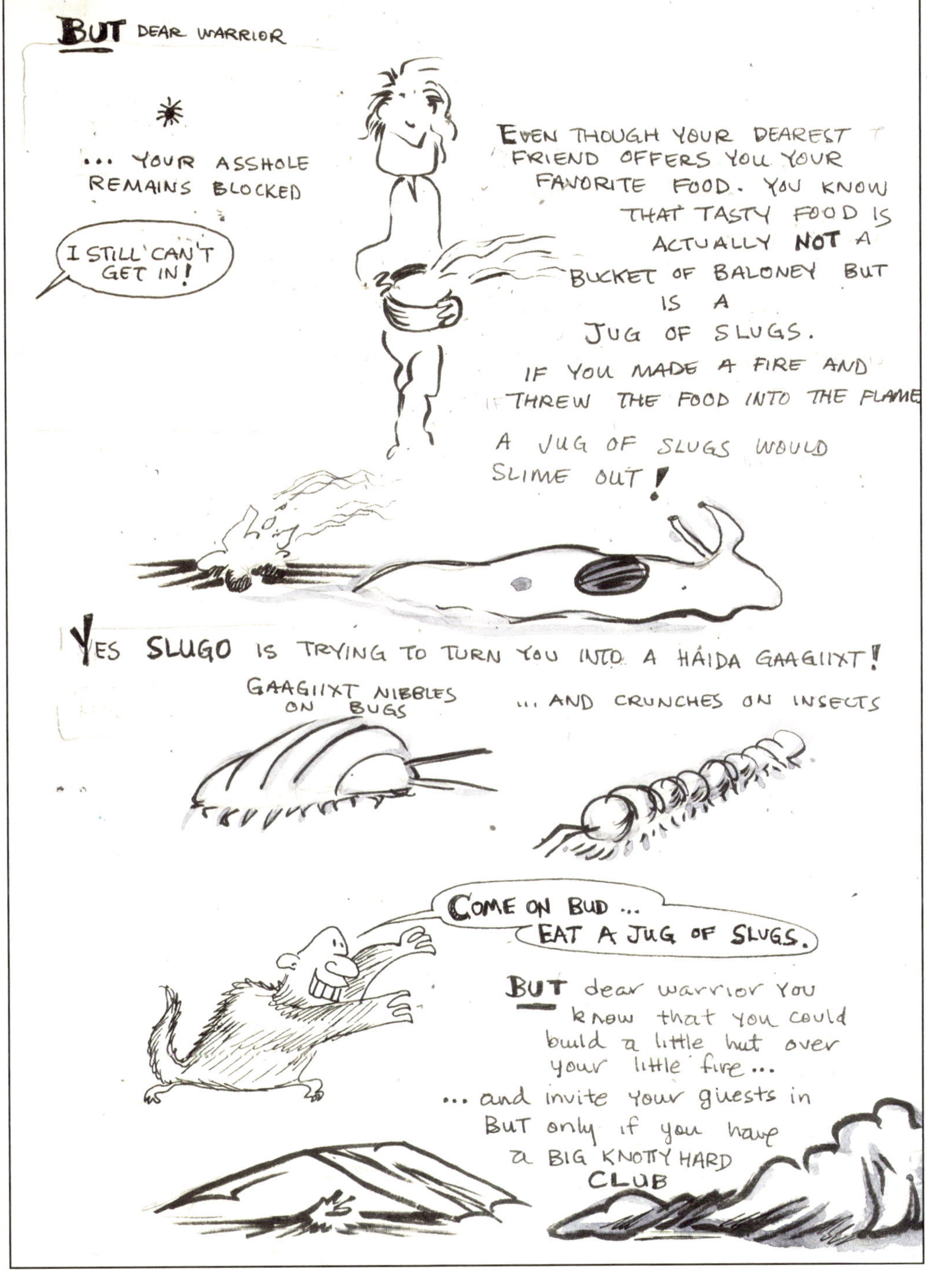
BUT DEAR WARRIOR
... YOUR ASSHOLE REMAINS BLOCKED
I STILL CAN'T GET IN!
EVEN THOUGH YOUR DEAREST FRIEND OFFERS YOU YOUR FAVORITE FOOD. YOU KNOW THAT TASTY FOOD IS ACTUALLY NOT A BUCKET OF BALONEY BUT IS A JUG OF SLUGS.
IF YOU MADE A FIRE AND THREW THE FOOD INTO THE FLAME
A JUG OF SLUGS WOULD SLIME OUT!
YES SLUGO IS TRYING TO TURN YOU INTO A HÁIDA GAAGIIXT!
GAAGIIXT NIBBLES ON BUGS
... AND CRUNCHES ON INSECTS
COME ON BUD ... EAT A JUG OF SLUGS.
BUT dear warrior You know that you could build a little hut over your little fire...
... and invite your guests in BuT only if you have a BIG KNOTTY HARD CLUB

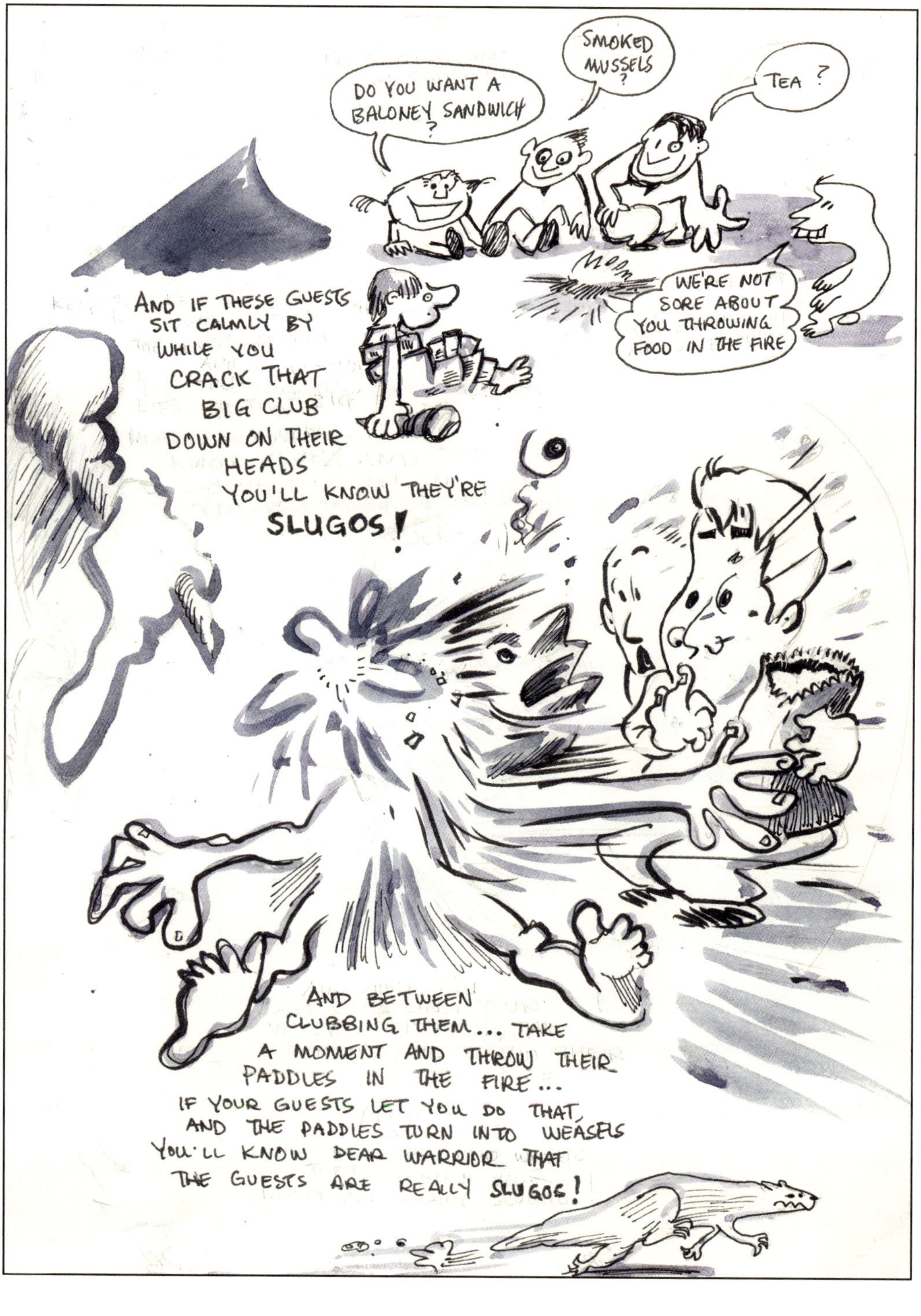

DO YOU WANT A BALONEY SANDWICH?
SMOKED MUSSELS?
TEA?
WE'RE NOT SORE ABOUT YOU THROWING FOOD IN THE FIRE
AND IF THESE GUESTS SIT CALMLY BY WHILE YOU CRACK THAT BIG CLUB DOWN ON THEIR HEADS YOU'LL KNOW THEY'RE SLUGOS!
AND BETWEEN CLUBBING THEM... TAKE A MOMENT AND THROW THEIR PADDLES IN THE FIRE... IF YOUR GUESTS LET YOU DO THAT, AND THE PADDLES TURN INTO WEASELS YOU'LL KNOW DEAR WARRIOR THAT THE GUESTS ARE REALLY SLUGOS!

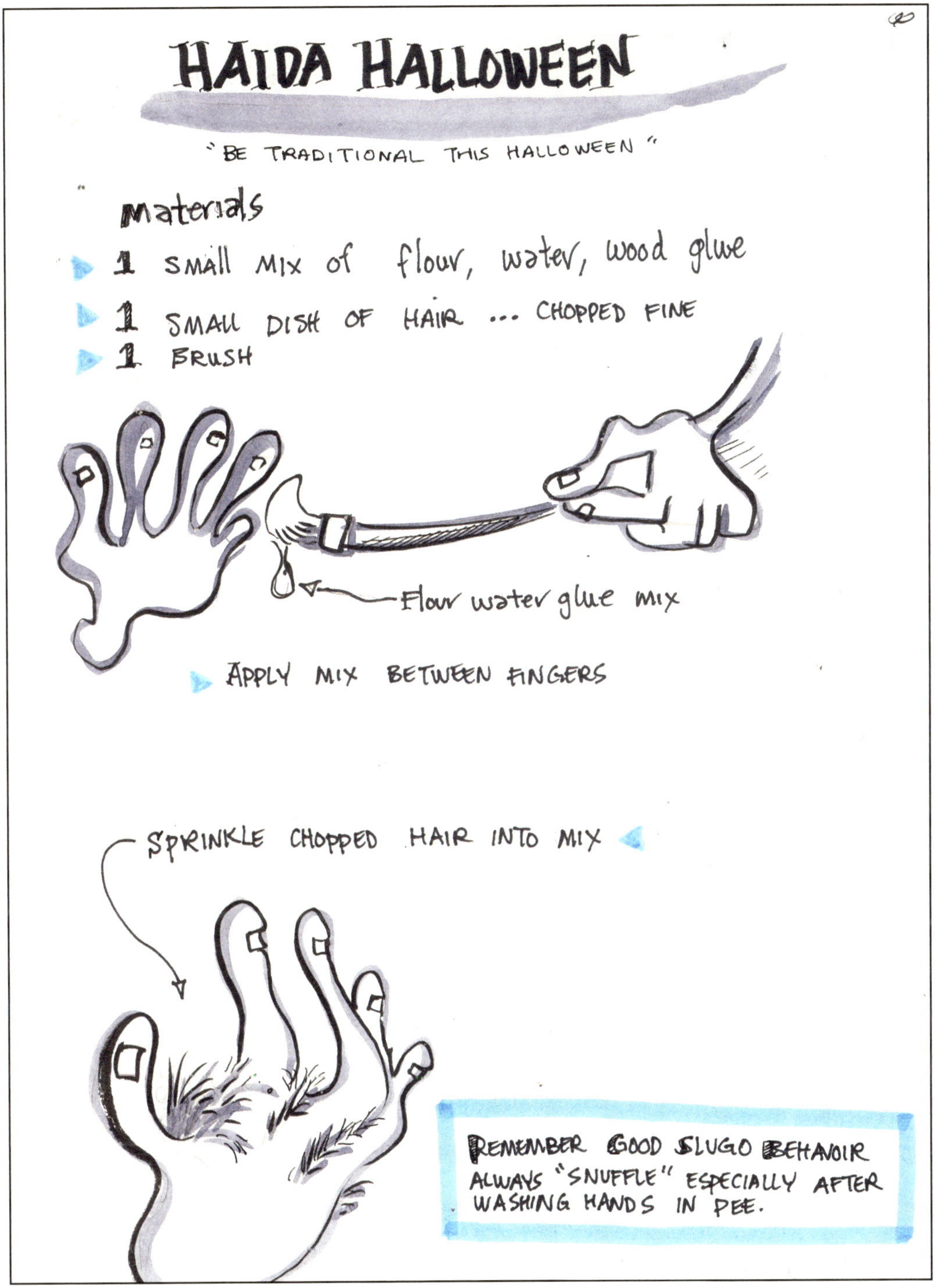
HAIDA HALLOWEEN
"BE TRADITIONAL THIS HALLOWEEN"
materials
1 SMALL MIX of flour, water, wood glue
1 SMALL DISH OF HAIR ... CHOPPED FINE
1 BRUSH
Flour water glue mix
APPLY MIX BETWEEN FINGERS
SPRINKLE CHOPPED HAIR INTO MIX
REMEMBER GOOD SLUGO BEHAVOIR
ALWAYS "SNUFFLE" ESPECIALLY AFTER WASHING HANDS IN PEE.

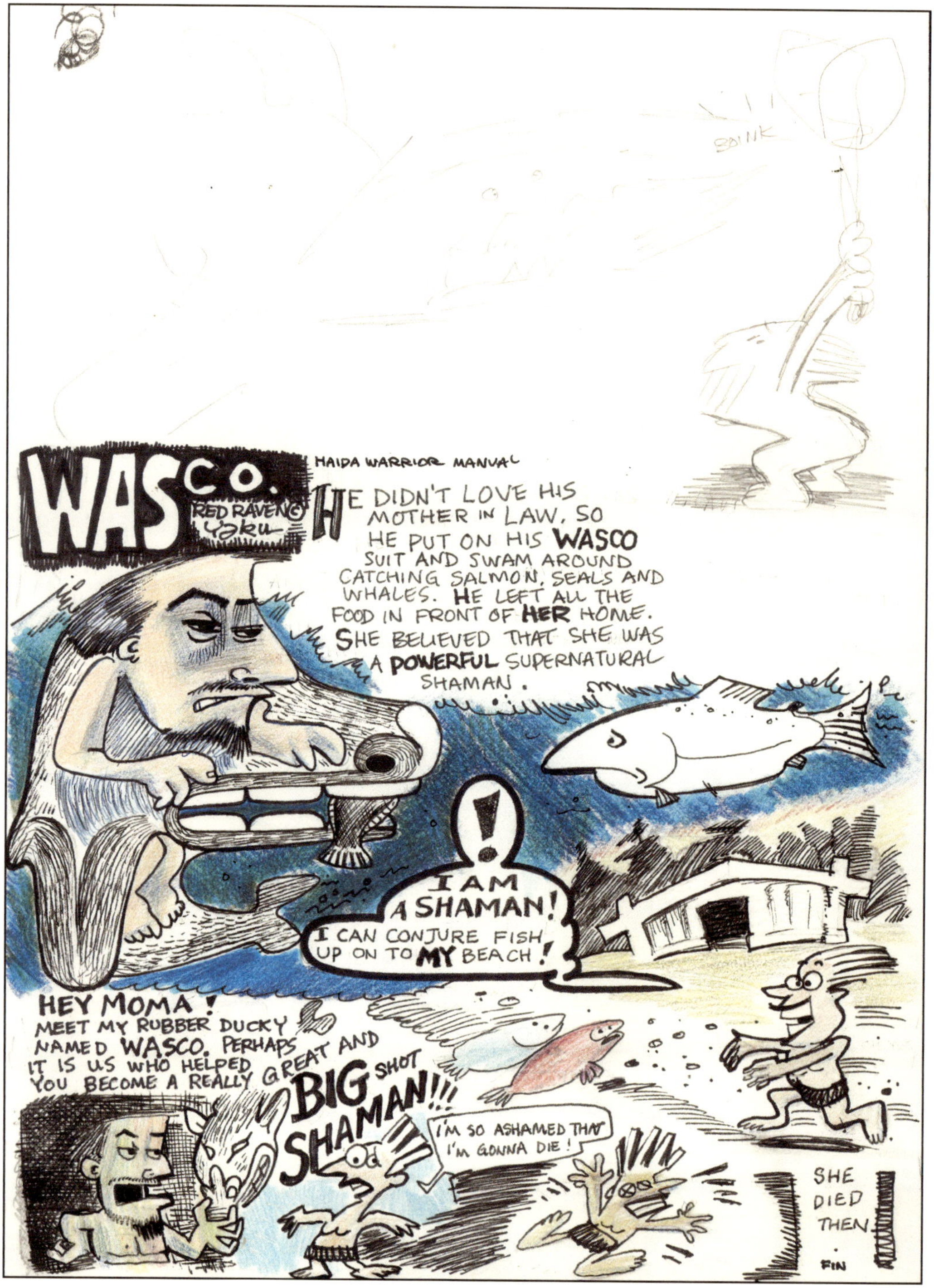
BOINK
WASCO.
RED RAVEN ©
HAIDA WARRIOR MANUAL
HE DIDN'T LOVE HIS MOTHER IN LAW, SO HE PUT ON HIS WASCO SUIT AND SWAM AROUND CATCHING SALMON, SEALS AND WHALES. HE LEFT ALL THE FOOD IN FRONT OF HER HOME. SHE BELIEVED THAT SHE WAS A POWERFUL SUPERNATURAL SHAMAN.
!
I AM A SHAMAN! I CAN CONJURE FISH UP ON TO MY BEACH!
HEY MOMA! MEET MY RUBBER DUCKY NAMED WASCO. PERHAPS IT IS US WHO HELPED YOU BECOME A REALLY GREAT AND BIG SHOT SHAMAN!!!
I'M SO ASHAMED THAT I'M GONNA DIE!
SHE DIED THEN.
FIN

Comics

Raven Kept Walking

Raven Kept Walking *is a well known Haida story of epic length, in which Raven embodies the push and pull and vices and virtues that characterize the ambivalence of human nature. Many unpublished chapters from this story remain in Michael Nicoll Yahgulanaas' personal archives, and many more chapters remain unfinished. Some chapters were previously published in publications as varied as* What Right? *2002,* Crank, *2002-2004,* Vancouver Special, *2002, and* A Lousy Tale, *2004.*

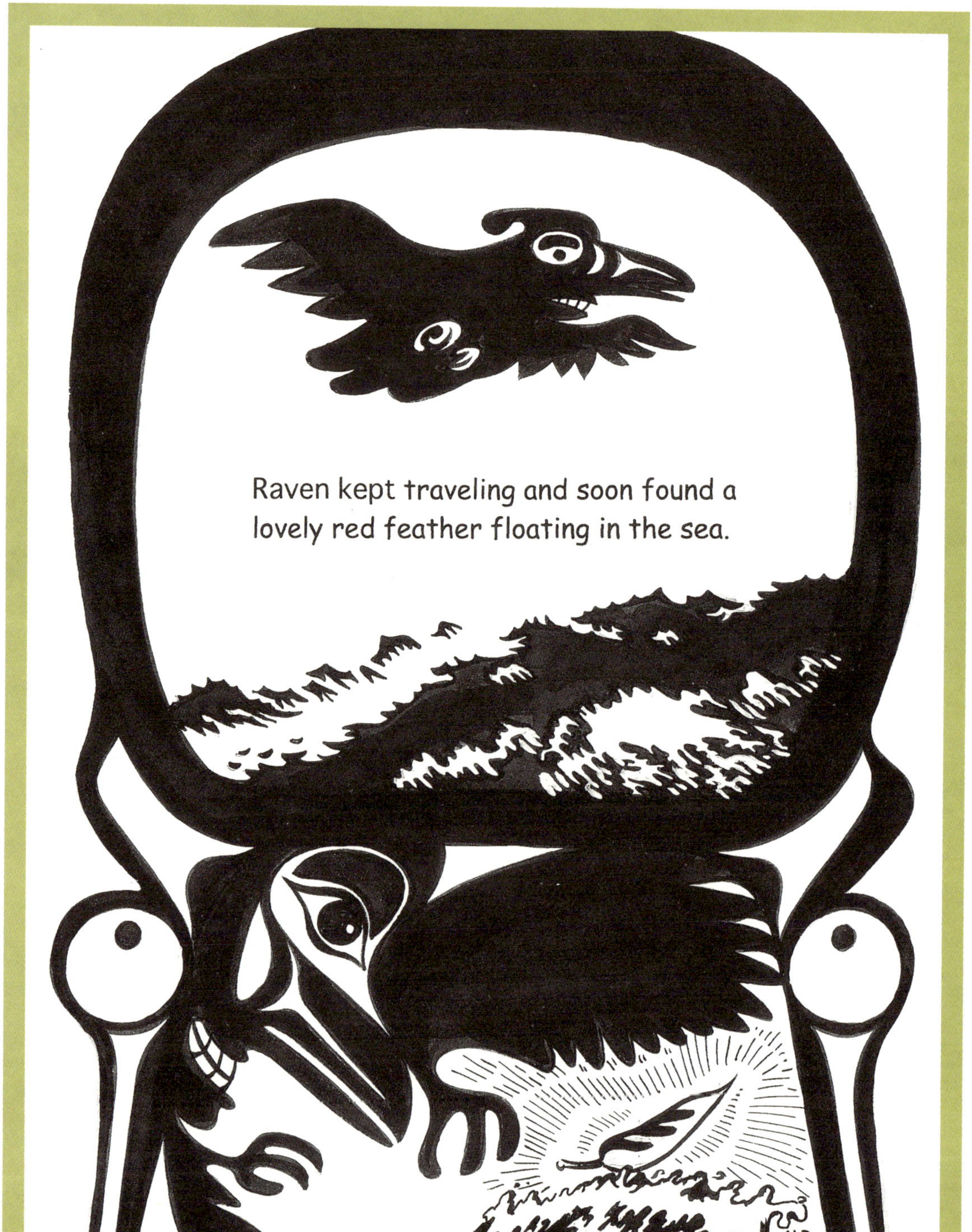
Raven kept traveling and soon found a lovely red feather floating in the sea.

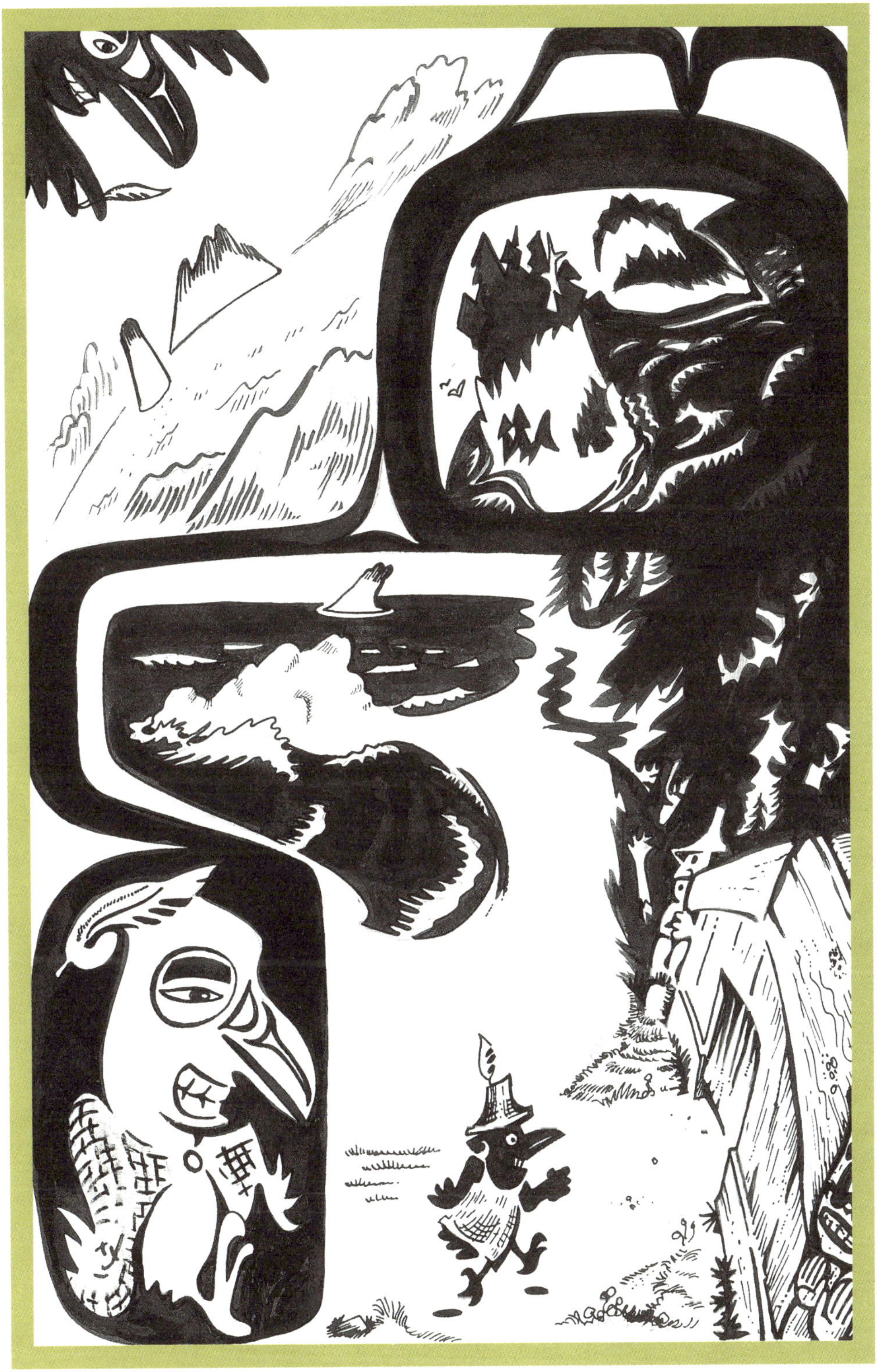

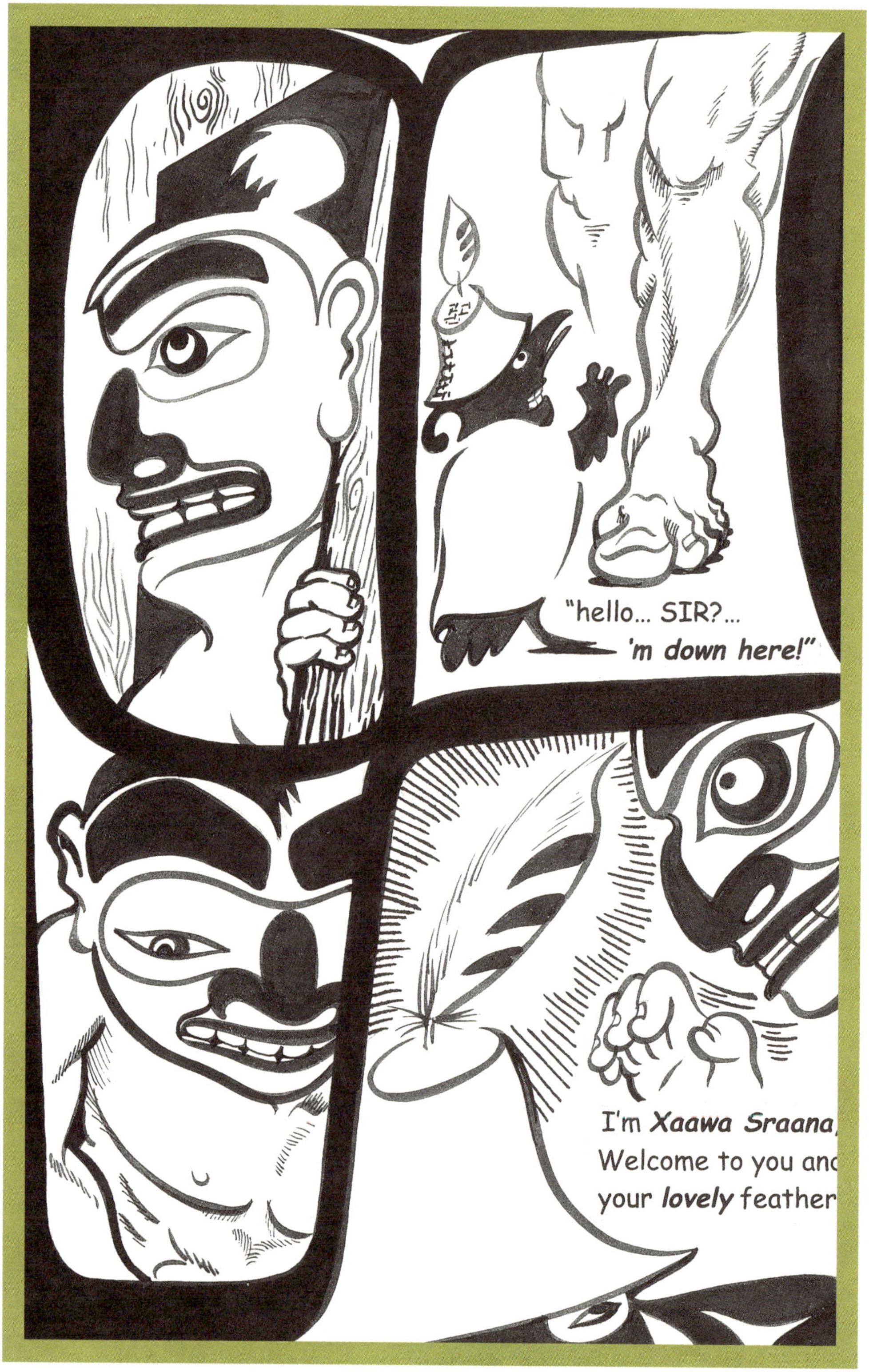
"hello... SIR?...
'm down here!"
I'm Xaawa Sraana,
Welcome to you and
your lovely feather

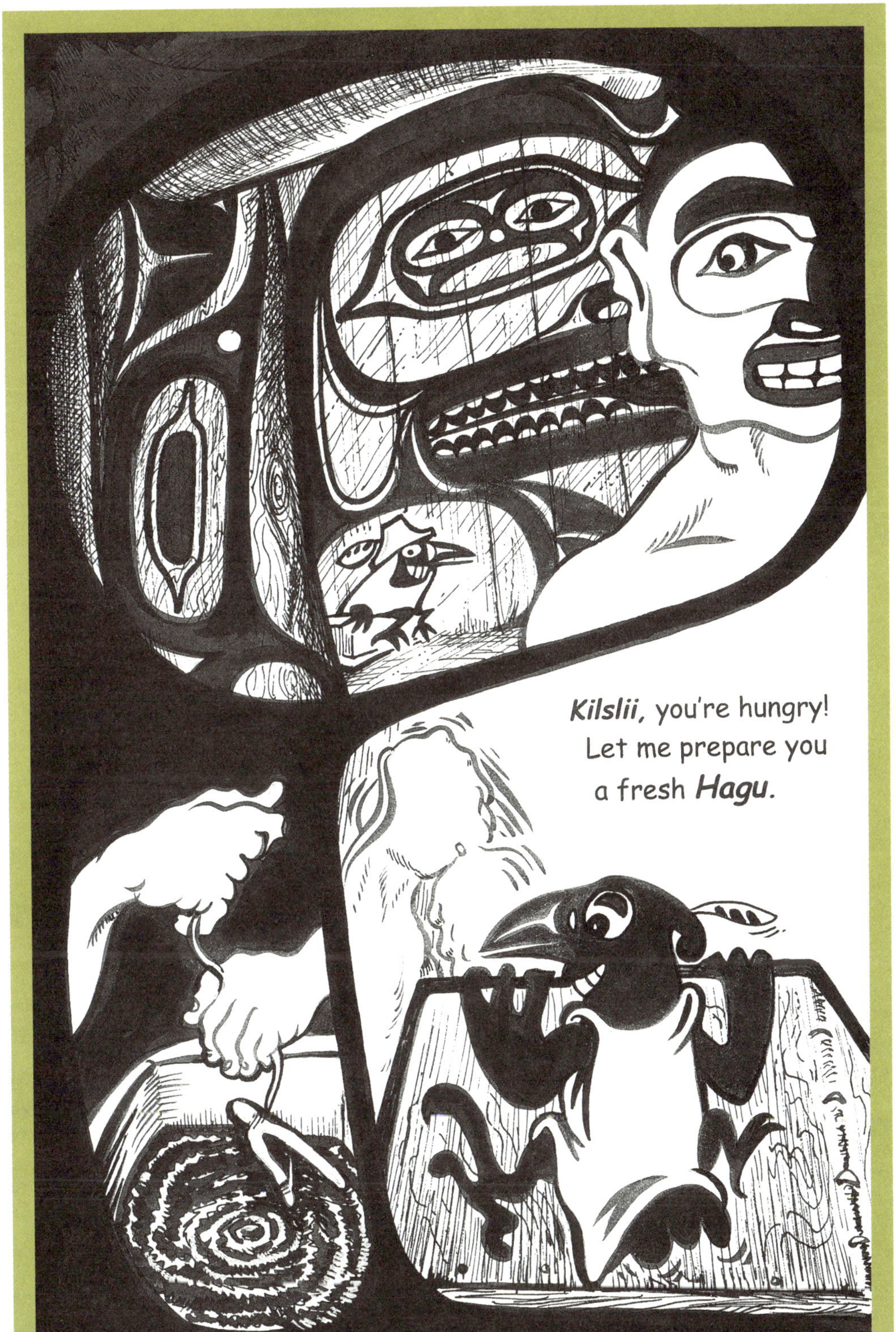
Kilslii, you're hungry! Let me prepare you a fresh ***Hagu.***

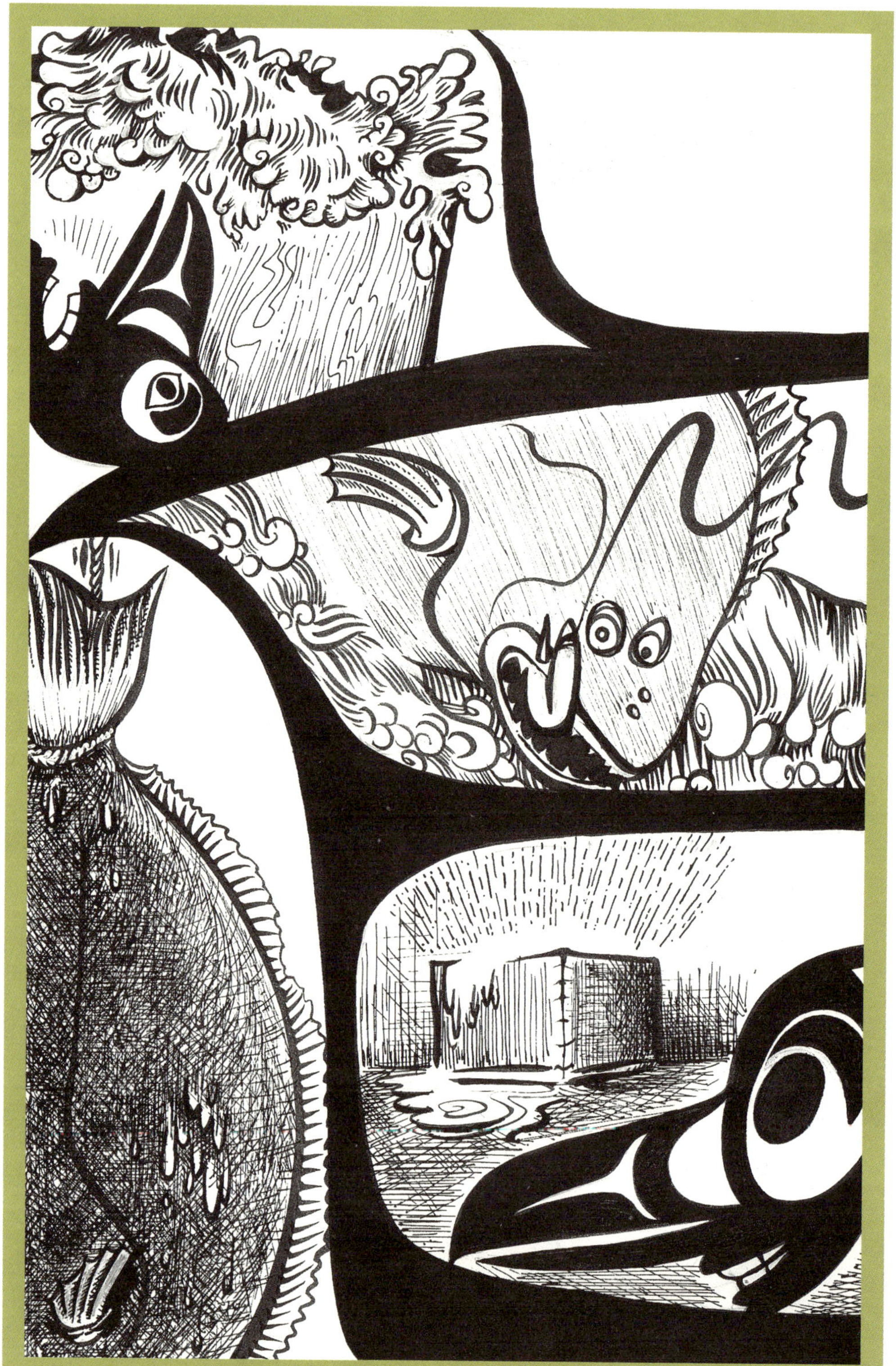

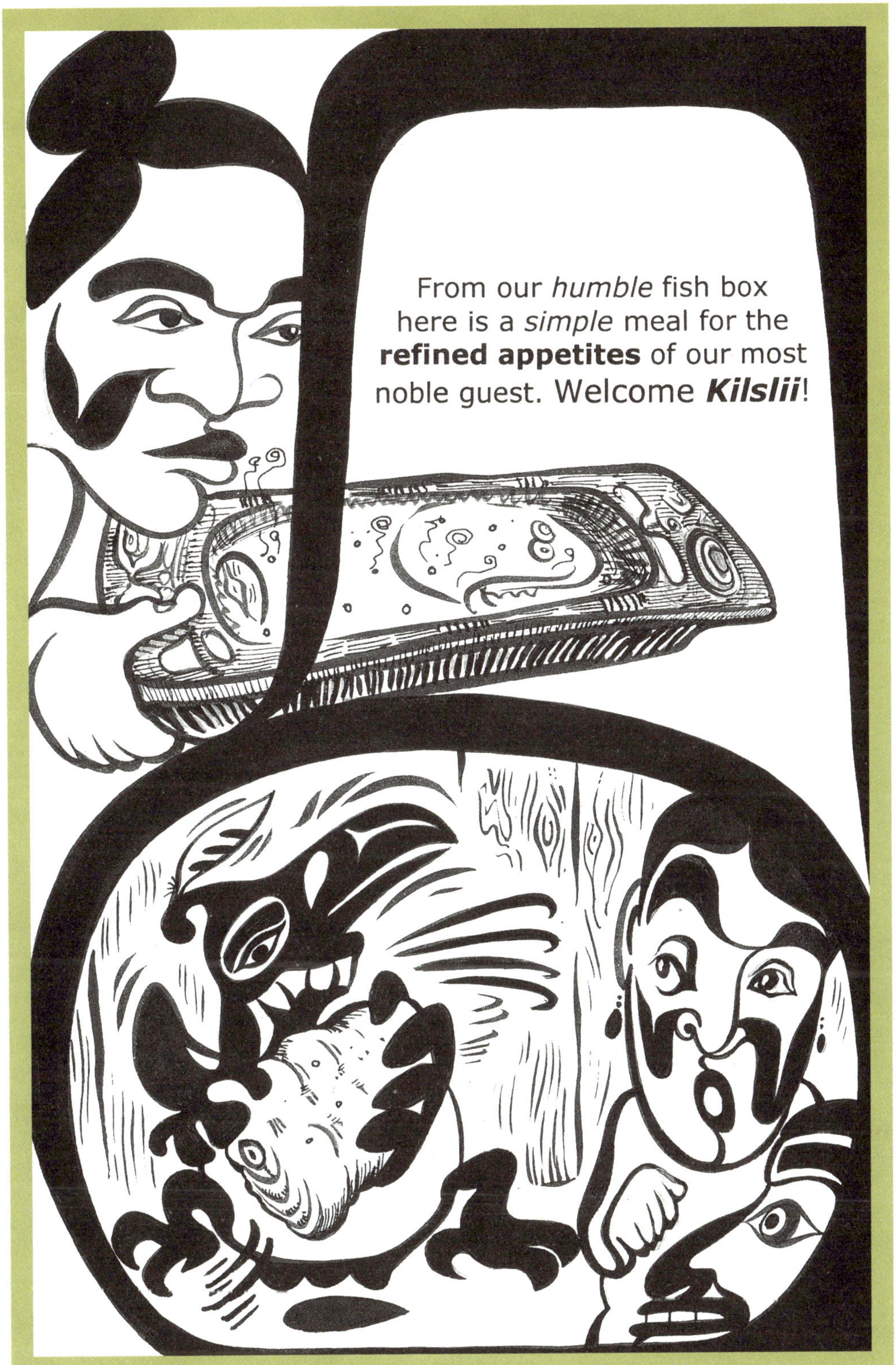
From our *humble* fish box here is a *simple* meal for the **refined appetites** of our most noble guest. Welcome ***Kilslii***!

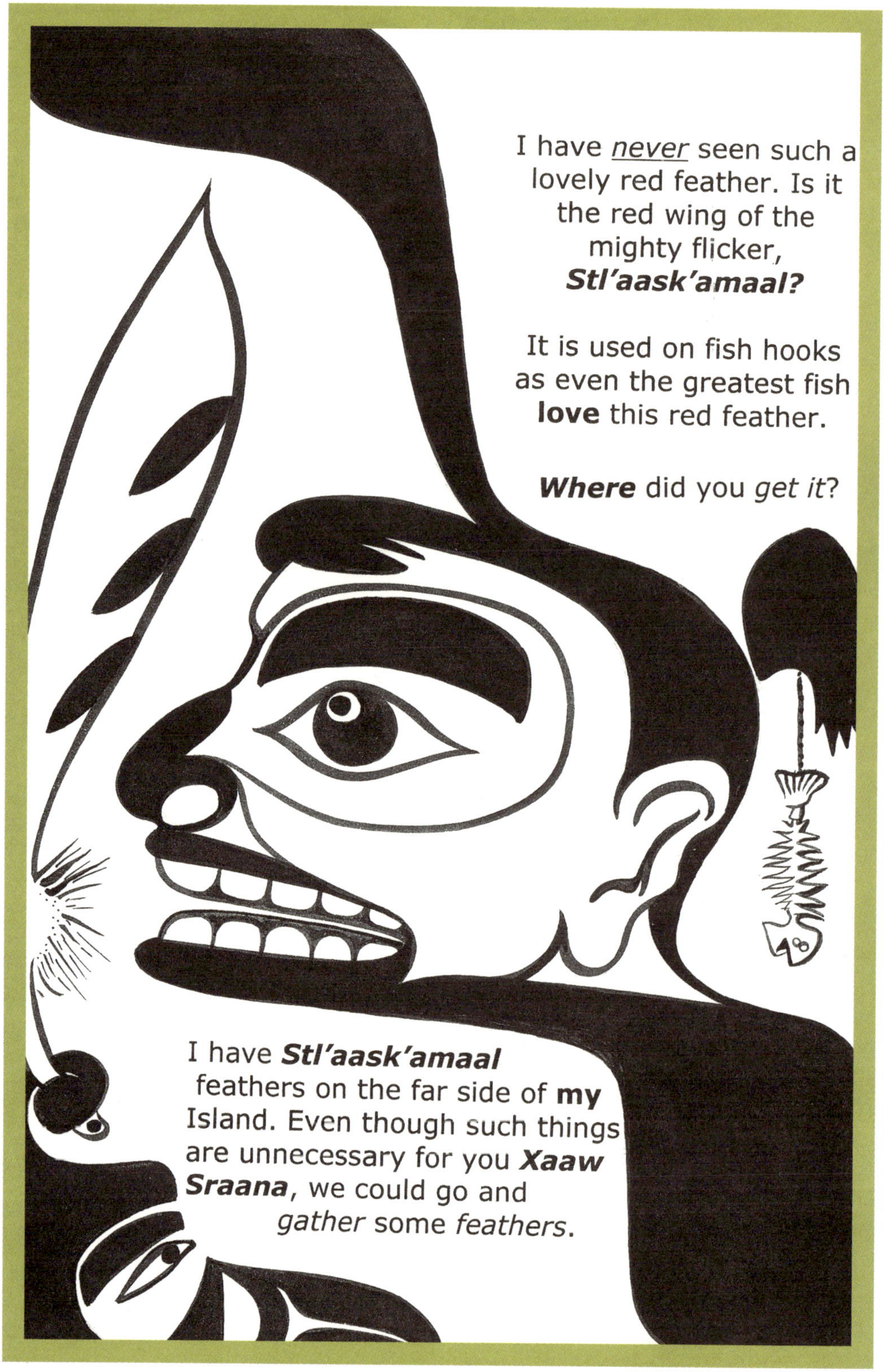
I have never seen such a lovely red feather. Is it the red wing of the mighty flicker, Stl'aask'amaal?
It is used on fish hooks as even the greatest fish love this red feather.
Where did you get it?
I have Stl'aask'amaal feathers on the far side of my Island. Even though such things are unnecessary for you Xaaw Sraana, we could go and gather some feathers.

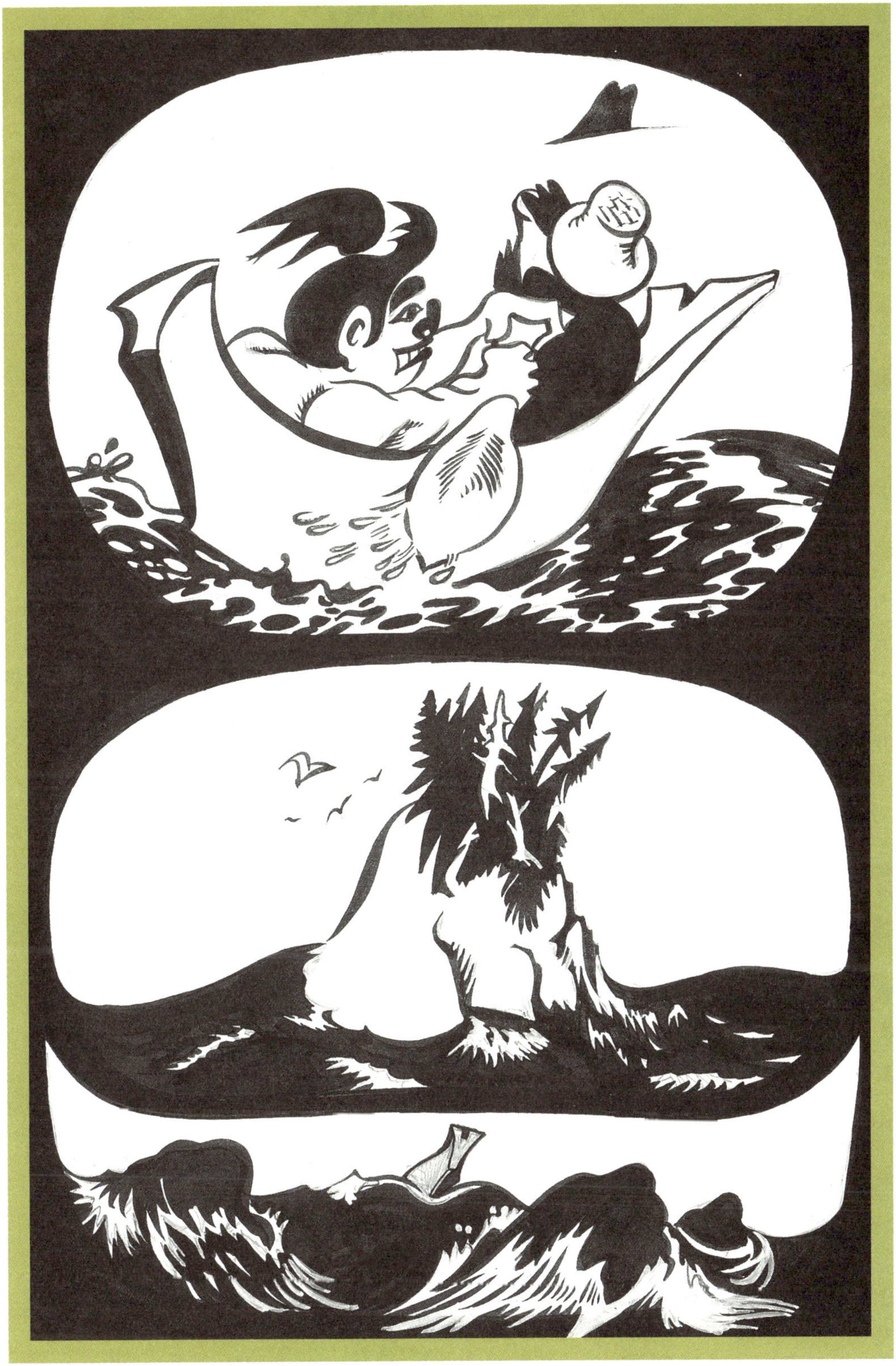

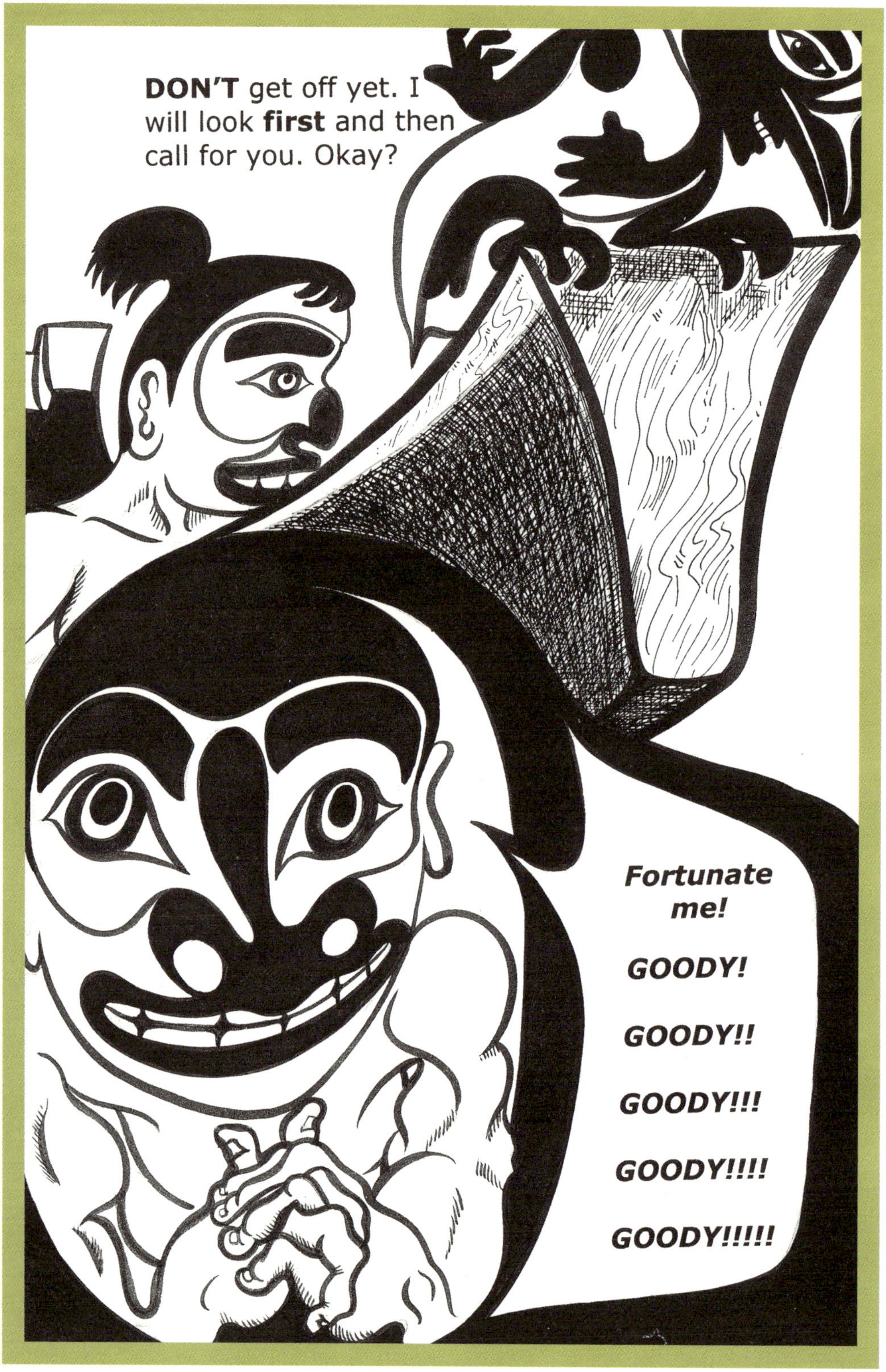
DON'T get off yet. I will look **first** and then call for you. Okay?
Fortunate me!
GOODY!
GOODY!!
GOODY!!!
GOODY!!!!
GOODY!!!!!

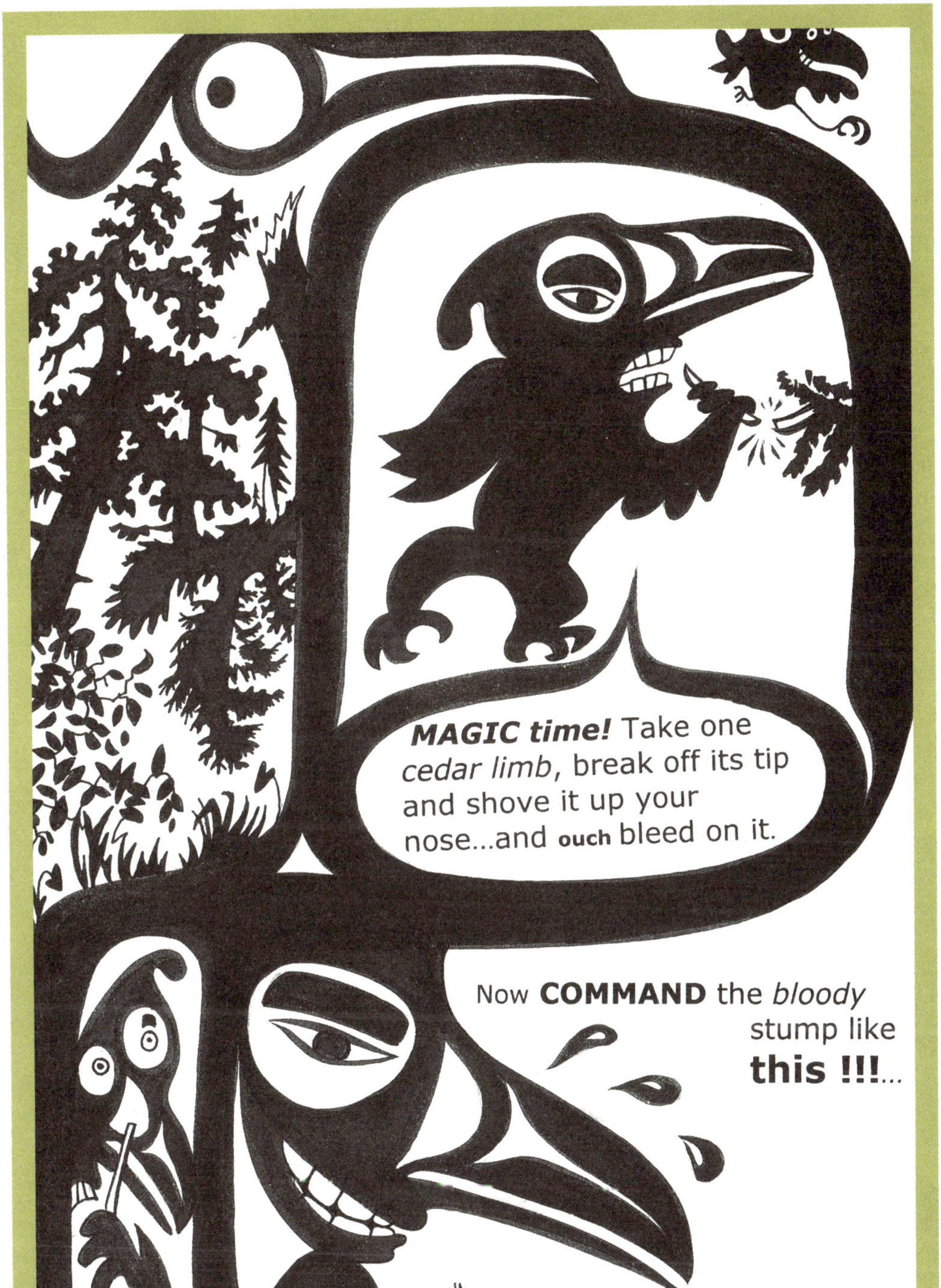
MAGIC time! Take one cedar limb, break off its tip and shove it up your nose...and ouch bleed on it.
Now COMMAND the bloody stump like this !!!...

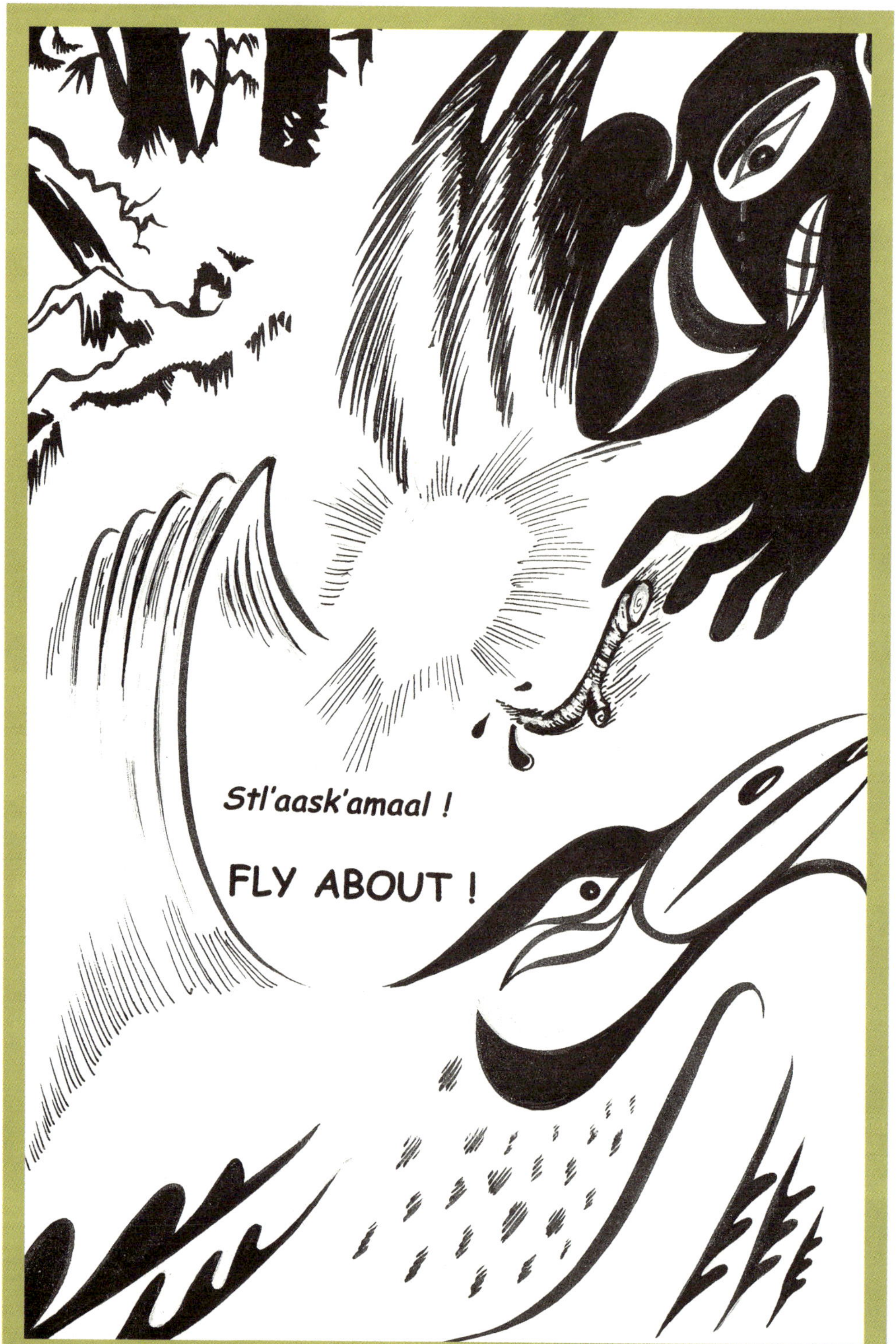
Stl'aask'amaal !
FLY ABOUT !

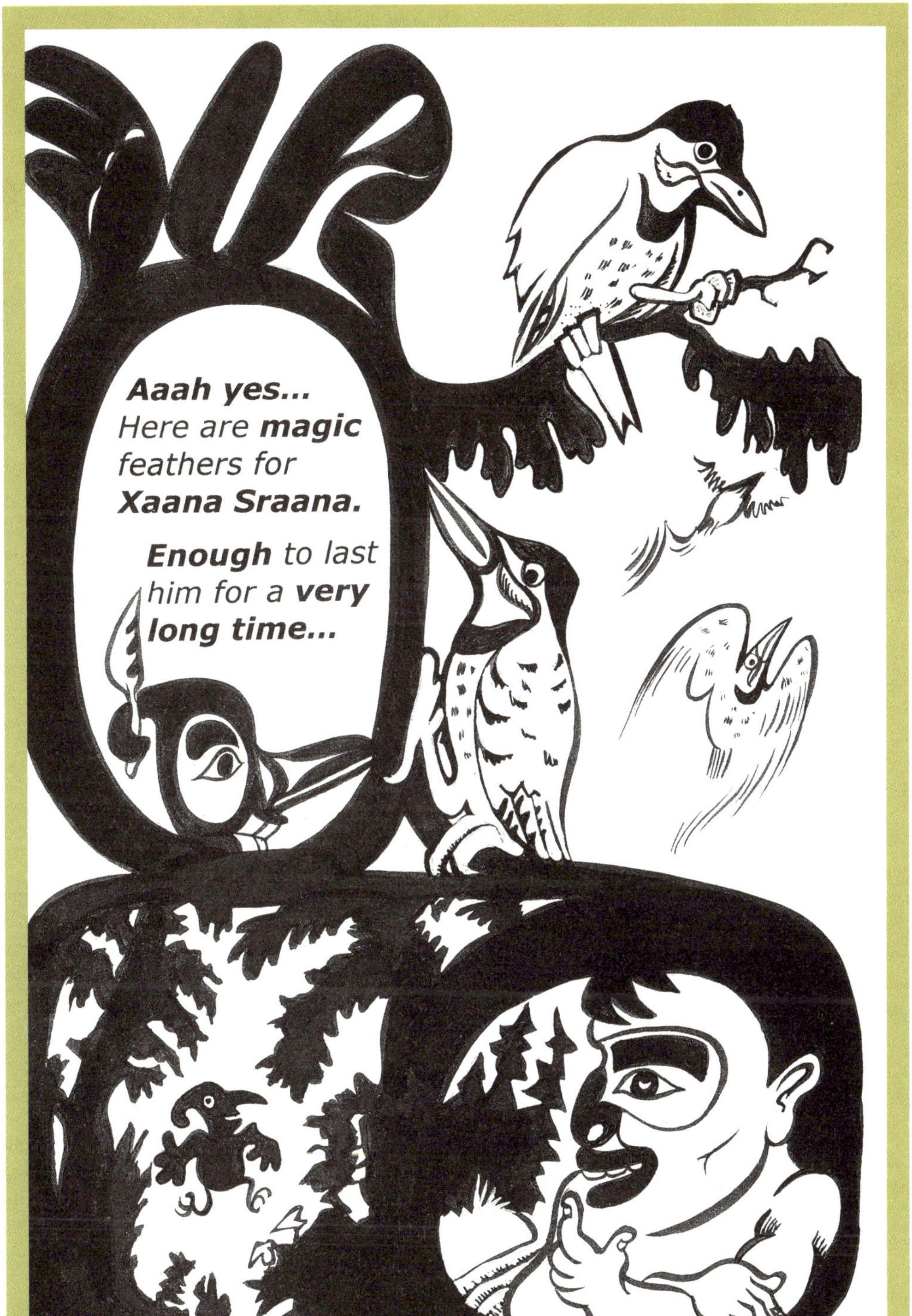
Aaah yes...
Here are **magic** feathers for **Xaana Sraana.**
Enough to last him for a **very long time...**

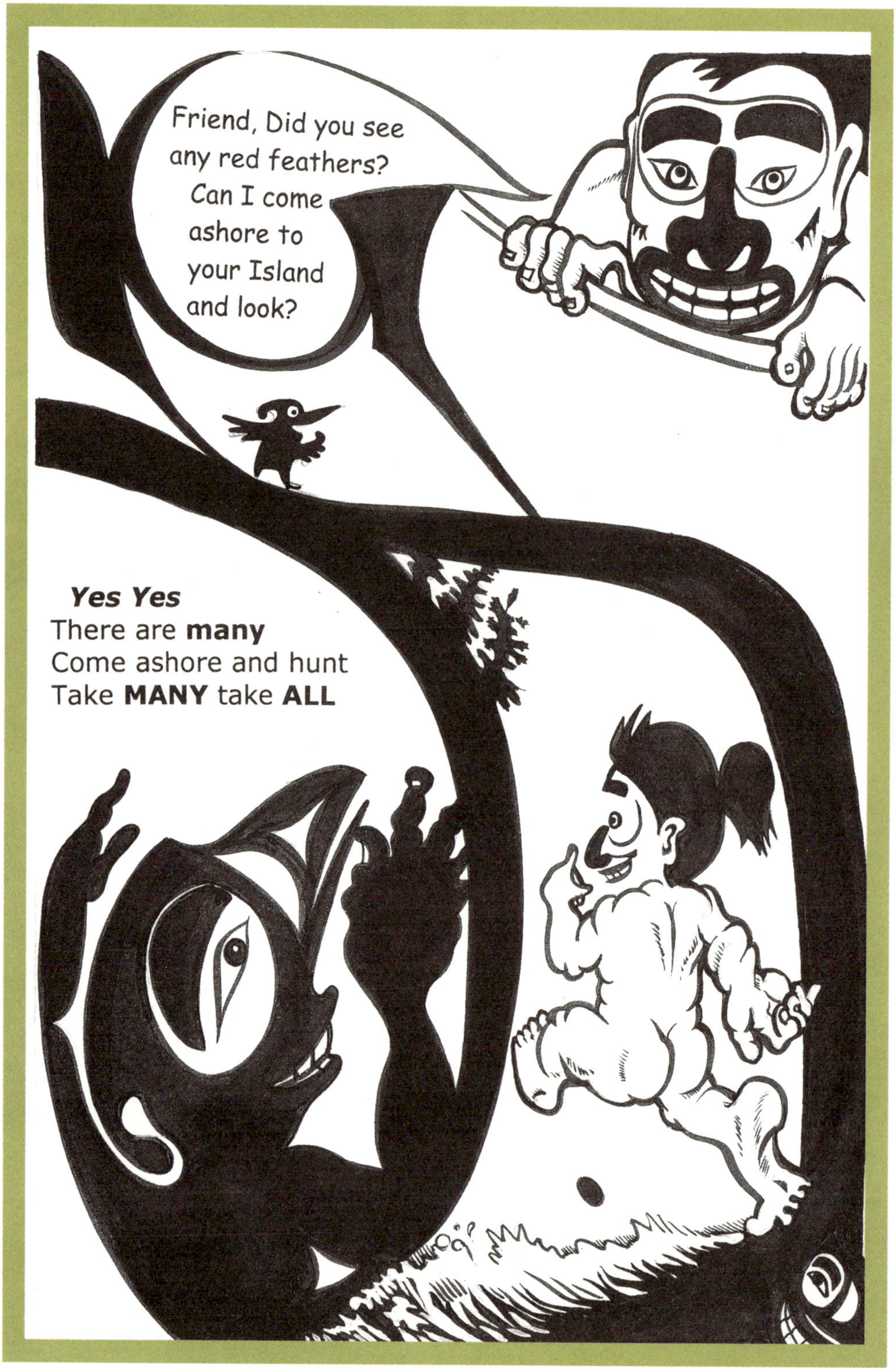
Friend, Did you see any red feathers? Can I come ashore to your Island and look?
Yes Yes
There are many
Come ashore and hunt
Take MANY take ALL

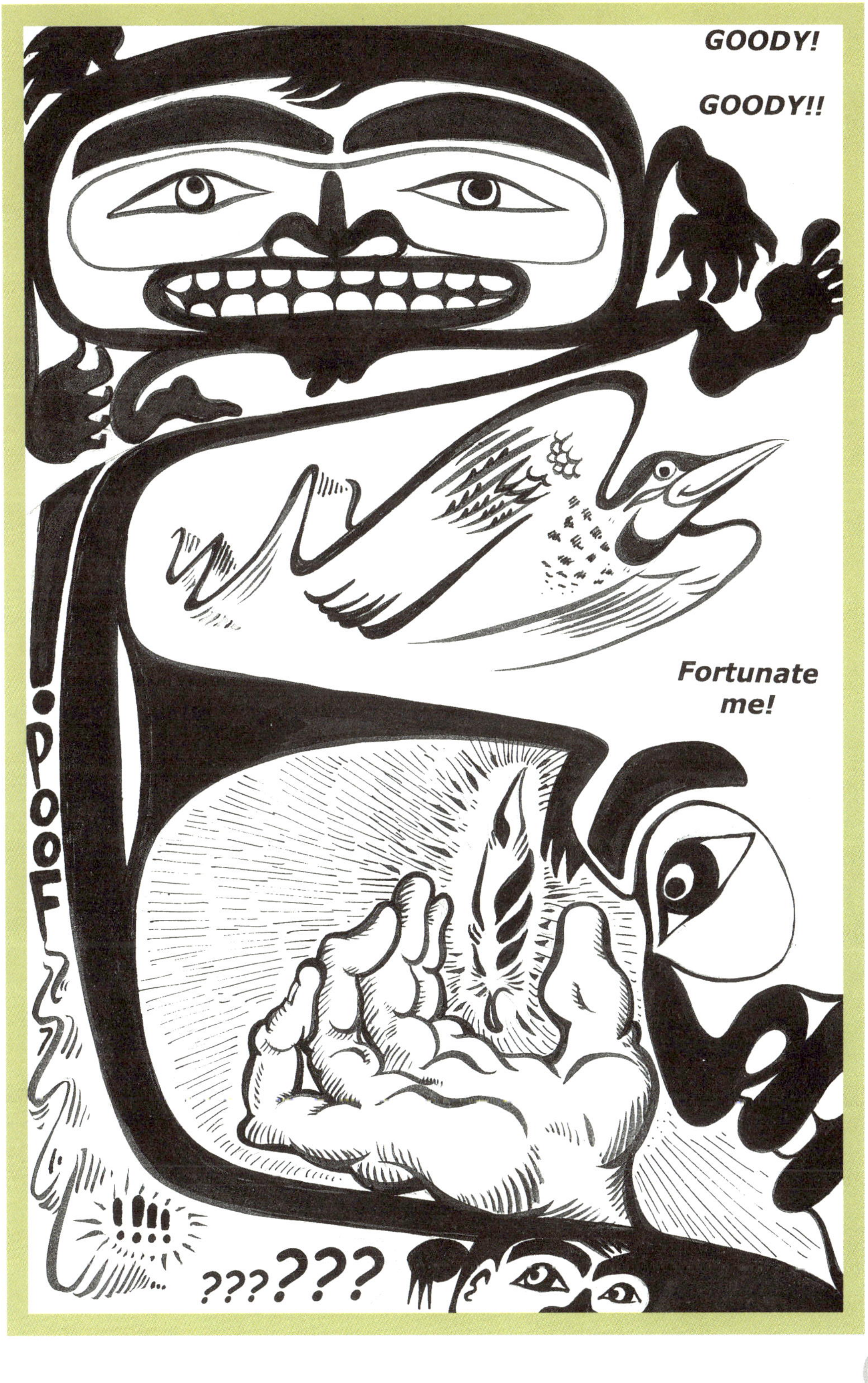
GOODY!
GOODY!!
Fortunate me!
POOF!!
!!!!
??????

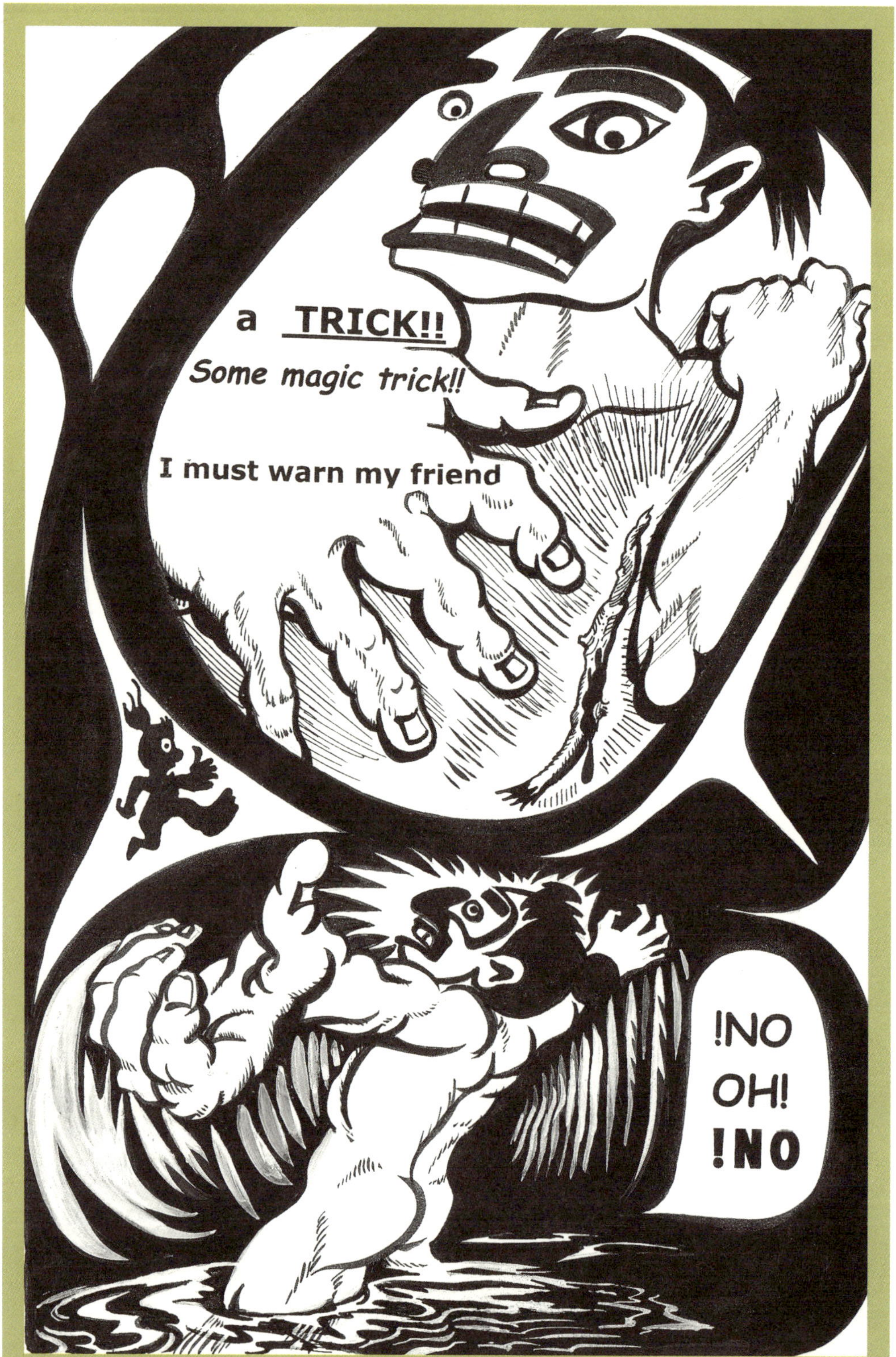
a TRICK!!
Some magic trick!!
I must warn my friend
!NO
OH!
!NO

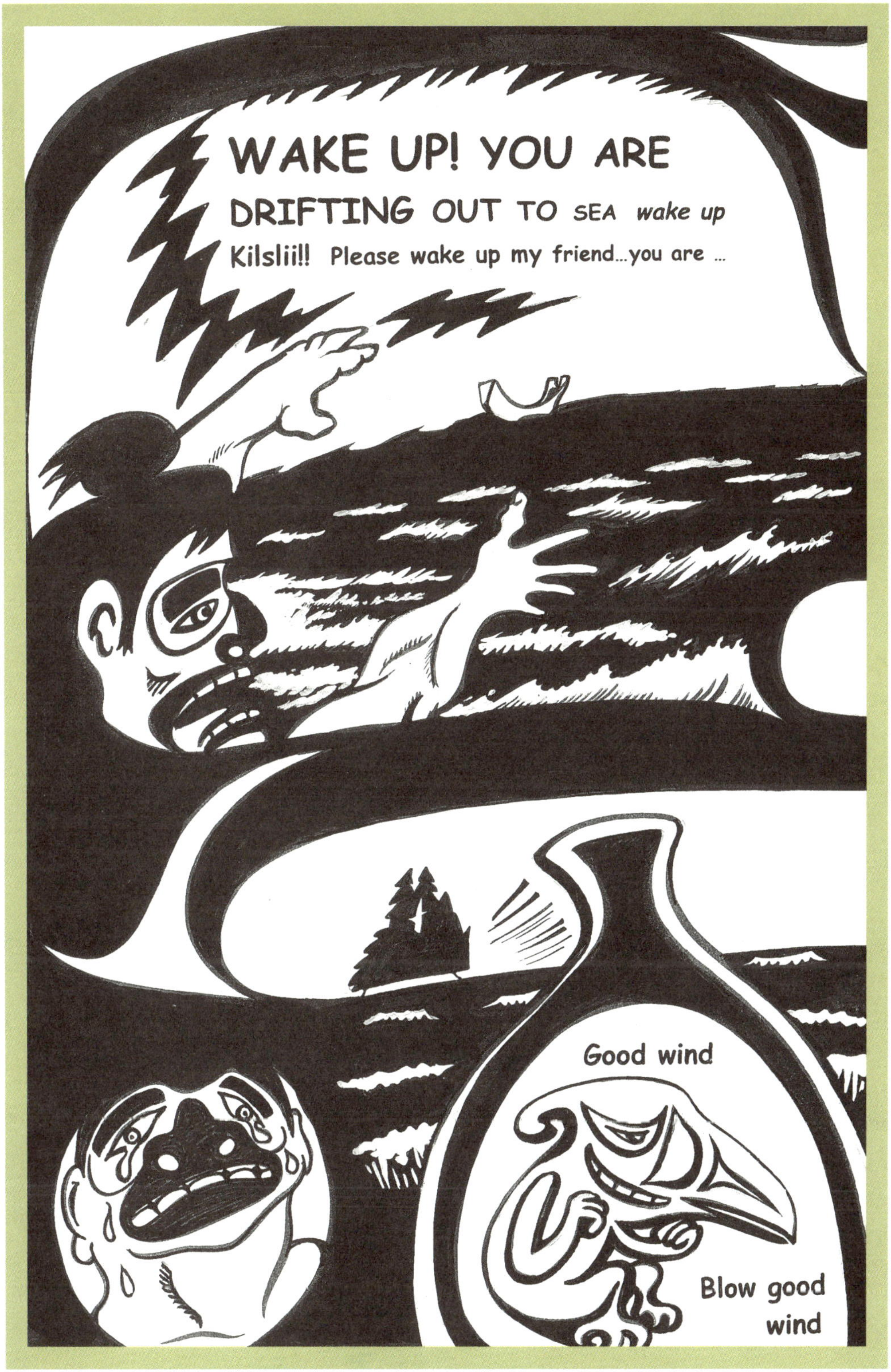
WAKE UP! YOU ARE DRIFTING OUT TO SEA wake up Kilslii!! Please wake up my friend...you are ...
Good wind
Blow good wind

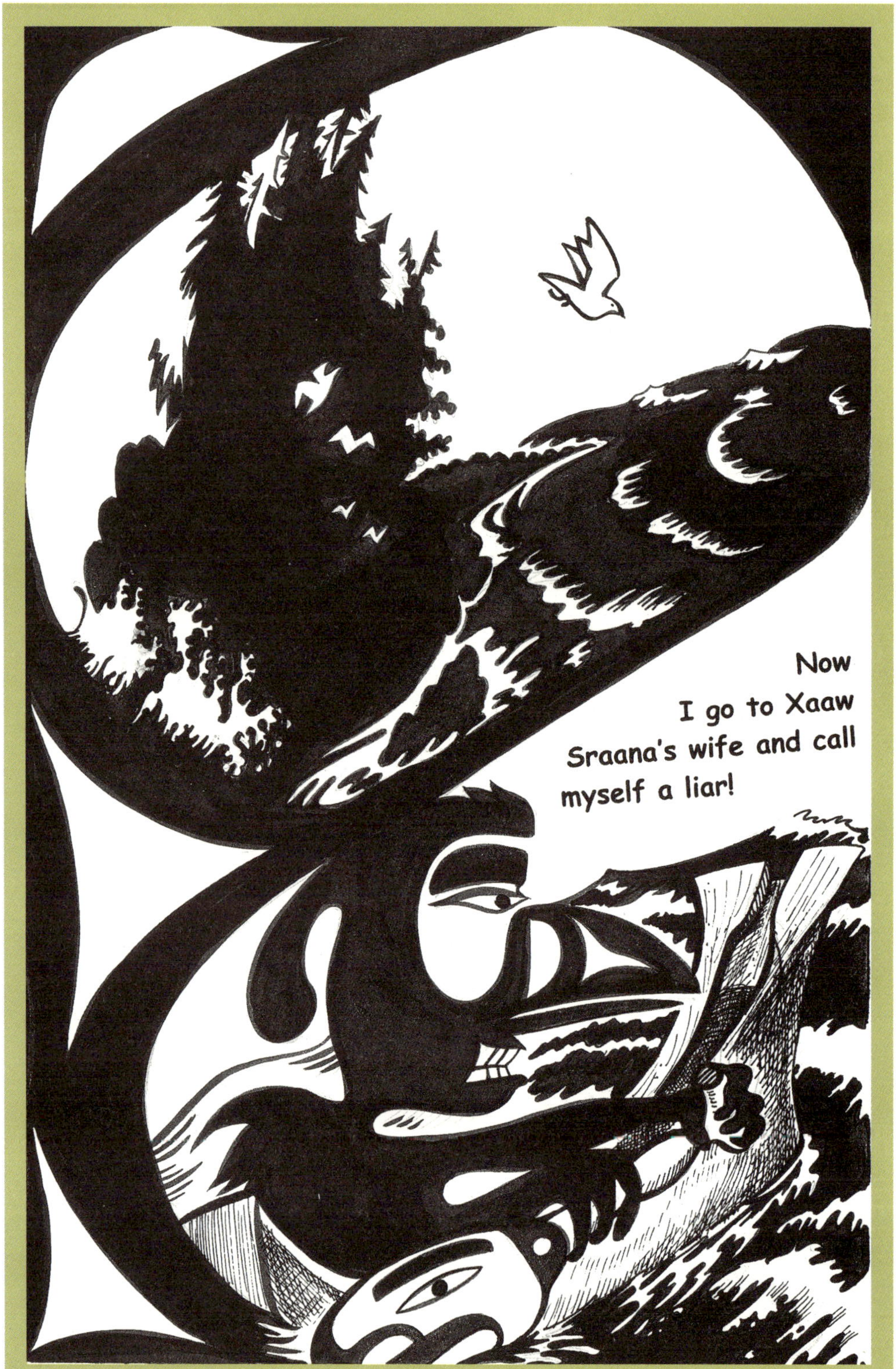
Now
I go to Xaaw
Sraana's wife and call
myself a liar!

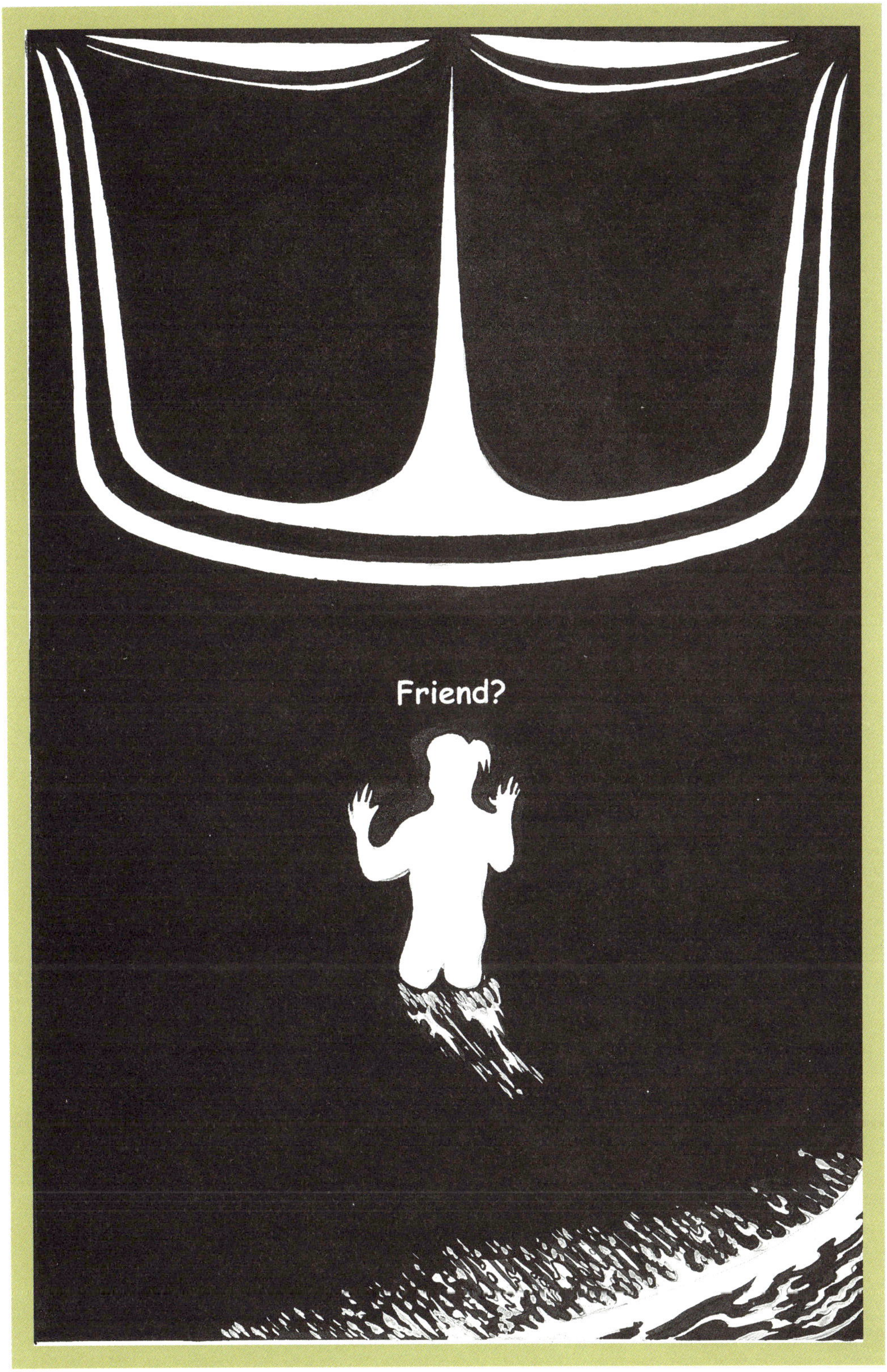
Friend?

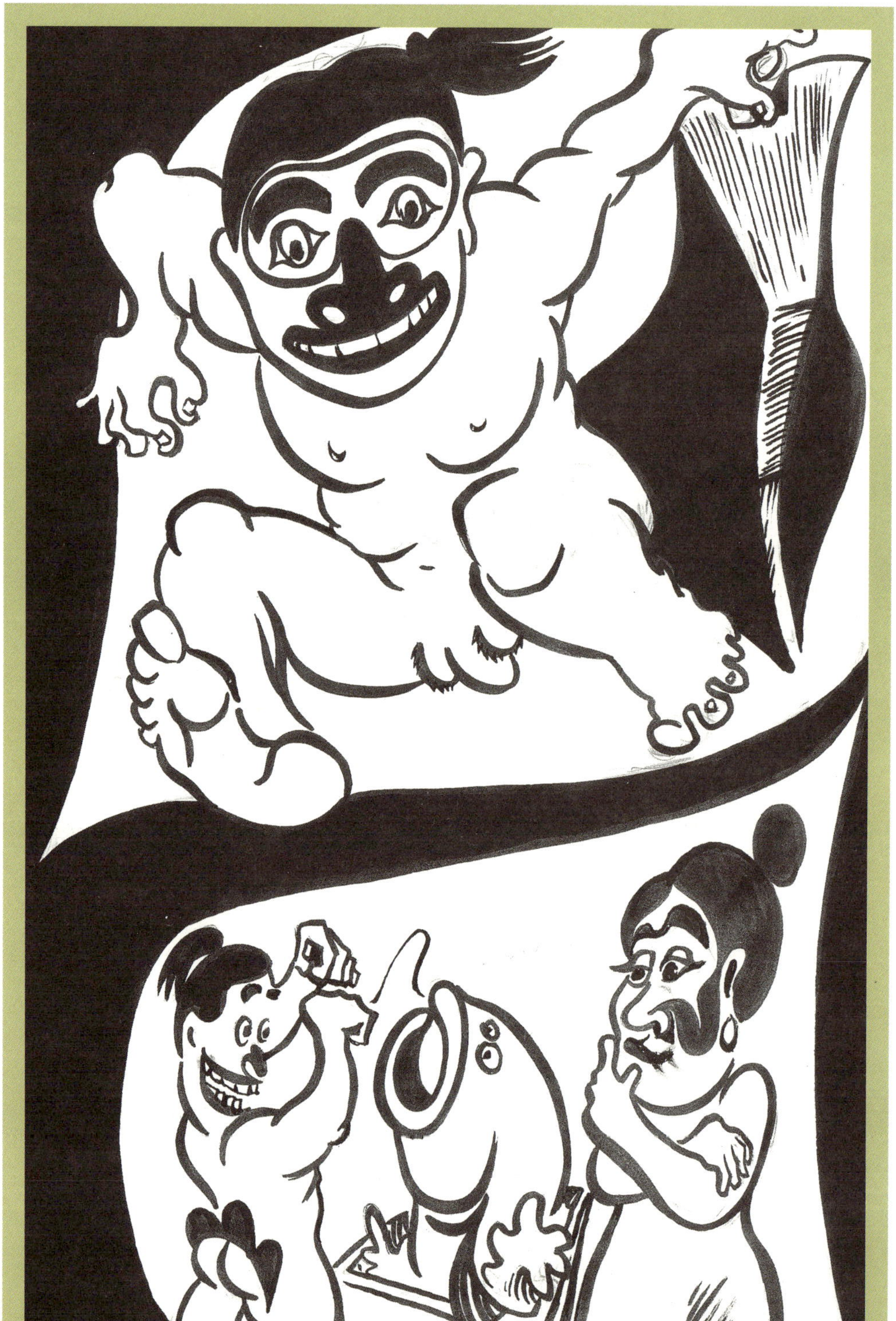

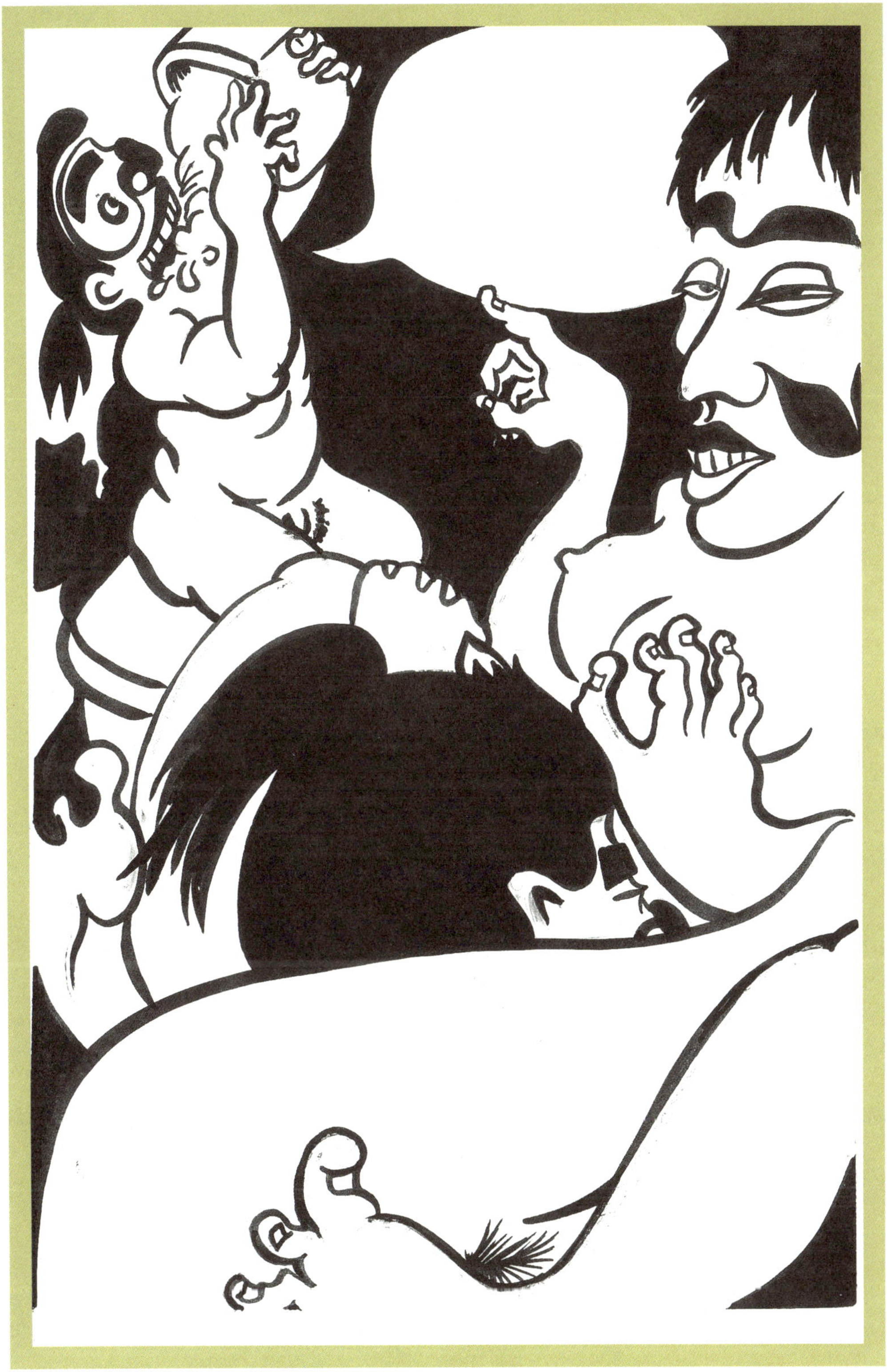

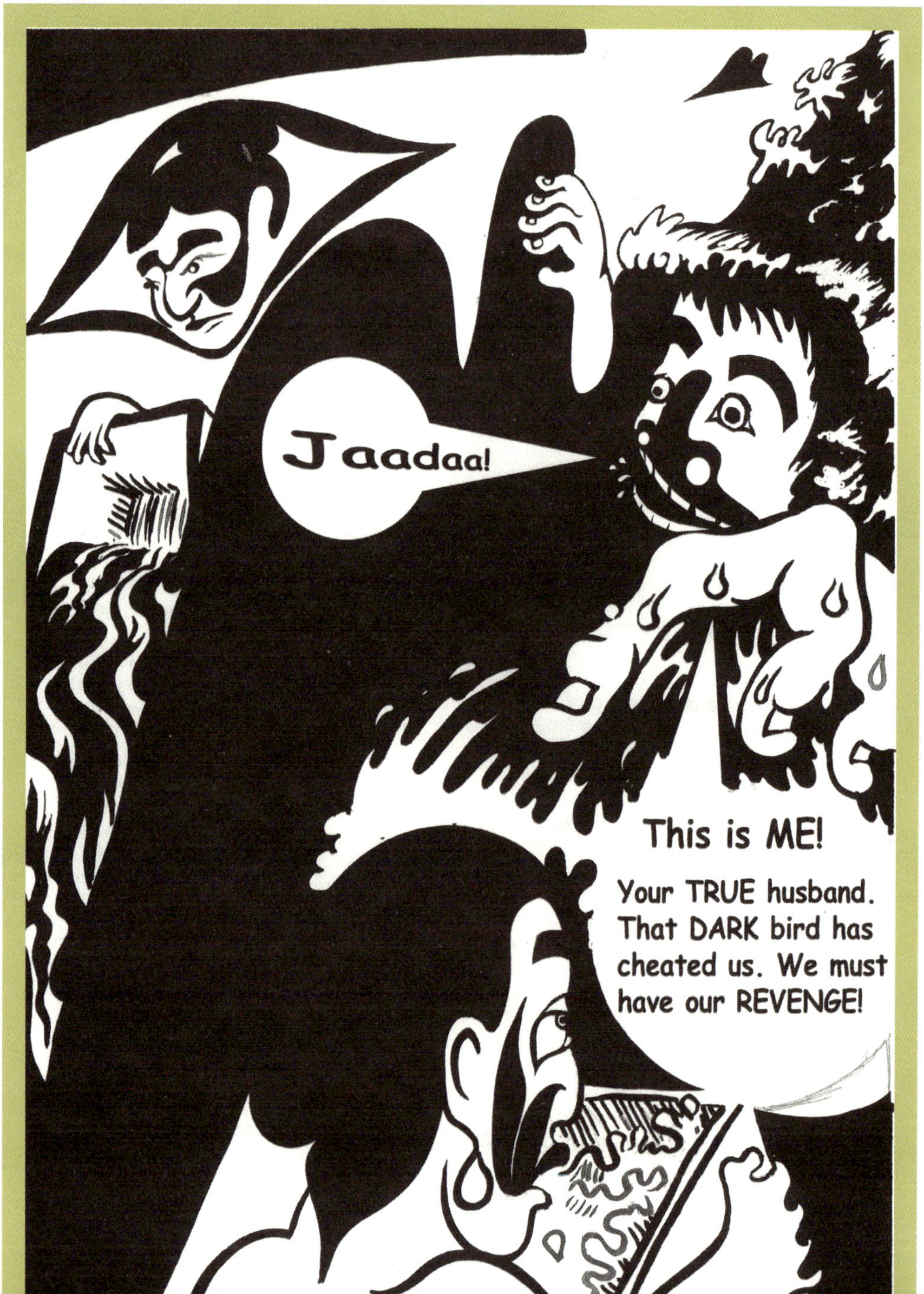
Jaadaa!
This is ME!
Your TRUE husband. That DARK bird has cheated us. We must have our REVENGE!

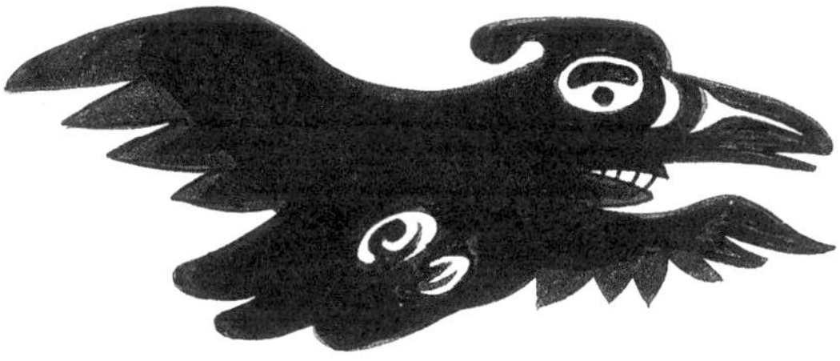

Index of Images

Page 101. Untitled, 1984.

Page 102. **Top**. *Trophy Loggers*, 1998. Originally published in *SpruceRoots Magazine* (Haida Gwaii).
Bottom. Untitled, 1985.

Page 103. **Top & Bottom**. Untitled, 1983/84.

Page 104. **Top Left.** Untitled, 1996.
Top Right. Untitled, 1984. Originally published in *The Ubyssey* (Vancouver, BC).
Bottom Left. Untitled, 1985. Originally published in *Kahtou* (Sechelt, BC).
Bottom Right. Untitled, 1984. Originally published in *The Ubyssey* (Vancouver, BC).

Page 105. Untitled, 1984. Originally published in *The Ubyssey* (Vancouver, BC).

Pages 106 - 107. **Top & Bottom.** Untitled, 1996/97. Originally intended for publication as part of Haida Watchmen Program training manual for Gwaii Haanas National Park Reserve and Haida Heritage Site. Previously unpublished.

Page 108. **Top Left**. Untitled, 1982. Originally published in *Kahtou* (Sechelt, BC).
Top Right. *The Cult that Speaks to the Young*, 1984. Originally published in *The Ubyssey* (Vancouver, BC).
Bottom Left & Right. Untitled, 1988. Originally published in *Kahtou* (Sechelt, BC).

Page 109. **Top**. Untitled, 1996. Originally published in *SpruceRoots Magazine* (Haida Gwaii).
Bottom. *Yaku Goes to Calgary*, 1988. Originally published in *Kahtou* (Sechelt, BC).

Page 110. **Top Left**. Untitled, 1983. Originally published in *Kahtou* (Sechelt, BC).
Top Right. *National Liberation Day*, 1998. Originally published in *Pacific News Bulletin* / Pacific Concerns Resource Centre (Suva, Fiji).
Bottom Left. *Free Trade*, 1998. Originally published in *SpruceRoots Magazine* (Haida Gwaii).
Bottom Right. Untitled, 1998. Originally published in *SpruceRoots Magazine* (Haida Gwaii).

Page 111. **Top Left, Top Right, Bottom Left & Bottom Right**. Untitled, 2000. Originally published in *SpruceRoots Magazine* (Haida Gwaii).

Page 112. **Top & Bottom**. Untitled, 1996. Originally published in *SpruceRoots Magazine* (Haida Gwaii).

Page 113. Untitled, 1996/97. Originally intended for publication as part of Haida Watchmen Program training manual for Gwaii Haanas National Park Reserve and Haida Heritage Site. Previously unpublished.

Page 114. **Top Left & Top Right.** Untitled, 2000. Originally published in *SpruceRoots Magazine* (Haida Gwaii).
Bottom. Untitled, 1998.

Pages 115 - 119. *Dunee*, 1992.

Page 120. *Slegootsanue*, 1992.

Page 121. *The Jealous Canoe*, 1998.

Page 122. *Culturally Modified Trees* (CMT), 1998.

Page 123. *An Ocean of Ideas*, 1993. Originally published in *Old Massett Newsletter* (Haida Gwaii).

Pages 124 - 125. Untitled, 1998. Studies for *Bear in the Bar*.

Page 126. *Bear in the Bar*, 1998. Originally published in *SpruceRoots Magazine* (Haida Gwaii).

Pages 127 - 141. Untitled, 1999/2000. Studies for *The Last Voyage of the Black Ship*.

Pages 142 - 146. *How Not to Become a GAAGIIXT*, 2001.

Page 147. *Haida Halloween*, 2001.

Page 148. *Wasco*, 2001.

Acknowledgments

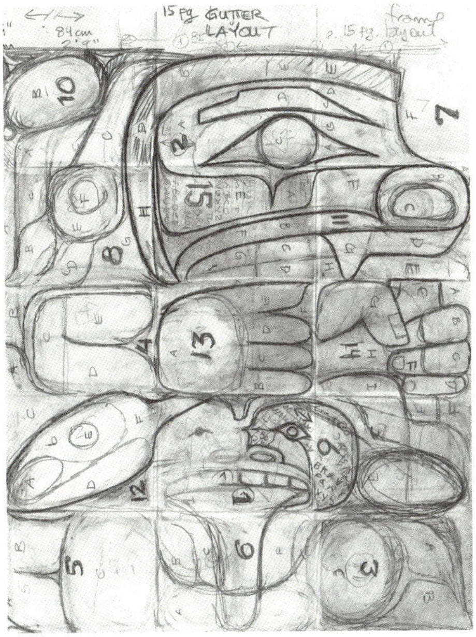

Michael Nicoll Yahgulanaas' *Old Growth* documents his important contribution over the past thirty years. The fight to save old growth forests in BC has been one of the province's most important political battles and one that crosses many cultural communities. The documentation of this history through Yahgulanaas' work is an exciting take on these events and we at grunt are honoured to be able to facilitate this project.

When Liz Park first approached us with this idea we were excited to host this exhibition and publication. grunt has a history of engaging with Indigenous artists working with contemporary art dating back over twenty years. *Old Growth* exists between Indigenous Art and activism, both being major touchstones at grunt, ones we have returned to again and again.

On behalf of the board and staff at grunt I would like to thank Michael for his wonderful, visionary work, Liz Park for her curatorial insight and writing, Tania Willard for her design and the staff from Simply Read Books for publishing this book. I'd also like to thank staff members Meagan Kus, Mary Ann Anderson, Demian Petryshyn and Venge Dixon for their support of this project.

Finally, I'd like to thank our funders: The Vancouver Foundation, for their generous support to this and other projects, and the Hamber Foundation.
Thank you.

grunt

Glenn Alteen
Program Director
grunt gallery, 2011

First published in 2011 by Read Leaf

Library and Archives Canada Cataloguing in Publication

Yahgulanaas, Michael Nicoll
Old growth / art by Michael Nicoll
Yahgulanaas ; edited by Liz Park.

Includes bibliographical references.
Co-published by: grunt gallery.
ISBN 978-1-897476-96-3

1. Yahgulanaas, Michael Nicoll.
I. Park, Liz, 1983- II. grunt gallery III. Title.

PN6733.Y34A6 2011 741.5'971 C2011-903005-5

ISBN: 9781897476963

10 9 8 7 6 5 4 3 2 1

Book design by Tania Willard, Red Willow Designs
Back Cover artist photograph courtesy of Yukiko Onley

Printed in China

We gratefully acknowledge for their financial support of our publishing program the Canada Council for the Arts, the BC Arts Council, and the Government of Canada through the Canada Book Fund (CBF).

Thank you to the following funders for their generous support:
The Vancouver Foundation and the Hamber Foundation.

The Hamber Foundation
Bettering the lives of British Columbians

vancouver foundation